ON THE NATURE
OF GRAMMATICAL
RELATIONS

Linguistic Inquiry Monographs
Samuel Jay Keyser, general editor

ON THE NATURE OF GRAMMATICAL RELATIONS

Alec Marantz

The MIT Press
Cambridge, Massachusetts
London, England

This book was set in VIP Times Roman by Village Typographers, Inc., using disks prepared by the author on an Apple III computer, and printed and bound by Halliday Lithograph Corporation in the United States of America.

Library of Congress Cataloging in Publication Data

Marantz, Alec.
  On the nature of grammatical relations.

  (Linguistic inquiry monographs; 10)
  Revision of thesis (Ph.D.)—MIT, 1981.
  Includes bibliography and index.
  1. Grammar, Comparative and general. I. Title.
II. Series.
P151.M3 1984   415   83-43018
ISBN 0-262-13193-5
ISBN 0-262-63090-7 (pbk.)

Contents

Contents

Contents   vii

Series Foreword

We are pleased to present this monograph as the tenth in the series *Linguistic Inquiry Monographs*. These monographs will present new and original research beyond the scope of the article, and we hope they will benefit our field by bringing to it perspectives that will stimulate further research and insight.

Originally published in limited edition, the *Linguistic Inquiry Monograph* series is now available on a much wider scale. This change is due to the great interest engendered by the series and the needs of a growing readership. The editors wish to thank the readers for their support and welcome suggestions about future directions the series might take.

Samuel Jay Keyser
for the Editorial Board

Preface

This book is a heavily revised version of my 1981 MIT doctoral dissertation. Although the topics discussed and the order of their presentation remain almost unchanged from the earlier work, substantial improvements have been made throughout. Chapter 3, including my analysis of raising and Move Alpha constructions, is entirely new, as are sections 7.3 and 7.4. The details of morphological merger in chapter 7 differ conceptually and technically from the earlier version. The material in chapters 4 and 5 is basically unmodified, as is most of chapter 6, with the exception of the analysis of Dyirbal dative shift.

In the two years it took to get things straight, I had the assistance of numerous individuals and audiences. Noam Chomsky, my thesis adviser, read everything in countless versions and insisted I get it right. But my debt does not end there: more by example than instruction, Noam showed me how to do linguistics. To single out some individuals who provided particular help with the manuscript, I would like to thank Paul Kiparsky, Ken Hale, Marion Johnson, R. M. W. Dixon, Tony Woodbury, Lori Levin, K. P. Mohanan, Joan Bresnan, Mamoru Saito, Barry Schein, Malka Rappaport, Jeremy Benstein, D.-W. Yang, Paula Pranka, Richard Sproat, Richie Kayne, and Kasuko Inoue and her students. Providing challenging questions and insightful (even devastating) criticism at presentations of material from this book were audiences at MIT, Harvard, the University of Texas at Austin, UCLA, UC Irvine, Tsukuba University, and ICU in Tokyo. For assorted support and encouragement I thank the organizers of the San Francisco marathon, Jay Keyser and the MIT Linguistics Department, Bruce Katz at MIT Press, the Harvard University Society of Fellows—especially my fellow Junior Fellows, and, in position of utmost emphasis, my parents.

Chapter 1
The Nature of Grammatical Relations

This book explores the nature of grammatical relations. In the linguistic literature, one finds a great deal of confusion over what an account of grammatical relations should be. Some theorists believe that what is required is a definition of grammatical relations in terms of other concepts of syntactic theory. Other linguists try to prove that grammatical relations are primitives, that is, not definable within linguistic theory. Most linguists who take either of these views share the assumption that it is reasonable to ask, "Are grammatical relations such as subject and object definable?" This assumption is based on the belief that grammatical relational terms have clear referents outside particular syntactic theories. The only way to test a particular definition of "subject" is to have some notion of "subject" with which to compare the implications of the definition.

In fact linguists lack any grounds for assuming that the definability of grammatical relations is a coherent issue. Although they operate with concepts, varying in clarity, that relate to grammatical relations, there is no firm ground to stand on in evaluating accounts of grammatical relations per se. Linguists have fairly clear theory-neutral notions of "antecedent of a reflexive," "case marking," "word order," "agent of an action," and other concepts that seem related to the notion of "subject." But "subject" itself does not fall into this class of theory-neutral concepts. How then may one propose to evaluate an account of grammatical relations or a definition of subject or object?

In practice, theories of grammatical relations are criticized in two ways. First, it is pointed out that the definition or account of, say, "subject" in a theory does not in fact apply to something identified as a subject in some other theory or according to someone's intuitive notion of what a subject is. This criticism is only partially coherent. Linguists who use it seem caught up with the notion that because they talk about subjects, there must be some class of subjects out there, a class that at least includes what they consider to be canonical subjects. Nevertheless, the philosophical considerations of Wittgenstein (1958) and the psychological findings of Eleanor Rosch and associates (see the references in Smith and Medin 1981) warn against assuming that words pick out clear classes of entities or have reductive definitions. What makes linguists think that their notion of "subject" is any different from that of "chair" or "game"? If they cannot provide a definition or account of "game" that picks out all and only the entities considered to be games, they should not expect to discover a definition of "subject" that accounts for their intuitive concept of "subject." Moreover, why should a term in a theory have to pick out just those constituents one believes to be subjects? An account of one's knowledge of grammar does not necessarily include an account of one's use of grammatical vocabulary. The study of "subject," "object," and "grammatical relation" as concepts and words that linguists and others use to talk about language should be reserved for those investigating word meanings and concepts in general. Such an investigation falls outside the syntactician's responsibility.

A second criticism leveled at accounts of grammatical relations is that a theory in question does not account for the same range of data that some other theory of grammatical relations handles. This criticism is valid if taken broadly. If a theory of grammatical relations is embedded in an inadequate syntactic theory, then one has reason to criticize that theory. However, the so-called data brought up in disputes over grammatical relations are often theory-internal generalizations about the grammatical relational terms in a particular theoretical framework. That, for example, "only subjects undergo syntactic raising" is not a simple fact that every syntactic theory must capture. Rather, it represents a network of connections among pieces of data. These connections are what competing theories are responsible for, not a generalization about "subjects."

Although grammatical relational terms do not designate unique referents outside particular theories, linguists writing about grammatical relations do tend to discuss a similar range of phenomena. There is enough agreement about the sort of data associated with grammatical relations that the subject matter of this book should be fairly clear from the title. Nevertheless, it will not be a valid criticism of my work that I have failed to capture someone's intuitive notion of grammatical relations. Although it is a challenge to the theory I develop here to capture all the significant generalizations accounted for by other theories of grammatical relations, it is clearly not necessary that the generalizations be captured in the same way. For example, if some rule of, say, Relational Grammar attributes a set of data to a condition on subjects whereas the present theory accounts for the same data without reference to grammatical relations at all, this does not count a priori against the present theory. Or if some construction some linguist calls a "passive" for taxonomic reasons does not fall under the definition of "passive" in the present theory, nothing should hinge on this fact. There can be no right definition of "subject" or "passive," only a correct (or better) syntactic theory.

Grammatical relations of some sort appear in virtually every grammatical theory from Pāṇini to the present. Within a grammar they are intimately connected with thematic or semantic roles such as agent or theme on the one hand, and with cases and structural relations such as nominative or accusative case or "NP immediately dominated by S" on the other. Often linguists define grammatical relations in terms of, or give them up in favor of, semantic or structural relations or morphological case marking. In this work, I develop and support a theory of grammatical relations that places them as intermediaries in the connection between semantic roles and dependencies and the expression of these roles and dependencies in structural and positional relations and in case marking and agreement.

Consider sentence (1.1):

(1.1)
Elmer threw the porcupine to Hortense.

The porcupine appears as the NP immediately dominated by VP ([NP, VP]) because it is the object of the verb, *threw,* and it is the object of the verb because it names the bearer of the "throwee" role in the action described by *threw.* Conversely, because it is the [NP, VP], *the porcupine* is interpreted as the object of *threw,* and because it is the object, it is interpreted as the "throwee." Grammatical relations such as subject and object stand between the semantic roles and relations constituents bear with respect to argument-taking words and phrases and the expressions of these semantic roles and relations in sentences. The diagram in (1.2) represents this central idea, around which the present work is based.

(1.2)

semantic roles and dependencies

↕

grammatical relations

↕

expressions of semantic roles and dependencies

The conception of grammatical relations as mediating the connection between semantic roles and their expression can be found in Pāṇini (see Kiparsky 1981, Kiparsky and Staal 1969, and Shibatani 1977).

Grammatical relations are not objects of study that can be identified outside a particular theory of grammar, and terms like "subject" and "object" have no clear pretheoretical reference. Given the absence of general agreement over what grammatical relations are, one cannot ask such questions as whether rules of verb agreement refer to grammatical relations without specifying some theory of grammatical relations to identify the objects of inquiry. It is widely believed that a crucial question for linguistics is whether grammatical relations are definable or primitive. But because grammatical relations have different characterizations—and grammatical relational terms have different extensions—in different theories, the question of the definability of grammatical relations arises only within particular theories of grammar.

So one may ask whether in theory T the grammatical relational terms are primitive or defined. As Chomsky (1981) points out, this question is of some interest when the theory of grammar is considered to represent the child's innate linguistic knowledge. Whatever the primitives of a linguistic theory qua innate linguistic knowledge are, the child must be able to associate them with the stream of speech that constitutes his linguistic experience. If grammatical relations are primitives in a theory, children must still have some means to pick subjects and objects out of the utterances that confront them. Any theory is suspect that postulates primitive grammatical relations but does not provide a reasonable account of how children manage to learn the extensions of grammatical relational terms.

The definability of grammatical relations within particular theories is thus an important issue from the standpoint of language acquisition. The debate in the literature over whether grammatical relations are primitive covers important issues as well, but they are not in fact issues of definability. When linguists appear to be arguing over whether grammatical relations are definable or primitive, they are often really arguing over whether the connection between semantic roles or relations and structural positions or case marking is direct or indirect in language. If this connection is direct in a theory, grammatical relations are said (without proper justification) to be defined in the theory because rules that are often believed to refer to grammatical relations (e.g., subject-verb agreement) will refer instead within the theory to groups of constituents classified according to their semantic roles or relations or according to their structural positions or case marking. When the mapping between semantic roles and their expressions is indirect in a theory (i.e., mediated by grammatical relations as shown in (1.2)), the theory's grammatical relations are considered primitive, again without justification.

The issue of whether grammatical relations are defined or primitive is also confused with the issue of how a theory should account for alternations in the expression of a verb's semantic arguments like the passive alternation illustrated in (1.3).

(1.3)
a. Elmer threw the porcupine to Hortense.
b. The porcupine was thrown to Hortense.

It is clear that the "thrown" argument in (1.3a) and (1.3b)—*the porcupine*—is expressed in different structural positions in the two sentences. If a theory accounts for alternations like the passive with a rule that refers only to semantic roles or with a rule that maps phrase markers onto phrase markers, the theory is considered (without proper justification) to have defined grammatical relations in semantic or structural terms. If a theory accounts for the passive alternation with a rule that refers directly to grammatical relations, the grammatical relations in the theory are (perhaps improperly) said to be primitive.

The important problems to be addressed by a theory of grammatical relations include the nature of the connection between semantic roles and relations and their expressions and the proper account of alternations in the expression of semantic roles and relations like the passive alternation illustrated in (1.3). The technical question of whether grammatical relations are defined or primitive arises only within particular theories and is of general interest only in connection with the acquisition problem. In claiming that grammatical relations are primitives within their theory, Relational Grammarians like Perlmutter (see Perlmutter 1983) really mean to emphasize that the association of semantic roles with their expressions is mediated by grammatical relations in Relational Grammar and that alternations like the passive are handled by rules referring directly to grammatical relations. In fact it is quite likely that the grammatical relations of Relational Grammar may be defined in terms of primitives of the theory (see Marantz 1982b). Nevertheless, in evaluating the merits of Relational Grammar, the crucial consideration is not whether grammatical relations are primitives in the theory but whether the theory provides the best account of the connection between semantic roles and relations and their expressions in the syntax of language.

To repeat, a theory of grammatical relations is a theory about the connection between semantic roles and relations and their expressions in sentences. This book presents one such theory and demonstrates its explanatory power; some alternative theories are discussed in chapter 8.

What is the nature of grammatical relations in the theory to be presented? Grammatical relations are the syntactic counterparts—the grammaticalizations, so to speak—of certain logico-semantic relations such as the predicate–subject and modifier–modifiee relations. Associated with each sentence is a "logico-semantic structure" (l-s structure) which displays the logico-semantic relations or interdependencies among the constituents of the sentence. The l-s structure of a sentence is not its semantic representation in the usual sense; it merely represents (a certain set of) the syntactically encoded semantic dependencies among sentential constituents. Logically, it would be possible for languages to connect l-s structures directly to the surface structures of sentences, that is, to express the logico-semantic relations directly in surface structure case marking, structural configurations, and so on. Although a direct mapping between l-s structures and surface structures cannot be ruled out a priori, I claim that a structure called "syntactic structure" similar in form and make-up to l-s structure stands between the l-s structure and surface structure in the analysis of any given sentence. Corresponding to each type of logico-semantic relation and constituent in l-s structure there is a type of grammatical relation and constituent in syntactic structure. Just as the l-s structure of a sentence displays the logico-semantic relations among constituents, so the syntactic structure of a sentence displays the grammatical relations constituents bear with respect to one another.

The model of grammar I adopt in this book is schematized in (1.4). I have drawn (1.4) to emphasize its similarities with the model proposed in Chomsky 1980b and elaborated in Chomsky 1981. In chapter 8 I discuss a few, but important, differences between the two models.

(1.4)

l-s structure

Move Alpha ←——— a general principle

surface structure ———— s structure

phonological structure

On the right-hand side of the grammar in (1.4), the logico-semantic (l-s) structure provides a representation of the compositional semantics of a sentence relevant to syntax (excluding quantifier-scope relations). Technically, an l-s structure displays the logico-semantic relations among constituents of a sentence. These include the relation between a predicate and its subject and that between a verb and a constituent for which the verb determines a semantic role in a sentence, that is, to which the verb assigns a semantic role. In (1.1) the verb *threw* determines that *the porcupine* will bear the theme role; in other words, *threw* assigns the theme role to *the porcupine*.

An l-s structure is essentially a list of l-s constituents and the relations that hold between them. Nevertheless, l-s structure may be represented as a constituent structure tree in which only the dominance relations, and not linear order, are significant. In chapter 2 I explain what the theory of syntax gains by including a structural representation of l-s structure in addition to the list of constituents and relations. Each phrasal constituent at l-s structure consists of a logico-semantic operator, like a predicate, and its l-s dependents, like the subject of the predicate. The l-s relations are represented in the tree structure by asymmetrical sisterhood: when A bears an l-s relation with respect to B, A and B are structural sisters but B is singled out as the operator.

The syntactic (s) structure of a sentence displays the grammatical relations among constituents, such as the relation between a verb phrase and its subject or the relation between a verb and its object. Recall that grammatical relations are grammaticalizations of l-s relations. An s structure is also essentially a list of constituents and the relations that hold between them; but an s structure, like an l-s structure, may be represented as a constituent structure tree in which linear order has no interpretation. Each phrasal constituent at s structure consists of a grammatical operator (e.g., a VP) and its grammatical dependent(s) (e.g., the subject of the VP).

For technical reasons, I view the grammar in (1.4) as strictly nonconstructive. That is, the grammar provides well-formedness conditions on each level of syntactic analysis and each syntactic representation at each level. The genesis of a syntactic representation is unimportant for the grammar; each representation may be built in any random manner employing items from the lexicon. The grammar also includes mapping conditions that indicate whether two distinct representations may be syntactic representations for the same sentence. The theory does not generate an s structure from an l-s structure but rather determines whether a given l-s structure and a given s structure stand in a valid mapping relationship.

In a sanctioned mapping between l-s and s structure, every l-s constituent finds a counterpart at s structure. The grammar must include certain definitions and principles to determine the s structure counterpart to each constituent at l-s structure. Once the correspondence between l-s and s structure constituents is fixed, one general principle governs the mapping between l-s and s structures (called principle M for Mapping principle):

(1.5)
Principle M (preliminary version):
If X bears an l-s relation with respect to Y, Y the operator in the relation, then the s structure counterpart of X must bear a grammatical relation with respect to the s structure counterpart of Y, or with respect to a phrase headed by the s structure counterpart of Y. A constituent is the head of a phrase if it determines the category of the phrase.

The mapping between l-s and s structure is also strictly governed by lexical properties of constituents. For example, only if a verb is grammatically transitive may it take an object at s structure. If a constituent, X, bears a relation with respect to a verb, V, at l-s structure, and the s structure counterpart of verb, V′, is *in*transitive, then the s structure counterpart of the constituent, X′, may not be the object of V′ although this correspondence is allowed by Principle M. Since Vs head VPs, X′ could correspond to the subject of the VP headed by V′ at s structure. Passivization occurs when a logical object of a grammatically intransitive verb corresponds to the subject of the VP that the verb heads at s structure.

No grammatical rules in the usual sense forge the connection between l-s and s structure in (1.4); there are no movements, substitutions, promotions, demotions, or clause unions, only the general principle M. Nor do I posit lexical rules, in the usual sense, to handle such constructions as passives or sentences containing morphologically derived causative forms. Rather, I assume that the only truly productive process in the lexicon is affixation. Affixes, such as the passive affix and the causative affix, carry features just like any other morpheme with a lexical entry. The features of a derived word are determined from the features of its constituent parts according to simple "percolation" conventions described and independently motivated in Lieber 1980. Features of constituent morphemes percolate up in a word tree, which displays the internal structure of a derived word, to become the features of the derived word. The features of affixes take precedence over the features of roots in percolation, although where an affix is unspecified for a feature, that feature percolates up from the root morpheme to become a feature of the derived word. For example, a derived word consisting of a transitive verb and an intransitive affix will be intransitive because the transitivity feature of the affix will take precedence over the transitivity feature of the root in percolation. If the affix were unmarked for transitivity, however, the derived word would be transitive, receiving the transitivity feature of the root. Assigning the correct features to affixes like the passive affix accounts in the present framework for the constructions analyzed in other theories as implicating lexical rules, relation changing rules, rules of clause union, or structure preserving NP movement transformations.

I call the level of structure between l-s and surface structure "syntactic" or "s" structure to emphasize its association with the S-structure of Government-Binding (GB) theory (Chomsky 1981). The principles of GB theory that apply at S-structure and that make crucial reference to the notion "government" will apply to s structure in the present theory; "X governs Y at S-structure" in GB theory is roughly equivalent to "Y bears a grammatical relation with respect to X" in the present framework. One set of GB principles that should apply to s structure in the present framework is "binding theory," which deals with possible reflexive–antecedent connections and with the possibilities of coreference among pronominal and nonpronominal noun phrases in a sentence.[1] In addition, the principles that determine the antecedent for PRO, called "control theory" in the GB framework, should apply at the s structure of (1.4) (on control theory, see especially Manzini 1983).

In the present theory, surface structure, like l-s and s structure, is essentially a list of constituents and relations. The constituents at surface structure are the surface phrase structure constituents of the language. The relations include the structural relations of constituent structure government and string adjacency and the morphology-connected relations of case marking and agreement. Structural government is a tree structure relation of asymmetric sisterhood: X structurally governs Y if X and Y are sisters in a phrase structure tree and X is designated as the operator.

The relations of surface structure constrain the construction of the surface phrase structure tree. Although languages may include additional constraints on surface phrase structure, constraints linguists encode in phrase structure rules, recent work (see Stowell 1981 for example) has indicated that a great deal of surface phrase structure follows from general principles, once surface structure relations are established. Unlike the structural representations of l-s and s structure, linear order in surface phrase structure is significant, as the surface tree serves as input to the phonology. An important principle, related to the Case filter of Government-Binding theory, implies that only constituents that bear relations with respect to lexical items, not to phrases, will appear in the surface structure tree. This principle interacts with other parts of the theory to explain the distribution of PRO and constraints on raising constructions, among other generalizations.

The principle mapping between s and surface structure states simply that every s structure relation must find a counterpart at surface structure: If X bears a relation with respect to Y at s structure, then the surface structure counterpart of X must bear a relation with respect to the surface structure counterpart of Y at surface structure. Since s structure relations may correspond either to structural relations or to case-marking or agreement relations at surface structure, although all relations at s structure are mapped to surface structure, there may be less constituent structure at surface than at s structure. If X bears a case-marking relation with respect to Y at surface structure, for example (that is, Y case marks X), then X need not be a constituent in the surface structure tree. Since the case-marking relation shows up as morphology on the head of X in the surface structure tree, the sub-constituents of X need not hang together in surface constituent structure. A language is "configurational" to the extent that its s structure relations correspond to structural relations at surface structure, rather than to case-marking and agreement relations. As these structural relations represent constraints (or descriptions) of surface constituent structure, they demand that constituents bearing them appear as constituents in the surface structure tree.

Within the present theory, constituents and relations may appear in surface structure that have no s structure counterparts. These are sanctioned in the list of constituents and relations at surface structure by the Move Alpha relation that holds at the surface structure tree. A constituent not corresponding to any s structure constituent may be sanctioned at surface structure if it occupies a nonprojected position in the surface structure tree and binds a trace in a projected position. A projected phrase structure position is a position that expresses some s structure relation; a nonprojected position is the expression of no s structure relation. The relation between binder and trace is called the Move Alpha relation and is constrained by subjacency.

In this work I do not consider issues related to what has been called "logical form." It seems that rules of the logical form component (see Chomsky 1981 and the references cited there) should apply to the pair consisting of the s structure and the surface structure of a sentence to derive a logical form for the sentence. Since syntactic relations determined by Move Alpha are represented at surface structure in (1.4) and since these relations affect the scope of elements, information about surface structure is crucial for logical form. I assume that logical form is basically a representation of scope relations, for example, the scope relations of quantifiers. These scope relations are precisely the semantic relations that are not represented at l-s structure and thus are not projected through s structure to surface structure.

I have nothing to say in the present work about the existence or nature of a level of "semantic interpretation." All four levels, l-s structure, s structure, surface structure, and logical form, contain information relevant to the semantics of a sentence: l-s structure is a representation of semantic relations—compositional semantics—of a certain sort; s structure is the level at which binding theory helps determine possibilities of coreference; surface structure encodes information about topics and foci; logical form represents certain sorts of scope information. I do not think that anyone has argued seriously for a unified level of semantic representation, and I have no idea what such a level would be used for. Linguists are still operating under the misconception that it makes sense for linguistic theory to say that a sentence *has* a meaning. On this view, a linguist must provide a representation of the meaning and relate it to the various syntactic representations of the sentence. But if meaning is not a *thing*, linguists need not capture it. They need only make sure that their account of a speaker's knowledge of a sentence correctly includes the proper information necessary to explain his behavior with respect to the sentence, including his intuitions about it.

Chapter 2
Levels of Syntactic Analysis

In these next six chapters, I develop that section of the model of grammar in (1.4) that leads from logico-semantic (l-s) structure through syntactic (s) structure to surface structure. I describe and discuss the types of constituents found at each level of analysis and the sorts of relations that interconnect the constituents at each level. I also present and explore the consequences of a few general principles that constrain the mapping between l-s and s structures and between s and surface structures.

In addition, I argue for two syntactic distinctions and two features of lexical items. The first distinction is that between the two basic relations "is an argument of" and "receives a {semantic, grammatical} role from." This distinction underlies the intuitive contrast between direct and indirect arguments of a verb or other argument-taking item. The direct argument of a verb takes (so-called) grammatical case marking and depends entirely on the verb for its incorporation into the semantics of a sentence. Indirect arguments, on the other hand, take (so-called) semantic case marking or are arguments of adpositions (prepositions or postpositions) which help determine their semantic role in a sentence.

The second distinction essential to the present theory is that between arguments of phrasal constituents and arguments of lexical items. This distinction underlies the contrast between subjects of verb phrases and arguments of predicative adjective, noun, and adpositional phrases on the one hand, and objects and oblique arguments of verbs and other lexical items on the other.

In addition to these two distinctions, the theory makes crucial use of two lexical features. One feature distinguishes two classes of predicate-forming lexical items: those that head predicates that take arguments and those that head predicates that do not. The second feature distinguishes lexical items that assign a syntactic role from those that do not. The first feature separates passive, raising-to-subject, unaccusative, and impersonal verbs from others. The second divides verbs into transitives and intransitives. Showing how these distinctions and features interact with a few general principles to explain a wide range of syntactic phenomena constitutes the major portion of my contribution to the theory of grammatical relations.

2.1. Logico-Semantic (l-s) Structure

Linguists generally agree that there are semantic relations that hold among sentential constituents, more particularly, among the morphemes and phrases in a sentence. I shall argue that there are two basic semantic relations which have syntactic significance. A major thesis of this book is that the semantic interrelations among morphemes determine the grammatical relations in a sentence, which, in turn, determine the surface structure of the sentence. Borrowing terminology from Chomsky (1981), I characterize the syntactic theory of this book as falling within the class of theories containing "projection principles." A projection principle determines how the argument structures of lexical items project into the syntactic structure of a sentence.

By definition, logico-semantic structure is a representation of certain semantic constituents of a sentence and of their semantic interdependencies. One can conceive of a variety of representations that would explicitly display these constituents and relations, perhaps the simplest being a list of the constituents and of the relations that interconnect them. I assume that l-s structure is essentially such a list. It is important to ask whether a structural representation of the semantic interrelations among morphemes, as in a constituent structure tree, holds any significance over and above a simple listing of the (semantically interacting) morphemes and phrases and the relations that connect them. As we shall see, there is a role for such a representation—that is, for l-s structure as a *structure*—but it is not to serve as input to rules mapping to grammatical relations—as input to the rules mapping to s structure.

In this section I introduce the types of constituents that are found at l-s structure and the sorts of relations in which these constituents stand with respect to one another.

2.1.1. Semantic Roles and l-s Relations

A verb is associated with some number of inherent semantic roles, roles inextricably connected with the meaning of the verb. Although locative, benefactive, temporal, and other such phrases may be interpreted freely with a wide range of verbs, certain roles are implicated in the semantics of verbs themselves, and arguments bearing these roles appear only with the verbs that select them. In (2.1) I list some verbs with their associated semantic roles (see section 2.1.2 for a discussion of the semantic role terms).

(2.1)

a. *touch:* agent, patient

b. *give:* agent, theme, goal

c. *buy:* source (seller), goal (buyer), theme (thing bought), means (money exchanged)

Although it may be difficult in practice to tell whether or not a constituent in a given sentence bears one of the inherent semantic roles of the verb heading the sentence, the distinction between inherent and noninherent semantic roles may be clearly stated: The verb dictates how to incorporate the constituents bearing its inherent semantic roles into the semantics of the clause of which it is the head. Noninherent semantic roles are adverbial in the sense that the semantic effect on the clause of the constituents bearing them is not determined by the head of the clause.

The inherent semantic roles associated with a verb constitute its "case frame" in the terminology of Case Grammar.[1] Although they argue about specific examples, case grammarians and others who work on thematic or semantic roles[2] more or less agree on the number and sorts of semantic roles to attribute to verbs. (Ostler 1979 surveys the literature on thematic/semantic roles; Abraham 1978 contains a number of articles on case frames.) According to general consensus, verbs possess from zero to perhaps a maximum of four inherent roles. English weather verbs like *rain* fall at the low end of the spectrum with no inherent semantic roles; transactional verbs like *buy* and *sell* fall at the high end with four roles each—see (2.1c).

Various attempts have been made to provide an adequate account of the semantic roles that seem to be involved in verb semantics. The work of Jackendoff (1976), Ostler (1979), and Carter (1976) illustrates one of the most interesting of the approaches. Although I will argue for a radically different conception of semantic roles from that offered by these authors, an understanding of their approach is an indispensable prerequisite to an appreciation of mine.

Jackendoff (1976) and Ostler (1979) decompose the meanings of verbs into complexes of primitive predicates such as CAUSE (x, y) and GO (x, y, z) (I follow Jackendoff's 1976 notation in this discussion). Constituents bear one or another semantic role by virtue of appearing in a particular slot in one of these primitive predicates. For example, a constituent falling into the first slot of the GO (x, y, z) predicate bears the theme role, that appearing in the third slot the goal role. To say that the subject of, for example, *fly* bears the theme role is to say that the GO predicate appears in the semantic decomposition of *fly* and that *fly*'s subject is inserted into the first slot of this predicate. Jackendoff (1976, 94) gives (2.2) as a semantic representation for *fly*.

(2.2)

$$fly: \begin{bmatrix} \text{GO } (x,y,z) \\ \text{THROUGH THE AIR} \end{bmatrix}$$

In Jackendoff's system, a verb's inherent semantic roles are simply the roles associated with the slots in the primitive predicates that constitute the verb's semantic decomposition.

The issue of whether words are semantically decomposable is irrelevant to this book (but see Fodor, Fodor, and Garrett 1975, Fodor et al. 1980), although I must assume that the linguistically relevant representation of a verb's argument structure generally involves no decomposition. Each verb is viewed as a function[3] from arguments bearing certain specified semantic roles to predicates, which may assign an additional semantic role to their subjects. The semantic roles borne by the arguments that serve as input to the function that the verb names plus the semantic role assigned by the predicate that is the output of this function constitute the verb's inherent semantic roles. Consider a verb like *give,* which I claimed in (2.1) to have for its inherent semantic roles a giver (or agent), a receiver (or goal), and a given (or theme). The function that *give* names ('give') takes as input an argument bearing the goal role and an argument bearing the theme role and yields a predicate which we might paraphrase as the open sentence (x give theme-NP to goal-NP). The predicate assigns the agent, or more properly, the "giver of theme-NP to goal-NP" role to its subject—that constituent which substitutes for its free variable to form a proposition.

One may represent a verb's semantics in the functional notation shown in (2.3).

(2.3)

'give' (,   )
          theme   goal

The representation in (2.3) indicates that the 'give' function requires an argument bearing the theme semantic role to fill its first slot and an argument bearing the goal role to fill its second slot. The value of the function in (2.3) is a predicate that assigns the giver role to its subject. For typographical convenience, I place the names of the semantic roles borne by arguments filling each slot in a function like (2.3) inside rather than underneath the slots, as shown in (2.4).

(2.4)

'give' (theme, goal)

I call representations such as (2.4) "predicate-argument structures" or P-A structures.

2.1.1.1. Direct vs. Indirect Arguments   One essential difference between P-A structures and Jackendoff's notation for primitive predicates is that whereas constituents in Jackendoff's framework receive their semantic roles by virtue of occupying positions within predicates, the constituents inserted in the slots of a P-A structure like (2.4) already bear the indicated semantic roles. These semantic roles must be assigned to them in some manner independent of the verb's function from arguments to predicates. Thus I distinguish the argument-taker–argument relation (the relation between the function and its arguments) from the semantic-role-assigner–semantic-role-assignee relation. The role-assigner–role-assignee relation holds between a constituent bearing a semantic role and the item that determines which semantic role the constituent will bear. The 'give' function in (2.4) is defined only over ordered pairs of constituents, the first bearing the theme role, the second the goal role. For a constituent to serve as argument to 'give,' it must be assigned the theme role or goal role first. In the present theory, I separate the organization of arguments into a predicate, performed by the function that a verb names, from the assignment of semantic roles to these arguments.

Since it is crucial to this book, the notion of semantic role assignment warrants further clarification. Consider sentence (2.5).

(2.5)

Elmer gave a porcupine to Hortense.

Speakers of English know from sentence (2.5) that *Elmer* denotes a giver, that *a porcupine* denotes something that underwent a transference of possession, and that *Hortense* denotes the recipient of *a porcupine*. One general approach to accounting for this knowledge is to suppose that the verb *gave* in (2.5) names a machine that organizes the NPs of (2.5) into some sort of structure suitable for semantic interpretation. On this account, speakers may deduce the semantic roles of the various NPs from the semantic interpretation of the sentence. This is basically Jackendoff's approach. I adopt the alternative view that constituents in sentences assign semantic roles to—determine the semantic roles of—other constituents independent of the semantic organization of the entire sentence or clause in which the constituents appear. For example, the preposition *to* assigns the goal or recipient role to *Hortense* in (2.5) independent of the fact that *Hortense* serves as an argument of *gave*. On this view a speaker's knowledge of the semantic role of a constituent need not be deduced from the semantic representation of a sentence but may be computed directly from a syntactic analysis of the sentence. A determination of the semantic roles borne by constituents is in fact logically prior to the derivation of a semantic representation since verbs, for example, name functions from constituents *bearing certain semantic roles* to predicates.

In sentence (2.5), in addition to naming a function from arguments to a predicate, *gave* assigns the given, or theme, role to *the porcupine*. The preposition *to* assigns the goal role to *Hortense,* and the predicate (x give the porcupine to Hortense) assigns to *Elmer* the role of "giver of the porcupine to Hortense." I will italicize within the P-A structure of a verb the semantic role or roles the verb assigns, as in (2.6).

(2.6)
'give' (*theme,* goal)

The marking of oblique arguments in English provides direct support for the assignment of semantic roles independent of the filling of argument positions in P-A structures. Consider verbs like *give, put,* and *steal,* which I assume to have P-A structures something like those shown in (2.7).

(2.7)
a. 'give' (*theme,* goal)
b. 'put' (*theme,* location)
c. 'steal' (*theme,* source)

Note that the prepositions used to mark the second arguments of these verbs assign the semantic roles of these arguments to their objects when they are used to head adjectival PPs and not to mark the arguments of verbs. Compare the sentences in (2.8) and (2.9).

(2.8)

a. Elmer gave two porcupines to *Hortense*.

b. Elmer put the porcupine on *the table*.

c. Elmer stole a porcupine from *the zoo*.

(2.9)

a. The train to *Pittsburgh* arrived at the station.

b. The porcupine on *the table* slipped its leash.

c. The porcupine from *the zoo* was tamer than the rest.

The italicized NPs in the sentences in (2.8) bear the same semantic roles as those borne by the italicized NPs in the corresponding sentences in (2.9). If one assumed that arguments receive their semantic roles simply by virtue of filling argument slots in P-A structures, then it would be an accident that the same items (e.g., the same prepositions) that are used to mark a verb's arguments also independently assign the semantic roles of these arguments when not being used for this purpose. If the source argument of *steal,* for example, received its semantic role simply by occupying the second slot in P-A structure (2.7c), it would be an accident that *from,* which assigns the source role in other constructions as evidenced by (2.9c), is used to mark *steal*'s source argument. Since *steal* in this case would, in effect, be assigning the source role itself, *from* would be unnecessary.

Joan Bresnan has pointed out (personal communication) that one can explain the use of semantically appropriate prepositions to mark a verb's arguments even if these arguments are treated on par with a verb's subject or object. Within Lexical-Functional Grammar, for example, what I have been calling direct and indirect arguments are all associated with essentially equivalent slots in a predicate-argument structure. However, some slots may be linked to semantically unrestricted grammatical functions like subject and object, while others are linked to semantically restricted functions like oblique object, marked by various prepositions. For an argument position to be linked to a semantically restricted grammatical function, the argument occupying that position must bear a semantic role appropriate to the restriction. For example, in order for an argument of a verb to be associated with the oblique *from*-object function, it must bear the source role.

It should be clear that, at the present level of discussion, the Lexical-Functional notion of an argument bearing a semantically restricted oblique function and my notion of an indirect argument of a verb are equivalent. In both cases, the semantic role of the argument in question is constrained not only by the verb (the verb takes only certain types of arguments) but by something else—the preposition *from* for example. In the framework of this book, the preposition assigns a certain semantic role; in Bresnan's terms, the preposition marks a constituent bearing a grammatical function that is restricted to a certain semantic role. In both frameworks the explanation for the data in (2.8)–(2.9) is that the verb alone is not the only constituent that may provide information about the semantic role of certain of its arguments.

If all of a verb's arguments received their semantic roles from the verb, one might expect all the arguments to be marked in the same manner, or with some arbitrary marking to specify which argument goes in which slot in a P-A structure. That some arguments of a verb are marked in the same manner as NPs bearing identical semantic roles but not serving as arguments of a verb is the strongest evidence for viewing the assignment of semantic roles to arguments as independent of P-A structures. In fact, the data in (2.8)–(2.9) display exactly what I mean when I talk about independent semantic role assignment, that is, the determination of semantic roles of arguments independent of their status as arguments.

The distinction between the assignment of a semantic role to a constituent and that constituent's serving as an argument to an argument-taking item is crucial in distinguishing direct arguments of argument-taking items (arguments that also receive their role from their argument takers) and indirect arguments (arguments that do not receive their roles from their argument takers). Although the particular cutting point between the classes differs, the direct/indirect argument distinction finds its way into most linguistic theories. Relational Grammar distinguishes between pure grammatical relations like 1's and 2's and impure relations like benefactives and locatives. Lexical-Functional Grammar (Bresnan 1982b) employs a similar classification of relations.

Although there are a number of ways of formulating the basic distinction between direct and indirect arguments, the particular formulation chosen for the present theory plays a central role in the explanation of a range of grammatical phenomena. For example, the treatment of passivization provided in chapter 4 interacts with my characterization of direct and indirect arguments to explain why only

direct arguments passivize in most situations, that is, show up as subjects of passive verbs.

So in the present theory constituents do not receive semantic roles
by virtue of occupying slots in predicates like GO (x, y, z) but rather
are assigned their semantic roles. Semantic roles may be assigned by at
least the items listed in (2.10).

(2.10)
a. lexical items (verbs, prepositions, nouns, adjectives)
b. predicates
c. case markings
d. certain structural positions

The verb's assignment of a semantic role to its logical object is the
canonical case of semantic role assignment. Similarly, other argument-
taking lexical items may assign semantic roles to their direct arguments. For example, I assume that some derived nominals assign
semantic roles to their *of*-objects (but see Rappaport 1983). So in (2.11),
destruction assigns the destroyed role to *the city* (see section 2.2.3.2 for
some discussion of derived nominals).

(2.11)
the destruction of the city

I also assume that a predicate assigns a semantic role to its subject.

Although a general principle yet to be discussed ensures that the argument of a predicate will always be a direct argument—that is, it cannot receive its semantic role from some constituent other than the
predicate—the separation of semantic role assignment and argument
taking in the case of the subject proves essential to the analysis of certain derived causative constructions in chapter 7. In the most normal
situation, the case markings that assign semantic roles are the markings
usually called the semantic cases, such as locative, benefactive, or instrumental case. When a case marking is associated with a certain
semantic role and the constituent bearing the case also bears the role,
then one says, usually, that the case marking assigns the constituent its
semantic role.

Like a particular case marking, when a structural position becomes
associated with a particular semantic role, it too may assign this role.
Consider sentence (2.12). In chapter 5, I claim that the theme NP, *a
porcupine,* receives its role from the structural position [NP, VP] ("NP
of VP," or the NP immediately dominated by VP in a phrase structure

tree), which is the canonical expression of themes and patients in English.

(2.12)
Elmer gave Hortense a porcupine.

According to this account, *a porcupine* in (2.12) is an indirect argument of the verb *gave* and should display precisely the same syntactic behavior it would if it were marked by a preposition.

   It seems that, in the unmarked case, each semantic role assigner may assign only one semantic role. To derive some results in chapters 5 and 7 concerning double object constructions and applied verbs, I need to elevate this observation to the status of a principle:

(2.13)
The One Role/Role Assigner Principle:
In the unmarked case, a semantic role assigner may assign only one role.

Moreover, an argument-taking item tends to assign a role to its argument, if it can. I incorporate this apparent tendency into principle (2.14).

(2.14)
The Direct Argument Principle:
In the unmarked case, an argument-taking item will assign a semantic role to its argument.

Principle (2.14) implies that unmarked arguments are direct arguments.
   The One Role/Role Assigner and Direct Argument principles are restrictive principles formulated by noting observable tendencies in the world's languages. In contrast, principle (2.15) is a stipulative constraint essential to the present theory.

(2.15)
The Lexical Exception Principle:
Exceptions (to markedness principles) must be encoded in the lexical entries of lexical items.

Since predicates are phrases, not lexical items, they lack lexical entries, which might contain exceptional features. Thus, by the One Role/Role Assigner and Lexical Exception principles, predicates will assign at most one semantic role each, and by the Direct Argument and Lexical Exception principles, the argument of a predicate will receive its semantic role from the predicate; that is, the subject of the predicate will be a direct argument.

The notions of semantic role assignment and argument structure provide definitions for the two basic semantic relations of l-s structure: that between an argument-taking item (like a verb or predicate) and its arguments, and that between a semantic role assigner and the constituent to which it assigns a semantic role. Other semantic relations may be defined in terms of these basic relations and the constituent types of l-s structure. For example, I define the logical object of a verb as the constituent that both serves as argument to and receives a semantic role from the verb. The logical subject of a predicate is the constituent serving as argument and semantic role assignee of the predicate.

2.1.1.2. l-s Subject-Object Asymmetries   To repeat, constituents are assigned their semantic roles in the present theory; they do not receive roles by virtue of occupying slots in predicates. Another important difference between P-A structures of this book and the sort of predicate notation employed by Jackendoff and others is that the former but not the latter imply an asymmetry among the inherent semantic roles associated with a verb. In the Jackendoff (1976) framework and in many current theories all semantic dependents of a verb simply fill slots in n-ary predicates such as GO (x, y, z). This equality of arguments characterizes Bresnan's Lexical-Functional Grammar, Williams's argument structures (Williams 1981), and Montague Grammar (Dowty 1982a, 1982b) as well. In a theory with symmetric argument structures, the choice of one argument can in no way affect the semantic role assigned to another argument of the predicate. All arguments are independent and on par. In contrast to the symmetric argument structures of these other frameworks, the asymmetric P-A structures incorporated into the present theory assure that the choice of arguments to fill P-A slots will affect the semantic role assigned to the (logical) subject. Since the P-A structures of verbs are functions from arguments to predicates, which arguments one inserts into the P-A structures determines what predicate the function will yield. As the predicate assigns the logical subject its semantic role, choice of arguments for P-A structures determines the semantic role of the logical subject.

By way of illustration, consider the sentences in (2.16a) and (2.17a). The verb *give* provided with the arguments in (2.16a) will yield the predicate in (2.16b); *give* provided with the arguments in (2.17a) will yield the predicate in (2.17b).

(2.16)
a. Elmer gave the porcupine to Hortense.
b. 'give' (the porcupine, Hortense) = (x give the porcupine to Hortense)

(2.17)
a. Elmer gave two aardvarks to Horace.
b. 'give' (two aardvarks, Horace) = (x give two aardvarks to Horace)

Since the different choice of arguments as theme and goal in (2.16a) and (2.17a) produce different predicates, *Elmer,* the logical subject of both sentences, will bear a distinct role in each, the "giver of the porcupine to Hortense" role in (2.16a) and the "giver of two aardvarks to Horace" role in (2.17a). But regardless of what NP is chosen as subject of *give the porcupine to Hortense, the porcupine* will be assigned the same theme role by *give*.

The proposed distinction between the logical subject and the verb's arguments implies an asymmetry between the effects of changing the arguments of a verb and the effects of changing the logical subject of a predicate. Choice of arguments for a verb can affect the semantic role assigned to the logical subject, but in no way may the choice of logical subject affect the semantic roles assigned to the verb's arguments. Although the predictions of this asymmetric treatment of a verb's semantic dependents are clear, they are not easy to test. Compare sentences (2.16a) and (2.17a) with sentences (2.18).

(2.18)
a. Elmer sold two porcupines to Hortense.
b. Horace sold two porcupines to Hortense.

I claimed without argument that *Elmer* bears the "giver of the porcupine to Hortense" role in (2.16a) but the "giver of two aardvarks to Horace" role in (2.17a)—two clearly distinct roles assigned to *Elmer* by the distinct predicates that the 'give' function produces when handed distinct sets of arguments. One could with equal justification claim that *two porcupines* bears the "sold by Elmer" role in (2.18a) but the "sold by Horace" role in (2.18b) instead of bearing simply the sold or theme role in both sentences. Clearly, being sold by Elmer differs from being sold by Horace. What is not clear is whether this difference demonstrates that *two porcupines* is assigned different roles in (2.18a,b).

If I restricted attention to examples like (2.16)–(2.18), I could not argue for the proposed asymmetry among verb dependents. In such examples, changing the logical subject seems to have as much effect on the semantic role borne by the verb's logical object as changing the logical object has on the semantic role borne by the verb's logical subject, and the effect in both cases is minimal. Expanding the data base, however, yields convincing evidence in English for the predicted asymmetry. Just about every simple transitive English verb expresses a wide range of predicates depending on the choice of direct object. The predicates in (2.19) illustrate this phenomenon.

(2.19)
a. throw a baseball
b. throw support behind a candidate
c. throw a boxing match (i.e., take a dive)
d. throw a party
e. throw a fit
f. take a book from the shelf
g. take a bus to New York
h. take a nap
i. take an aspirin for a cold
j. take a letter in shorthand
k. kill a cockroach
l. kill a conversation
m. kill an evening watching T.V.
n. kill a bottle (i.e., empty it)
o. kill an audience (i.e., wow them)

One might distinguish the basic or literal uses of the verbs in (2.19) from their metaphoric and idiomatic uses, yet no clear lines divide the classes. Although the different predicates formed by adding different direct objects to most simple transitive verbs assign different semantic roles to their subjects, one would be hard pressed to argue that a different predicate implies a different (homophonous) verb in each case. The person throwing a baseball propels it through the air with a motion of his arm; the person throwing a party may do no more than telephone a few guests; the person throwing a fit thrashes about on the floor. Despite these differences in subject semantic role, may one not maintain that the verb *throw* in at least the majority of its uses names the same function from arguments to predicates, with the variety of predicates displayed in (2.19) being attributable to the variety of input arguments to this function? Killing a cockroach involves causing it to become not alive; killing an evening may be accomplished by sitting motionless in front of a T.V.; and killing a bottle implies causing it to become empty, yet some thread of meaning ties these uses of *kill* together, a thread we may weave into a single function, 'kill,' from arguments to predicates. For present purposes, the importance of the range of predicates illustrated in (2.19) lies in the dependence of the predicate on the choice of arguments for the verbs.

It might be claimed that the semantic roles borne by the direct objects in (2.19) also differ from use to use of the verbs. Thus *a book* in (2.19f) may be called a theme since it undergoes a change in position, whereas *a letter* in (2.19j) is something created, undergoing a change in state, perhaps, but not necessarily a change in position. Although the identification of the particular semantic or thematic roles assigned by verbs is a vexing problem (see section 2.1.2), regardless of whether the direct objects in (2.19) do differ in semantic role from use to use of the verbs, the choice of subject for the verbs does not determine the semantic role of their objects. Consider the sentence schemas in (2.20).

(2.20)
a. The policeman threw NP.
b. The boxer threw NP.
c. The social director threw NP.
d. Aardvarks throw NP.
e. Throw NP!
f. Harry killed NP.
g. Everyone is always killing NP.
h. The drunk refused to kill NP.
i. Silence can certainly kill NP.
j. Cars kill NP.

Although the more material these sentence fragments contain and the more elaborate the context one sets them in, the more they suggest particular direct objects and therefore particular predicates, the different subjects for the verbs do not imply different semantic roles for the object NPs. Note that certain subjects may violate the selectional restrictions of certain predicates, thereby limiting the range of predicates that may happily cooccur with them. Thus *Silence threw NP* does not readily support a reading in which *throw* produces the predicate it does in *Harry threw the baseball*. Varying the subject of a transitive verb, however, simply does not produce a range of predicates on objects similar to the range of predicates on subjects produced by varying the objects of transitive verbs. This is the asymmetry that confirms my conception of verb semantics: choice of object (or other argument of a verb) affects the semantic role of the logical subject whereas choice of logical subject does not affect the semantic role of the object.

The compositional asymmetry between the logical subject and a verb's arguments explains another striking property of English. New predicates in English are created by modifying a verb's function from arguments to predicates. That is, new values are given to the function for certain special input arguments. As a result of the asymmetric compositional semantics of sentences, then, there are countless object idioms in English like *kick the bucket* while subject idioms that are not also full phrasal idioms are rare, if they exist at all. Object idioms are combinations of verb plus object with slightly or highly unusual semantics from what one would expect from the canonical uses of the verb. A subject idiom would be an idiomatic combination of subject and verb. I know of only one such idiom with a free object position. Bresnan (1982a), in a criticism of an earlier version of this work, points out *What's eating NP,* meaning 'what's bothering NP,' as a possible example. This particular idiom has a peculiar property not always associated with object idioms: its sentential syntax is fixed. One can change the idiom to the past tense—*What was eating NP yesterday?*—but no sentence internal modifications are allowed (it is argued in sections 2.3.3 and 3.1 that tense should be considered a sentence-external modifier). For example, the idiom requires progressive aspect; *What ate NP?* lacks the idiomatic reading. From the point of view of the present theory, it is important that this apparent subject idiom has no S-internal syntax, for it is precisely S-internal syntax that is at issue. *What's eating NP?* is not a combination of subject and verb, forming a predicate on the object, but rather a combination of *wh-* question syntax, progressive aspect, plus subject and verb—that is, a complete sentence frame—with an open slot for an argument. Apart from the sentence frame *What's eating x,* although one does find idiomatic expressions with fixed subjects—for example, *The shit hit the fan*—the objects in such expressions are also fixed. One cannot say, *The shit hit the air conditioner* when things really go wrong.[4]

The evidence from the preponderance of object over subject idioms simply reinforces the conclusions derived from the range of predicates in (2.19). Predicates are created by functions on objects and other arguments excluding the logical subject.

Bresnan (1982a) has objected to the claims of this section on two grounds: that my argument depends on faulty logic and that its conclusions are factually inaccurate. On the first point, Bresnan is simply being unfair. She attributes a conclusion to me that I do not support, then points out that my argument does not prove this conclusion.

The assumption is that if the subject is always the *last* argument to be semantically composed with the predicate, one can explain the generalization that the choice of nonsubject arguments does not depend on the choice of the subject argument. By suppressing the subject argument from the verb's predicate argument structure, one prevents the subject from being combined directly with the verb before the verb and its nonsubject arguments have been assembled into a predicate; the subject can then be semantically composed only with a completely formed predicate. But the issue of whether or not the subject argument has a special role in the semantic composition of the sentence is logically independent of the issue of whether or not a subject argument position should appear in lexical predicate argument structure. For example, in Dowty's theory [Dowty 1982a], the subject is always the last argument to be semantically composed with the predicate; yet the lexical function that expresses the meaning of a transitive verb in his theory contains variables for both the subject and the object arguments. In short, one could capture the subject/nonsubject generalization without affecting the lexical representation of predicate argument structure, simply by giving the subject a distinguished role as final argument in the semantic composition of the sentence. (Bresnan 1982a, 350)

Bresnan somehow takes the foregoing discussion as an argument for a particular representation of semantic subject/nonsubject asymmetries. It should be clear that all I am doing at present is arguing for the asymmetries themselves. The arguments for the particular representation of the asymmetries within the present theory come from considerations of the operation of the theory as a whole. I choose the present form of representation for these asymmetries—excluding the subject from the P-A structure—because it both correctly captures the semantic asymmetries, as Bresnan points out in the quoted passage, and allows me to relate semantic subject/nonsubject asymmetries to parallel syntactic asymmetries. It also interacts with other principles to correctly constrain the possible syntactic effects of derivational morphology, as argued in chapters 4 through 7. In chapter 8 I argue specifically against Dowty's (1982a) representation of subject/nonsubject semantic asymmetries. In summary, Bresnan is correct in pointing out that the foregoing arguments alone do not choose a representation for semantic subject/nonsubject asymmetries, but this point is of little importance.

As Bresnan herself notes, my notation correctly predicts the asymmetries; this much is sufficient at this point in the presentation of the theory.

Turning now to Bresnan's factual quarrels with my arguments, I respond to each of her points in turn.

First, there are in fact subject idioms with free non-subject arguments: for example, *The cat's got x's tongue* ('x can't speak'), *What's eating x?* ('What is making *x* so irritable?'), *Time's up (for x)* ('The time (for *x*) has expired'), *x's goose is cooked* ('x is in trouble and there is no way out'). (Bresnan 1982a, 350)

Note that only *What's eating x?* actually meets the schema for a potential counterexample to the claim that there are no subject idioms with free object positions. Although they contain idiomatic subject material, the other idioms Bresnan lists do not have free objects. We may dismiss *x's goose is cooked* as irrelevant, as this is a passive sentence whose subject is presumably its logical object (cf. *They cooked his goose*). My arguments obviously imply that idiomatic material should not appear as a logical subject (in a sentence with a free, i.e., nonidiomatic predicate-internal argument position); the compositional semantics of a sentence are represented directly only at l-s structure, not at s structure, where grammatical relations are encoded. This leaves *The cat's got x's tongue* and *Time's up (for x)*. The latter example falls together with another set of examples Bresnan brings up and will be discussed with them later. The former raises some interesting questions, but is not relevant to the issue at hand (I in fact mention *The cat's got x's tongue* in Marantz 1981b, to which Bresnan is replying). A study of *A Dictionary of American Idioms* (Boatner and Gates 1975) reveals that idioms with a free possessive slot are perhaps the most common phrasal idioms with free argument positions. How one should represent the structure of these idioms is an open question. For example, in *Elmer got her goat*, what sort of argument is *her*? One has a free hand in the analysis of such idioms, at least currently; therefore, they cannot be used to argue against the subject/object asymmetries in idioms.

Bresnan continues:

Second, there are clear cases in which the semantic choice of a non-subject argument does depend upon the choice of the subject. Consider, for example, (6a–c).

(6)
a. The ceiling caved in on John.
b. The wall caved in on John.
c. The roof caved in on John.

Example (6c) has a figurative or metaphorical sense ('Everything went wrong for John') as well as the literal sense that part of the structure of a house collapsed on John; but examples (6a,b) are unambiguously literal. Thus, the choice of *the roof* as subject of *caved in* gives rise to a special meaning. Under this special meaning, one can choose as the object of *on* an abstract noun phrase which cannot occur with the literal meaning:

(7)
a. #The ceiling caved in on John's dreams.
b. #The wall caved in on John's dreams.
c. The roof caved in on John's dreams.

How do we know that it is not the object of *on* which gives rise to the special meaning and thereby determines the choice of the subject *the roof*? When we omit the *on* phrase altogether, we find that *The roof caved in* still has the figurative sense 'Everything went wrong' while *The ceiling caved in* and *The wall caved in* lack it. It is not difficult to find other examples which support the same conclusion (e.g. *A truck hit John* vs. *An idea hit John* . . .). (Bresnan 1982a, 350–351)

Bresnan's examples fail to support her point on a number of grounds. First, note that the free argument in *The roof caved in on NP* is not the object of the verb. Principles yet to be described in detail make it perfectly plausible that when a sentence lacks a syntactic object, the syntactic subject of the sentence may in fact be the logical object of the verb. There is good evidence that groups of verbs in many languages are syntactically intransitive but take logical objects—the unaccusative verbs of Relational Grammar. The logical objects of such verbs become syntactic subjects at s structure. So Bresnan has no argument that there is even a logical subject in her examples (6)–(7). Similar considerations hold for idioms like *Time's up for x* and *Fortune smiled on x* (pointed out to me by Probal Dasgupta). Oblique free arguments of intransitive idioms cannot be crucial to this issue.

Moreover, for both *The roof caved in (on x)* and *Time's up (for x),* as Bresnan points out, the free argument is optional in the idiom. Therefore, the idioms may be analyzed compositionally as [[The roof caved in] on NP] and [[Time's up] for NP], with the prepositions dictating the semantic effects of adding the free argument to an already complete full phrasal idiom.

Bresnan's putative counterexamples to my claim that subject idioms do not exist (pace *What's eating NP*) actually prove my point. That a linguist trying to settle an important issue could only come up with

examples in which the free argument is buried in an oblique prepositional phrase or as the possessive in an NP increases one's confidence
in the rarity of true subject idioms—idioms with fixed logical subjects
and free argument positions. Bresnan gives *A truck hit John* vs. *An idea
hit John* as a parting shot, but it is clear that the latter sentence contains
a metaphoric use of *hit* that permits a wide range of subjects and objects (*Misfortune hit Elmer, Inspiration hit Hortense, Apathy hit the city*,
etc.) Moreover, it simply is not true that "It is not difficult to find other
examples which support the same conclusion"—the conclusion that
there are no subject/object asymmetries in idioms and ranges of predicates. Bresnan provides no convincing examples and even pseudo-
examples are difficult to uncover, as I, a former skeptic about this sort
of argument, can attest after many hours of fruitless searching.[5]

2.1.2. Semantic Roles and the Construction of Predicate-Argument Structures

To this point I have been somewhat loose in my identification of the
semantic roles associated with verbs. The assumption motivating the
preceding discussion was that each semantic role assigner may, in principle, assign a unique role or a unique set of roles. For example, although their logical objects are both things acted upon so that they
move, *throw* and *push* need not assign precisely the same semantic
role; that is, the throwee and pushee roles may be distinct. Nevertheless, although semantic role assigners may assign their own unique
roles, there are, apparently, linguistically significant classes of semantic roles. I consider terms like "agent" and "theme" as naming such
semantic role classes.[6] On this view there is no reason to exclude a
given semantic role, say that role assigned by *swim down the river*, from
being both an agent and a theme, that is, from belonging to more than
one semantic role class.

The grammatical machinery that makes reference to semantic role
classes includes the notation of P-A structures. Consider a verb like
put, which requires some sort of locative argument in addition to a
theme, but does not specify exactly what sort of location. A variety of
prepositions may be used to express *put*'s locative argument, each assigning this argument a different semantic role, but *some* locative preposition must be used.

(2.21)

$$
\text{Elmer put the porcupine}
\left\{
\begin{array}{ll}
\text{a.} & \text{in the box} \\
\text{b.} & \text{on the table} \\
\text{c.} & \text{under the hedge} \\
\text{d.} & \text{through the window} \\
\text{e.} & \text{*during the movie} \\
\text{f.} & \text{*after the fall} \\
\text{g.} & \text{*on weekends} \\
\text{h.} & \text{*quietly} \\
\text{i.} & \text{*aardvarks}
\end{array}
\right\}
$$

The P-A structure for *put* must specify that it takes a locative argument without insisting on a particular prepositional phrase expression for the argument. Therefore, some semantic role class term, "location," is needed in P-A structures, as shown in (2.22).

(2.22)
'put' (*theme,* location)

From the fact that classes of semantic roles have linguistic significance, one should not conclude that all semantic roles fall into one or more linguistically significant classes. It is quite possible that the semantic roles assigned by some items are not classifiable. For example, the logical object of *like* is neither theme (thing moved) nor patient (thing affected by the action of the verb). Perhaps the only linguistically significant piece of information an English speaker knows about the role assigned by *like* is that it is the role assigned by *like*.

In addition to appearing in P-A structures, semantic role classes seem necessary to express generalizations about the organization of P-A structures within a language. In English and many other languages, it is generally true that if one of the inherent roles associated with a verb is an agent role (the role of an active, animate being who intentionally causes something), then this role will be assigned to the logical subject of the predicate that the verb produces. It is also generally true in these languages that theme inherent roles (roles of objects which the verb specifies to undergo a change of state or location or of which the verb indicates a location) and patient inherent roles (roles of objects that bear the brunt of the action described by the verb) are assigned by verbs—that is, they are borne by logical objects. These generalizations must be stated within the grammar of a language, where "grammar" is taken broadly to mean the representation of a speaker's knowledge of his language. A straightforward statement of the generalizations for English is given in (2.23).

(2.23)
a. agent roles—logical subject
b. theme/patient roles—logical object

The existence of generalizations like (2.23) raises two important questions. First, why should languages incorporate such generalizations at all; that is, why shouldn't some verbs assign agent roles to their logical objects and have theme/patient roles assigned to their logical subjects while others conform to (2.23)? Second, assuming that a grammar incorporating generalizations like (2.23) is somehow more highly valued than a grammar without them, why do English and many other languages employ the particular generalizations in (2.23) and not, say, the reverse generalizations in (2.24)?

(2.24)
a. agent roles—logical object
b. theme/patient roles—logical subject

In Marantz 1982a I report the results of two experiments that I conducted with 3- to 5-year-old children which suggest an answer to the first question. These experiments support the hypothesis that, until about the age of 5, children's knowledge of language connects semantic roles directly to their surface structure expressions. For example, English-speaking children know that agents are placed preverbally and theme/patients postverbally. The experiments show that 3- and 4-year-old children have greater difficulty learning to use verbs whose P-A structures lead the verbs to violate these generalizations about the connection of semantic roles and surface positions (in active declarative sentences) than verbs whose P-A structures lead the verbs to conform to these generalizations. Consider the made-up verb *moak*, meaning 'to pound with the elbow,' with P-A structure (2.25).

(2.25)
moak 'pound with the elbow' (*agent*); logical subject = patient

Sentences like (2.26) containing *moak* violate English-speaking 3- and 4-year-olds' generalizations that agents come preverbally, patients postverbally.

(2.26)
The book is moaking Larry.

My experiments demonstrate that English-speaking 3- and 4-year-olds have more difficulty learning to use verbs like *moak* than made-up verbs conforming to the generalizations in (2.23). When 3- and 4-year-olds are shown a videotape of Larry pounding a book with his elbow and are told, "The book is moaking Larry," they tend to make *moak* conform to their generalizations about the association of semantic roles and surface positions. For example, they tend to say, "Cindy is moaking the ball," when shown Cindy pounding a ball with her elbow. For the child's spontaneous use of *moak* to be correct in the adult language, *moak* would have to be given the P-A structure in (2.27), which accords with the generalizations in (2.23).

(2.27)
moak 'pound with the elbow' (*patient*)

The performance of the children in these experiments suggests that verbs violating the generalizations in a language corresponding to generalizations (2.23) in English would be regularized to conform to these generalizations through the acquisition process. Children's early linguistic knowledge establishes a direct connection between semantic roles and their expressions in sentences. Generalizations like (2.23) ensure that most verbs in a language will conform to the young child's linguistic knowledge, at least in the simple active declarative sentences he most often produces.

Returning now to the second question, given that, due to the language acquisition process, languages should change to include generalizations like (2.23), why should they come to employ the generalizations in (2.23) and not those in (2.24)? Nothing in my characterization of P-A structures would demand or even suggest that predicates but not verbs should assign agent roles while verbs but not predicates assign theme/patient roles. The l-s relations subject and object are tied not to semantic roles themselves but rather to the assignment of semantic roles.[7] Therefore, one might expect to find languages in which the generalizations of English (2.23) are reversed. The answer to the second question, then, would be that it is an accident that English employs generalizations (2.23) in place of (2.24). In chapter 6 I claim that languages employing (2.24) do exist; they are the true ergative languages. In that chapter I examine the consequences within the present theory of choosing one or the other of the sets of generalizations (2.23) and (2.24), and demonstrate that Dyirbal and Central Arctic Eskimo are true ergative languages: they choose set (2.24). Languages choosing

(2.23) are nominative-accusative languages. The P-A structure for a verb meaning 'hit' in a nominative-accusative language is shown in (2.28a); that for 'hit' in an ergative language is given in (2.28b).

(2.28)
a. 'hit' (*patient*); logical subject = agent
b. 'hit' (*agent*); logical subject = patient

Note that the existence of ergative language still leaves quite a lot unexplained about generalizations like (2.23) and (2.24). For example, why should themes and patients group together; do these classes of semantic roles share some semantic property? Why should agents, patients, and themes, and not other semantic role classes, like location or instrument, be canonically associated with logical subjects and objects, that is, with verbs? Also, why are there so few true ergative languages compared with nominative-accusative languages? I return to this last question in chapter 6.

The incorporation of generalizations like (2.23) and (2.24) within a grammar leads one to expect the existence of two sorts of verbs associated with a single inherent semantic role. If the only role associated with an intransitive verb in a nominative-accusative language falls into the agent class, by (2.23a) one expects the verb's P-A structure to look like (2.29a). If, on the other hand, the sole role falls into the theme or patient class, generalization (2.23b) indicates that this role should be assigned by the verb, necessitating the P-A structure in (2.29b).

(2.29)
a. 'intransitive-V-1' ($\emptyset$); logical subject = agent
b. 'intransitive-V-2' (*theme/patient*); no logical subject

The verb in (2.29a) is a degenerate function; it takes no argument into predicates. The predicate returned by the P-A structure in (2.29a) when given no arguments assigns an agent role to its logical subject. The predicate returned by the P-A structure in (2.29b), however, assigns no semantic role; it is a degenerate predicate, requiring no arguments to make a proposition. English *swim* might be a verb of type V-1; English *arrive* a verb of type V-2.

(2.30)
a. 'swim' ($\emptyset$)
b. 'arrive' (*theme*)

Relational Grammar should be credited with first distinguishing in this manner the two classes of intransitive verbs whose P-A structures are schematized in (2.29) (see Perlmutter 1983 and the references cited there). Relational Grammarians call type V-1 intransitives "unergative" and type V-2 intransitives "unaccusative." Throughout the RG literature one finds convincing evidence for the validity of this distinction (see, e.g., Perlmutter 1978b; Perlmutter and Postal 1978a; Harris 1982). Burzio (1981) provides considerable support from Italian for the proposed distinction between intransitive verb classes. See also Pesetsky (1982) with similar data from Russian. In section 4.1.3, I demonstrate how the characterization of the distinction between unergative and unaccusative verbs implicit in (2.30), which is essentially the characterization supported by Relational Grammar and Burzio (1981), correctly predicts one contrasting property of these verbs within the present theory.

It is necessary to have some formal means for distinguishing verbs whose P-A structures produce predicates that assign no semantic role from verbs whose P-A structures produce role-assigning predicates. Verbs of the former sort (e.g., *arrive* in (2.30b)) will be assigned the negative value of the feature [±log sub]; those of the latter sort (e.g., *swim* in (2.30a)) will be given the positive value. Technically, for a verb to be [+log sub] is for it to form a phrase that takes a logical subject at l-s structure. A [−log sub] verb heads an l-s phrase that does not take a logical subject.

Encoding the unaccusative/unergative distinction between intransitive verb classes in a lexical feature has clear consequences in the present theory. Lexical features like [±log sub] may be carried by affixes and thus play a role in derivational morphology. Because [−log sub] is a lexical feature in the present theory, passivization may be analyzed as the affixation of a [−log sub] morpheme to a verb, as explained in detail in chapter 4. In chapter 4 I also explore strong evidence that the feature [±log sub] cross-classifies verbs in a language. For example, Albanian (Hubbard 1979) has two distinct conjugational paradigms, one for [+log sub] verbs, one for [−log sub] verbs.

The existence of generalizations referring to semantic role classes like agent and patient is supported by the simple fact that in English, if a verb is associated with an agent and a patient as I have defined these roles, chances are overwhelming that the agent argument will behave grammatically like the agent argument associated with *hit* and the patient argument will behave grammatically like the patient argument of *hit*. Evidence for the particular formulation of these generalizations as in (2.23) and (2.24) will be drawn from the existence and behavior of unaccusative verbs and ergative languages (see section 4.1.3 and chapter 6).

Although classes of semantic roles do figure into generalizations like (2.23) and (2.24) and are mentioned in P-A structures, as shown in (2.21)–(2.22), it is not at all clear that any rule of grammar must refer to such classes. In the present theory, these role classes appear only in P-A structures and in generalizations like (2.23). As far as the rest of the grammar is concerned, what is important to know about semantic roles is which constituents receive semantic roles from which semantic role assigners; the identity or classification of semantic roles is irrelevant.

2.1.3. Categories at l-s Structure

Although I have introduced and discussed the two basic relations that I assume exist at l-s structure—that between an argument taker and its arguments and that between a semantic role assigner and its semantic role assignee—I have yet to discuss the sorts of constituents that bear these relations. The account of constituent categories that I develop here molds together leading ideas of Montague Grammar (Dowty et al. 1981) and X-bar syntax (see, e.g., Jackendoff 1977). With Montague Grammar, I assume that there are just a few basic constituent types, the remaining types being "categorially" or "functionally" defined in terms of these basic types. With X-bar syntax, I assume that the notions "head of a phrase" and "maximal projection" enter into principles of constituent structure which constrain the possible internal structure of different categories.

I assume that the two basic l-s categories are the "proposition" and the "nominal." Propositions canonically make statements and nominals canonically refer to entities in the domain of discourse. As far as the syntax is concerned, however, these categories are primitive; that is, the semantic basis of these categories will not figure into any syntactic rule or principle. As for the nonprimitive categories, I define "predicate" as the (functional) constituent type that takes an argument into a proposition. The l-s "verb" is a function from arguments to a predicate.

I define "projection" as follows:

(2.31)
A projection of a constituent X is a phrase whose category type is determined by X.

Since a predicate is defined as a function from an argument to a proposition, the predicate determines the category type—proposition—of the phrase consisting of itself and its arguments; thus the proposition is the projection of the predicate. The notion of "head" of a phrase receives the following definition:

(2.32)
The head of a phrase Y is
i. the immediate constituent of Y that determines the category of Y, or
ii. the head of this constituent.

The second part of the definition in (2.32) makes the head relation transitive; if A heads B and B heads C, then A also heads C. By (2.32) a predicate heads a proposition, a verb heads a predicate, and thus, by (2.32ii), a verb also heads a proposition.

The last X-bar type term to be defined is that of a "maximal projection":

(2.33)
A maximal projection is a constituent that will not by its definition alone determine the constituent type of a phrase of which it is an immediate constituent. All other categories are nonmaximal projections.

Thus a predicate, which is defined as a function from an argument to a predicate, is not a maximal projection because it is defined so as to determine the constituent type—proposition—of the phrase of which it is an immediate constituent. On the other hand, as primitive categories the proposition and nominal are not defined so as to determine the category type of any constituent containing them and thus qualify as maximal projections.

In addition to verbs and predicates, another important functionally defined category is the "modifier":

(2.34)
Modifiers are functions from constituents of type X to constituents of type X.

For example, a nominal modifier, such as an adjective phrase or restrictive relative clause, takes nominals into nominals. I call the argument of a modifier the "modifiee." By the definition in (2.34), it is the modifiee that determines the category type of the constituent consisting of the modifier and its modifiee; whatever the category type of the modifiee, this will be the category type of the combination of modifier and modifiee. Therefore, by the definition of "head" in (2.32), the modifiee heads the constituent immediately dominating modifier and modifiee. Also, by the definition of "projection" in (2.31), modifiers cannot project and must be maximal projections.

I assume that the arguments of modifiers, unlike the arguments of constituents that head phrases, are not assigned semantic roles. This assumption finds some intuitive justification in the behavior of restrictive nominal modifiers. The arguments of such modifiers (like *the porcupine* in the phrase *the porcupine under the table*) are not referring expressions independent of the restrictive modification. It is the modifier that picks out the object of reference in restrictive modification. Thus it would be strange to say that *the porcupine* alone bears some sort of locative role in the phrase *the porcupine under the table*. Only the full nominal, with the PP modifier, is the sort of entity that could be located.

Most categorial grammars would allow, say, a predicate to serve as the argument of a function from predicates to, say, nominals. In the present system, however, I assume the X-bar-like principle in (2.35).

(2.35)
The Nonmaximal Head Principle:
Nonmaximal projections must head phrases.

Among other consequences, principle (2.35) assures that predicates and verbs, nonmaximal projections, cannot be arguments, except of a modifier. Only as the argument of a modifier could a predicate, for example, simultaneously head a phrase and serve as an argument. As a modifiee, the predicate would determine the phrase type—predicate—of the combination of modifier and modifiee and thus head this combination. In all other situations a predicate must take an argument, possibly null, and form a proposition. From the Nonmaximal Head principle (2.35) one may derive the constraint that only maximal projections may serve as arguments of anything but modifiers. By this principle nonmaximal projections must head phrases but only modifiees among arguments head phrases. In chapter 3, we shall see that this constraint holds important consequences for the analysis of raising constructions.

Note that the definitions of "head," "projection," and "maximal projection," plus the Nonmaximal Head principle, are not intended to duplicate the constraints of X-bar theory. Rather, they replace these constraints. Universal grammar does not need both a categorial theory of the compositional semantics of a sentence and a set of arbitrary conditions on constituent structure, the conditions of X-bar theory. The present categorial theory subsumes the X-bar principles and in part explains their validity. As described in the sections to follow, the category types of l-s structure will project to s and surface structures. Therefore, the principles of l-s constituent structure will also constrain surface constituent structure.

It will prove useful to develop some notation for talking about relations and constituent types at l-s structure. If X assigns Y a semantic role, I refer to the relation between X and Y as role(X, Y). If Y is an argument of X, I write arg(X, Y). If both role(X, Y) and arg(X, Y), then I call Y a direct argument of X. If arg(X, Y) but not role(X, Y), I call Y an indirect argument of X. Since modifiers take arguments that are not assigned semantic roles, there is no distinction between direct and indirect arguments of modifiers.

If Y is a direct argument of X when X belongs to a lexical category (i.e., is not a phrase), I call Y the direct logical object (or logical object) of X and write obj(X, Y). If Y is the direct argument of X, X a predicate, then Y is the logical subject of X and sub(X, Y). In the case that Y is the argument of X and X is a modifier, I call Y the modifiee of X and write mod(X, Y). Recall that a modifier is a function from a constituent of type X to a constituent of type X.

In drawing and talking about l-s structures, I use standard category and phrase nodes in a nonstandard way. Unless otherwise noted, I reserve the label "V" for an l-s lexical item that heads a predicate and the label "N" for an l-s lexical item that heads a nominal. I use the label "P" for an l-s lexical item that assigns a semantic role but does not take an argument (e.g., *to* in *Elmer gave a porcupine to Hortense*) and for the head of certain adverbial modifiers expressed as prepositional phrases in English (e.g., *after* in *Elmer will arrive after three weeks*). The label "A" indicates the head of a nominal modifier. The phrase node "VP" will be used for predicates, the node "PP" for most adverbial modifiers, the node "NP" for nominals, the node "AP" for nominal modifiers, and the node "S" for propositions.

Table 2.1 lists the relations and the constituent types, both primitive and defined, introduced in this chapter, along with their abbreviations.

2.1.4. Structural Representation of l-s Structure

What is the logico-semantic structure of a sentence? I take it as given that sentential constituents stand in semantic relations with respect to

Table 2.1

Basic relations:	role(X, Y) semantic-role-assigner–semantic-role-assignee
	arg(X, Y) argument-taker–argument
Defined relations:	direct argument = role(X, Y) and arg(X, Y)
	indirect argument = arg(X, Y) but not role(X, Y)
	obj(X, Y) = direct argument(X, Y), X a lexical category
	sub(X, Y) = direct argument(X, Y), X a predicate
	mod(X, Y) = arg(X, Y), X a modifier
Basic categories:	NP nominal
	S proposition

Functionally defined categories:

Lexical:	N head of NP
	V head of VP
	A head of AP
	P head of PP or semantic role assigner without argument structure
Phrasal:	VP (predicate) head of S
	AP nominal modifier (function from NPs to NPs)
	PP adverbial modifier (function from Vs to Vs, VPs to VPs, or Ss to Ss)

one another. Hierarchical (i.e., constituent structure) relations are implicit in semantic relations. For example, a verb takes in arguments to form a predicate. Thus the verb plus its arguments constitute a predicate and the predicate immediately dominates the verb plus its arguments in a clear sense of immediate domination. If one claims that there is a linguistically significant level of structure that encodes the semantic interrelations among sentential constituents, one should be claiming more than just that semantic relations or semantic constituent structure exist. One posits a level of structure, like l-s structure in the present system or S structure in the Government-Binding theory, because of evidence that rules, constraints, or other generalizations are to be stated at this level. The linguistic evidence for semantic relations must be separated from the evidence for a level of l-s structure. One posits semantic relations because they can be shown to play an essential role in determining the syntax of sentences. One posits l-s structure as a structure because it encodes certain linguistic constraints.

For example, suppose that the list of constituents and relations that constitute l-s structure must be representable in a constituent structure tree, where the linear order of constituents is uninterpreted—irrelevant for all concerns. This condition on the representability of semantic relations already imposes constraints on the semantic relations of an l-s structure. For example, a given nominal cannot serve both as the logical object of a verb and as the logical subject of the predicate that this verb heads. If it did bear both these relations, the nominal would have to appear in two positions in the constituent structure representation of l-s structure simultaneously: within the predicate headed by the verb and as sister to this predicate. But a given item cannot be in two places at the same time. The constraints I impose on the structural representation of l-s structure will be substantive constraints on the set of constituents and semantic relations that may underlie a grammatical sentence.

So the structural representation of l-s structure can prevent a given nominal from serving as the logical object of a verb and simultaneously as the logical subject of the predicate the verb heads. In the GB theory of Chomsky 1981, this possibility is ruled out by the theta criterion, which limits nominals to one semantic (thematic) role each. Similar conditions have been imposed in other theoretical frameworks. I wish to claim that the only purpose of a structural representation for l-s structure—for a distinct level of analysis called l-s structure—is to impose theta-criterion-like constraints on semantic relations. In fact, following Schein (1981, 1982, in press), I reject the GB version of the theta criterion entirely, relying on independent constraints to derive the same effects. There are constraints on the ability of constituents to bear multiple semantic roles, but these constraints may be encoded in restrictions on the structural representation of semantic relations.

The constituent structure representation of l-s structure obeys one basic condition:

(2.36)
If X bears a semantic relation with respect to Y, then X and Y must be sisters at l-s structure. X and Y are sisters if they are immediately dominated* by the same constituent node.

The notion of sisterhood relevant for (2.36) is fairly standard, with the exception that it requires a slightly refined notion of immediate domination: immediate domination*. I define immediate domination* recursively as in (2.37).

(2.37)

X is immediately dominated* by Y iff

a. it is immediately dominated by Y or

b. it is immediately dominated* by a lexical category node that is immediately dominated* by Y or

c. it is immediately dominated* by a node Y' that is immediately dominated* by Y, where Y' and Y are of identical category type.

Part (b) of definition (2.37) is necessary if a verb, for example, is to be a sister to the nominals in a predicate even though it is dominated by a category node V, which intervenes between the verb and the predicate node.

(2.38)

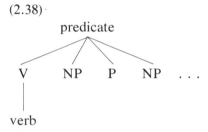

In (2.38) the category node V immediately dominates the verb and thus, by (2.37a), immediately dominates* the verb. Since "verb" is immediately dominated* by a category node V which is immediately dominated* by "predicate," "verb" in (2.38) is immediately dominated* by "predicate." Thus, by the definition in (2.36), "verb," NP, and P are all sisters in (2.38). Part (c) of definition (2.37) proves necessary to allow for certain cases of a constituent bearing multiple semantic relations (see chapter 3 and the discussion surrounding (2.39)) and for the merger constructions discussed in chapter 7. The treatment of these two sorts of constructions in a single clause of the definition of immediate domination* may represent a spurious generalization.

Note that it is not necessary to assume that lexical categories are dominated by category nodes in the structural representation of l-s structure. A lexical item itself can serve as its own category node if it bears a lexical feature identifying its category. Definition (2.37b) merely allows one to draw l-s constituent structure trees in accordance with common conventions governing such trees.

Having established the basic constraint on the construction of l-s structure representations in (2.36), I am prepared to state the manner in which constituent structure representations of l-s structure enforce constraints on the l-s structure of a sentence. First, I assume that the constituent structure representation consists of a well-formed constituent structure tree headed by a single S or proposition node. No crossing branches or multiple parents are allowed. Second, I assume that the set of lexical items making a contribution to the compositional semantics of a sentence (excluding quantifier scope) is just the set of items appearing as terminal nodes in the constituent structure representation of l-s structure. This constraint ensures that lexical items are individuated at l-s structure. If a given lexical item appears twice in an l-s tree, then there must be two tokens of the item in the compositional semantics of the sentence.

We shall see why it is not necessary to stipulate that a given constituent may bear only one semantic role or may serve as argument to only one lexical item. However, some sort of condition may be required to make sure that an item appearing in semantic structure assigns all its roles or receives all its obligatory arguments. This sort of condition should be considered definitional of a well-formed representation of compositional semantics.

Clear cases of an item bearing more than one semantic role at l-s structure are easy to find, but their significance is difficult to interpret. Sentences like (2.39) illustrate this phenomenon.

(2.39)
a. Elmer ate the porcupine raw.
b. Hortense painted the porcupine purple.
c. The porcupine arrived at the party terribly drunk.

Although it is clear that *the porcupine* in sentences (2.39) bears more than one role in each sentence (e.g., the eaten and raw roles in (2.39a)), it is not clear that *the porcupine* should be represented as bearing both these roles at l-s structure. Instead, one might suppose that some element like GB's PRO bears the roles assigned by the APs in (2.39), with *the porcupine* linking up to the PRO at s structure. I do want to say that in cases like (2.40), in which an NP seems to be receiving two semantic roles with one from a predicate, one of these roles is assigned to a PRO—to a phonologically null pronominal element.

(2.40)
Elmer persuaded Hortense [PRO to paint the porcupine].
Elmer bought that brush [PRO to paint the porcupine].

In chapter 3 I examine some evidence that motivates distinguishing the two sorts of cases illustrated by (2.39) and (2.40). At the moment, I wish to show only how I represent the distinction within the grammar. For the cases in (2.39), the APs assign a role to *the porcupine* but do not take *the porcupine* as argument. Rather, they act as predicate modifiers, taking the predicates as modifiees. The structural representation of sentence (2.39a) is shown in (2.41).

(2.41)

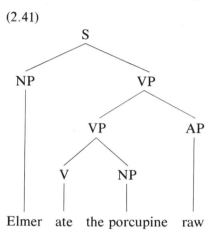

Elmer   ate   the porcupine   raw

Since the NP *the porcupine* is immediately dominated* by the lower VP, since the lower VP is immediately dominated* by the upper VP, and since the two VPs are of the same category type, *the porcupine* is immediately dominated* by the upper VP according to the definition in (2.37c). Therefore, *the porcupine* and *raw* are sisters according to the definition in (2.36) and the semantic-role-assigner–semantic-role-assignee relation between these constituents is properly represented in (2.41), along with the modifier–modifiee relation between the predicate modifier *raw* and its modifiee *ate the porcupine*. *Raw* says something about the temporal location of the eating of the porcupine event; the porcupine was eaten at the time when it was raw.

It would not make sense to suppose that *the porcupine* served as argument to *raw* in (2.39a). A modifier is a function from constituents of type X to constituents of type X. So a nominal modifier takes in nominals and produces nominals. If *the porcupine* were the modifiee of *raw*, *raw* would be acting as a restrictive modifier on the nominal, creating a nominal with the meaning of 'raw porcupine.' But (2.39a) does not claim that Elmer ate the raw porcupine; rather, he ate the porcupine when it was raw. I return to this point in chapter 3.

2.2. Syntactic Structure

In diagram (1.4) I proposed a model of grammar in which a level of syntactic analysis, the syntactic (or s) structure, stands between l-s structure and surface structure. As l-s structure encodes the logico-semantic relations between constituents of a sentence, so s structure displays the grammatical relations between constituents. Recall that the present theory belongs to the class of theories incorporating projection principles. What characterizes this class of theories is the direct projection of the compositional semantics of a sentence into syntactic structure. In this section I propose a particular sort of projection principle to govern the relation between logico-semantic and syntactic structure.

To each l-s relation and constituent type of l-s structure there corresponds a grammatical relation and constituent type of s structure; that is, there is a one-to-one type correspondence between semantic and grammatical relations and constituent categories. This principle assures that, although a constituent bearing l-s relation type R may not map onto or be associated with a constituent bearing the corresponding type of grammatical relation, R′, there will be such a corresponding type within grammatical theory.

It is logically possible that s structure could always be entirely isomorphic to l-s structure.[8] Nevertheless, in natural languages, s structure differs from l-s structure only in certain heavily constrained ways. Recall that the binding theory, which determines possibilities of co- and disjoint reference among nominals, applies (at least) at s structure. Also, s structure must map directly onto the surface structure of sentences. Given these assumptions, the existence of, in particular, passive and raising constructions reveals the need for some level of syntactic representation distinct from l-s structure.

Consider first passive constructions. Recall the arguments in section 2.1.1.2 for the semantic asymmetry between logical objects and logical subjects. In particular recall that the predicates that a verb will produce depend on the logical object given to the verb as an argument. Thus by providing distinct logical objects for a verb like *throw,* one derives the range of predicates illustrated in (2.19). As explained in detail later (see especially chapter 4), passive sentences characteristically have their logical objects appear as syntactic subjects. Under passivization, it is still the logical object, appearing as syntactic subject, that combines with the passive verb to form the predicate (which may take, as logical subject, the object of the preposition *by* in an agentive *by*-phrase—see section 4.1.1.2). Varying the syntactic subject of the passive verb yields the same range of predicates as varying the syntactic object of its active counterpart.

(2.42)
a. A baseball was thrown (by Elmer)
b. Support was thrown behind that candidate
c. The boxing match was thrown
d. A party was thrown
e. A fit was thrown

To the extent that the argument in section 2.1.1.2 revealed the compositional semantics of sentences, in semantic relational terms the subject of the passive verb is equivalent to the object of the active verb. As far as the surface syntax of sentences is concerned, however, what is called the grammatical subject of the passive verb behaves just like the grammatical subjects of active verbs. Therefore, if l-s structure is a transparent representation of semantic relations and s structure maps directly into surface structure, then l-s and s structure cannot be isomorphic.

  It seems that raising constructions also involve a serious breach of isomorphism between l-s and s structure. Consider a sentence like (2.43):

(2.43)
Elmer appears to himself to be certain to win that porcupine.

The proper compositional semantics for (2.43) is an open question. But, as is usually assumed and as is argued in chapter 3, *appears* does not produce predicates that take a logical subject. Rather, raising to subject verbs like *appear* take a proposition, a modifier, or, perhaps, a predicate (see section 3.1) to produce degenerate predicates; that is, raising verbs are [−log sub]. *Elmer* is a semantic dependent of the lower predicate in (2.43), that is, of the l-s counterpart to *to win that porcupine*. In order to be in a proper position to c-command the reflexive *himself* at s structure and thus to serve as its antecedent, *Elmer* must bear a grammatical relation in the upper clause (compare the ungrammatical, *It appears to himself that Elmer is certain to win that porcupine*). But, since *Elmer* bears no l-s relation in this clause, l-s and s structure may not be isomorphic.

These arguments for a nonisomorphism between l-s and s structures are both highly theory-dependent and nondemonstrative. They depend on a particular characterization of l-s and s structure, on the one hand, and on assumptions about possible rule types and the locus of application of principles such as the binding conditions, on the other.

I will propose one general projection principle, which both defines and constrains the mapping between l-s and s structure. This principle is weak enough to allow for the nonisomorphic mapping exhibited in passive and raising constructions while remaining powerful enough to prohibit deviations from an isomorphic mapping that we do not observe in the world's languages.

2.2.1. Syntactic Roles and Grammatical Relations

I have introduced and argued for two basic semantic relations, that between an argument-taking item and its arguments and that between a semantic role assigner and its semantic role assignee. According to the hypothesis of a one-to-one relation between semantic and grammatical relations, there should be two basic grammatical relations, that between a syntactic argument-taking item and its arguments and that between a syntactic role assigner and its syntactic role assignee.

The notion of a syntactic role deserves some comment. It was suggested in section 2.1.2 that each semantic role assigner assigns (or may assign) a unique role; nevertheless, the roles fall into linguistically significant classes, such as agent or goal. The relation between a semantic role assigner and its semantic role assignee is a semantic dependency that is logically independent of semantic constituent structure. While the argument-taker–argument relation is tied up in the functional definition of constituent types—argument takers are functions from their arguments to certain constituent types—the semantic-role-assigner–semantic-role-assignee relation is independent of these definitions. One may look at the syntactic-role-assigner–syntactic-role-assignee relation as a syntactic dependency which is logically independent of syntactic constituent structure. A syntactic argument taker will be a function from arguments (bearing syntactic roles) to a certain constituent type and thus will determine syntactic constituency. For example, a syntactic verb is a function from syntactic arguments to a verb phrase—the s structure counterpart to the l-s predicate. The verb thus determines the constituency of the verb phrase. A syntactic role assigner does not determine constituent structure in this manner. It is a hypothesis of both Government-Binding theory and the current work that there are constituent structure constraints on the assignment of semantic and syntactic roles. However, this is a substantive hypothesis that cannot be derived from the characterizations of role assignment and argument structure within the theory.

The assignment of syntactic roles strongly resembles the assignment of abstract Case in the GB framework. Just as semantic roles fall into linguistically significant classes, so syntactic roles may be seen as making up categories corresponding to the abstract Case classifications of GB. So perhaps verbs canonically assign objective syntactic roles, whereas prepositions in many languages may assign oblique roles. I do not pursue this line of thought further in this book. I mention the possible correspondence between syntactic roles and abstract Case both to facilitate the incorporation of GB work into the present framework and to provide a possible interpretation of syntactic roles over and above their identification as the s structure projection of semantic roles.

I provide lexical items with a feature, [±transitive], to indicate whether or not they assign a syntactic role. Syntactically transitive— [+transitive]—verbs assign roles; intransitive—[−transitive]—verbs do not. The distribution of the [±transitive] feature is highly predictable. For example, it seems that only verbs and prepositions among lexical category types may be [+transitive], adjectives and nouns may not. Moreover, as argued in Burzio 1981, markedness principles determine the value of the feature for a verb in the unmarked case. If a verb assigns a semantic role and is [+log sub], it will be [+transitive]. If it either does not assign a semantic role or is [−log sub], the verb will be [−transitive] in the unmarked case. Prepositions are generally [+transitive].

The treatment of syntactic transitivity as a lexical feature dividing, for example, verbs into two classes receives direct support from the behavior of the conjugational system in some languages. For example, the Eskimo languages (discussed in chapter 6) employ different sets of agreement suffixes for transitive and intransitive verbs. Less straightforward evidence for this feature comes from its role in the analyses presented in chapters 4 through 7.

Just as the two basic semantic relations project to two basic syntactic relations, so each sort of semantic constituent type finds a corresponding constituent type at s structure. To begin with the basic (undefined) constituent types: corresponding to the l-s proposition is the s structure sentence, to the l-s nominal the s structure noun phrase. Each functionally defined l-s constituent also projects an s structure counterpart. The predicate corresponds to the verb phrase: a function from an argument to a sentence. The l-s verb corresponds to the syntactic verb: a function from arguments to a verb phrase. The other l-s constituents are similarly matched to s structure counterparts.

The same terminology used to discuss l-s structure constituents and relations can be used for s structure. An argument of argument-taking item X which also receives its syntactic role from X is a direct argument of X. Arguments of X that do not receive a role from X are indirect arguments. The direct argument of a lexical item is the direct object of that item. The direct argument of a VP (of the s structure counterpart to a predicate) is the subject of the VP.

Recall the One Role/Role-Assigner and Direct Argument principles ((2.13)–(2.14)), which state that in the unmarked case a constituent will take one argument and that this argument will be direct. Since the features of l-s structure are projected into s structure, an s structure constituent will also take one argument in the unmarked case, and this argument will be direct. Since, according to the Lexical Exception principle (2.15), exceptions to (markedness) principles must be encoded in the lexical entries of lexical items, it follows that each VP will have at most one subject and that the argument of a VP must be a direct argument. Since the VP is a phrase, not a lexical item, it will not have a lexical entry in which to record the marked property that it takes more than one argument, or that its argument need not be a direct one.

I employ basically the same notation for s structure as for l-s structure, with the exception that the relational terms are capitalized to distinguish them from the corresponding l-s terms. The s structure notation is summarized in table 2.2.

2.2.2. Constituent Structure Representation of s Structure

Recall from section 2.1.4 that the constituent structure representation of a set of relations among constituents may be used to encode constraints on the set of representations. For l-s structure the constituent structure representation encodes what I have claimed to be the correct portions of Chomsky's theta criterion. As for s structure, the constraints of binding theory, which determine possibilities of coreference among sentential constituents (see Chomsky 1981), are defined in terms of a constituent structure representation of s structure. For example, a structural c-command condition on the relation between a reflexive and its antecedent determines that a reflexive serving as a subject of a

Table 2.2

Basic relations:	ROLE(X, Y) syntactic-role-assigner–syntactic role assignee
	ARG(X, Y) argument-taker–argument
Defined relations:	direct argument = ROLE(X, Y) and ARG(X, Y)
	indirect argument = ARG(X, Y) but not ROLE(X, Y)
	OBJ(X, Y) = direct argument(X, Y), X a lexical item
	SUB(X, Y) = direct argument(X, Y), X a verb phrase
	MOD(X, Y) = ARG(X, Y), X a modifier
Basic categories:	NP noun phrase
	S sentence

Functionally defined categories:

Lexical:	N head of NP
	V head of VP
	A head of AP
	P head of PP or syntactic role assigner that does not take arguments
Phrasal:	VP (verb phrase) head of S
	AP noun phrase modifier (function from NPs to NPs)
	PP adverbial modifier (function from Vs to Vs, VPs to VPs, or Ss to Ss)

verb phrase will never have an object within this verb phrase as its antecedent.

The constituent structure representation of s structure need not impose a theta-criterion-like constraint on s structure, preventing an s structure constituent from occupying multiple positions in an s structure tree. Recall that an l-s constituent could not serve as both (logical) subject and object in the same l-s clause because this would require it to occupy two positions simultaneously at l-s structure, and two positions implies two distinct l-s constituents. The parallel line of reasoning fails when applied to s structure. An s structure constituent may in fact appear in more than one position in the constituent structure representation. Appearance in two distinct locations at surface structure implies two distinct phonological entities—two distinct tokens of phonological constituent types. Appearance in two distinct locations at l-s structure implies two distinct logical entities—two distinct tokens of semantic constituent types. But s structure is merely an intermediary level between these two interpreted structures. There is no compelling reason to prevent a constituent from appearing in more than one location at s structure, and so I shall not do so.

The constituent structure representation of l-s structure helps constrain the semantic roles a constituent may bear while the constituent structure representation of surface structure serves as input to the rules of phonology. Although one may choose to state such principles as the binding conditions on a constituent structure representation of s structure, such a constituent structure both is mechanically determinable from the list of constituents and relations at s structure and has no independent constraints imposed upon it such that the constituent structure representation may be said to constrain the class of possible s structures.

I use the same conventions for constructing constituent structure representations of s structure as I used for constituent structure representations of l-s structure. In particular:

(2.44)
If X bears a grammatical relation with respect to Y or vice versa, then X and Y must be sisters at s structure. X and Y are sisters iff they are immediately dominated* by the same node Z.

2.2.3. Mapping to s Structure
What is the relation between the s structure and l-s structure of a given sentence? Recall that I consider each level of syntactic structure to consist essentially of a list of constituents and relations. The constituent structure representation of each level imposes constraints on the possible sets of constituents and relations that may underlie a grammatical sentence. Whereas GB theory describes a transformational mapping between the constituent structure trees at each syntactic level, in the present theory I must assume that the mapping holds between the lists of constituents and relations constituting each level.

I also assume that each level of analysis is independently generated—that is, each level of syntactic analysis is simply an arbitrary assemblage of constituents and relations. The mapping between levels of analyses merely determines whether two lists may be structures for the same sentence. If two lists of constituents and relations may be related by the mapping principles of the grammar, then they may be different levels of analysis for a single sentence.

2.2.3.1. Mapping Principles   Lexical items anchor the connection between the l-s structure and s structure of a sentence. In most syntactic theories, a lexical entry contains a list of features and specifications. Some features in this list (e.g., semantic role assigning and argument taking features) are relevant for l-s structure; some (e.g., the [±transitive] feature) are relevant for s structure; and some (e.g., phonological features) are relevant for surface structure. In the present theory, instead of viewing lexical entries as a list of features relevant at different levels of analysis, I consider a lexical entry to encode a mapping between features at difference levels. For example, consider the lexical entry for *hit* in (2.45).

(2.45)
hit, V, 'hit' (*patient*), [+log sub], [+transitive], /hɪt/

One may view (2.45) as specifying a mapping between l-s features like the P-A structure 'hit' (*patient*) and s structure features like [+transitive], and a mapping between s structure features like [+transitive] and surface structure features like /hɪt/. Thus lexical items provide a basis for the mapping between l-s and s structure.

One might ask whether it is conceivable that an l-s structure lexical item of type X would *not* map onto an s structure category of the corresponding s structure category type X'—for example, whether an l-s verb could map onto something other than an s structure verb. Although it would be possible to play with the fundamental principles and definitions of the theory to rule out such category changing in principle, I will simply state the condition that lexical items map categories at l-s structure onto the corresponding s structure categories.

Although each l-s lexical item maps onto some s structure lexical item, there is not a one-to-one correspondence between constituents at l-s and s structure. Pleonastic elements like the dummy *it* of extraposition constructions bear grammatical but not semantic relations:

(2.46)
It seems that Elmer will buy this porcupine.

Thus there may be more constituents at s structure than at l-s structure. But each morpheme at l-s structure will find a counterpart at s structure; that is, each morpheme will project some s structure features. As far as the lexical items at l-s structure are concerned, then, the mapping between constituents at l-s and s structures may be considered an identity mapping in the sense that each lexical entry itself determines a mapping between a set of l-s and a set of s structure constituents. On the other hand, phrasal constituents at s structure are not mapped from l-s constituents by information found in lexical entries but are built up from lexical constituents according to the definitions of category types at s structure. So a verb at s structure will take in arguments to form a verb phrase.

The identity mapping between lexical items at l-s and s structure leaves open the problem of determining the s structure counterparts of particular l-s phrases. Depending on the idea that phrases are projections of lexical items in the sense of X-bar theory, the s structure counterpart of an l-s phrase may be defined recursively as in (2.47).

(2.47)
Definition:
The s structure counterpart of an l-s phrase X with immediate head Y is the s structure constituent whose immediate head is the s structure counterpart of Y.

Since the s structure counterpart of an l-s verb will be an s structure verb, definition (2.47) ensures that the s structure counterpart of an l-s predicate, headed by an l-s verb, will be an s structure verb phrase, a constituent whose immediate head is an s structure verb. The principles I have proposed thus determine that the s structure counterpart of an l-s phrase will be of the s structure category corresponding to the l-s category of the phrase—nominal to noun phrase, proposition to sentence, and so on.

As an example of the operation of definition (2.47), consider the l-s structure (2.48a) and its s structure counterpart, (2.48b).

(2.48)

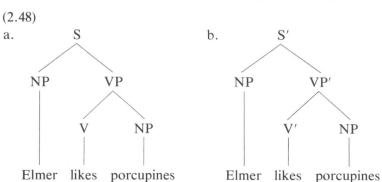

The lexical item *likes* in (2.48) serves as its own s structure counterpart in accordance with the basic principle that the identity of lexical items in l-s and s structure anchors the connection between the two levels of structure; that is, *likes* projects a bundle of l-s features that we label "like" onto a bundle of s structure features we also label "like." By definition (2.47), the s structure counterpart of the VP in (2.48a) is the phrase headed by the s structure counterpart of its immediate head, the verb *likes*.[9] Since the s structure counterpart of *likes* (V in (2.48a)) is *likes* (V' in (2.48b)), the s structure counterpart of VP is VP', which is headed by V'. The immediate head of S in (2.48a) is VP and the s structure counterpart of VP is VP'. Therefore, by definition (2.47), the s structure counterpart of S is S', which is headed by VP'.

In l-s structure, constituents bear l-s relations with respect to lexical items or with respect to phrases headed by lexical items. Given that it is possible to identify the s structure constituents corresponding to l-s constituents through the identity of lexical items in both structures and through definition (2.47), then for each l-s constituent X bearing l-s relation R, what grammatical relations will the corresponding s structure constituent X' bear? Informally put, the basic principle constraining the mapping between l-s (semantic) and grammatical relations runs as follows: If constituent X bears an l-s relation with respect to constituent Y, the constituent corresponding to X in s structure, X', will bear a grammatical relation with respect to the constituent corresponding to Y in s structure, Y', or with respect to a phrase that Y' heads at s structure.

A convenient and precise statement of the principle governing the mapping between l-s and s structures requires some easily definable notions. First, it will be useful to have some way to say, "X bears a logico-semantic/grammatical relation with respect to Y, Y an operator."

(2.49)
Definition:
Y *governs* X iff X bears a logico-semantic relation with respect to Y, Y an operator.
Y *Governs* X iff X bears a grammatical relation with respect to Y, Y an operator.

The head of a phrase is the constituent that determines the category type of the phrase. Thus operators are generally heads, with the exception of modifiers. Since modifiers are functions from constituents of type X to constituents of type X, the argument of the modifier (the modifiee) determines the constituent type of the resulting phrase. The head relation is transitive: If X is the head of Y and Y is the head of Z, then X is also the head of Z. Thus an X that heads a predicate VP, or its s structure counterpart VP', will also head the proposition or sentence headed by VP or VP'. An extended notion of Government, keying on the concept of "head of a phrase," plays a crucial role in the principle mapping from l-s to s structure.

(2.50)
Definition:
X *head-Governs* Y iff X Governs Y *or* a phrase that X heads Governs Y.

The principle that constrains the connection between l-s and s structure may now be precisely stated as in (2.51).

(2.51)
Principle M:
If X governs Y at l-s structure, then the s structure counterpart of X head-Governs the s structure counterpart of Y.

Since I will have numerous occasions to refer to the principle in (2.51), I have named it principle M, for Mapping from l-s to s structure.

Principle M and idiosyncratic information about lexical items, such as whether or not they are transitive, determine the mapping between l-s and grammatical relations. It is not necessary to postulate special mapping rules of the form "associate the logical object with the grammatical object" or promotion rules of the form "associate the logical object with the grammatical subject" (e.g., for passive sentences). *Some* principle is needed to govern the connection of l-s and s structures; for example, any theory would have to prevent the logical object of a verb from freely corresponding to the grammatical object of a verb several clauses up in l-s structure. There is no reason to believe that the principle in question does not take some general form, like that in (2.51), which obviates the need for more specific rules. The relative attractiveness of principle M over rules that connect specific l-s with specific grammatical relations lies in the restrictiveness of the general principle approach. If one allowed into a grammar a rule explicitly connecting a logical object of a verb with its grammatical object, one would have to explain why no rule exists to associate the logical subject of a verb with its grammatical object. When we examine the phenomena accounted for by the relation-changing rules of Relational Grammar, we shall see that many rules conceivable in a framework that incorporates rules like "associate the logical object with the grammatical object" simply are not instantiated in the world's languages. Rather, principle M proves necessary and sufficient to account for relation-changing phenomena—and does not lead one to expect rules that do not occur cross-linguistically.

2.2.3.2. Correspondences Between l-s and s Structure Relations   The mapping principles (2.47) and (2.51) greatly constrain the possible correspondences between l-s and s structures. Given certain auxiliary assumptions and hypotheses, it is possible to prove exactly what correspondences in relations are allowed by the present theory, as I showed in Marantz 1981b. But since new data could lead to the modification of any of the auxiliary assumptions, changing the results, it seems unnecessary to repeat these proofs here. Instead, I explore a few cases of correspondences which are determined directly by the general principles and which will prove of importance for what follows.

Consider a constituent X that stands in the modifier-modifiee relation with respect to Y at l-s structure (i.e., mod(Y, X)), as shown in (2.52).

(2.52)

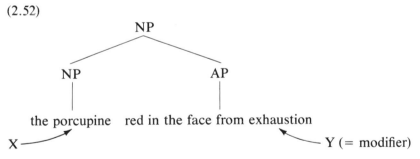

Recall that mod(Y, X) if and only if arg(Y, X) and *not* role(Y, X), where Y is a modifier. That is, X is an argument of Y but does not receive a semantic role from Y. To satisfy principle M, Y', the s structure counterpart of the modifier Y, must head-Govern X', the s structure counterpart of X. According to the assumption that each l-s lexical constituent maps onto an s structure constituent of the corresponding type and to definition (2.47), which fixes the s structure counterpart of l-s phrases, Y' will be a grammatical modifier. As a modifier, Y' will head a phrase only if it is the modifiee in a modifier-modifiee relation. Consider first the case in which Y' is *not* a modifiee at s structure. Then

Y' will not head a phrase and the only way in which Y' could head-Govern X' would be by Governing it. And the only way in which a modifier may Govern X' is by taking X' as its argument. So in this case the mod(Y, X) relation would correspond to the MOD(Y', X') relation.

I will now show that, in fact, in the situation under consideration Y' may *not* be a modifiee, thus may *not* head a phrase, thus must head-Govern X' by Governing X'. That is, I will demonstrate that mod(Y, X) *must* correspond to MOD(Y', X'). Demonstrating that Y' may not be a modifiee at s structure requires considering in more general terms what conditions must be met for some constituent Y' to serve as the argument to modifier Z' (the s structure counterpart of some l-s modifier Z) at s structure. A situation in which the s structure counterpart of a constituent Y, Y', is a modifiee in a modifier-modifiee grammatical relation is illustrated in (2.53), in which Z' is the modifier.

(2.53)

Y'* (= some constituent of the same category type as Y')

Y'   Z' (= modifier)

Now it is clear that there cannot be degenerate modifiers at l-s structure (modifiers that take no argument into a constituent of type T). Modifiers are defined as functions from constituents of type X to constituents of type X. A modifier that took in no argument would produce nothing.

Given that there are no degenerate modifiers, the l-s counterpart of Z', the modifier Z, must have some modifiee—call it "W"—at l-s structure. Now according to principle M, Z' must head-Govern W' at s structure, where W' is the s structure counterpart to W. If Z' head-Governs W' by Governing W', the diagram in (2.53) makes it clear that W' is Y' and therefore that W must be Y. But it is also clear from diagram (2.53) that Z' does not head a phrase (the modifiee heads the phrase consisting of a modifier and a modifiee and Y' is the modifiee in (2.53)). So the only way Z' may head-Govern W' is by Governing it. Since Z' Governs Y', W' must be Y' and W must be Y. "W" was the name given to the l-s modifiee of Z, so mod(Z, Y), as shown in (2.54).

(2.54)

Y* (= some constituent of the same category type as Y)

Y   Z (= modifier)

But if mod(Z, Y), then Y is an argument at l-s structure. It should be clear that the requirement that the list of l-s constituents and relations be represented as a well-formed constituent structure tree prohibits arguments from serving as argument takers. An argument taker (a-t) is defined as a function from arguments (args) to a constituent of type X. Suppose an argument arg′ of a function from arguments to a constituent of type X itself served as an argument taker from arguments to a constituent of type Y. The l-s tree structure required to represent this state of affairs would look something like (2.55), not a well-formed constituent structure tree.

(2.55)

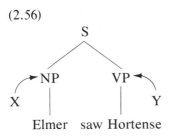

a-t arg arg . . . arg′ arg arg . . . , for some arg′ serving
                                                 as a function from arguments
                                                 to a constituent of type Y

In general, if arg(Y, X), then the s structure counterpart of Y, Y′, will not be modified. I have shown that if Y′ were modified, then mod(Z, Y) for some modifier Z, and mod(Z, Y) is incompatible with arg(Y, X) since Y may not be both argument taker and argument.

Returning to the specific situation relevant to this section in which mod(Y, X), the discussion of the last paragraph proved that there is no case in which Y′ is a modifiee. If Y′ were a modifiee, Y would have to be a modifiee at l-s structure. But since Y is an argument taker at l-s structure, it cannot be a modifiee. Therefore, mod(Y, X) must correspond to MOD(Y′, X′), the conclusion from the situation in which Y′ is not a modifiee.

Consider next the case in which X stands in the subject relation with respect to Y—sub(Y, X), as in (2.56).

(2.56)

```
            S
          /   \
      →NP      VP ↖
  X      |      |     Y
      Elmer   saw  Hortense
```

Recall that sub(Y, X) if and only if role(Y, X) and arg(Y, X). By principle M, if sub(Y, X), then Y′, the s structure counterpart to Y, must
head-Govern X′, the s structure counterpart to X. Recall that the mapping principles determine that the s structure counterpart to a predicate
like Y will be a verb phrase; therefore, Y′ is a verb phrase and will take
a grammatical subject.

When a verb phrase takes a subject it heads a constituent (the sentence) that will not Govern, or head-Govern, anything; therefore Y′
may not head-Govern X′ by heading a sentence that head-Governs X′.
Rather, Y′ will head-Govern X′ by Governing X′ or by serving as head
of a verb phrase consisting of Y′ and a modifier that head-Governs X′,
two situations illustrated in (2.57).

(2.57)

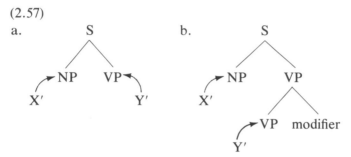

Consider first the case in which Y′ head-Governs X′ by Governing
X′, as in (2.57a). The Direct Argument principle (2.14) states that the
unmarked case for any argument taker is for the argument taker to take
a direct argument; that is, the unmarked case is for both arg(X, Y) and
role(X, Y) (or ARG(X, Y) and ROLE(X, Y)). Since, according to the
Lexical Exception principle (2.15), only lexical items may bear exceptional features, a phrasal argument taker (which takes arguments bearing roles—recall that modifiers take arguments without roles) must
take a direct argument. So if Y′, a verb phrase, Governs X′, both
ARG(Y′, X′) and ROLE(Y′, X′); that is, SUB(Y′, X′). Therefore, in
this case sub(Y, X) corresponds to SUB(Y′, X′). I will now show that
this is the only possible case.

Consider the situation in which Y′ serves as the head of a verb phrase
consisting of Y′ and a modifier, as illustrated in (2.57b). I have just
shown that Y′ may not in fact serve as a modifiee at s structure. If it
did, then Y would be a modifiee at l-s structure, and a modifiee cannot
take arguments. But Y takes a subject. So sub(Y, X) must in fact correspond to SUB(Y′, X′).

Suppose now X receives a semantic role from some constituent Y but
does not serve as argument for Y; that is, role(Y, X) but not arg(Y, X).
Two situations in which this might arise are of interest here. One is the
case of an X that is the indirect argument of some argument taking item
at l-s structure, say the indirect object of a verb like *give*. *Hortense* in
(2.58a) receives its role from the preposition *to* but does not serve as
argument to *to*, but rather to *give*. The l-s structure of (2.58a) is represented in (2.58b).

(2.58)
a. Elmer gave a porcupine to Hortense.
b.

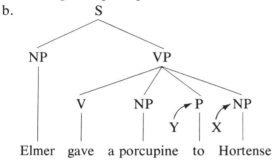

The second case of this sort involves a construction to be examined
at greater length in chapter 3. In contrast to the sort of construction
exemplified in (2.58), in this latter type some constituent receives two
semantic roles, one from a predicative modifier. An example of this
sort is given in (2.59).

(2.59)
Elmer ate the porcupine raw.

As the direct argument of *eat* in (2.59), *the porcupine* receives a semantic role from the verb. However, it also is interpreted as the thing that is
raw. In chapter 3 I claim that *raw* is a predicate modifier—a function
from predicates to predicates—that also may assign a semantic role.
The l-s structure of (2.59) is displayed in (2.60).

(2.60)

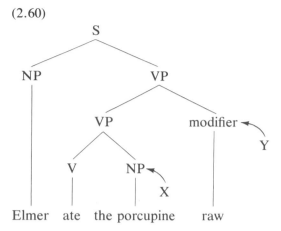

Elmer   ate   the porcupine   raw

Recall that modifier and the lower NP count as sisters on the definition of sisterhood provided in (2.36). Thus (2.60) may serve as the constituent structure representation of an l-s structure in which modifier assigns a role to *the porcupine*.

In the two cases under consideration in which role(Y, X) but not arg(Y, X), Y does not head anything. Therefore, in order for Y', the s structure counterpart of Y, to head-Govern X', the s structure counterpart of X, Y' must Govern X'. In both cases it is easy to see that Y' must Govern X' by assigning X' a syntactic role. In the first case, that of Y a semantic role assigner marking an indirect argument, Y' will be a syntactic role assigner without argument structure, which is only capable of Governing by assigning a (syntactic) role. In the second case, that of Y a modifier assigning a semantic role to the argument of a verb, although Y' (as a modifier) does take an argument, this argument must be the s structure counterpart to the modifiee of Y at l-s structure. Thus if role(Y, X) but not arg(Y, X) in the two sorts of cases under consideration, then ROLE(Y', X') but not ARG(Y', X').

Let us now examine the situation in which X is a direct argument (logical object) of some verb Y at l-s structure.

(2.61)

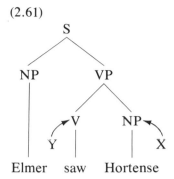

Elmer   saw   Hortense

To satisfy principle M, Y′, the s structure counterpart of Y, must head-Govern X′, the s structure counterpart of X. Since Y is an argument-taking item at l-s structure, Y′ will be an argument-taking item, an s structure verb. In accordance with principle M, X′ could be an indirect grammatical argument of Y′, a direct object of Y′ (if Y′ is transitive), or the grammatical subject of a phrase Y′ heads. Each of these possibilities is in fact instantiated, but under different conditions, and we shall examine each in turn.

Consider first l-s constituents X and Y such that obj(Y, X), for Y a verb, where Y heads a predicate that takes no logical subject.

(2.62)

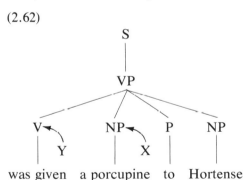

was given   a porcupine   to   Hortense

It was shown above that if a verb is [+log sub], the logical subject of the predicate it heads will correspond to the grammatical subject of the s structure counterpart to this predicate. Therefore, if X′, the s structure counterpart of X, is to correspond to the subject of the phrase headed by Y′, the s structure counterpart of Y, Y must be [−log sub].

In section 4.1, I analyze English passivization as the affixation to a verb of the passive affix, *-en,* carrying the features [−log sub], [−transitive]. The lexical entry in (2.63) approximates that for the passive participle of *give, given,* the verb in (2.62).

(2.63)

[[give]en] 'give' (*theme,* goal) [−log sub], [−transitive]

The s structure counterpart of the logical object of *given* must be head-Governed by *given;* the verb *given,* being [−transitive], takes no s structure object; and English has no general means for making the s structure counterpart of the logical object of a verb an s structure indirect argument by providing some syntactic role assigner. Therefore, the logical object of *given* must correspond to the grammatical subject of an s structure phrase that *given* heads. In (2.64) *a porcupine,* the s structure counterpart of *given*'s logical object in (2.62), is head-Governed by the verb's s structure counterpart, serving as subject to the VP that the verb heads.

(2.64)

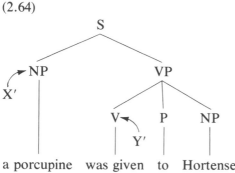

a porcupine   was given   to   Hortense

Compare the lexical entry (2.63) with the entries assumed for unaccusative verbs like (2.30b). Clearly, whatever mechanism tells us that the sole semantic role associated with an unaccusative verb will be borne by the syntactic subject of the phrase headed by the verb will account for the promotion of the logical object to subject in passive constructions as well. My claim is that this mechanism is just the general principle, principle M, which constrains the association of l-s and s structure.

If obj(Y, X), where Y is a [+transitive] verb, then X′, the s structure counterpart of X, may bear the grammatical object relation with respect to Y′, the s structure counterpart of Y: OBJ(Y′, X′). At the moment I have not introduced any principles that will prevent the s structure counterpart to a logical object from only receiving a syntactic role from its Governing verb without also serving as an argument to the verb or to any other constituent. To put it another way, no principle prevents two l-s relations, arg(V, X) and role(V, X), from corresponding to a single s structure relation, ROLE(V', X'), where V, V' is a verb. It is unclear to me whether or not the lack of any such principle holds any empirical consequences—I have found nothing that appears to hinge on it. Nevertheless, it seems that a constituent at any level of structure that does not serve as either an argument taker or an argument would not be integrated into the constituent structure of a sentence. That is, one could not identify it as being part of any constituent. A natural constraint to place on a level of structure would be that every constituent must be either an argument taker or an argument—or the root S or proposition node. If every constituent must constitute part of some phrase at every level of structure, then obj(Y, X), for Y a verb, could not correspond simply to ROLE(Y', X'). Rather, X' would have to be an argument of Y' and thus its direct object: OBJ(Y', X').

Consider again l-s constituents X and Y such that obj(Y, X).

(2.65)

As the theory has been developed, X', the s structure counterpart of X, may serve as argument to Y', the s structure counterpart to Y, but receive its syntactic role from some syntactic role assigner Z, perhaps introduced at s structure.

(2.66)

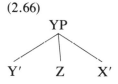

Since X' serves as argument to Y' in (2.66), Y' Governs X' and principle M is satisfied. Moreover, I have supposed that a constituent qualifies as an argument to a verb only if it is assigned a role. Since X' receives a syntactic role from the syntactic role assigner Z in (2.66), this requirement too is satisfied.

Languages exploit the possibility of a direct logical argument's corresponding to an indirect syntactic argument in antipassive constructions (see section 4.3). English seems to make use of this possibility in certain derived nominals. For example, consider the well-known case of *destruction*.

(2.67)
a. The clay porcupine's destruction by Elmer lasted four hours.
b. Elmer's destruction of the clay porcupine lasted four hours.
c. The destruction of the clay porcupine lasted four hours.
d. Elmer's destruction lasted four hours.
e. Elmer's destruction was horrible to behold.

In sentences (2.67a,b,c), which contain some mention of the "de-stroyed" nominal, *destruction* has an event reading, but for most speakers the derived nominal in (2.67d,e), where *Elmer* is taken as the destroyer, has only the result reading. Thus (2.67d) is somewhat anomalous if *Elmer* is interpreted as destroying something. The nominal *destruction* in (2.67d) refers to some result of the destruction, not to the event of destroying, and it is hard to imagine how the result of a destruction could last for four hours. Thus (2.67e) has a natural reading in which *Elmer's destruction* refers to the clay shards left after he broke apart the clay porcupine.

The data in (2.67) make sense if we suppose that *destruction,* in its event use, has the nominal-argument structure (function from argu-ment(s) to a nominal) in (2.68a), parallel to the P-A structure for the related verb *destroy,* which is given in (2.68b).

(2.68)
a. *destruction,* N, 'destroy' (*patient*)
b. *destroy,* V, 'destroy' (*patient*)

On the event reading, the nominal *destruction* takes an obligatory ar-gument, just like the related verb. However, all nouns in English are inherently [−transitive]. Also, nouns do not form predicates or other phrasal constituents that might take subjects. Therefore, if a noun gov-erns an argument at l-s structure, it must head-Govern the s structure counterpart of the argument at s structure by Governing it, and the noun must Govern this constituent by taking it as an indirect grammati-cal argument. An l-s structure for the nominal in (2.67c) is shown in (2.69a). The corresponding s structure is displayed in (2.69b).

(2.69)

a. l-s structure

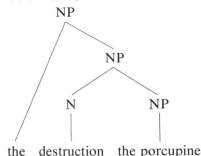

b. s structure

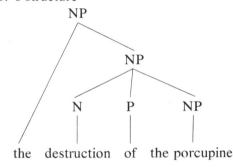

Note that a syntactic role assigner comes in at s structure to assign the indirect argument of *destruction* its syntactic role.

This analysis of derived nominals is not forced by principles of the theory presented to this point. One might say, for example, that nouns do not take direct semantic arguments, that is, do not assign semantic roles. In this case, one would be forced to suppose that *of* assigns *the porcupine* its *semantic* role in the nominals in (2.67b,c). Or, following Rappaport (1983), one might suppose that nouns do not take arguments at all. Rather, all the constituents that look like semantic dependents of the noun are actually modifiers of the nouns. On some ways of looking at nominals, saying that nominals take arguments means giving up an explanation for why derived nominals created from raising to object verbs are not raising to object nominals (see Williams 1982, for example).

Consider finally the situation in which X is an indirect l-s argument of Y, Y a verb; that is, arg(Y, X) but not role(Y, X), as in (2.70).

(2.70)

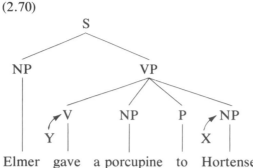

Elmer   gave   a porcupine   to   Hortense

The semantic role assigner that assigns X its role at l-s structure and thus qualifies X as a potential argument—the preposition *to* in (2.70)—will correspond to a syntactic role assigner at s structure and assign a syntactic role to X', the s structure counterpart to X. Principle M tells us that Y', the s structure counterpart to Y, must head-Govern X'. One possibility consistent with these considerations is that X' will be an indirect syntactic argument of Y'. In this case, the s structure for (2.70) would look just like (2.70), with Y' and X' substituted for Y and X, of course.

Two other possibilities should be considered. First, suppose that X' is a direct syntactic argument of Y' at s structure; that is, ARG(Y', X') and ROLE(Y', X'). We have just seen that X' will receive a syntactic role from the s structure counterpart to the semantic role assigner that assigns a role to X. Therefore, X' will receive two syntactic roles from lexical (nonphrasal) constituents. But as I show in section 2.3.3, a general constraint on surface structure, necessary to explain the distribution of PRO, for example, prohibits a single constituent from receiving two syntactic roles from nonphrasal constituents. So, given my assumptions, an indirect l-s argument of a verb will not correspond to a syntactic direct object of the verb.

Suppose, however, that Y' head-Governs X' by virtue of the fact that the VP headed by Y' Governs X'; that is, suppose that X' serves as grammatical subject to this VP. Again, the s structure counterpart to X's semantic role assigner will assign a syntactic role to X', as will the VP of which X' will also be an argument. A structural representation of this state of affairs is shown in (2.71).

(2.71)

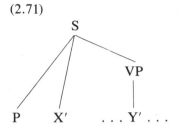

Thus far I have not introduced any constraints or principles that will rule out in all cases the sort of situation indicated in (2.71). Readers are invited to work out for themselves why this sort of situation would arise in only very special cases. For example, for the same reasons that the verb heading a passive clause must be [−log sub], so Y, the l-s counterpart to Y' in (2.71), must head an l-s predicate that takes no logical subject. In addition, the sentence in (2.71) must appear in an environment such that there would be no overt subject in the clause were it not for the presence of the P. If the sentence in (2.71) were a tensed English sentence, for example, it would be ungrammatical for the same reason that an l-s indirect argument cannot correspond to an s structure direct object. Tensed sentences in English, it will be argued in chapter 3, contain a lexical tense/aspect marker that assigns a syntactic role to the sentential subject. But, again, a principle to be discussed in section 2.3.3 has the effect of prohibiting a single s structure constituent from receiving syntactic roles from more than one lexical role assigner. Since X' receives a syntactic role from the P in (2.71), it may not receive one from tense/aspect and thus cannot appear in a tensed English sentence. Other considerations further narrow the possible cases one might examine to discover whether situations like (2.71) actually occur in natural languages. It would be easy to fine-tune our principles to exclude cases like (2.71), but in the absence of any real data to decide the issue, I leave this hypothetical construction as an allowed possibility.

2.3. Surface Structure

The theory of grammatical relations I have been developing is intended to be universal. No matter what the sentences of a language look like in terms of the ordering of constituents or phrase structure regularities, the language will have s structures and l-s structures like those described. Though the theory makes claims about constituency in the syntactic analysis of sentences, it does not, as thus far developed, imply anything about constituency in the phrase structure of languages. For example, every language has s structure VPs (grammaticalizations of predicates), but a language may lack phrase structure VPs. I have assumed that the surface structure of a sentence in a given language, like the other syntactic levels in the present model, consists of a list of constituents and relations accompanied by an associated constituent structure tree. It is the surface constituent structure tree that is mapped onto phonological structure. The principles of the present theory allow the surface constituent structure trees of a language to be quite flat in comparison with the constituent structure representations of l-s and s structure. The theory also allows a language to place few constraints on the ordering of constituents in a surface structure tree. Unlike the constituent structure trees of l-s and s structure, the ordering of elements within a surface structure tree is significant and is phonologically interpreted.

The list of constituents and relations at surface structure is constrained not only by the mapping relation between s and surface structure but also by the relation of Move Alpha. Move Alpha sanctions the presence in surface structure of constituents and relations not directly related to s structure constituents and relations. Basically, Move Alpha is the relation between a constituent bearing a relation not mapped from s structure and a trace standing in a relation that is mapped from s structure.

The possible surface structures for a given language are determined by the rules mapping from s to surface structure. In a highly configurational language, s structure Government (i.e., grammatical relations; see the definition in (2.49)) is expressed in surface structure government and in linear order—in certain types of structural relations within a constituent structure tree. In the so-called nonconfigurational languages, s structure Government is expressed via case marking and agreement rather than structural government. Thus the mapping between s and surface structures in these languages places fewer demands on the constituency of surface structure, allowing for more freedom in the ordering of words.

Within this framework, there is no reason to see the distinction between configurational and nonconfigurational languages as a dichotomy rather than a continuum. The more a language strictly expresses grammatical relations configurationally—in terms of structural government and linear order—the more configurational the language.

Perhaps owing to a concentration on English in transformational linguistics, the connection between relational structure and constituent structure has until recently received little attention in the transformational-generative tradition. It is generally possible to represent a relational structure such as s structure in constituent structure trees resembling the phrase structure trees of English. Because English seems to encode grammatical relations in phrase structural relations in a transparent manner, it has been tempting to claim that the connection between surface—or surfacy—structures and relational structures is trivial. Nevertheless, recent studies of languages with widely different or impoverished phrase structure compared with English have forced linguists working within the transformational-generative framework to examine more closely the possible mappings between relational and constituent structure representations (e.g., the work of Hale 1980, Nash 1980, and the studies in Bresnan 1982b). Even if I had the space, I could not hope to present a complete story about the mapping between s structure and surface structure encompassing the range of languages studied over the past few years. No one has completed the necessary preliminary work describing the possible range of surface structures in universal grammar. Instead, I discuss some general principles governing the mapping between s and surface structures and provide some remarks about this mapping relevant to the central issues of this book.

2.3.1. Surface Structure Constituents and Relations

Grammatical relations seem to be expressed in four main ways in surface structure: through the structural relations of linear precedence, or more precisely, linear adjacency, and structural government, as well as the relations of case marking and agreement. These relations are the surface structure counterparts of the role assigning and argument taking relations of l-s and s structure.

Of the constituent structure relations that appear in the list of constituents and relations at surface structure, structural government is simply a relation of asymmetric sisterhood (the notion of "sister" in (2.72) is defined in (2.36)).

(2.72)
X structurally governs Y iff X and Y are sisters and X is the operator of the phrase consisting of X and Y (and, possibly, other constituents); X is an operator iff X is the surface structure counterpart of an argument taker or role assigner at s structure.

Given the organization of a phrase structure tree, the structural government relation establishes proximity (or locality) relations between the terminal elements of constituents standing in the relation. A closer proximity relation is that of (string) adjacency. Since both adjacency and structural government determine phrase structure nearness, one might reduce the inventory of relations at surface structure by eliminating the adjacency relation. Instead of postulating a separate adjacency relation, I could suppose that the mapping between s and surface structure may establish only a structural government relation between constituents, where this relation may be further realized as an adjacency relation; consideration of certain apparently aberrant interactions between phonology and syntax in section 7.3 leads me to distinguish between adjacency and government, however. For example, the situations in French in which certain prepositions combine with the articles of a following NP to create special suppletive forms like *du* (from *de* + *le*) and *au* (from *à* + *le*) seem to require the postulation of a distinct adjacency relation.

Since there are usually cross-categorial generalizations within a language as to the order of an argument-taking word and its complements, it seems that linear precedence between elements standing in an adjacency relation at surface structure need not be specified individually with each pair standing in this relation (see Stowell 1981). Surface structure need only specify that X and Y are adjacent; general rules within the language will determine whether X or Y comes first. For example, a language might specify that all arguments of Governers must precede the Governer, as in a strictly SOV language with postpositions and postnominal adjective phrases. In such a language, the linear precedence relations between an argument taker and its arguments are fixed once for the entire language.

In addition to structural relations, languages use case marking and agreement to express grammatical relations in surface structure. When A and B stand in some relation at s structure, where A is the operator, then the surface structure counterparts of A and B, A' and B', can stand in surface structure relations such that A' bears some morphology associated with B' or B' bears some morphology associated with A'. When the surface counterpart to the operator bears the morphology, the relation is one of agreement; where the operand bears the morphology, the relation is called case marking.

An enormous range of issues arise in the discussion of case marking and agreement. For the purposes of this book, these terms refer to morphological case and agreement, not the abstract Case and AGR of GB theory. I shall examine constraints on case marking that greatly limit the use of case marking to express grammatical relations, but the discussion will barely scratch the surface of the important issues. As for agreement, the present work is even more deficient. In chapter 7 I suggest that at least some overt agreement arises not as the direct expression of grammatical relations from s to surface structure but rather as the result of morphological merger, in which case the agreement itself stands in some grammatical relation.

Formally, it seems quite easy to do without agreement as an expression of grammatical relations, leaving case marking alone as a nonstructural expression. For example, following GB theory, one could suppose that some agreement elements are abstract Case assigners. The AGR element of S, associated with tense, could be said to assign nominative case to the subject of S. Continuing with this idea, one could say that any time agreement looks to be expressing a grammatical relation, agreement is actually a case marker, assigning abstract Case to the item with which it agrees. It is also possible to subsume some apparent agreement phenomena under the principles of binding theory and Move Alpha. Some agreement elements can be treated as pronominal elements bound to the agreeing NP; others, in particular, object (often clitic) agreement markers, can be treated as variable binders subject to the same constraints as the wh- words moved by Move Alpha. As these approaches to agreement reduce the number of independent mechanisms within the grammar, placing agreement phenomena under the constraints of independent components of grammar (see Chomsky 1981), this sort of analysis has its intuitive appeal. But at the present general level of discussion, nothing hinges on the decision whether or not to distinguish agreement as an independent expression of grammatical relations. For ease of discussion, I treat agreement and case assignment separately.

I have given the l-s relations of arg(X, Y) and role(X, Y) some interpretation in terms of compositional semantics or meaning in a nontechnical sense. The s structure relations ARG(X, Y) and ROLE(X, Y) have been defined simply as the s structure counterparts of the corresponding l-s relations. The surface structure relations of structural government, adjacency, agreement, and case marking have a direct connection with phonological interpretation, but it seems that they are not directly tied up with the s structure relations; in some sense the s structure of a sentence is closer to l-s than to surface structure.

To change perspectives, consider the relation between l-s and surface structure relations. Structural government and agreement are metaphorically related to the arg(X, Y) relation. Structural government is a relation of asymmetric sisterhood, as is the arg(X, Y) relation, in which X and Y are specified to be immediate constituents of the same phrase, with X singled out as the operator. Agreement simply affixes a placeholder for an argument on the argument taker. Adjacency and case marking seem to be metaphorically associated with the role(X, Y) relation. All three are relations established independent of constituent structure. Case and role assignment consist in an operator's determining a feature of the operand. Adjacency without implication of constituency is perhaps the most basic way a system of communication that depends on linear order could express a dependency between two items like the role(X, Y) dependency.

From this new perspective, then, the s structure relation of ARG(X, Y) may be seen as the projection or grammaticalization of structural government and agreement while the s structure relation of ROLE(X, Y) serves as the projection of adjacency and case marking. That is, grammatical relations truly stand between l-s and surface structure relations in the present theory. Their existence as abstract, uninterpreted entities is supported from both sides, both by l-s and by surface structure relations.

As in the mapping between l-s and s structure, each s structure constituent type will find a corresponding type at surface structure, and the X-bar-like principles of constituent structure described in section 2.1.4 will apply to the constituents of surface structure as well. I therefore eschew phrase structure rules in favor of general constituent structure principles, language specific generalizations about the order of heads and their complements, and any language-particular surface structure constraints a language might impose. Including phrase structure rules in a grammar—in particular, those of X-bar theory—can be seen as making a substantive claim about natural languages: that the distribution of phrases depends on their internal structure (see Marantz 1978, 1980). In a phrase structure grammar, the distribution of constituents is specified in terms of the names of the constituents (e.g., NP); in X-bar theory, the name of a constituent strictly determines its internal structure, most directly, its head. Thus the grammar fixes distribution of a phrase according to its internal structure. In the present theory, the distribution of a phrase depends most directly on its function, that is, on the grammatical relation(s) it bears.

Until recently, theories of syntax have not been sufficiently developed to test the competing claims of an X-bar-like phrase structure grammar and the sort of approach adopted here. A verdict on this issue is still awaited, but studies such as Stowell 1981 indicate how far the sort of principles I have mentioned will correctly determine the phrase structure of a language in the absence of stipulated phrase structure rules. On the other hand, Horvath 1981 and Huang 1982 argue strongly for a language-particular phrase structure rule or stipulation in the grammars of Hungarian and Chinese. The balance between functional and relational determination of phrase structure and stipulated phrase structure rules has yet to be established. The present theory makes the exploitation of phrase structure rules the marked case in universal grammar.

2.3.2. Mapping Between s and Surface Structures

Every lexical item in s structure must map onto a lexical item at surface structure. This principle anchors the association of s and surface structures as the parallel principle anchors the association of l-s and s structure, allowing one to identify the surface structure counterparts of s structure constituents. As with the mapping between l-s and s structure, each lexical entry may be seen as a mapping rule, associating features relevant at s structure (say [±transitive]) with features relevant at surface structure (e.g., phonological features). In the mapping between l-s and s structure, I have stipulated that lexical category type is preserved in the sense that a constituent of l-s category X will map onto a constituent of the corresponding s structure category X'. It is an open question whether to adopt a similar principle to constrain the mapping between s and surface structure. Hinging on the decision in this case is the question whether or not, for example, prepositional phrases acting as indirect arguments have the same internal structure as prepositional phrases acting as VP and NP modifiers.[10] If all these phrases share identical internal structure and this structure does not follow from general constituent structure facts about the language in question, then some specific phrase structure rule or constraint must refer to a unified class of surface structure PPs in the language, and the various functionally defined constituent types must all map onto surface structure Ps and PPs. In this case, the prepositional head of a predicate modifier and the prepositional role assigner without argument structure would have to correspond to a single surface structure category type.

Although the identity of lexical items in s and surface structures establishes a correspondence between the constituents of the two structures, some additional principle is required to guarantee that the grammatical relations of s structure find counterparts in surface structure. Because a complete theory of surface structure is wanting, the principle governing the mapping between s and surface structure relations (corresponding to principle M) may only be given a general, imprecise formulation, something like (2.73).

(2.73)
Principle:
Grammatical relations must be expressed in surface structure.

Principle (2.73) may be interpreted to imply that to each grammatical relation of s structure R(X, Y), there must correspond a relation of surface structure R'(X', Y'), where X' and Y' are the surface structure counterparts of X and Y and where R' is chosen from the list of structural (structural government and adjacency), case marking, and agreement relations. I will examine some constraints on the choice of surface structure relations to correspond to particular s structure relations.

A crucial difference between (2.73) and the corresponding principle M lies in the role played by head-Government in principle M. Whereas (2.73) ties a grammatical relation between X and Y directly to a relation between the surface structure counterparts of X and Y, principle M allows an l-s relation between X and Y to correspond to a grammatical relation between the s structure counterpart of Y and some constituent headed by the s structure counterpart of X.

Although principle (2.73) does not heavily constrain the possible correspondences between the s structure relations of ARG(X, Y) and ROLE(X, Y) and the four surface structure relations, work in other grammatical frameworks points to the strengthening of the principle for certain specific situations, making interesting predictions about some languages. Within the present framework, the GB theory of Chomsky 1981 may be interpreted as making a very strong claim about the mapping between surface and s structure *when s structure grammatical relations are expressed in surface structure configurational relations.* Following the spirit of Chomsky 1981, one could claim that the principle that constrains the mapping between s and surface structure when s structure relations are expressed structurally demands a strict correspondence between structural government, as defined in (2.72), and Government, as defined in (2.49).

(2.74)

The Configurationality Principle:

If X Governs Y in s structure and the relation(s) between X and Y is (are) expressed structurally, then the surface structure counterpart of X must structurally govern the surface structure counterpart of Y.

The insight captured by the GB framework, an insight encoded in (2.74), is that English and other highly configurational languages express grammatical relations (Government) in structural relations (structural government).

The Configurationality principle places heavy constraints on the expression of grammatical relations in structural configurations. Another principle adapted from Chomsky 1981 restricts the possible expression of grammatical relations in case marking.

(2.75)

The Case Marking Principle:

Case is determined under government/Government.

Principle (2.75) implies that although a verb can determine case marking on its l-s or s structure object, it may not determine the case on a subject of a phrase it heads. Although a verb may determine the case marking on some element it governs at l-s structure, by the logic of the grammar such case marking may not be seen as satisfying principle (2.73). Principle (2.73) is satisfied only by case marking that expresses grammatical relations in the mapping between s and surface structure. Case marking under government at l-s structure is thus superfluous from the point of view of the complete mapping from l-s to surface structure.

In general it is difficult to observe the operation of the Case Marking principle in natural languages. Languages with overt case marking include general case marking rules that decide the case marking of nominal arguments in unmarked situations. Subjects in tensed clauses might usually be marked nominative, for example, whereas objects of most verbs might be marked accusative. When these general case marking rules are in operation, there is no obvious evidence that case marking is being determined under government/Government, that is, by an operator.

The Case Marking principle shows its predictive power in cases of idiosyncratic violations of the general case marking rules in a language. For example, although the usual expression of the OBJ relation in a language may be the appearance of accusative case on the surface structure counterpart of the OBJ, a verb in the language might require an unusual case on its OBJ. The Lexical Exception principle (2.15) ensures that exceptions to general rules must be carried in lexical entries. This principle taken with the Case Marking principle constraining the expression of relations in surface structure guarantees that a verb can specify unusual case only on one of its grammatical dependents and that there is no way in which unusual case could be assigned to a SUB by virtue of its being a SUB. A SUB bears its relation with respect to a phrase, not a lexical item. By the Case Marking principle, case marking is performed under Government/government; therefore, the SUB could receive its case only from the VP with respect to which it bears its relation. However, VPs do not have lexical entries in which one might store information about unusual case marking. Therefore, case marking on SUBs must be regular.[11]

Japanese provides an example of verb-specified unusual case-marking on OBJs. Japanese normally marks OBJs with the accusative particle *o,* as in (2.76).

(2.76)
Mary ga okasi o taberu.
Mary NOM cake ACC eat
'Mary eats cake.'

Nevertheless, as explained in Marantz 1981a, drawing on the analysis by Kuno 1973, certain Japanese verbs, such as *soodan suru* 'consult,' require the dative particle *ni* on their object.

(2.77)
a. John ga Mary ni soodansita.
        NOM   DAT consult-PAST
   'John consulted Mary.'

b. Mary ga John ni soodans-(r)are-ta
        NOM   DAT consult-PASS-PAST
   'Mary was consulted by John.'

One indication that the consulted argument is an OBJ in (2.77a), even though it is marked with the dative particle, is that it passivizes, as shown in (2.77b) (see Kuno 1973 for discussion of such verbs). Note that when the logical object of the verb in (2.77a) shows up as a subject in (2.77b), it bears the expected nominative case, not the dative case that it bears as OBJ in (2.77a). This fact indicates that the verb in

(2.77a,b) demands dative case on its grammatical OBJ, not on some particular semantic argument that might show up as OBJ or SUB. Since there is no OBJ in (2.77b), no constituent bears the dative case.

Since the specification of an unusual expression of a grammatical relation is found in the lexical entry of the operator of the relation, grammatical relations with phrasal operators, like SUB(X, Y), should not have exceptional expressions. Phrases do not have lexical entries in which an exceptional expression of a grammatical relation might be recorded. Moreover, the lexical head of a phrase could not dictate the expression of a constituent that the phrase governs/Governs because an item may only make demands about a constituent that the item governs or Governs itself. These restrictions on the specifications of unusual expressions of grammatical relations predict that, although an OBJ may have an unusual expression dictated by the item that Governs it, as in the Japanese (2.77a), a SUB may not be expressed unusually.

Rather than disconfirming this prediction about the exceptional expression of SUBs (as wrongly claimed in Bresnan 1982a), the phenomenon of "quirky case marking" (see Andrews 1981), which appears to involve verb-determined exceptional case marking on subjects, actually provides striking support for it. The Case Marking principle allows case marking under either Government or government. The Japanese example in (2.77) illustrates the effects of unusual case marking by a verb under s structure Government. Suppose a verb demanded unusual case on an l-s structure logical object under government. Just in the case that the verb was [−log sub], this unusually case-marked logical object could show up as a SUB of the VP that the verb heads at s structure. One should expect verb-specified unusual case marking on SUBs, then, only when the these SUBs are logical objects of the verbs in question, which must also be [−log sub]. In addition, since the case marking determined at l-s structure is independent of the grammatical relations borne by the unusually case-marked constituent, one should expect this constituent to bear the unusual case marking no matter what grammatical relation(s) it bears at s structure.

Unusual (quirky) case marking in Icelandic displays exactly the features that the present theory predicts for case marking determined at l-s structure under government by a verb. In a discussion of case marking in Icelandic, Andrews (1981) points out that Icelandic verbs may demand unusual case marking on their subjects or on their objects. For example, although objects are usually accusative and subjects (of matrix clauses) nominative, *hjálpa* 'help' requires a dative object and *batna* 'recover from' requires a dative subject (in matrix clauses), as illustrated in (2.78).

(2.78)

a. Ég hjálpa honum.
   I help him-DAT
   'I help him.'

b. Barninu batnaði veikin.
   child-DAT recover-from disease-NOM

An unusual feature of Icelandic quirky case, the feature that sets it off from the exceptional case marking illustrated in the Japanese example, is the "case preservation effect." Note that the dative object of Japanese *soodan suru* in (2.77a) corresponds to a nominative subject of the passive in (2.77b); that is, the consulted argument bears the dative case as an OBJ but the nominative case as a SUB. The verb *soodan suru* 'consult' demands that its grammatical OBJ be expressed in the dative case, not that its logical object appear in the dative case; if it made the latter demand, its logical object would appear in the dative case as SUB of the passive in (2.77b).

In contrast to the behavior of Japanese exceptional case marking on objects, Icelandic quirky case is preserved in passivization and raising. In (2.79a–c) the dative object of *hjálpa* 'help' corresponds to a dative subject of the passive, (2.79a), a dative object of a raising to object verb when the passive is embedded under such a verb, (2.79b), and a dative subject of a raising to subject verb when the passive is embedded under this sort of verb, (2.79c).

(2.79)

a. Honum er hjálpað.
   he-DAT is help-PASS
   'He is helped.'

b. Ég tel honum hafa verið hjálpað.
   I believe him-DAT to-have been help-PASS

c. Honum virðist hafa verið hjálpað.
   he-DAT seems to-have been help-PASS

Similarly, the dative subject of *batna* 'recover from' corresponds to a dative object in a raising to object construction, (2.80a), and a dative subject in a raising to subject construction, (2.80b).

(2.80)

a. Hann telur barninu hafa batnað veikin.
   he-NOM believes child-DAT to-have recovered-from disease-NOM
   'He believes the child to have recovered from the disease.'

b. Barninu virðist hafa batnað veikin.
   child-DAT seems to-have recovered-from disease-NOM
   'The child seems to have recovered from the disease.'

In (2.81) a normal, nominative subject (2.81a) corresponds to an accusative OBJ in a raising to object construction, (2.81b), and to a nominative subject in a raising to subject construction, (2.81c).

(2.81)

a. María hafi skrifað ritgerðina.
   Mary-NOM has written dissertation-ACC
   'Mary has written her dissertation.'

b. Þeir telja Maríu hafa skrifað ritgerðina.
   they-NOM believe Mary-ACC to-have written dissertation-ACC

c. María virðist hafa skrifað ritgerðina.
   Mary-NOM seems to-have written dissertation-ACC

Since lexical items may make demands only on elements that they govern or Govern, and since *batna* 'recover from' in (2.78b) does not Govern its SUB *barninu* 'child-DAT,' *batna* must govern *barninu* at l-s structure to specify that it receives dative case. As seen in section 2.2.3.2, for a constituent that is not the logical subject of a predicate to correspond to the SUB of the s structure counterpart of the predicate, the verb that heads the predicate must be [−log sub] and the constituent in question must be the logical object of the verb. So in order to govern *barninu* 'child-DAT' in (2.78b) yet allow it to correspond to the SUB of the sentence, *batna* 'recover from' in (2.78b) must be [−log sub] and must assign the recoverer role to *barninu*. In section 4.1.3, we shall see that [−log sub] verbs do not undergo passivization or impersonal passivization. Since the Case Marking principle forces the analysis of verbs taking quirky case marked subjects as [−log sub], I predict that these verbs should not undergo passivization or impersonal passivization. Levin (1981) confirms this prediction for Icelandic and explains at length why quirky case marked subjects should be treated as P-A structure internal arguments (see also Levin and Simpson 1981). Ultimately, it is the asymmetry between logical subjects and logical objects that demands the [−log sub] analysis of verbs that take quirky case marked subjects. Since Levin's (1981) passivization data independently identify the verbs taking quirky case marked subjects as [−log sub], Icelandic quirky case marking provides additional support for the l-s subject/object asymmetry.

Because quirky case remains with an argument regardless of the grammatical relation it bears, quirky case must be linked directly with a particular argument in the lexical entry of a verb that demands it. Levin (1981) suggests associating quirky case with argument slots as shown in (2.82).

(2.82)
a. *hjálpa* 'help' (*helped*) [+log sub], [+transitive]

DAT

b. *batna* 'recover from' (*recoverer,* theme) [−log sub], [−transitive]

DAT

The double lines connecting an argument position to the dative case symbol indicate a constraint on the expression in surface structure of the argument filling this slot.

The dative case assigns neither a semantic nor a syntactic role to the helped or recoverer arguments (see Levin 1981); rather, the constituents bearing these roles are constrained to appear in the dative case in surface structure. Suppose the DAT case did assign a semantic role to the helped argument of *hjálpa* or the recoverer argument of *batna*. Then the constituents bearing these roles would not be logical objects of the verbs in question but only indirect arguments of these verbs, assigned their semantic roles independent of the argument-taker that governs them. But arguments of verbs that are not also logical objects of these verbs cannot (uniformly) correspond to the SUB of the VPs the verbs head at s structure. Since the helped argument is the SUB of the passive of *hjálpa* (see (2.79a)) and the recoverer is the SUB of the active of *batna* (see (2.78b)), the helped and recoverer arguments must be logical objects of *hjálpa* and *batna* and the DAT case may not assign these roles.

Neither could DAT case assign a syntactic role to the constituents bearing the helped and recoverer roles of *hjálpa* and *batna*. If the helped argument could satisfy principle M by receiving a syntactic role from DAT case and corresponding to an indirect grammatical argument of the verb, then it would not have to correspond to the SUB of the passive of *hjálpa*. But the helped argument must be the SUB of the passive of *hjálpa*, demonstrating that the constituent bearing the helped role does not receive a syntactic role from the DAT case. Similarly, if the recoverer argument of *batna* received a syntactic role from DAT case, it would not have to correspond to the SUB of active *batna* to satisfy principle M, appearing instead as a grammatical indirect argument of the verb. Since the recoverer argument must appear as SUB in this situation, DAT case must not assign it a syntactic role.

Just as the semantic asymmetries pointed out in section 2.1.1.2 support the asymmetry between the logical subject and a verb's P-A structure-internal arguments, so the absence of Japanese-type exceptional case marking on SUBs supports the grammatical asymmetry between the SUB and the s structure arguments of a verb. A verb does not Govern the SUB of the VP it heads at s structure and so may not demand an unusual case marking on the SUB. It does Govern its OBJ and may demand an unusual case marking for this constituent, as in the Japanese example. Where it seems as if a verb is demanding a quirky case marking on its SUB, as in Icelandic, the verb is actually stipulating a connection directly between the case and a slot in its P-A structure. In such a situation, one expects the case preservation effect illustrated in (2.79)–(2.80). One also expects to find evidence that the quirky case marked subjects are not logical subjects, such as the failure of Icelandic verbs taking quirky case marked subjects to undergo (impersonal or personal) passivization.

2.3.3. Visibility and the Construction of Surface Structure Trees

To this point I have discussed only what constituents and relations appear in surface structure and how s structure maps onto these constituents and relations. I turn now to the question of how the list of constituents and relations at surface structure relate to the constituent structure tree that will serve as input to the phonology. Given the highly developed apparatus for the remainder of the grammar, I am in a position to answer this question more by observation and hypothesis than by stipulation or conjecture.

First, certain elements that the theory's principles force to appear in s structure do not seem to show up in surface structure; that is, they exhibit no phonological reflexes. Consider the subjects of the bracketed clauses in the following sentences, indicated as PRO.

(2.83)
a. [PRO to sell porcupines] was his lifelong ambition.
b. Elmer forced Hortense [PRO to sell porcupines].

The principles demand some element to serve as logical subject in the sentential subject in (2.83a), and the mapping principles guarantee that this logical subject will correspond to a grammatical subject at s structure. Yet there is no overt element in (2.83a) that could serve as the logical subject. In (2.83b), *Hortense* is interpreted as the logical subject of the embedded sentence, but the grammar does not permit a single element such as *Hortense* to serve both as logical object to a verb and as logical subject to a predicate; therefore, there must be some element serving as logical subject to the embedded clause that is interpreted as coreferent with *Hortense* at some level of analysis. Of course, there is a long literature on why one should believe that some phonologically null pronominal element serves as subject in sentences like (2.83). (The location of PRO in (2.83) is chosen for expository reasons; if the strings are to represent surface constituent structures, no element would appear in subject position where I have placed PRO.)

In addition to cases like those in (2.83), there are other situations in which one can identify missing constituents.

(2.84)
a. Elmer seems sick.
b. Hortense considers Elmer sick.
c. Elmer and Hortense arrived drunk.
d. Elmer painted the porcupine red.

In (2.84a,b), raising constructions, *Elmer* is a semantic argument of *sick* but bears a grammatical relation with respect to the higher verb. Particularly in the case of (2.84a) it is important to ask what s structure constituent is standing in what relation to correspond to *Elmer*'s standing in its l-s relation with respect to *sick;* that is, how is principle M being satisfied with respect to the relation between *Elmer* and *sick?* In (2.84c,d) a single constituent bears multiple semantic roles: in (2.84c) *Elmer and Hortense* are both the arrivers and the drunkards; in (2.84d), *the porcupine* is both painted and red. Only the relation between *Elmer and Hortense* and *the porcupine* and the verbs in (2.84c,d) seem to be represented at s structure. What happens to the relations between these constituents and the adjectives?

As Schein (1981, in press) has made explicit, and as I will review in chapter 3, it is important to separate constructions of control, as in the sentences of (2.83), from raising constructions like (2.84a,b) and structures of predication like (2.84c,d). Nevertheless, I would like to claim that a single principle makes all these constructions possible and explains why one does not find similar constructions with slightly different properties. For example, there is no control of grammatical objects in English, no raising from object, and no predication structures like (2.84c,d) only off objects rather than subjects.

(2.85)

a. *Elmer persuaded Hortense (for) Horace to kiss PRO.

    (i.e., Elmer persuaded Hortense to be kissed by Horace.)

b. *Elmer seems (for) Hortense to like.

    (i.e., It seems that Hortense likes Elmer.)

c. The porcupine [O[PRO to beat t]] is number 32.

d. Elmer found the porcupine [O[PRO to beat t]] in the zoo.

The string in (2.85a) is the sort of construction that would be grammatical if languages could control object positions (in other terminology, if Equi-NP deletion could take an object as its target). The structure in (2.85b) represents what would be allowed if raising occurred from object position. The predication structures in (2.85c,d) look parallel to structures in sentences (2.84c,d), but the predication is from an object position in the predication clause. In such constructions there is reason to believe that the relation of Move Alpha holds between a phonologically empty operator, indicated as O in (2.85), and a position marked by a t, or trace. This operator creates a structure of predication, whose properties are discussed in Chomsky 1982. In section 3.3 I briefly discuss the motivation for an empty category analysis of predication structures like (2.85c,d).

In (2.86) I propose a principle that I believe makes the proper cut between permissible and impermissible structures involving the missing elements under discussion.

(2.86)

The Surface Appearance Principle:

A constituent X will appear in the surface structure tree by virtue of bearing a relation with respect to some item Y iff Y is a lexical item (i.e., not a phrase).

Owing to the nature of mapping principle (2.73), a constituent will bear a relation with respect to a lexical item at surface structure if and only if its s structure counterpart bears a relation with respect to a lexical item, that is, if and only if its s structure counterpart is lexically Governed. Therefore, I could rewrite (2.86) to read "a constituent X will appear in the surface structure tree by virture of bearing a relation if and only if this relation corresponds to an s structure relation of lexical Government."

The Surface Appearance principle is written with the qualificatory "by virtue of." Although a phrase not bearing a relation with respect to a lexical item may not appear in surface structure by virtue of bearing a relation with respect to a phrase, it may appear in surface structure for other reasons. For example, it seems that the lexical content of all operators (e.g., verbs, modifiers, verb phrases) will appear in surface structure.

Subjects and constituents bearing relations with respect to modifiers are precisely the constituents that bear relations with respect to phrases, not lexical items. The Surface Appearance principle thus permits control of subjects, raising from subject and modifiee, and the bearing of multiple relations if one of these relations is borne with respect to a phrase (predicate, verb phrase, or modifier). That is, this principle permits exactly the missing constituents in the constructions exemplified in (2.83)–(2.84) to be phonologically absent from their expected positions in surface structure. If a constituent bears an OBJ relation, then by the Surface Appearance principle it must appear as OBJ and cannot be missing from the surface structure tree in OBJ position; that is, it must be expressed as objects are usually expressed. If constituents bore multiple relations with respect to lexical items (e.g., multiple OBJ relations), by the Surface Appearance principle they would have to appear in surface structure by virtue of bearing each of these relations. But, as surface structure trees are phonologically interpreted, surface structure constituents are individuated by their appearance in these trees and a single constituent may not appear more than once. Therefore, a surface structure constituent may not bear multiple relations with respect to a lexical item and an s structure constituent may not be multiply lexically Governed.

In the structures in (2.83) containing PRO, the PRO bears relations only with respect to a VP (it is subject of the VP) and thus does not appear in surface structure. The theory's principles thereby allow control of the subject of a tenseless clause. Now the subjects of tensed clauses in English certainly appear in surface structure, most often in the position expected for the argument of the verb phrase, given principle (2.74) for configurational languages. Since the Surface Appearance principle prohibits the subject's appearing by virtue of being a subject, it must appear in surface structure for some other reason. Following Chomsky and others, I assume that the subject of a tensed sentence also receives a syntactic role from tense/aspect, which serves as a semantic operator on the entire sentence or on the verb phrase (see chapter 3). I shall return to the mechanics of this suggestion in section 3.1 on raising, for the analysis given the expression of the subject in tensed English clauses is precisely that for raising to object constructions. What must be emphasized here is that subjects of tensed English clauses are grammatical objects of some lexical item (tense/aspect) and thus are expected to appear in surface structure in accordance with the Surface Appearance principle.

An important question for further research is how much structure should appear in the constituent structure representation of surface structure; that is, how much articulation should be given to surface structure trees. When should an s structure VP correspond to a surface phrase structure constituent, for example? At a minimum, if an s structure relation maps onto a structural relation between constituents, these constituents must be surface phrase structure constituents. It would not make any sense to suppose that A may structurally govern B at surface structure, where structural government is defined as in (2.72), if A and B are not structural constituents in the surface structure tree. The structural relations of surface structure should be taken as direct descriptions of the corresponding surface structure tree. On the other hand, agreement and case marking do not seem to imply anything about surface constituency. If X and Y stand in an agreement relation, then agreement morphology appears, at least, on the head of X. This implies nothing about the tree structure constituency of X or Y. Similarly, if X and Y stand in a case marking relation, then case marking appears, at least, on the head of Y. But again, this case marking relation does not imply that Y must be a phrase structure constituent. It is simply an observation that some languages that express grammatical relations through case marking and/or agreement do not keep subconstituents of, say, grammatical arguments together in surface structure (see Nash 1980).

The surface phrase structure articulation of a language depends, then, on its configurationality; a language is configurational, and thus displays articulated surface structures, to the extent that it maps s structure relations onto the surface structural relations of structural government and adjacency. The degree of articulation—the complexity of structure—that a language may display in surface structure is directly constrained by the grammatical relations at s structure. With the exception of the structures sanctioned by Move Alpha, a surface constituent structure tree may look no more complex than the constituent structure representation of the corresponding s structure. In addition, constituent structure may not be completely distinct at s and surface structure. For example, a SUB may not appear within the surface structure VP corresponding to the s structure VP with respect to which it bears the SUB relation. Thus s structure constituent structure places strong constraints on surface constituent structure. A language may have less articulation at surface structure as compared with s structure, but it may not have more or different articulation (pace Move Alpha).

The connection between surface constituency and the expression of grammatical relations in structural relations does make predictions about what might be found in the world's languages. For example, one should never find a language in which the head noun of an object must immediately follow the governing verb but in which the complements and modifiers of this noun may appear anywhere.[12] If an adjacency relation is established between a verb and its object NP, then this object NP must be a surface phrase structure constituent and its internal members should not appear scattered around the clause. Unlike agreement and case marking relations, structural relations are established between constituents, not between heads of phrases. It would be premature to propose other sorts of principles or constraints in this area, as the pertinent data are simply not available.

Recall that I assume two sources of constraints on the list of constituents and relations that make up the surface structure of a sentence—the mapping between surface and s structure and the relation of Move Alpha. (In chapter 3 I discuss Move Alpha in more detail.) I assume that each level of syntactic analysis is independently generated in the sense that the mapping between levels does not establish a generative relation between the levels but rather determines whether level L and level L′ may serve as analyses of the same sentence. Thus the surface structure of a sentence is simply some list of constituents and relations, whose provenance is irrelevant as far as the grammar is concerned.

Certain of the constituents and relations at surface structure are related to s structure constituents and relations. Because the s structure constituents and relations are in turn connected to l-s constituents and relations and l-s structure has a certain semantic interpretation, surface structure constituents and relations mapped onto s structure counterparts are integrated into the semantics of a sentence. Nothing prevents constituents and relations from appearing at surface structure even though they are not connected to s structure, but, unless something else is said, such constituents will not be integrated into the sentence. Move Alpha provides a means for relating surface structure constituents lacking s structure counterparts to surface structure constituents with such counterparts, thus allowing the former constituents to be integrated into the interpretation of a sentence.

Consider the question in (2.87).

(2.87)
What did Elmer see?

The question word *what* bears a structural relation in (2.87)—it structurally governs the clause *(did) Elmer see*—that does not correspond to any s structure relation. Moreover, the object of *see*, which, by the normal conventions of English syntax one expects to find immediately following *see*, is not overt. Suppose that the OBJ of *see* is a trace or variable—one of a set of phonologically null constituents to be discussed in chapter 3. Move Alpha will relate the question word *what* to the trace in (2.87), accounting for the fact that *what* bears the semantic role assigned by *see* and serves as semantic argument to this verb although it does not appear in a position in which one would expect to find the logical object of *see*.

Move Alpha is a relation between constituents A and B in a surface constituent structure tree such that A and B are coindexed. The connection between A and B is constrained by a locality condition called "subjacency"—they must be as structurally close as subjacency demands (see Chomsky 1981 for one formulation of subjacency). One of the constituents standing in a Move Alpha relation is the operator and one the variable. A general condition on operator–variable binding demands that the operator structurally c-command the variable; that is, the variable must be dominated by the node that immediately dominates the operator. The surface constituent structure for (2.87) is represented in (2.88), in which the Move Alpha relation is displayed.

(2.88)

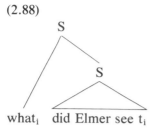

what$_i$ did Elmer see t$_i$

The assumption is that Move Alpha is a relation defined over surface tree structures. In effect, then, the list of constituents and relations at surface structure is sanctioned both by the mapping between this list and s structure and by relations represented in the constituent (tree) structure representation of this list.

In most languages, the relation of Move Alpha is defined only between a binder in a nonprojected position and a trace in a projected position. A nonprojected position is a position that would not be the structural expression of some grammatical relation. In practice, this limits the location of binders to sisters of maximal projections that are not the surface structure counterparts of modifiers. Nonmaximal projections and modifiers are operators, and the position of sister to an operator is a projected position, the position in which one expects to find the operand of the operator. In section 3.3, I examine some evidence that at least one language allows Move Alpha to relate binders and traces that both occupy projected positions.

Chapter 3
Bearing Multiple Relations

I explained in section 2.1.4 that a constituent may be assigned multiple semantic roles at l-s structure, but constraints on the formation of a structural representation of l-s structure limit the situations in which such assignment may occur. In addition, a constituent may bear multiple grammatical relations at s structure. Here, however, different constraints are at work. If bearing multiple semantic relations required a single l-s constituent to appear in more than one place in the structural representation of l-s structure, the resulting tree structure would be ill-formed. Constituents are individuated by their occurrence at l-s structure; a single constituent cannot appear in more than one place in an l-s tree at the same time. On the other hand, s structure is an uninterpreted structure. It stands between l-s structure, which has some semantic interpretation, and surface structure, which is phonologically interpreted. An s structure constituent may appear in more than one position in an s structure tree, as long as the principles of grammar do not force this constituent to correspond to a constituent appearing in more than one place in l-s or surface structure.

The possibility of a single constituent's appearing in more than one position in an s structure tree is exploited in raising constructions, in which a single constituent bears multiple grammatical relations. In this chapter I try to motivate a new analysis of raising constructions, an analysis that clearly separates raising from *wh-* movement constructions. The possibility of raising constructions and constraints on raising are shown to follow from well-motivated principles of grammar. Although raising is related to passivization on this analysis, it is not related to constructions involving Move Alpha and traces.

The discussion in this chapter leads to a consideration of the nature of empty constituents in syntax, phrase nodes lacking phonological

and/or other features. I argue that the PRO of control (Equi-NP) constructions is an empty element that occurs only at l-s and s structures,
receiving features at s structure. The trace of *wh-* movement is an
empty element that appears in surface structure and receives its features there. Following Chomsky 1982, I acknowledge only a single
truly empty element, which is either PRO or *wh-* trace. The theory
does, however, allow for another sort of empty element: a constituent
with all the semantic and grammatical features of a regular pronoun
lacking only phonological features. Only a subset of natural languages
contain such pronouns in their lexicons. The cases of phonologically
empty pronominals, exhibited in languages such as Japanese, must be
distinguished from the cases of phonologically null subjects, discussed
by Chomsky (1981) under the heading of "the pro-drop parameter" (see
section 7.4).

3.1. Raising

Consider first cases in which a constituent bears multiple semantic relations at l-s structure (other than just one argument and one semantic
role assignee relation). In (3.1) the italicized constituents are assigned
more than one semantic role.

(3.1)
a. Elmer ate the *fish* raw.
b. Naked, *Elmer* entered the room.
c. Elmer hammered the *fish* flat.

The theory allows constructions like these if one of the operators involved in providing the italicized constituents with one of their semantic roles is a modifier standing in a particular relation with respect to the
sentence.

   The theory requires a different analysis for sentences like (3.2).

(3.2)
a. Elmer found (just) *the porcupine* [to run the race].
b. [Eating smoked salmon], Elmer read the Sunday *Times*.
c. Elmer asked *Hortense* [to leave the room].

Unlike adjective phrases (modifiers), verb phrases (predicates) are not
maximal projections. Predicates take an argument into a proposition.
The constraints on the construction of l-s structures that permit a constituent to serve both as the semantic role assignee of a modifier and

also as the argument of a verb will not permit the constituent to both receive a semantic role from a predicate and serve as the argument to a verb. Although the italicized constituents in (3.2) are interpreted as if they were the subjects of the bracketed verb phrases, the theory prevents these constituents from actually being logical subjects of these phrases at l-s structure. Instead, some constituent, call it PRO, must serve as subject to the bracketed phrases and be linked to the italicized phrases at some point in the grammar. If indeed a sentence like (3.2c) were analyzed in such a manner that the italicized constituent served as argument both to the higher verb and to the lower predicate, the l-s structural representation of the sentence, given in (3.3), would not be a legitimate constituent structure tree. If a constituent could serve as argument to two separate operators, it would be multiply parented in the constituent structure representation, as shown in (3.3).

(3.3)

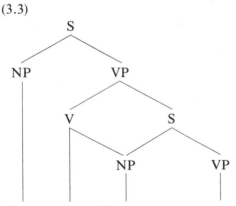

Elmer   asked   Hortense   to leave the room

Nor could the lower VP in (3.3) simply be a sister to *asked* and *Hortense* under the matrix VP node. According to the Nonmaximal Head principle (chapter 2), the VP, as a nonmaximal projection, must head its own S.

In raising sentences, as opposed to the constructions in (3.1) and (3.2), a single constituent bears multiple grammatical relations without necessarily bearing multiple semantic relations (other than one role assignee and one argument relation). In the canonical raising constructions in (3.4), *Elmer* bears a grammatical relation in the matrix clause although semantically this constituent is an l-s dependent of only the phrase *fond of porcupines*.

(3.4)
a. Elmer seems fond of porcupines.
b. Hortense considers Elmer fond of porcupines.

The problem for any theory of syntax is to allow the sort of mismatch between compositional semantics and grammatical structure found in raising constructions like (3.4) while ruling out mismatches that do not occur in the world's languages. In the case of raising, the theory must limit the ability of constituents to take on grammatical relations at s structure independent of the relations they must bear to satisfy mapping principle M.

Recall that lexical items anchor the mapping among levels of syntactic analysis. Each lexical entry acts as its own mapping rule, dictating, for example, what set of semantic features map onto what set of grammatical features. The structural representation of l-s structure individuates l-s constituents; the constituents of l-s structure are just those that appear in the structural representation. Identifying constituents at s structure, an uninterpreted level of analysis, is a different matter. Since s structure depends for its existence on the mappings to l-s and surface structure, it is reasonable to suppose that s structure constituents are identified by these mappings.

Suppose l-s constituent X bears relations r-1 and r-2 at l-s structure. Suppose further that the mapping principles discussed in chapter 2 determine that X' is the s structure counterpart of X and that X' must bear s structure relations R-1 and R-2, relations corresponding to r-1 and r-2. Could X' also bear relation R-3 at s structure? Consider s structure as a list of constituents and relations. In the situation under consideration, this list would include R-1(Y, X'), R-2(Z, X'), and R-3(W, X') for some operators Y, Z, and W. How would the grammar encode the fact that the X' in R-3(W, X') is *the* X' that bears relations R-1 and R-2? This is a problem for the identification of constituents at s structure, a task that should be reserved for the principles mapping between l-s and s structure and between s and surface structure. Thus the X' in R-1(Y, X') is identified with the X' in R-2(Z, X') by the principles mapping between l-s and s structure. To this point we have not encountered any principle that would identify the X' bearing R-3 with the X' bearing R-1 and R-2.

In a canonical raising sentence, a constituent bears a grammatical relation outside the clause in which it bears its semantic relations. From the considerations outlined in the preceding paragraph, one may conclude that the theory as developed thus far rules out raising construc-

tions. If one tried to encode the fact that an s structure constituent X',
corresponding to l-s X, bears a grammatical relation not predicted by
the rules mapping from l-s to s structure, one could not identify X' with
the s structure counterpart of some l-s constituent bearing semantic
relation(s). Some additional principle is required to allow the grammar
to make this identification.

Examination of raising constructions in the world's languages leads
me to adopt the principle in (3.5), a transitivity condition on grammatical relations.

(3.5)
The Government Transitivity Principle:
Government is transitive such that, if X Governs Y and Y Governs Z,
then X head-Governs Z.

The Government Transitivity principle may be seen as an identification
principle; it allows the grammar to identify as a single constituent an
element bearing grammatical relations at least one of which is not
predicted by the principles mapping from l-s to s structure. Suppose
s structure constituent Z bears relation R-1(Y, Z) and suppose R-2(X,
Y) is predicted by the mapping principles. The relation R-3(W, Z) is
also on the list of s structure relations. Now R-3(W, Z) satisfies the
Government Transitivity principle for Z if one assumes that Z bears R-1
and if X is W or heads W; X Governs Y, Y Governs Z, therefore X
head-Governs Z—the same Z that Y governs. Therefore, given these
assumptions, the grammar identifies the constituent Z bearing R-3 with
the constituent Z bearing R-1, and one may say that the same s structure constituent bears R-1 and R-3.

Given the Government Transitivity principle, raising will occur when
an argument-taking item takes as argument a constituent itself capable
of Governing at s structure. Consider the canonical raising verbs *seem*
and *consider*. Both these verbs may take propositional arguments, as in
their uses in (3.6).

(3.6)
a. It seems that Elmer has sold his last porcupine.
b. Elmer considered that Hortense had been with his firm for five
   years.

According to the theory, no raising or exceptional case marking may
take place in situations where verbs take propositional arguments.

These same verbs *seem* and *consider* may also take modifiers as arguments. This option is illustrated in the raising constructions of (3.7).

(3.7)
a. Elmer seems fond of porcupines.
b. Hortense considers Elmer fond of porcupines.

First note that the theory prohibits analyzing sentences (3.7) as containing some sort of propositional argument to the raising verbs—a "small clause" (see Schein in press, Stowell 1980, Williams 1983) consisting of *Elmer* and *fond of porcupines*. If the arguments to the raising verbs were propositions, no raising would take place. Since sentences (the s structure counterparts to propositions) themselves do not Govern, a propositional argument will not trigger the application of the Government Transitivity principle. Nor can one analyze the phrase *fond of porcupines* as a predicate in (3.7). According to the principles of constituent structure outlined in section 2.1.3, only maximal projections may serve as arguments of anything but modifiers. Since predicates are not maximal projections, they may not serve as arguments to verbs. Thus the argument of the matrix verbs in (3.7) must be the modifier phrase *fond of porcupines*—a maximal projection. Finally, *Elmer* may not be analyzed as the *argument* of this modifier phrase. If *Elmer* served as argument to a modifier, the resulting constituent would be a nominal; by definition, modifiers of nominals take nominals to nominals. But there is no nominal corresponding to *Elmer fond of porcupines* in (3.7) that might be parallel either to *the man fond of porcupines* in *The man fond of porcupines is likely to succeed in all endeavors* or to *Elmer fond of porcupines* in *Elmer fond of porcupines is a lovely sight*.

From these considerations, I conclude that *fond of porcupines* is a maximal projection in (3.7) serving as argument to the raising verbs. Although it does not take *Elmer* as an argument, it assigns *Elmer* a semantic role, the "fond of porcupines" role.

It might be objected here that this analysis fails to capture the semantics of raising constructions. What "seems" in (3.7a), for example, is not a modifier but a modifier applied to a nominal; it seems that the modifier does in fact apply to the nominal. For purposes of discussion, I will call a modifier that applies to a nominal as in (3.7), assigning it a semantic role, a "predication" (to borrow terminology of B. Schein). To reply to the objection that this modifier analysis of raising constructions does not suitably account for the semantics of such constructions, I must take a broader view of the function of modifiers. Modifiers may form predications when accompanied by the copula. The copula in such situations takes a modifier and creates a predication. In (3.8), the modifier *fond of porcupines* is behaving exactly as it does in (3.7).

(3.8)
Elmer is fond of porcupines.

The copula may create a predication; in (3.8) predication-creating is the copula's only role. Raising verbs also make predications from modifiers. The point is that all nominal modifiers have this dual potency— they may serve as functions from nominals to nominals (the modifier function) or they may serve as predications, for example, with the copula. Since it is reasonable to assume that raising verbs, like the copula, create predications, it is also reasonable to say that they take modifiers as arguments. The predication readings are derived by the functions that the raising verbs name.

Given that raising verbs take modifiers as arguments, the principles of the theory interact to predict the syntax of raising constructions and to explain some cross-linguistic phenomena associated with raising. The l-s structures for sentences (3.7a,b) are shown in (3.9a,b).

(3.9)
a.

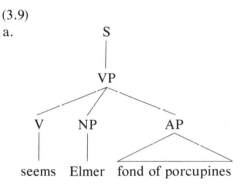

b.

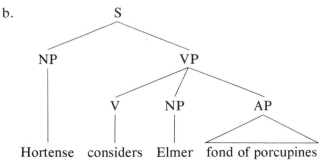

Elmer bears no semantic relations with respect to either *seems* or *consider* in (3.9a,b). This NP appears in the VPs of both sentences as the semantic role assignee of the AP, in order to satisfy the sisterhood condition on the structural representation of semantic relations given in (2.36). As l-s direct arguments of the verbs in (3.9), the modifiers will correspond to arguments of the corresponding s structure verbs; that is, the s structure counterparts of the raising verbs must Govern the s structure counterparts of their modifier arguments. The s structure counterparts to the modifiers will serve as indirect syntactic arguments of the verbs, receiving their syntactic roles from the structural position X of VP ([X, VP]), a structural position available to assign syntactic roles to any non-NP complement.[1]

Since *Elmer* bears an l-s relation with respect to the AP in both sentences of (3.9), its s structure counterpart must be head-Governed by the s structure counterpart of the AP. The s structure counterpart of *fond of porcupines* will not head any constituent at s structure; thus it must Govern *Elmer* directly. Since the verbs in (3.9) must Govern the modifiers and the modifiers must Govern *Elmer,* the Government Transitivity principle demands that the verbs head-Govern *Elmer* at s structure. In (3.7a), *seems* is a [−transitive], [−log sub] verb. In order for *seems* to head-Govern *Elmer, Elmer* must be the SUB of the VP that *seems* heads at s structure. That is, *Elmer* stands in the same situation relative to *seems* in (3.7a) as the logical object of a passive verb stands relative to the verb (see chapter 4). In (3.7b), *considers* is [+transitive], [+log sub]. Thus the verb will head-Govern *Elmer* by taking *Elmer* as direct object. The s structures corresponding to (3.9) are shown in (3.10).

(3.10)
a.

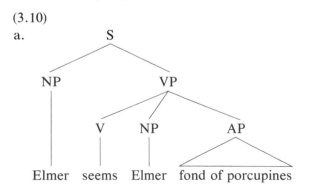

b.

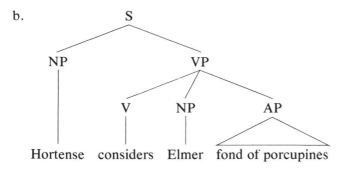

(I have left out of (3.10) the structural position [X, VP] that assigns the APs their syntactic roles.)

In (3.10a) *Elmer* must appear twice in the constituent structure representation of s structure, once to satisfy the sisterhood condition on the structural representation of relations with respect to the subject relation it bears, once to satisfy this principle with respect to its relation to the modifier. Since s structure, unlike l-s structure, is not an interpreted representation, there is no problem in having a single constituent, individuated either semantically by its appearance at l-s structure or phonologically by its appearance at surface structure, appear more than once in s structure representations. The identity of the *Elmer*s in (3.10a) is determined by the mapping principles and the Government Transitivity principle. Since the *Elmer* within the VP does not bear a grammatical relation with respect to a lexical item, the Surface Appearance principle will determine that this *Elmer* does not appear in surface constituent structure by virtue of bearing the grammatical relations that place it within the VP at s structure. Thus only one phonological *Elmer* will appear in the surface phrase structure of (3.10a), as required.

This analysis of raising cannot be extended to the raising sentences in (3.11).

(3.11)
a. Elmer seems to have sold his last porcupine.
b. Hortense believes Elmer to have sold his last porcupine.

As pointed out in section 2.1.3, the theory implies that only maximal projections may serve as arguments to anything but modifiers. For the analysis of raising with modifiers to extend to sentences like (3.11), the arguments of the raising verbs would have to be predicates. But predicates, functions from an argument to a proposition, are not maximal projections and thus may not serve as arguments without violating the Nonmaximal Head principle.

Data presented in Neidle 1982, whose importance in this context was first brought out by B. Schein (1982), indicate that raising should be allowed only with modifiers in the unmarked case, raising from full clauses as in (3.11) requiring some marked violation of a universal principle. As Neidle points out, Russian raises to object only from AP, NP, and PP—never from VP. This state of affairs seems to be the common situation for the (non-Germanic) languages that allow what has been analyzed as raising to object with verbs like *believe* and *consider*. For example, (3.12a) is a grammatical Russian raising to object sentence with the verb meaning 'consider' and an AP complement; (3.12b) is representative of the fact that Russian prohibits such raising constructions when they contain VPs (predicates).

(3.12)

a.   Ivan sčitaet ego bol'nym.
        considers him(ACC) sick(INST)
     'Ivan considers him sick.'

b.   *Ivan sčitaet ego byt' bol'nym.
        considers him(ACC) to-be sick(INST)
     'Ivan considers him to be sick.'

Bhojpuri (Shukla 1981, pp. 264ff) displays the same restriction as Russian on the complements to raising to object verbs, as shown in (3.13) (where OM is the object marker, GM the genitive marker).

(3.13)

a.   lalit gʰo:Da: ke sunnar ma:n-a:la:.
     Lalit horse OM beautiful believe(3sg, m., pres.)
     'Lalit believes the horse beautiful.'

b.   *lalit gʰo:Da: ke sunnar ho:-b ma:n-a:la:.
     Lalit horse OM beautiful be-INF believe(3sg, m., pres.)
     'Lalit believes the horse to be beautiful.'

c.   lalit gʰo:Da: kæ sunnar ho:-b ma:n-a:la:.
                 GM

The sentences in (3.13a,b) illustrate the generalization that verb-headed constituents (predicates) in Bhojpuri may not serve as arguments in raising to object constructions (OM marks direct objects in Bhojpuri). Sentence (3.13c) illustrates the fact that verb-headed constituents may be arguments of raising to object verbs as long as the subjects of these constituents remain grammatical dependents of only the lower clause, and thus bear genitive marking; that is, verb-headed constituents may serve as arguments to raising to object verbs only if they are full propositions or nominals and thus maximal projections.

I have argued (Marantz 1983) that a restriction on Japanese raising to object constructions noted by Kuno (1976) also follows from the restriction that maximal projections must head phrases and thus may not serve as arguments to verbs. (The situation in Japanese is too complex to summarize here; the reader is directed to the cited paper for details.)

In addition to correctly restricting the source of raising to modifiers in the unmarked case, the present analysis of raising clearly separates the use of raising to object verbs with full clausal arguments from their use in raising constructions. It has usually been claimed as an advantage for the (transformational) raising to object analysis that this analysis simplifies the subcategorization of raising verbs—they always take a sentential complement. Nevertheless, it is clear that (3.14a) is not similar in meaning to the corresponding sentence with a full sentential complement, (3.14b).

(3.14)
a. I considered Elmer fond of porcupines.
b. I considered that Elmer is fond of porcupines.

When *consider* takes a sentential complement, as in (3.14b), it has a meaning something like 'think over'; when it appears in a raising construction like (3.14a), its meaning is close to that of *believe*. Thus one must distinguish two uses of *consider* based on the choice of complement; one would not in general want to assimilate the cases of raising to object with the cases of selection of a clausal complement. Rather, in each case that a raising to object verb takes a sentential complement, it also takes a noun phrase with propositional type meaning, as in (3.15).

(3.15)
I considered his statement.

Sentence (3.15) means 'I thought over his statement'; that is, it contains the same sense of *consider* as does (3.14b). Sentences like (3.14) and (3.15) show that categorial theories of subcategorization capture the wrong generalization in assimilating cases like (3.14a) and (3.14b) while failing to capture the right generalization in not being able to assimilate cases like (3.14b) and (3.15).

The present analysis wrongly predicts the impossibility of sentences like (3.11) in English, in which raising involves predicates rather than maximal projections. Of the marked properties I could attribute to English to account for (3.11), the one that is closest to traditional accounts within transformational grammar seems the least promising: I could allow English raising verbs to take a proposition semantically but to exceptionally Govern the VP heading the s structure counterpart to this proposition. Then the Government Transitivity principle would ensure that the subject of the VP would become a grammatical dependent of the raising verb. It is clear from a comparison of (3.16) with (3.14) and (3.15), however, that raising sentences like (3.11) share the semantics of raising sentences with modifiers, not the semantics of clausal complement constructions.

(3.16)
a.   Hortense considered Elmer to have sold his last porcupine.
b.   *Hortense considered Elmer to sell his last porcupine (today).
c.   Hortense considered that Elmer sells his last porcupine today.

In (3.16a), Hortense is said to believe a predication, that the property of having sold his last porcupine applied to Elmer; when *consider* takes a sentential complement, as in (3.16c), the considerer is thinking over some statement; (3.16b) shows that the VP complement to *consider* must contain some tense/aspect (usually perfect, progressive, or habitual) that allows it to take on a property reading.

In light of sentences (3.14)–(3.16), I am led to propose that English allows some verbs to take predicates as if they were modifiers and turn them into predications. That is, English must be seen as allowing a marked violation of the Nonmaximal Head principle. English raising verbs treat predicates as if they were maximal projections, take them as arguments, and thus prevent them from heading phrases.[2]

It should be clear that the Government Transitivity condition makes the correct predictions about multiple raising as well as raising of dummies like *it*. Consider first the s structure, (3.17b), of raising construction (3.17a).

(3.17)
a. Elmer seems to appear to run every time he hears the sound of a wounded porcupine.

b.

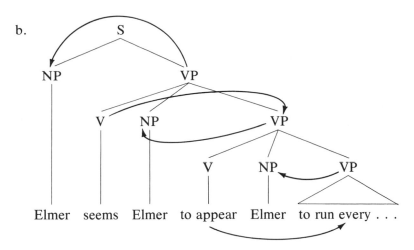

I have drawn lines in (3.17b) to indicate the essential chain of head-Government that, by the Government Transitivity principle, determines the grammatical relations *Elmer* will bear. According to mapping principle M, *Elmer* need correspond only to the subject of the VP *to run every*. . . . The VP, however, bears a relation with respect to *appear,* which starts the chain of head-Government.

As for the raising of dummy or pleonastic elements, most analyses of the source of such elements will interact with the present analysis of raising to yield the correct predictions. Consider sentences (3.18).

(3.18)
a. It seems obvious that Elmer is fond of porcupines.
b. I consider it obvious that Elmer is fond of porcupines.

If predications (in the sense I have defined) in English require syntactic role assignees at s structure, then *it* may appear in the s structures of (3.18) as this required role assignee without corresponding to any s structure constituent. Since *it* is Governed by the predications at s structure in (3.18), the Government Transitivity principle demands that it be head-Governed by the raising verbs. Other accounts of dummy *it* will yield the same results.

One of the important insights captured in the GB framework is that the expression of the subject in natural languages seems dependent on the tense and/or aspect of a sentence in a manner in which the expression of the object is not. The Surface Appearance principle provides the means to capture this insight in the present framework. This principle makes the appearance of a constituent in the surface constituent structure of a sentence depend on the lexical item with respect to which it bears a grammatical relation. Since subjects bear relations with respect to phrases (verb phrases), the Surface Appearance principle ensures that the expression of subjects in sentences must depend on something other than their subject relation. On the other hand, objects of verbs are grammatical dependents of lexical items—verbs—which will determine their expression in sentences.

Although the Surface Appearance principle sets up a situation in which the expression of a subject may depend on tense/aspect, no principle introduced to this point has indicated why the subject should depend on tense/aspect in this way. Clearly, if tense/aspect can be seen as Governing verb phrases at s structure, the Government Transitivity principle will ensure that the subjects of the verb phrases are head-Governed by tense/aspect. If subjects end up as objects of tense/aspect, which is lexical not phrasal, then the Surface Appearance principle will determine that the expression of subjects depends on tense/aspect. The question becomes, then, why should tense/aspect be seen as governing verb phrases?

The answer to this question that seems most plausible within the present theory is not without conceptual difficulties. Although one could view tense/aspect as assigning a role to a predicate, linguists have argued that tense at least should be considered a propositional, not a predicate, operator semantically. The connection between tense marking and the complementizer system supports this view (see Stowell 1981); complementizers stand in a structural position in which one would expect to find proposition (sentential) operators.

Taken as a sentential modifier, tense/aspect would have to exceptionally Govern the VP heads of the sentences that it modifies. Then, by the Government Transitivity principle, tense/aspect would head-Govern the subjects of these VPs. We have seen, however, that such exceptional Government was not motivated by an analysis of raising constructions. Rather, in the marked cases of raising illustrated in (3.11), raising verbs take predicates, not propositions. If tense/aspect does exceptionally Govern the VP head of a sentence that it Governs, the mechanism involved in this exceptional Government would stand independent of the phenomenon of raising.

On the other hand, auxiliary verbs in English seem to require an analysis distinct from the one I have offered for raising constructions but precisely parallel to that required for English tense/aspect. Recall that true raising verbs canonically take modifier arguments and exceptionally take predicate (VP) arguments. In contrast, auxiliaries take only VPs syntactically, and must take propositions, or perhaps predicates, semantically. Whatever mechanism allows for apparent raising to subject with English auxiliaries, this should be the mechanism that allows tense/aspect to Govern a VP.

Suppose English tense/aspect (and auxiliaries) takes propositional arguments and exceptionally Governs the VP head of the s structure counterpart of its argument. The l-s structure for sentence (3.19a) on this analysis is shown in (3.19b), with the corresponding s structure shown in (3.19c).

(3.19)
a. The porcupines rebelled.

b.

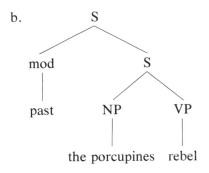

c.

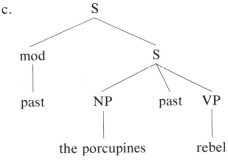

The tense morphology in (3.19c) merges with the head V of its VP argument at s or surface structure according to the principles of merger described in chapter 7. The analysis represented by (3.19) places tense/aspect in a position exterior to the sentence occupied by complementizers in English, making it possible to account for the connection between complementizers and the tense/aspect system.[3]

To summarize: tense/aspect—and auxiliaries—take propositions and, through some mechanism not directly implicated in canonical raising constructions, Govern *into* the sentences that they Govern at s structure.[4]

This analysis of raising places stringent constraints on the distribution of raising constructions. Not only must raising take place from subject, but it is also limited to constructions where certain types of modifiers, or, in the marked case, predicates analyzed on par with modifiers, serve as arguments to higher operators. Unlike the Projection Principle of Chomsky 1981, the present theory does not limit raising to raising to subject. Data discussed in a number of sources indicate that the lack of such a restriction is an advantage rather than a disadvantage of the present analysis. I predict raising to object with verbs like *consider;* exactly what is found.[5] Although in English various factors conspire to make it difficult to decide whether the raised object is a syntactic argument of the raising verb, in other languages the arguments for object status are more clear-cut. Furthermore, one would expect raising to indirect argument when the raising constituent is [−transitive] but is associated with a case marking or adposition that might assign a syntactic role to one of its grammatical arguments. If a raising constituent Governs a VP or modifier at s structure and therefore by the Government Transitivity principle must head-Govern the argument of the VP or modifier, this argument stands in the same position relative to the raising constituent as the s structure counterpart to the logical object of an antipassive verb stands relative to this verb (see sections 2.2.3.2 and 4.2). The raising constituent could Govern the argument in question if the argument served as an indirect syntactic argument of the raising constituent, assigned its syntactic role by some independent means. Data from modern Irish (McClosky 1983) indicates that this possibility of raising to indirect argument is realized in at least one language.

The present analysis correctly connects raising constructions to a variety of other constructions. Thus the relatively peculiar nature of modifiers that allows them to assign semantic roles in predication constructions without taking their semantic role assignees as arguments permits both the predication cases in (3.1) and the raising cases in (3.4). The possibility of passivization in natural languages depends on the presence of head-Government in place of Government in principle M mapping from l-s to s structure. Similarly, raising to subject requires that the Government Transitivity principle involve head-Government rather than simply Government. Finally, the Surface Appearance principle directly associates raising and control constructions. This principle allows a constituent to bear multiple grammatical relations and therefore permits raising constructions; at the same time, it limits the situations in which multiple relation-bearing is possible, thereby restricting raising to the cases actually observed. As shown in section 3.2.1, the Surface Appearance principle is also responsible for allowing control of subjects, which the principle implies will not appear in surface structure by virtue of being subjects. The Surface Appearance principle claims that one should find raising only from phrasal operators (semantic role assigners that are maximal projections) for the same reason that only the arguments of phrasal operators (predicates) are controlled.

The analysis of raising presented here differs essentially from the picture of raising that has dominated transformational grammar for the past 25 years.[6] In the conventional picture, raising is something that happens to verbs taking propositional arguments—traditionally, propositional subjects or objects; more recently, propositional complements alone. This conception of raising reaches its most refined state in Government-Binding theory, where raising to subject occurs when a verb takes a propositional complement but the verb phrase it heads at d structure takes no subject (the verb does not indirectly theta-mark the subject). The subject of the complement clause may be governed but not Case marked by the raising predicate. Unless this subject moves, via NP movement, into the subject position of the higher clause, it will not receive Case and the sentence will fail to satisfy the Case filter. Thus raising applies. To summarize, this traditional picture has raising predicates take propositional arguments but leave the subject position open to be filled by transformational movement. In the case of raising to object, again the verb takes a propositional complement and may govern the subject of the complement. But raising to object verbs, being Case assigners, are also able to assign Case to the downstairs subject. This Case assignment constitutes raising to object because the downstairs subject now is governed and Case marked by the raising verb, just as a direct object would be.

Although I have rejected the traditional conception of raising constructions for the canonical cases of raising cross-linguistically, the traditional analysis is in fact instantiated, but not in English. There are languages in which verbs taking sentential complements allow some constituent of these complements to move into the matrix clause, becoming either the subject or object of this clause. In these languages the verbs do in fact take sentential complements, not modifiers, as arguments. Unlike the relation between a raised constituent and the source position (as semantic dependent of an embedded modifier) in the true raising constructions, the relation between the moved constituent and its source position in these other constructions shares crucial properties with the corresponding relations in questions and topicalizations. That is, the raising constructions that conform to the traditional picture of raising involve the relation of Move Alpha. In particular, movement in these constructions may occur from any properly governed position, including direct object position in the complement clause. The clearest example of such raising is described for Niuean by Seiter (1980, 1983), though the same phenomenon is observed in some of the Bantu languages (see Trithart 1981 on Chichewa). A discussion of this sort of raising must be postponed until after the presentation of the analysis of *wh-* type movement constructions in section 3.2.2.

3.2. Null Constituents

As I have shown, raising in languages like English does not involve empty categories such as traces or PRO in the present theory. Rather, raising constructions simply contain a single constituent bearing multiple grammatical relations at s structure as a result of the Government Transitivity principle. Nevertheless, the principles of the theory do require the postulation of three sorts of empty constituents (see Chomsky 1982). The first is a pronoun without phonetic features. In languages such as Japanese, what would be considered an obligatory argument of a verb in other languages may be freely omitted in the sense that no overt NP appears in the Japanese sentence to serve as this argument. When the principles of grammar predict that the argument should appear in surface structure, such an argument is interpreted as if some overt pronoun appeared in the sentence. The null pronoun that stands in for an overt pronoun in such cases is crucially different from what has been called PRO in the literature. In particular, it may not take arbitrary reference and may be interpreted as 'I/me' or 'you' in the proper context.

The theory simply allows languages to contain lexical pronouns that lack phonological features. These pronouns appear in surface structure (by the Surface Appearance principle), but, lacking phonological content, they are not phonologically interpreted. More research is required to determine constraints on these phonologically null pronouns.

3.2.1. PRO

The second sort of null constituent allowed by the theory is PRO. This is the NP that appears in structures of obligatory control, like (3.20).

(3.20)
a. Elmer tried [PRO to open the porcupine cage].
b. Elmer persuaded Hortense [PRO to open the porcupine cage].

The Nonmaximal Head principle demands that there be some constituent in (3.20), which is not *Elmer* or *Hortense*, to appear as the subject of the embedded clauses. According to this principle, the embedded predicates, which are not maximal projections, must head some phrase at l-s structure. According to principle (2.36) the logical subjects of these predicates must be sisters to them at l-s structure. But the constituents that are interpreted as the subjects of the lower predicates, *Elmer* in (3.20a) and *Hortense* in (3.20b), cannot appear as their logical subjects in the constituent structure representation of l-s structure since they must appear as arguments of the upper verbs or predicates and l-s constituents may not appear in more than one place at a time. In order for sentences like (3.20) to be grammatical, some constituent, some place holder, must serve as subject in the lower clauses and some principle or theory must hook this place holder up with the proper constituent of the upper clause.

That place holder is PRO and the theory that determines the antecedent for PRO is control theory. (See Chomsky 1981, 1982, and especially Manzini 1983 for details of control theory within the Government-Binding theory.) I assume that PRO is a completely featureless empty constituent that receives features at s structure through the principles of control theory.

It has been tempting to many linguists to collapse the analysis of raising with the analysis of control constructions (see Bresnan 1982a, Dowty 1982b). Manzini (1983) provides strong evidence that the principles governing control constructions form an independent system not applicable to raising. In addition to the considerations Manzini raises, an important contrast between raising and control is illustrated in (3.21), a contrast whose relevance was brought to my attention by B. Schein.

(3.21)

a. Hortense considered Elmer fond of porcupines.

b. *Hortense persuaded Elmer fond of porcupines.

c. Elmer seems the best man for the job.

d. *Elmer tries the best man for the job.

At a surfacy level of analysis, raising verbs take NPs, APs, and PPs—in fact, canonically take only these types of complements—but control verbs like *persuade* and *try* take only VP complements. In the present theory, the contrast in (3.21) follows from the fact that control verbs take propositional arguments canonically. There are tense, aspect, and modal implications in the complements to the control verbs that the complements to raising verbs lack, and tense, aspect, and modality are properties of propositions. Given that the theory demands a propositional argument for the canonical control verbs, I predict the presence of some sort of logical subject for these propositional arguments which cannot be identical to any argument of the control verbs. Control theory dictates the interpretation of these embedded subjects as coreferential with an argument in the matrix clause.

Any theory collapsing raising and control will have to develop an independent explanation for this basic asymmetry: raising verbs canonically take nonsentential (non-verb-headed) complements while control verbs canonically exclude any but verb-headed complements.

3.2.2. Trace

The third sort of empty constituent found in the present theory is the trace of Move Alpha. This constituent, abbreviated ''t,'' is found in sentences like (3.22).

(3.22)

a. Porcupines, I can't stand t.

b. What does Elmer like to put t in the porcupine cages?

Traces appear in positions in which the principles that map from s to surface structure and that constrain the constituent structure representation of surface structure indicate that one should find some constituent. In (3.22b) the logical object of *put* should appear as its grammatical object at s structure and should project to a constituent immediately following the verb, a constituent not overtly present in the sentence. In fact, it has been argued that traces like those in (3.22) have phonetic importance in some languages and thus most definitely should occur in surface constituent structure, which serves as input to phonological interpretation (see Jaeggli 1980). Like PRO at s structure, the surface structure trace serves as a placeholder for a constituent that the principles of grammar predict should occupy a particular location but that does not patently appear there. It was Chomsky's insight that if these two sorts of placeholders are not given distinct essential properties, one can explain their complementary distribution: traces appear in surface constituent structure, that is, in positions that are mapped to surface constituent structure by general principles, whereas PROs stand in precisely those grammatical relations whose bearers are predicted not to appear in surface phrase structure.

Let us return to the description of the left side of the grammar sketched lightly in chapter 1 and section 2.3.3. Recall that surface structure, like the other levels of syntactic analysis, is a set of constituents and relations with a corresponding constituent structure tree. Some of the constituents and relations at surface structure correspond to constituents and relations at s structure, but the presence of other constituents at surface structure is sanctioned not by the mapping from s structure but by the relation of Move Alpha defined over the constituent structure representation of surface structure. Move Alpha connects a surface structure constituent (a binder) not projected from s structure with a trace (variable) that is so projected. The relation between binder and trace integrates the binder into the sentence. The binding relation in the surface structure tree is constrained by some locality condition (subjacency) that guarantees that the binder will be structurally close to its trace.

Consider sentence (3.23).

(3.23)
What did Elmer see t?

The question word *what* does not occupy the position of direct objects in English. Therefore, if it is to be interpreted as, or associated with, the logical object of *see,* it cannot be assigned its surface structure position through the usual mapping from l-s to surface structure. Rather, the rules of English demand that some constituent follow the main verb in the verb phrase in (3.23) and that this constituent correspond to *see*'s logical object. In order for *what*'s presence to be sanctioned in (3.23)—in order for it to be integrated into the sentence—it must be linked to a position that is independently sanctioned by the mapping rules, namely the position of t.

This linking is described by movement in standard transformational grammars. In the present theory, I assume that *what* is a surface structure constituent not corresponding to any constituent at s structure. It bears a structural relation at surface structure such that it structurally governs the sentence that it precedes. The conventions and principles for constructing constituent structure representations of surface structure will yield (3.24) as the surface constituent structure of (3.23).

(3.24)

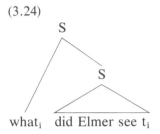

what$_i$ did Elmer see t$_i$

The relation of Move Alpha allows for the coindexing of *what* and the trace in (3.24), integrating the binder *what* into the sentence. I assume here that the binding relation of Move Alpha obeys the same principles and constraints that the relation between a moved constituent and its trace obeys in the GB framework. In particular, a binder must structurally c-command its trace.

Some condition constrains the occurrence of empty categories in the constituent structure representation of surface structure, prohibiting a PRO from appearing in this representation. That is, an empty category that appears in surface constituent structure may not be subject to the theory of control at s structure. All empty categories at surface constituent structure should stand in the Move Alpha relation with respect to some binder. Given certain reasonable assumptions, the required constraint on empty categories follows from the structure of grammar as outlined to this point.

To see this, consider again the nature of lexical items. I have assumed that each lexical entry serves as a set of mapping rules, indicating the mapping between features relevant at the various levels of syntactic analysis. The empty category "ec" will map a limited set of features from l-s to s to surface structure, perhaps simply category features. Since the same ec serves for PRO and trace, it must have no inherent phonological features (PRO does not appear in surface constituent structure and thus is not phonologically interpreted) and no inherent pronominal features (traces do not pattern with true pronouns). Since surface constituent structure is phonologically interpreted, all the constituents that appear in the surface structure of a sentence must be visible to the phonology; that is, all surface constituent structure constituents must be phonologically interpretable. Regardless of how the theory of control works to interpret PROs at s structure, the surface structure counterpart to the empty category is the empty category. That is, the theory of control does not change or add features to the empty category; it merely identifies and interprets the empty category. An empty category making an appearance at surface structure must be provided with features—with an interpretation—that make it visible to the phonological component. Since the principle that identifies empty categories at surface structure is the relation of Move Alpha, an empty category at surface structure must be a variable. If an empty category were interpreted as PRO at s structure and as a variable at surface structure, an inconsistent interpretation would result.

Note what does the work in this account of the complementary distribution of PRO and trace. First, I assume that there is a single ec, which may be interpreted as a PRO at s structure and/or as a trace at surface constituent structure. Second, I assume that an ec without features may not serve as input to phonological interpretation. Third, I assume that all constituents at surface constituent structure must be phonologically interpreted. Finally, I assume that a single ec cannot be interpreted both as PRO and as trace. From these assumptions, it follows that a constituent interpreted as PRO may not appear at surface constituent structure. The Surface Appearance principle makes it possible to derive from this conclusion the constraint that PRO may not be lexically Governed at s structure, for this principle ensures that lexically Governed constituents appear in surface constituent structure. Since ec's are identified as traces at surface constituent structure, traces must appear in this structure and so must be lexically Governed.

Although variable-binding at surface structure is not of major concern to the main themes of this work, it is useful to explore some of the reasons that the most popular alternative conception of Move Alpha offers no particular advantages over the present approach. Suppose Move Alpha were an actual transformational movement. If in fact the relation between variables and variable-binding at surface structure were one-to-one, then movement would be an elegant formulation of Move Alpha. One could look at some structure, call it A, as the constituent structure representation of surface structure, now defined as that list of constituents and relations that is projected from s structure.

Move Alpha would create new structure by adjoining constituents to categories in the constituent structure tree A. The positions to which Move Alpha moves constituents may be called "A-bar" (nonargument) positions, to employ the vocabulary of GB theory. An A-bar position is precisely a structural position that does not map onto an s structure grammatical relation—a position not in structure A. A transformational movement analysis of Move Alpha would capture the one-to-one relation between variables and binders and also the fact that movement is always into A-bar positions.

However, the phenomenon of parasitic gaps, discussed in Chomsky 1982 based on the data in Engdahl 1981, shows that the relation between binders and variables is not one-to-one. Consider the sentences in (3.25).

(3.25)
a. Which porcupine did Elmer sell t before cleaning t?
b. That's the professor whom stories about t in the newspapers upset t so much.

Although sentences like (3.25) sound strange to some speakers, they are generally considered grammatical. In such sentences, a single binder is associated with two traces. If Move Alpha is a movement transformation, as in Chomsky 1982, then some traces must be inserted into tree structures independent of the transformation to account for (3.25). Since the relation between binders and traces is not one-to-one, it is not an advantage of the movement analysis that it is able to capture such a one-to-one relation. Furthermore, Move Alpha may in fact relate a binder in an A position (a surface constituent structure position that serves as the counterpart to some grammatical relation) to a trace in an A position (see section 3.3). Thus the other possible advantage of the movement analysis also supplies no support for it.

A conceptual problem with a transformational Move Alpha concerns the complementary distribution of PRO and trace. In order to account for this complementary distribution on Chomsky's theory and in the present analysis I need to assume that the empty category PRO and the empty category variable are one and the same item. One should ask why a transformational movement should leave an empty category of the same sort as a PRO. There is no a priori concept of transformational movement to appeal to in order to establish the nature of what is left after movement removes a category or the contents of a category. A movement theory must stipulate that movement leaves *the* empty category—the category that is both PRO and trace.

In short, there is nothing wrong in assuming that the relation of Move Alpha is established by a syntactic movement, but there is nothing particularly elegant or compelling about this assumption either.

3.3. The Move Alpha Relation Between Projected Positions

It seems likely that the Move Alpha relation is canonically defined for semantic operators, that is, for words with semantic scope. The relation between an operator in a Move Alpha relation and the constituent over which it has scope overlays the relations expressing the semantic relations represented at l-s structure. Given this canonical use for the Move Alpha relation, it is not surprising that most languages limit the relation to holding between a trace and an operator in a nonprojected position, a position that is not the (ultimate) expression of an l-s semantic relation. Nevertheless, one might ask whether the Move Alpha relation might also hold between projected positions in some languages.

I have suggested that the traditional view of raising, although incorrect for the constructions and languages for which it was developed, is instantiated in Niuean and Chichewa. In this traditional view there is a movement relation, here a Move Alpha relation, between some constituent head-Governed by the raising verb and a trace within a sentential complement to the raising verb. In the canonical raising constructions of English, the missing element in the complement to a raising verb bears a grammatical relation—subject to a tenseless verb phrase or syntactic role assignee of a maximal projection—which the trace of Move Alpha may not bear, since the trace of Move Alpha must appear in the surface constituent structure tree and grammatical dependents of phrases do not appear in this tree. If the traditional account of raising as involving movement is appropriate for some language, one would expect the missing element to be in positions where trace could occur, for example, subject of a tensed clause and direct object of a verb.

The Niuean raising predicates include *maeke* 'can, be possible' and *kamata* 'begin.' In (3.26) these verbs are used with full sentential complements. In (3.27), the subjects of the complements have been raised to subject of the raising verbs; in (3.28) the objects of the complements are raised to subject.

(3.26)

a. To maeke ke lagomatai he ekekafo e tame ē.
   FUT possible SBJ help ERG doctor ABS child this
   'The doctor could help this child.'

b. Kua kamata ke hala he tama e akau.
   PERF begin SBJ cut ERG child ABS tree
   'The child has begun to cut down the tree.'

(3.27)

a. To maeke e ekekafo ke lagomatai e tama ē.
   FUT possible ABS doctor SBJ help ABS child this
   'The doctor could help this child.'

b. Kua kamata e tama ke hala e akau.
   PERF begin ABS child SBJ cut ABS tree
   'The child has begun to cut down the tree.'

(3.28)

a. To maeke e tama ē ke lagomatai he ekekafo.
   FUT possible ABS child this SBJ help ERG doctor
   'The child could be helped by the doctor.'

b. Kua kamata e akau ke hala he tama.
   PERF begin ABS tree SBJ cut ERG child
   'The tree has begun to be cut down by the child.'

Clearly my analysis of raising in English will not extend to the constructions illustrated in (3.27) and (3.28). This analysis claims that the raised constituents bear multiple grammatical relations at s structure. If the analysis could apply to the raising constructions in (3.28), the raised subject would also bear an object relation at s structure. But the matrix subjects do not appear as objects in (3.28), implying that they are not Governed by the lower verbs.

Instead of extending the analysis of canonical raising to Niuean raising constructions, suppose that the Niuean raising verbs simply take sentential arguments and allow Move Alpha to hold between traces and binders in projected positions, like that of the subject of a sentence. I suppose that the raised subjects are simply s structure constituents that do not correspond to l-s constituents; they come in at s structure bearing the subject relation. They are integrated into the semantics of a sentence by bearing the Move Alpha relation at surface structure, binding a trace that bears an l-s semantic relation. On this analysis, sentence (3.27b) has an l-s structure like that in (3.29a), an s structure like that in (3.29b), and a surface structure like that in (3.29c).

(3.29)

a.

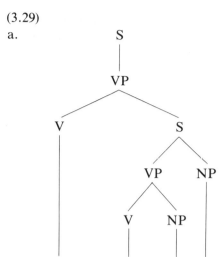

b.

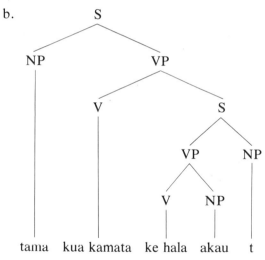

c.

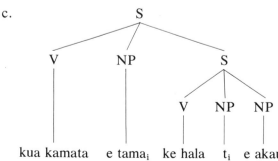

Although Niuean seems to allow the Move Alpha relation to hold between projected positions, the data I have presented are not sufficient for one to conclude that a binder must be allowed to occupy a projected position. English, for example, apparently allows raising from object to subject in tough-movement sentences like (3.30), but analyses have been motivated in which the movement relation holds not between the subject and the object trace but between some operator, indicated as O in sentence (3.30), and the trace.

(3.30)
Elmer is tough [O[to sell porcupines to t]].

The operator in (3.30) forms a type of predication (see Williams 1980 and Chomsky 1982). Evidence for the analysis in (3.30) over an analysis that moves a constituent directly into an empty subject position includes the following.

First, where direct movement, but not predication, is involved, as in *wh-* question formation, constructions obey the weak-crossover constraint illustrated in (3.31a). Structures like relative clauses involving an overt operator, the relative pronoun, and patent predication do not exhibit weak crossover, as shown in (3.31b). Tough-movement constructions pattern with the relative constructions, not the question constructions, with respect to weak crossover, as illustrated in (3.31c).

(3.31)
a. *Which porcupine$_i$ does his$_i$ owner love?
b. I bought the porcupine$_i$ that his$_i$ owner loved.
c. That porcupine$_i$ is tough for his$_i$ owner to love.

Second, the predication analysis accounts for the fact that the subject in a tough-movement construction may not be a dummy. The null operators that appear in tough-movement constructions must bind a thematic position. It is not important to speculate here on the reasons for this constraint. For present purposes it is sufficient to note that this property of tough-movement constructions, illustrated in (3.32), finds no counterpart in true raising constructions.

(3.32)
a. *There is tough to believe to be too many porcupines in Massachusetts.
b. *It is easy to consider important that Elmer give you a porcupine.

(3.33)

a.   There seem to be too many porcupines in Massachusetts.

b.   It is likely to be important that Elmer gave you a porcupine.

In Niuean, tough-movement constructions share an important property with relative clause constructions, a property not shared by the raising constructions illustrated in (3.27)–(3.28). This fact supports an analysis that posits a null operator in the tough-movement but not the raising constructions. This null operator makes the tough-movement constructions parallel to the predication structures of relative clauses. As Seiter demonstrates, the raised constituent in tough movement may bind a resumptive pronoun bearing some oblique relation in an embedded clause, whereas in the true raising constructions the raised constituent must bind a trace (either subject or object) and may not bind a pronoun.

Note that if one gives a Move Alpha analysis to raising in Niuean, one must allow a single constituent to operate as both binder and trace. Seiter reports that multiple raising is allowed in Niuean. This is schematized in (3.34), where a subject raises to subject of an embedded raising verb, then raises again to subject of a matrix raising clause.

(3.34)

[subject raising-V [t raising-V [t Verb]]]

Given the Move Alpha analysis, (3.34) is ruled out unless the upper trace may also serve as a binder. On this analysis, the lower trace in (3.34) may not be grammatically bound to an operator other than the upper trace. There cannot be a Move Alpha relation between the upper subject and the lower trace because, as Seiter points out, long-distance Move Alpha is not permitted in Niuean raising—the trace of raising must find a binder in the next clause up. If the higher trace is a trace, bound by the subject of the matrix clause, and if traces cannot also be binders, then this trace may not bind the lower trace. Thus, if the higher trace is bound and therefore may not bind, the lower trace will be unbound. So traces must be permitted to be binders as well. It is not possible for the subject in the matrix clause to bind both traces in (3.34), with the lower trace operating as a parasitic gap. Chomsky (1982) points out that a parasitic gap may not be c-commanded by the trace in a parasitic gap construction, and the upper trace c-commands the lower in (3.34). One might explain the c-command condition in a variety of ways,[7] but as an observational fact it rules out a parasitic-gap analysis of (3.34).

Suppose some mechanism could be devised to allow canonical raising to raise an object in Niuean. Would a canonical-raising analysis be preferable to an analysis that allows Move Alpha to hold between projected positions? If one treated Niuean raising in line with the analysis of canonical raising in English, there would be no explanation for the fact that the set of raising verbs in the two languages have different semantic properties. As expected under the analysis of this chapter, canonical raising verbs take predications semantically. The raising verbs of Niuean, as pointed out by Seiter, are various sorts of propositional operators or other semantic functions that take propositions, not predications.

Chapter 4

Affix-Mediated Alternations in the Expression of Arguments I

A wide range of grammatical phenomena are often thought to implicate grammatical relations, including passive and antipassive constructions, lexical reflexive verb forms, dative movement alternations, applied verb constructions, and causative sentences. These phenomena involve alternations in the syntactic behavior of verbs, often signaled by morphology on the verbs. In chapters 4 through 7, the analysis of these phenomena will be shown to follow from the theory of grammatical relations developed in chapter 2 coupled with independently motivated principles of morphology. With an important class of exceptions to be discussed in chapter 5, what have been called lexical rules in the Lexical-Functional framework of Bresnan 1982b (and elsewhere) reduce in the present framework to affixation. Two lexical items, a root or stem and an affix, each with its own set of features, combine according to the subcategorization restrictions of the affix to yield a derived word whose features are a predictable combination of the features of the constituent morphemes. For example, passivization in English, considered as a process, is the creation of a passive participle via affixation of the passive suffix to a transitive verb. The features of passive constructions are determined by the general principles discussed in chapter 2 and by features of the passive participles that passive constructions contain. The features of passive participles are in turn determined by the theory of morphology and by the features of the constituent transitive verb and passive affix.

I adopt those aspects of the theory of morphology described by Lieber (1980) that are relevant to present concerns. Within this theory there are no word formation rules in the sense of Aronoff 1976. Rather, affixes as well as roots have their own lexical entries and all morphemes are inserted into unlabeled binary branching word structure trees (alternatively, the word structure tree may be created by the affixation; nothing hinges on these aspects of the mechanics of word formation). The insertion of morphemes into word trees respects the subcategorization features contained in their lexical entries.[1] For example, since the passive suffix in English attaches to verbs, it carries the subcategorization feature, $]_V$——, indicating it is to be inserted into a word tree to the right of a verb. Features of the morphemes inserted into the unlabeled trees percolate up through the tree according to the percolation conventions Lieber details. Feature percolation labels the nodes of the word tree and determines the features of the derived word, that is, of the entire tree.

Two of Lieber's percolation conventions play an important role in what follows (for further support of these conventions, see Marantz 1982d). First, the features of affixes take precedence over the features of roots in percolation. For example, the suffix -ment, although it attaches to verbs, is itself nominal. By the convention that features of affixes take precedence over features of roots in percolation, the words derived by combining -ment and verbs become nouns.

(4.1)

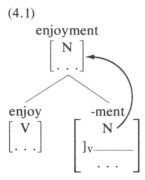

The percolation of the (nominal) features of an affix over the (verbal) features of a root is shown in (4.1), the internal structure for the derived noun *enjoyment*.

A second percolation convention ensures that when an affix is unspecified for the value of some feature, that feature of the root percolates to become the value for the combination of root plus affix. Consider the behavior of the Russian diminutive suffix, *-ushka, -ushek*. The majority of Russian nouns ending in *-a* are feminine, but a few, although they decline like feminine nouns in *-a*, take masculine adjectives, indicating that they carry a masculine feature.

(4.2)

d'ad'a 'uncle'

a. moj drugoj d'ad'a
    my-masc other-masc uncle
b. *moja drugaja d'ad'a
    my-fem other-fem uncle

The variant of the diminutive suffix *-ushka* attaches to nouns in *-a* regardless of their gender. When *-ushka* attaches to a feminine noun in *-a*, such as *baba* 'grandmother,' the result, *babushka*, is feminine; when it attaches to a masculine noun in *-a*, such as *d'ad'a* 'uncle,' the result, *d'ad'ushka*, is masculine.

(4.3)

a. moj drugoj d'ad'ushka
    my-masc other-masc uncle-dimin
b. moja drugaja babushka
    my-fem other-fem grandmother-dimin
c. *moja drugaja d'ad'ushka
d. *moj drugoj babushka

Clearly, the diminutive suffix carries no gender feature of its own. Rather, since the diminutive suffix is unmarked for gender, the gender feature of the root noun percolates up to become the gender feature of the Russian derived diminutive. The internal structures of the derived diminutives in (4.3a,b) are displayed in (4.4), where the arrows indicate feature percolation.

(4.4)

a.

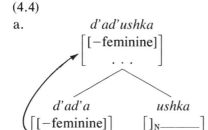

b.

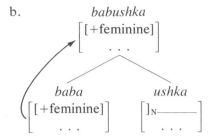

In this chapter I discuss a set of alternations in the expression of a verb's semantic dependents that is signaled by affixation on the verb but in which the affixes themselves are semantically neutral in the sense that they lack either argument structures or semantic role assigning features. In chapter 5 I turn to alternations in the expression of a verb's semantic dependents that cannot be explained by endowing affixes with features and hypothesizing that these affixes mediate the alternations. Chapter 6 discusses the differences between nominative-accusative and ergative languages that follow from the results of chapters 4 and 5. In chapter 7, I analyze alternations in the expression of a verb's semantic dependents that are mediated by affixes which, in constrast to the affixes discussed in the present chapter, do carry their own argument structures.

In section 2.2.3.2, I proved that within the present theory the correspondence between l-s and s structure relations is extremely limited for all l-s relations save obj(X, Y). The various options for the s structure counterpart of the obj(X, Y) relation depend on features of X: If X is [−log subj], obj(X, Y) may correspond to SUB(Z, Y′) where Y′ is the s structure counterpart of Y and the s structure counterpart of X heads Z. If X is [+transitive], the obj(X, Y) relation may correspond to OBJ(X′, Y′) where X′ and Y′ are the s structure counterparts of X and Y. And if the language in general or the lexical entry of X in particular provides a syntactic role assigner without an argument structure to give Y′, the s structure counterpart of Y, a syntactic role, then obj(X, Y) may correspond to arg(X′, Y′) but not role(X′, Y′), where X′ is the s structure counterpart of X (i.e., Y′ is an indirect argument of X′).

Suppose affixation is to affect the correspondence between the l-s and s structure relations in a sentence. If the affix neither assigns a semantic role nor takes arguments, it will not be an independent l-s constituent and thus will not merge with an l-s constituent, nor will its s structure counterpart merge with some s structure constituent (on morphological merger, see chapter 7). Rather, the affix will appear on the root to which it attaches at l-s structure. The affix affects the expression of the root's semantic dependents by, in effect, transferring features to the root. That is, the affix carries certain features which, by the feature percolation conventions, become features of the derived verb that it forms. This derived verb inherits the argument structure and semantic role assigning features of the verb root. The derived verb thus has the same semantic properties as the root verb but perhaps distinct syntactic features, provided by the affix, which may determine a syntactic behavior for its semantic dependents that is different from the behavior of the dependents of the root.

If affixation is to allow the logical object of a [+log sub] verb to correspond to the SUB of the VP that the verb heads at s structure, the affix must carry the feature [−log subj]. The addition of a [−log sub] morpheme (without semantic role assigning features or argument structure) to a verb is called passivization. If affixation is to force the logical object of a verb to correspond to an indirect argument at s structure, the affix must carry the feature [−transitive] and must provide a syntactic role assigner to assign the indirect argument its syntactic role (unless the language generally provides such syntactic role assigners for indirect arguments). The [−transitive] feature prevents the logical object from corresponding to the OBJ of the verb. The addition to a verb of a [−transitive] affix unmarked for the feature [±log sub] is called antipassivization.

Alternations in the expression of a verb's arguments mediated by the affixation of morphemes that are not independent l-s constituents are limited by the theory to alternations in the expression of a verb's logical object as either its OBJ, the SUB of the VP it heads, or an indirect argument of the verb. Productive affixation processes are further restricted by the markedness principles discussed in chapter 2. Thus even antipassivization is marked in the theory because it produces derived verbs that are [−transitive] although they both assign a semantic role and carry the feature [+log sub]. As expected within the theory, antipassivization as defined here is extremely rare cross-linguistically, especially in comparison with passivization.

A theory that postulates relation-changing rules in the syntax or lexicon must add constraints to account for the limited examples of alternations in the expression of a verb's arguments which are actually observed across languages. The present theory, which includes only a general principle governing the mapping of l-s onto s structures, correctly constrains affix-mediated alternations to just those found in the world's languages.

4.1. Passivization

The structures called passives in different languages are a varied lot. I will give here an analysis of English passivization and extend it to passivization cross-linguistically. In effect, I will be defining the term "passivization." That some construction considered a passive by some linguist does not fall under my analysis cannot be counted against the analysis unless failing to relate this construction to those I have considered passives misses an important generalization.

4.1.1. Passivization in English

4.1.1.1. The Passive Affix   Simply put, English passivization involves the affixation to a verb of the passive morpheme *-en*. The passive suffix subcategorizes for verbs and carries the features [−log sub], [−transitive], and whatever features specify its participle nature.[2] The participle features of passive verbs are summarized here in the symbol [+participle].

(4.5)

-en,]$_V$＿＿＿＿, [−log sub], [−transitive], [+participle]

I will introduce a principle that ensures that the passive affix attaches only to [+log sub], [+transitive] verbs. Since the features of an affix take precedence in percolation over the features of a root, a derived passive verb will be [−log sub], [−transitive], [+participle].

Attaching the passive suffix to *write* derives the verb in (4.6a), which appears in (4.6b).

(4.6)
a. [[write]$_V$en]$_V$, 'write' (*written*), [−log sub], [−transitive],
   [+participle]
b. Elmer's book was written in twenty days.

As the passive affix lacks an argument structure, the derived passive verb inherits the P-A structure of the active root according to the convention that percolates root features where the affix lacks them. Since the passive participles of verbs like *write* are [−transitive], the logical object of the passive participle cannot correspond to its OBJ in s structure—the passive participle simply cannot take an OBJ at s structure. English provides no general mechanism for allowing the s structure counterpart of *written*'s logical object to become an indirect argument of *written*, and the passive participle is [−log sub], freeing the SUB of the VP that *written* heads from having to correspond to the logical subject of the predicate that *written* produces. Therefore, the logical object of *written* can, and by principle M must, correspond to the SUB of the VP headed by *written*. Thus the promotion of objects to subjects in passivization is just a natural by-product of principle M and the features of a passive participle.

Not only does this analysis of English passivization yield the correct results, but it is in fact forced by the theory of this book. I assume that the active and passive forms of an English verb are related by a productive affixation process. Since affixation does not change the argument structure or semantic role assigning properties of a verb, the passive and active forms of a verb should share a P-A structure and should assign the same role(s). To allow the logical object of a [+log sub] verb that assigns a semantic role to correspond to the SUB of the VP that it heads, affixation must make the verb [−log sub]. If the logical object of a verb may not correspond to its OBJ at s structure, the verb must be [−transitive]. Therefore, if an l-s argument of a verb is to correspond to the OBJ of the active verb but the SUB of the VP headed by the passive verb, then the passive affix must carry the features [−log sub], [−transitive].[3]

Although the English passive morpheme attaches only to [+log sub], [+transitive] verbs, it is not necessary to include this information in the subcategorization feature of *-en* in (4.5). If the passive morpheme attached to [−transitive] verbs, sentences like *It was danced,* meaning 'someone danced,' would be grammatical (see the discussion of impersonal passivization in section 4.1.2). It is not clear that there are any [−log sub], [+transitive] verbs in English. One candidate for [−log sub], [+transitive] status is the verb *strike* in sentences like (4.7) (see also section 4.1.3 on "sporadic advancements" in English).

(4.7)
a. It strikes me as being too hot for porcupines outside.
b. There strike(s) me as being too many porcupines in this room.

Like [−transitive] verbs, the [−log sub], [+transitive] *strike* in (4.7) may not be passivized, as shown in (4.8).

(4.8)
*I was struck by Elmer as selling too many porcupines.

The information that -*en* must attach to [+log sub], [+transitive] verbs was omitted from the subcategorization frame in (4.5) because it follows from a general principle governing affixation. Affixes carrying the alpha value of certain features may attach only to roots carrying the −alpha value of these features.

(4.9)
The No Vacuous Affixation Principle (NVAP):
For a certain class of features F, an [alpha F_i] affix may attach only to a [−alpha F_i] root.

Although the proper characterization of the features F in principle (4.9) is problematic, the application of the NVAP to the passive affix is clear. The features subject to the NVAP are features unmotivated by the argument structure or semantic role assigning properties of the affix. If, for example, the passive affix had a P-A structure that produced predicates that assigned semantic roles, it would be [+log sub] by virtue of its inherent properties. The [+log sub] feature of the affix would be motivated by its argument structure and thus not governed by the NVAP. Since the passive affix has no argument structure and assigns no semantic role, its [−log sub] and [−transitive] features are unmotivated and thereby subject to the NVAP. So the NVAP restricts English passivization to [+log sub], [+transitive] verbs.

Principle (4.9) may be seen as a principle against certain forms of vacuous affixation. For example, some principle is required to prevent the past participle affix from attaching to past participles. Since the past participle already contains all the features of the past participle affix, affixation of this morpheme to a past participle adds nothing but phonological features to the participle—it is vacuous in all but its phonological effects. The NVAP is intended to be the principle that prevents affixation of grammatical affixes like past participle endings to words that already contain these affixes.

4.1.1.2. The *by* Phrase If the semantic role that a predicate assigns is borne by no constituent in the passive sentence, as in (4.10), the bearer of that role is interpreted as being an indefinite someone or something.

(4.10)
The porcupine was sold for twenty dollars.

As made explicit by Fodor and Fodor (1980), the indefinite interpretation of the bearer of the logical subject role in passives exactly parallels the interpretation of the bearer of any inherent semantic role of a verb not mentioned in the sentence. For example, I have assumed that the source (or seller) role is inherently associated with the verb *buy*. If the source of *buy* is not expressed in a sentence, the bearer of this role is interpreted as someone or someplace unspecified—see (4.11).

(4.11)
Elmer bought the porcupine yesterday.

Similarly, the bearer of the inherent agent (or seller) role associated with *sell* is interpreted as someone indefinite in sentence (4.10). Fodor and Fodor (1980) present arguments that this indefinite interpretation of unexpressed bearers of inherent semantic roles must be distinguished from the explicit binding of these roles to the quantifiers *someone* or *something* (see also Dowty 1981).

Although the bearer of the logical subject role in a passive sentence need not be expressed, it may appear in a prepositional phrase headed by *by*. The simple fact is that the object in a *by* prepositional phrase within a VP headed by a passive participle bears the semantic role assigned by the predicate that the passive participle produces. Although there may be isolated examples of passive participles that cannot co-occur with *by* phrases, suggesting that *by* can assign only certain semantic roles, one can give no semantic characterization of the semantic roles borne by the object of *by* in passive sentences. Objects of *by* bear the full range of semantic roles carried by logical subjects in English. These roles include agents (*Hortense was pushed by Elmer*), experiencers (*Elmer was seen by everyone who entered*), themes (*The intersection was approached by five cars at once*), recipients or goals (*The porcupine crate was received by Elmer's firm*), and various other roles that seem to fit none of the classes that I have seen defined in the literature (*The house is surrounded by trees*). This point bears repeating since it is often overlooked: No semantic characterization of the objects of *by* as agents, save one that defines agents as those roles assigned by predicates (as the roles borne by logical subjects), can account for the semantic range of the *by* objects in passive constructions.

So it is a fact about *by* that its object may bear the semantic roles assigned by predicates. This fact must be captured in an adequate account of the semantics of *by*. Consider the l-s structure of the passive in (4.12), given in (4.13).[4]

(4.12)

Elmer was insulted by Hortense.

(4.13)

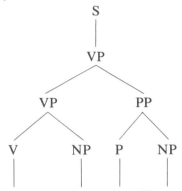

was insulted   Elmer   by   Hortense

The predicate *was insulted Elmer* in (4.13) is a function from arguments to propositions. The preposition *by* creates a modifier, the PP *by Hortense,* which is a function from predicates to degenerate predicates, that is, to predicates that are functions from *no* arguments to propositions. The predicate *was insulted Elmer* may be represented as the open sentence (x insulted Elmer). The preposition *by* performs a special task in English. It assigns to its logical object the semantic role assigned by the predicate that the modifier that it produces modifies. So in (4.13) *by* assigns to *Hortense* the role assigned by *was insulted Elmer,* which the modifier *by Hortense* modifies. The modifiers that *by* produces modify predicates by applying the predicates to *by*'s logical object, creating a proposition that is identified as a degenerate predicate.

  In (4.13) *by* applies the predicate *was insulted Elmer* to its logical object, *Hortense,* effectively substituting *Hortense* for the free variable in the predicate (x insult Elmer), to produce the proposition or degenerate predicate (Hortense insult Elmer).[5]

  One might ask why *by* appears only in passive sentences like (4.14a) and not in active sentences like (4.14b,c).

(4.14)

a.   The porcupine was sold by the last porcupine salesman in Boston.

b.   *Elmer sold the porcupine by the last porcupine salesman in Boston. (Ungrammatical with the reading that the porcupine salesman also sold the porcupine)

c. *It sold the porcupine by the last porcupine salesman in Boston. (Ungrammatical with pleonastic or dummy *it* and the reading that the porcupine salesman did the selling)

Recall that the modifiers produced by *by* modify predicates to yield degenerate predicates, predicates that are functions from no arguments to a proposition. Suppose one adds a *by* phrase to a predicate headed by a [+log sub] verb, as in (4.14b,c). Since it takes no arguments, the (degenerate) predicate that the *by* phrase produces may not be sister to a logical subject. Yet the [+log sub] feature on the verb that heads the predicate that the *by* phrase modifies demands that the verb head a predicate that is sister to a logical subject. Thus one cannot add a *by* phrase to a predicate headed by a [+log sub] verb in the l-s structure of a well-formed sentence.[6]

4.1.1.3. Passivization of Raising Verbs   When the passive ending is attached to a raising to object verb like *believe,* a raising to subject verb is automatically derived. Recall that raising to object verbs are [+log sub], [+transitive] and take modifier logical objects (and make these modifiers into predications, as explained in chapter 3). Raising to subject verbs are [−log sub], [−transitive] and take modifier logical objects. Adding the passive morpheme to a raising to object verb yields a [−log sub], [−transitive] verb that takes modifier logical objects, that is, a raising to subject verb.

Consider a sentence like (4.15a), parallel in structure to (4.15b).

(4.15)
a. Elmer was believed to have sold his last porcupine.
b. Elmer seems to have sold his last porcupine.

The present theory claims that *Elmer* in (4.15a), just like *Elmer* in (4.15b), is at no level of analysis and at no stage in a derivation an object of the raising verb. In both sentences, *Elmer* is the SUB of both the matrix and embedded clauses but an OBJ in neither.

4.1.1.4. Against a Promotion Analysis of Passivization   In "Whither Move NP?" (Marantz 1982e, written in 1980), I showed that an analysis of passivization similar to the one outlined here is required within the government-binding framework (that is, passive morphology must be stipulated to absorb structural Case and to prevent the verb phrase headed by the passive participle from assigning a semantic role to its subject; these properties of passives do not follow from independent principles[7]). Such an analysis was subsequently adopted explicitly by Chomsky (1980b, 1981). It is difficult to argue against other analyses of passivization within alternative theoretical frameworks since these analyses may be the best available within the frameworks and may be made to work mechanically. The most popular alternative analysis of passivization, supported in Relational Grammar among other frameworks, insists that passivization involves the explicit promotion of objects to subject. Within the present theory, allowing a rule that explicitly associates a logical object with a grammatical subject, for example, would increase the power of the theoretical mechanisms, forcing one to ask why the grammar employs this stipulated association of l-s and s structure relations and not other conceivable ones. In addition to these theoretical considerations, there are some data that lead one to reject the promotion analysis of passivization within the framework of this book. These same data call into question a promotion analysis in any theoretical framework.

Recall that the logical object of a verb must correspond to the SUB of the VP that its passive participle heads in most cases because passive participles must head-Govern the s structure counterparts of their logical objects but are [−transitive] and introduce no syntactic role assigner to make the s stucture counterpart of their logical object into an indirect grammatical argument. If some rule of English provided passive participles with such a syntactic role assigner, then their logical objects would not have to promote to SUB to satisfy principle M of chapter 2. In fact, I was led to assume for the analysis of raising constructions in chapter 3 that English allows the structural position [X, VP], X a modifier or sentence, to assign a syntactic role and provides this syntactic role assigner to any argument-taking item. Since it is restricted to modifiers and sentences, this structural position cannot assign a syntactic role to an NP argument. Thus one should expect that although nominal logical objects of passive verbs must promote to subject, sentential logical objects need not promote but may show up as indirect arguments at s structure assigned syntactic roles by [X, VP]. As explained in Williams 1979, what one expects is what one finds:

(4.16)
a. I believe that Elmer sold his last porcupine.
b. That Elmer sold his last porcupine was believed by everyone.
c. It was believed by everyone that Elmer sold his last porcupine.

(4.16c) shows that when no l-s constituent corresponds to the grammatical subject of an s structure clause, English provides a dummy NP, *it,* to serve as SUB.

The argument against the promotion analysis of passivization derives from the behavior of verbs that allow only the (4.16a,c) members of the pattern in (4.16); that is, the s structure counterparts of their l-s logical objects seem never to promote to SUB (here I follow Williams 1979).

(4.17)
a. I feel that Elmer should sell his last porcupine.
b. ?*That Elmer should sell his last porcupine was felt by everyone who saw the condition of his pet shop.
c. It was felt that Elmer should sell his last porcupine.

(4.18)
a. I reasoned that Elmer could sell ten porcupines a week.
b. ?*That Elmer could sell ten porcupines a week was reasoned by the accounting firm of Hummer, Hummer, Hummer, and Fred.
c. It was reasoned by everyone that Elmer could sell ten porcupines a week during an economic recovery.

(4.19)
a. I said that Elmer had the best porcupines in the business.
b. ?*That Elmer had the best porcupines in the business was said around the financial district.
c. It was said that Elmer has the best porcupines in the business.

In the present theory, the ungrammaticality of the (b) examples in (4.17)–(4.19), as compared with the grammaticality of (4.16b),[8] is explained by the mechanism that accounts for another peculiar property of *feel, reason,* and *say:* In their meanings in (4.17)–(4.19), these verbs do not take NP objects.

(4.20)
a. *I reasoned the outcome of that situation.
b. *I felt Elmer's obligation to sell his last porcupine. (Ungrammatical with the reading, 'I felt Elmer was obliged to sell his last porcupine')
c. *I said the announcement in a loud voice.

I propose to capture the fact that *feel, reason,* and *say* take only sentential complements in certain usages in the same manner that one would account for unusual or quirky case marked constituents in

Icelandic (Levin 1981; see also section 2.3.2). For present purposes, the important aspects of quirky case marking are these: A quirky case marked logical object in Icelandic retains its quirky case marking in passivization and raising, no matter what grammatical relation it bears. That is, the quirky case marking—say dative—that appears on the surface structure counterpart of the logical object of a transitive verb shows up on the constituent bearing the logical object semantic role in passive and raising constructions. So, if the OBJ of the active verb is unexpectedly marked dative (the usual object marking is accusative), the SUB of the corresponding passive will be marked dative, as will be the OBJ of a raising to object verb or the SUB of a raising to subject verb embedding this passive sentence. This case preservation effect is illustrated in (4.21a–d) from Levin 1981; see also (2.78)–(2.81).

(4.21)

a. Ég hjálpa honum.
   I help him-DAT

b. Honum er hjálpað.
   He-DAT is helped

c. Ég tel honum hafa verið hjálpað.
   I believe him-DAT to-have been helped

d. Honum er talið hafa verið hjálpað.
   He-DAT is believed to-have been helped

The case preservation effect and related phenomena demonstrate that the quirky case markings in Icelandic are associated not with grammatical relations but directly with a particular argument position in a P-A structure. No matter what grammatical relations the constituent assigned the helped role in (4.21) bears, it must appear in the dative case. Moreover, the quirky case markings play no role in the sentence other than to mark the constituent that fills the argument position with which they are associated. In particular, as explained in section 2.3.2, they assign neither semantic nor syntactic roles.

Just as the quirky case marked arguments in Icelandic seem exceptionally connected with their quirky cases, so the propositional logical objects of verbs like *feel, reason,* and *say* seem to be exceptionally connected with the structural position [S, VP]. Regardless of the grammatical relations (OBJ or indirect argument) borne by the constituent assigned the logical object semantic role, the logical object of these verbs appears in the surface structure position [S, VP].

Assigning the logical objects of these verbs the quirky case marking [S, VP] assures that no NP may become their logical objects—no NP could occupy this position. This method of accounting for the facts in (4.20) also immediately accounts for the failure of sentential objects of these verbs to promote in passivization. If the sentential arguments of the verbs must appear as [S, VP], they may not become subjects, which are not expressed as [S, VP] in English.

To account for the ungrammaticality of the (b) examples and the grammaticality of the (c) examples in (4.17)–(4.19), a promotion analysis of passivization would somehow have to require that the passive participles of *feel*, *reason*, and *say* trigger an obligatory rule of sentential subject extraposition.[9] The trouble with this move is that the extraposed sentences in the (c) examples of (4.17)–(4.19) behave like sentential complements of active verbs and not like extraposed sentential subjects. Clear cases of sentential subject extraposition are illustrated in (4.22); these involve postverbal sentences that clearly bear the semantic role of a logical subject.

(4.22)
a. That Elmer should be allowed a tax deduction on porcupine depreciation stinks in the minds of most pet dealers.
b. It stinks that Elmer should be allowed a tax deduction on porcupine depreciation.
c. That Elmer arrived late for dinner proved his point about the tardiness of pet dealers.
d. It proved his point about pet dealers that Elmer arrived late for dinner.

In general, sentential complements (sentential logical objects corresponding to constituents within the syntactic verb phrase) but not extraposed subjects (postverbal sentences bearing the logical subject role) may appear without the *that* complementizer and may permit extraction (*wh-* movement) from within.

(4.23)
a. Elmer believed porcupines mate in the spring.
b. Who did Elmer believe (that) Hortense likes most?
c. Elmer claimed porcupines mate in the spring.
d. What did Elmer claim (that) Hortense did with her spare time?

(4.24)
a. *It stinks Elmer should be allowed a tax break like that.
b. *Who did it prove his point that Elmer knew?
c. *What did it stink that Elmer bought?

The postverbal sentential complements of the (c) examples in (4.17)–(4.19) behave like the complements in (4.23), not like the extraposed subjects in (4.24).

(4.25)
a. It was felt Elmer could do a lot better in aardvarks.
b. It was reasoned Elmer could sell ten porcupines a week in an economic recovery.
c. It was said Elmer was overstepping his authority.
d. What was it felt (that) Elmer could afford to buy with his porcupine proceeds?
e. How many porcupines was it reasoned (that) Elmer could sell in a week?
f. What was it said (that) Elmer could do with his extra merchandise?

In fact, the postverbal sentential complements of the passive participles of all verbs taking sentential objects behave like the sentential complements in (4.23) and not like the extraposed subjects in (4.24), suggesting that these complements need not be promoted to subject then extraposed.

(4.26)
a. It was believed Elmer could save porcupines from extinction.
b. It was claimed Elmer sold puce porcupines after hours.
c. What was it believed (that) Elmer could sell instead of porcupines?
d. How many porcupines was it claimed (that) Elmer gave to the poor?

Another piece of evidence against the promotion analysis of the passives in (4.17c)–(4.19c) can be derived from the generalization in English that [−log sub] verbs taking sentential complements are raising verbs. Assume that English obeys this generalization because it allows any [−log sub] verb to take modifier arguments if its meaning is compatible with this sort of argument—for example, the verb must take an argument type compatible with a predication in the sense of chapter 3. I can now explain why the passive participles of verbs taking sentential objects raise to subject whereas mere subject extraposers do not raise. The passive participles of the verbs taking sentential complements in (4.27), being [−log sub] and compatible with predication arguments,

will raise in accordance with the generalization in English just described. The sentential subject extraposers, which may be [+log sub]
but which certainly do not take logical arguments compatible with
predications, may not take modifiers as arguments and so do not raise.

(4.27)
a. Elmer was felt to have overstepped his authority in this matter.
b. Elmer was reasoned overqualified for that position.
c. Elmer was said to sell imported porcupines below cost.

(4.28)
a. *Elmer proved his point about pet owners to have arrived late.
b. *Elmer stinks to have said that at the party.

Since the active versions of (4.27) are ungrammatical—see (4.29)—
any theoretical framework must give some special account of why passive participles of verbs that take sentential complements raise to SUB.

(4.29)
a. *I felt Elmer to have overstepped his authority in this matter.
b. *I reasoned Elmer overqualified for that position.
c. *They said Elmer to sell imported porcupines below cost.

Whatever mechanism determines that the passive participles of *feel,*
reason, and *say* will raise to subject, it must be able to distinguish these
verbs as a class from sentential subject extraposers like *stink.* If these
passive participles were analyzed as obligatory sentential subject extraposers, as required on a promotion analysis of passivization, it
would be difficult to explain why just these verbs but not sentential
subject extraposers in general allow raising to subject.[10]

4.1.2. Passivization Cross-linguistically

I have defined passivization as the addition to a verb of an affix without
argument structure or semantic role assigning properties which carries
the feature [−log sub]. In Marantz 1982e I argue that the English passive suffix attaches only to [+transitive] verbs and that the restriction
on passivization to transitive verbs is not uncommon among the world's
languages. The NVAP (4.9) accounts for this restriction on passivization in English if the English passive morpheme is provided with the
feature [−transitive]. According to the NVAP, an affix bearing an unmotivated [−transitive] feature will attach only to [+transitive] roots.
There are languages in which the passive affix may attach to [−transi-

tive] verbs. Since it prohibits an affix with an unmotivated [−transitive] feature from attaching to a [−transitive] verb, the NVAP demands that the passive morpheme in these languages not carry the feature [−transitive].

Suppose one attaches a passive affix carrying only the feature [−log sub] to a [+log sub], [−transitive] verb root. Such affixation would prevent the predicates that the derived passive verb produces from taking a logical subject, thereby freeing the SUB of the VP that the verb heads at s structure from having to correspond to the logical subject. A verb root that is [+log sub], [−transitive] will, in the unmarked case, not assign a semantic role; that is, it will not take a logical object. Since only l-s subjects and objects may generally correspond to s structure SUBs, the grammatical subject of the passive of the [+log sub], [−transitive] verb root will correspond to no l-s constituent. The passivization of a [+log sub], [−transitive] verb yields what has been called an "impersonal passive" in the literature, a passive sentence with a nonthematic subject.

Impersonal passivization in Dutch has been discussed by Perlmutter (1978b) and Comrie (1977). I suppose that the passive affix in Dutch carries only the feature [−log sub] (and the features of a participle), allowing it to attach to [−transitive] verbs. Affixation of the passive morpheme to the intransitive verb *fluiten* 'to whistle,' whose lexical entry appears in (4.30a), yields the passive participle, *gefloten,* whose lexical entry appears in (4.30b).

(4.30)
a. *fluiten,* V, 'whistle' (∅), [+log sub], [−transitive]
b. *gefloten,* V, 'whistle' (∅), [−log sub], [−transitive], [+participle]

Since an l-s structure proposition headed by the passive participle in (4.30b) will contain neither a logical subject nor a logical object to correspond to the syntactic SUB of the corresponding sentence in s structure, Dutch employs a dummy SUB, *er,* where independent rules of grammar demand an overt grammatical subject—see sentence (4.31b). Note that the preposition *door* in Dutch serves the same function that *by* serves in English (see section 4.1.1.2).

(4.31)
a. De jongens floten.
   'The boys whistled.'

b. Er werd door de jongens gefloten.
   it was by the boys whistled-PASS
   'The boys whistled.'

Sentence (4.31b) illustrates the impersonal passive construction. Again, the characteristic feature of this construction is that its SUB is not the s structure counterpart of a constituent bearing an l-s relation.

If one attaches the passive morpheme to a [+transitive] verb in Dutch, feature percolation would yield a [−log sub], [+transitive] derived passive verb. However, I pointed out in chapter 2 that [−log sub] verbs are [−transitive] in most if not all clear cases. It was suggested that the implication in (4.32) may be a universal markedness principle (see Burzio 1981 and section 4.1.3).

(4.32)
[−log sub] → [−transitive]

Suspending a decision on the status of (4.32) in universal grammar, one may hypothesize that (4.32) operates as a redundancy rule in the Dutch lexicon, changing the [+transitive] feature of the passive participles of [+transitive] Dutch verbs to [−transitive] (or verbs in Dutch could generally be unmarked for transitivity, with (4.32) merely adding the minus value of the transitive feature to [−log sub] verbs). Passivization of *verwoesten* 'to destroy,' whose lexical entry is shown in (4.33), yields the passive participle *verwoest* displayed in (4.34).

(4.33)
verwoesten, V, 'destroy' (*destroyed*), [+log sub], [+transitive]

(4.34)
verwoest, V, 'destroy' (*destroyed*), [−log sub], [−transitive], [+participle]

Although the Dutch passive affix does not carry the feature [−transitive], implication (4.32) provides the verb in (4.34) with this feature. As the passive participle of *verwoesten* is [−transitive], its logical object cannot correspond to its OBJ at s structure; instead, the s structure counterpart of its logical object becomes the SUB of the VP headed by the passive verb, as shown in (4.35b).

(4.35)
a. De soldaten verwoesten de huizen.
   'The soldiers destroyed the houses.'

b. De huizen werden door de soldaten verwoest.
   the houses were by the soldiers destroyed
   'The houses were destroyed by the soldiers.'

If (4.32) always provides the feature [−transitive] to the passives of [+transitive] verbs, then no language should exhibit impersonal passives of transitive verbs. The issue of whether universal grammar allows impersonal passives of transitive verbs has been debated in a different guise by Perlmutter (1978b), Perlmutter and Postal (1980), and Comrie (1977). Perlmutter and Postal take the position that, in my terms, a passive verb will not be [+transitive] and that therefore impersonal passivization is restricted to intransitives, whereas Comrie claims that some languages do exhibit [+transitive] passive verbs.

Because, in the present framework, the passive morpheme is merely a carrier of the feature [−log sub] and sometimes the feature [−transitive], one might expect to find the passive morpheme employed in constructions other than canonical passives which involve preventing a predicate from taking a logical subject or preventing a verb from assigning a syntactic role. It turns out that the passive morpheme in some languages is used in nonpassive constructions in which a predicate must not be sister to a logical subject in l-s structure, freeing the grammatical subject of the s structure counterpart of the predicate from having to correspond to the logical subject. Consider the use of the Japanese passive morpheme, -*rare*, in what has been called the indirect or adversity passive (see the papers in Shibatani 1976c). The sentence in (4.36b) is a straightforward Japanese passive corresponding to the active sentence in (4.36a). The Japanese passive morpheme, -*rare*, carries the feature [−log sub] and, since Japanese lacks impersonal passives, the feature [−transitive]. The dative case particle *ni* serves the same function in Japanese passives that *by* serves in English, assigning the semantic roles of the predicates with which it is associated.

(4.36)
a. Sensei wa John o sikar-ta.
   teacher TOP John ACC scold-PAST
   'The teacher scolded John.'

b. John wa sensei ni sikar-are-ta.
   John TOP teacher DAT scold-PASS-PAST
   'John was scolded by the teacher.'

The subjects of the verbs suffixed with *-rare* in (4.37), unlike the subject (also the topic) in (4.36b), do not bear the logical object semantic role but rather are interpreted as persons adversely affected by what the rest of the sentence describes.

(4.37)

a. Taroo ga doroboo ni zitensya o nusumareru.
   Taro NOM thief DAT bike ACC steal-PASS
   'A thief steals his bike, and Taro is adversely affected.'

b. John ga ame ni hurareta.
   John NOM rain DAT fall-PASS-PAST
   'It rained, and John was adversely affected.' (or, 'It rained on John.')

c. Hanako wa musuko ni sin-are-ta.
   Hanako TOP son DAT die-PASS-PAST
   'Her son died, and Hanako was adversely affected.'

Note that the passives in (4.37) have no direct active counterparts. If the verbs in (4.37) appear in sentences without the passive morpheme, the SUBs of the sentences bear the logical subject role and the OBJs, if the verbs are transitive, bear the logical object role. No constituent bears the role of the person adversely affected by what the sentence describes.

(4.38)

a. Doroboo ga zitensya o nusum-ru.
   Thief NOM bike ACC steal-PRES
   'A thief steals a bike.'

b. *Doroboo ga zitensya o Taroo o/ni nusum-ru.
   thief NOM bike ACC Taro ACC/DAT steal-PRES

c. Ame ga hur-ta.
   rain NOM fall-PAST
   'It rained.'

d. *Ame ga John o hur-ta.
   rain NOM John ACC fall-PAST

e. Musuko ga sin-ta.
   son NOM die-PAST
   'A son died.'

f. *Musuko ga Hanako o sin-ta.
   son NOM Hanako ACC die-PAST

The important thing to note here about sentences (4.37) is that the syntactic SUB does not bear the semantic role assigned by the l-s counterpart of the VP; rather, it bears the added adversity role. If the verbs marked -*rare* in (4.37) were [+log sub], the logical subjects of the predicates that they yield would necessarily correspond to the grammatical SUBs of the s structure counterparts to these predicates.[11] Therefore, the verbs in (4.37) must be [−log sub]. That they are [−log sub] accounts for the appearance in adversity passive sentences of a *ni*-marked NP bearing the logical subject semantic role. As pointed out, the dative case particle *ni* serves the same function in Japanese as *by* serves in English, and I have shown why a *by*-phrase is incompatible with a predicate headed by a [+log sub] verb. The present theory would claim that the passive morpheme -*rare* in (4.37) carries the feature [−log sub] just as it does in the true passive sentence (4.36b). The passive morpheme is used in the adversity passive constructions precisely to indicate that the verbs in these constructions are [−log sub].

Since the SUBs in (4.37) do not bear the semantic role of the logical subject, what assigns these constituents their adversity roles? A full account of the adversity passive would take me far off the track here. Let me simply reiterate that according to the present theory the verbs marked with -*rare* in (4.37) must be [−log sub] and that the passive morphology is used in (4.37) to carry this [−log sub] feature.

A construction in Chichewa, a Bantu language described in Trithart 1977, resembles the adversity passive of Japanese in interesting respects. The combination of passive and causative morphology on the Chichewa verb can indicate that an NP bearing the instrument semantic role appears as the SUB of the verb. In (4.39b,d) I display some true Chichewa passives, containing the passive morpheme -*dw*-. Note that the preposition *ndí* serves the same function in Chichewa that *by* serves in English.[12]

(4.39)

a. Jóni a-ná-(zí-)nyamul-a n-thóchí.
   John$_i$ he$_i$-PAST-(them$_j$)-carry-INDIC bananas$_j$
   'John carried the bananas.'

b. N-thóchí zi-ná-(zí-)nyamul-idw-a ndí Jóni.
   bananas$_i$ they$_i$-PAST-(them$_i$-)carry-PASS-INDIC by John
   'The bananas were carried by John.'

c. Jóni a-ná-(zí-)pats-a n-thóchí kwá a-máí́ á-ké.
   John$_i$ he$_i$-PAST-(them$_j$-)give-INDIC bananas$_j$ to mother his
   'John gave the bananas to his mother.'

d. N-thóchí zi-ná-(zí-)pats-idw-a kwá a-máí́ á-ké ndí Jóni.
   bananas$_i$ they$_i$-PAST-(them$_i$-)give-PASS-INDIC to mother his by
   John
   'The bananas were given by John to his mother.'

The sentences in (4.40) are examples of causative constructions, which
will be discussed in chapter 7. Note the causative morpheme -*ts*-.

(4.40)

a. Ḿ-phúzitsi a-ná-(wá-)lemb-ets-a á-ná.
   teacher$_i$ he$_i$-PAST-(them$_j$-)write-CAUSE-INDIC children$_j$
   'The teacher made the children write.'

b. Cátherine a-ná-(má-)kolol-ets-a mw-ăná wá-ké chí-manga.
   Catherine$_i$ she$_i$-PAST-(him$_j$-)harvest-CAUSE-INDIC child$_j$ her corn
   'Catherine made her child harvest the corn.'

Sentence (4.41) is an example of the instrumental construction under
consideration. The verb in (4.41) is marked with both the passive affix
-*dw*- and the causative affix -*ts*-, but the syntactic SUB of the sentence
is interpreted as an instrument, not as a causer or as the logical object
of the root verb.

(4.41)
Khásu lí-ma-(li-)lim-its-ídw-a chí-manga ndí Jóni.
hoe$_i$ it$_i$-HABIT-(it$_i$-)farm-CAUSE-PASS-INDIC corn$_j$ by John
'The hoe is used by John to farm corn with.'

Like the Japanese adversity passives in (4.37), the "passive" in (4.41)
has no active counterpart. A verb marked with the causative morpheme alone, as in (4.40), can be used only in a causative construction.
It cannot be used to indicate that an NP bearing the instrument role
appears somewhere in the sentence—see (4.42). The causative reading of (4.42) is blocked by a restriction in Chichewa that causers be
animate.

(4.42)
*Jóni á-ma-(yi-)lemb-éts-a pêni.
John$_i$ he$_i$-HABIT-(it$_j$-)write-CAUSE-INDIC pen$_j$
'John writes with a pen.'

Sentence (4.42) is ungrammatical because only the causative and passive morphemes together may signal the instrumental construction.

In (4.41), as in the Japanese adversity passive constructions, the verb must be [−log sub] to prevent the syntactic subject from bearing the semantic role of the logical subject of the predicate that the root verb produces. As in Japanese, the Chichewa passive morpheme carries the feature [−log sub] even when it appears in constructions other than simple passives, such as those in (4.39b,d). The passive morphology in (4.41) semantically vacates the subject position of a sentence headed by the passive verb, allowing this position to be occupied by a constituent bearing some semantic role other than that of the logical subject. A more complete analysis of the Chichewa instrumental construction illustrated in (4.41) is given in section 7.1.2.

4.1.3. The 1-Advancement Exclusiveness Law

One of the most interesting findings of Relational Grammar has been the set of restrictions on passivization and impersonal passivization accounted for within the theory by the 1-Advancement Exclusiveness Law (or 1AEX; a "1" is a subject in Relational Grammar). In Relational Grammar, all passivization processes promote (advance) an object to subject. Impersonal passivization involves the promotion of a dummy object to subject. The 1AEX (see Perlmutter 1978b, Perlmutter and Postal 1978a, 1980) states, in effect, that there may only be one advancement to subject per clause. Perlmutter 1978b shows how the 1AEX and the unaccusative hypothesis—basically the hypothesis that languages include unaccusative argument-taking items, which were introduced in section 2.1.2—explains the ungrammaticality of certain impersonal passives in Dutch and Turkish. Perlmutter and Postal (1978a) discuss several other applications of the 1AEX, in particular, its role in explaining the cross-linguistic ungrammaticality of double passivization within the same clause and the apparent impossibility of passivizing certain subclasses of English verbs in some constructions. In this section I demonstrate that some of the predictions of the 1AEX follow directly from the present theory without further statement. The remaining data accounted for by the 1AEX within Relational Grammar are handled by the theory given what seems to be a general principle governing morphological processes. The data associated with the 1AEX provide strong support for the present theory. What requires a special rule or stipulation in Relational Grammar follows from general principles in the present framework.[13]

Consider first cases of what Perlmutter and Postal (1978a) call sporadic advancements to 1. Within Relational Grammar, sentences like (4.43) are associated with a relational network in which a constituent that bears an initial impure grammatical relation, something like the means relation in (4.43a) and the time relation in (4.43b), advances to become the final subject of the sentence. These are called sporadic advancements because no general rule in English sanctions the advancement to subject of such impure relations. Compare sentences (4.43) with those in (4.44). In (4.44) the constituents that advance to subject in (4.43) still bear the initial impure grammatical relations assigned to them by an assumed universal initial assignment of grammatical to semantic relations.

(4.43)
a. Ten dollars buys this porcupine.
b. 1979 found the country at the brink of economic disaster.

(4.44)
a. A kind-hearted person may buy this porcupine for ten dollars.
b. We found the country at the brink of economic disaster in 1979.

In Relational Grammar every constituent bearing a given semantic role will be assigned the same initial grammatical relation. Because of this assumed universal connection between semantic and grammatical relations, if one knows the semantic relations associated with a verb, the initial grammatical relations borne by its grammatical dependents are fixed. Since *ten dollars* and *1979* in (4.43) and (4.44) are assumed to bear the same semantic relation in both sentences in which they appear, they must bear the same initial grammatical relation in both sentences: the impure means and time relations, respectively. Because the subjects in the relational networks associated with sentences (4.43) have advanced to subject (are not initial subjects), the 1AEX prevents the objects in these networks from advancing to subject in turn, explaining the ungrammaticality of sentences like (4.45).

(4.45)
a. *This porcupine {is bought, may be bought} by ten dollars.
b. *The country was found on the brink of economic disaster by 1979.

On the other hand, the 1AEX permits the promotion of the object to subject in the relational networks associated with (4.44), in which the subjects are initial subjects—see sentences (4.46).

(4.46)

a. This porcupine may be bought by a kind-hearted person for ten dollars.

b. The country was found by us in 1979 at the brink of economic disaster.

The present theory explains the ungrammaticality of (4.45), given some reasonable assumptions about the P-A structures of the verbs these sentences contain. Suppose that the P-A structures of *buy* and *find* do not differ significantly between (4.43) and (4.44). In particular, the predicates produced by *buy* and by *find* are assumed to assign the same semantic role in these sentences. Since English generally has predicates assign agent roles (see section 2.1.2), the predicates in (4.43, 4.44a) should assign a buyer role, those in (4.43, 4.44b) a finder role. However, the subject in (4.43a) is not the buyer and that in (4.43b) is not the finder. Therefore, the verbs in (4.43) must be [−log sub]; otherwise, the SUBs in these sentences would bear the semantic roles assigned by the predicates.

These suggestions constitute enough of an analysis to account for the ungrammaticality of sentences (4.45). The preposition *by* assigns the roles assigned by the predicates with which it is associated. Ex hypothesis, the predicates produced by the verbs in (4.45) are the same as the predicates produced by the verbs in (4.44). Thus the objects of *by* in (4.45) should receive the buyer and finder roles. There is no way in which *by* could assign the means or time roles. Second, even if the *by* phrases in (4.45) are deleted, the resulting sentences, given in (4.47), could not contain passive participles of the verbs in (4.43).

(4.47)

a. This porcupine may be bought.

b. The country was found on the brink of economic disaster.

Since the verbs in (4.43) are [−log sub], the NVAP prevents the attachment of the [−log sub] passive affix to these verbs.

Thus, adopting the assumption of Relation Grammar that the verbs in (4.43) and (4.44) are similar in that the predicates they produce assign the same semantic roles makes it possible to predict the ungrammaticality of sentences (4.45). These cases of sporadic advancement deserve more attention and a fuller analysis than has been provided here, but even a superficial account of sentences (4.43) explains the ungrammaticality of the passives in (4.45) without recourse to special laws or principles.[14]

Perlmutter (1978b) explains how the 1AEX predicts the ungrammaticality of impersonal passives formed from unaccusative verbs and confirms this prediction with data from Dutch and Turkish. Recall that unaccusative verbs are analyzed within Relational Grammar as verbs that take initial objects but no initial subject. The class of unaccusative verbs is identifiable in Relational Grammar through the assumed universal initial assignment of grammatical to semantic relations. If a verb is associated with the sort of semantic relation that is assigned the grammatical object relation but not with the sort assigned the grammatical subject relation, the verb will have an initial object but no initial subject and will thereby qualify as unaccusative. Impersonal passivization involves inserting a dummy as the object of a clause and advancing the dummy to subject. Since the objects of unaccusative verbs advance to subject, the 1AEX prohibits the additional advancement of a dummy to subject of unaccusative verbs (I am leaving out some assumptions of Relational Grammar that help make this analysis go through).

Employing semantic criteria to identify unaccusative verbs in Dutch, Perlmutter demonstrates the impossibility of impersonal passivization with Dutch unaccusatives. The examples in (4.48) include ungrammatical impersonal passives of unaccusative verbs.

(4.48)
a.   In dit weeshuis groeien de kinderen erg snel.
     'In this orphanage the children grow very fast.'

b.   *In dit weeshuis wordt er door de kinderen erg snel gegroeid.
     in this orphanage is it by the children very fast grown

c.   De bloemen waren binnen een paar dagen verflenst.
     'The flowers had wilted in a few days.'

d.   *Er werd door de bloemen binnen een paar dagen verflenst.[15]
     it was by the flowers in a few days wilted

Compare (4.48b,d) with the grammatical impersonal passives of "unergative" verbs in (4.49).

(4.49)
a.   Er wordt hier door de jonge lui veel gedanst.
     'It was danced here a lot by the young people.'

b.   Hier wordt (er) veel gewert.
     'It is worked here a lot.'

Within the current theory, unaccusative verbs are those whose P-A structures produce predicates that assign no semantic role, verbs that are inherently [−log sub]. Unlike Perlmutter and Postal, I assume no universal rules for arranging a verb's inherent semantic roles into P-A structures, rules that would be the equivalent in the present framework to Relational Grammar's universal initial assignment of grammatical to semantic relations. I provide extensive evidence against any such universal arrangement of P-A structures in chapter 6. Although the organization of semantic roles into P-A structures is not universally fixed, each language contains generalizations about which roles its predicates will assign, which roles its verbs will assign (see section 2.1.2). Assuming that Dutch incorporates generalizations similar to those described for English, having its predicates assign agent roles and its verbs assign theme and patient roles, I would analyze the verbs Perlmutter identifies as unaccusative as inherently [−log sub]. So a verb like *groeien* 'grow' in (4.48a) would have the lexical entry shown in (4.50).

(4.50)
groeien, V, 'grow' (*grower*), [−log sub], [−transitive]

If one attaches to *groeien* the Dutch passive morpheme, assumed to carry the features [−log sub], [+participle] (see the discussion of impersonal passivization in 4.1.2), the derived verb would have the lexical entry in (4.51).

(4.51)
gegroeid, V, 'grow' (*grower*) [−log sub], [−transitive], [+participle]

The verbs in (4.50) and (4.51) differ only in that (4.51) is a participle. One would not expect the passive participle in (4.51) to appear in sentences like (4.48b) since *door*, like English *by*, assigns the semantic role of a predicate and, as unaccusative verbs are [−log sub], the predicate in (4.48b) (and (4.48d)) does not assign a semantic role. Rather, one would expect the passives of unaccusative verbs like *groeien* to appear in sentences like (4.52), differing from the active sentences (4.48a,c) only in containing a passive participle.[16]

(4.52)
a. *In dit weeshuis werden de kinderen erg snel gegroeid.
b. *De bloemen werden binnen een paar dagen verflenst.

In the present framework then, the impossibility of creating impersonal passives with unaccusative verbs is evidenced by sentences like (4.52), not by sentences like (4.48b,d), and it is the ungrammaticality of (4.52) that needs explaining.

The NVAP, introduced to account for the restriction on English passivization to transitive verbs, automatically prevents the formation of the passive participle in (4.51). The passive affix in Dutch, carrying the unmotivated feature [−log sub], may not attach to the [−log sub] unaccusative verbs. In preventing the passivization of unaccusative verbs, principle (4.9) clearly exhibits its nature as a constraint against vacuous affixation. As one can see by comparing (4.50) and (4.51), the only difference between an unaccusative verb and its (ill-formed) passive participle is that the passive participle is a participle. Since passive verbs, like unaccusatives, are [−log sub] ([−transitive]), my explanation for the impossibility of forming passive verbs from unaccusatives explains the impossibility of forming passives from passives as well.[17]

In summary, the 1-Advancement Exclusiveness Law of Relational Grammar reduces within the current theory to a constraint that an affix carrying an unmotivated [−log sub] feature cannot attach to a [−log sub] root. I have argued that this constraint is a reflection of a broader principle governing affixation, the NVAP.

4.2. Antipassivization

An affix carrying the feature [−transitive] but not the feature [−log sub] will attach to a [+log sub], [+transitive] verb to create a [+log sub], [−transitive] derived verb. The logical object of this derived verb may not correspond to its OBJ at s structure because the derived verb, being [−transitive], may not take an OBJ. Since the derived verb is [+log sub], the predicate it produces will be sister to a logical subject, which must correspond to the SUB of the VP that the verb heads at s structure. So the verb's logical object is prevented from corresponding to a SUB. To satisfy principle M constraining the mapping between l-s and s structure, then, the logical object of the [+log sub], [−transitive] derived verb must correspond to an indirect grammatical argument of the verb at s structure. For a logical object of a verb to correspond to an indirect argument at s structure, a syntactic role assigner without an argument structure must be provided at s structure to assign the argument its syntactic role (see chapter 2). Antipassivization is the affixation to a verb of a [−transitive] morpheme unmarked for

[±log sub] that has no argument structure or semantic role assigning properties. Either the affix itself will specify a syntactic role assigner for the indirect argument of the derived antipassive verb, or the language will have some general mechanism for providing such a syntactic role assigner to [−transitive] verbs.

Antipassivization creates marked verbs with respect to the generalization that a [+log sub] verb that assigns a semantic role will be [+transitive]. Since antipassivization is marked within the current theory, the theory leads one to expect to find antipassivization in fewer languages than passivization, which produces completely unmarked verbs. In fact, antipassivization is extremely rare among the world's languages.[18]

One clear example of antipassivization in the literature is found in Greenlandic Eskimo (see Woodbury 1977a). I argue in chapter 6 that Greenlandic is a nominative-accusative language with ergative (type B) case marking. Basically, this classification means that Greenlandic shares generalizations (2.23) with English: its verbs canonically assign theme and patient roles and its predicates canonically assign agent roles. However, SUBs of Greenlandic [−transitive] verbs and OBJs of [+transitive] verbs are case marked in the same way, in contrast to the case marking on SUBs of [+transitive] verbs (see chapter 6 for further explanation of this classification schema).

A transitive Greenlandic verb (in a main clause) agrees with both the grammatical subject and the grammatical object. The subject of such a matrix verb appears in the ergative (also called the genitive) case and the OBJ in the absolutive (unmarked) case, as in the simple transitive Greenlandic sentence in (4.53) (the orthography is that of Woodbury 1977a).

(4.53)
Anut-ip arnaq-∅ taku-vaa.
man-ERG woman-ABS see-IND3sg3sg (IND=indicative)
'The man saw the woman.'

An intransitive Greenlandic verb agrees with one constituent, the subject, which appears in the absolutive case.

(4.54)
Anut-∅ autlar-puq.
man-ABS go away-IND3sg
'The man went away.'

The Greenlandic passive suffix -*tau*- carries the features [−log sub], [−transitive]. A range of case endings plays the role of *by* in English passives, marking the displaced subject of a Greenlandic passive. One such case is the ablative, whose use is illustrated in the passive in (4.55). Compare (4.55) with its active counterpart (4.53).

(4.55)
Arnaq-∅ anuti-mit taku-tau-puq.
woman-ABS man-ABL see-PASS-IND3sg
'The woman was seen by the man.'

Passivization makes *taku*- 'see' [−transitive]. The logical object of *taku*-, *arnaq*- 'woman,' corresponds to the SUB of the VP that *taku-tau*- 'see-PASS' heads at s structure and thus appears in the absolutive case and triggers (intransitive) verb agreement. The displaced subject of the predicate in (4.55) appears in the ablative case.

The antipassive construction is illustrated in (4.56b).

(4.56)
a. Anut-ip miirqa-t paar-ai.
   man-ERG child-PL(ABS) take care of-IND3sg3pl
   'The man takes care of the children.'

b. Anut-∅ miirqu-nik paar-si-vuq.
   man-ABS children-INST take care of-ANTIPASS-IND3sg
   'The man takes care of the children.'

The lexical entry for the active verb in (4.56a) is given in (4.57). The antipassive morpheme in Greenlandic is -*si*-. Antipassivization of (4.57) yields (4.58).

(4.57)
paar-, V, 'take care of' (*patient*) [+log sub], [+transitive]

(4.58)
paar-si-, V, 'take care of' (*patient*) [+log sub], [−transitive], INST

I include the notation "INST" in (4.58) to indicate that the antipassive suffix provides instrumental case as a syntactic role assigner for a verb's indirect argument at s structure. Since the antipassive verb in (4.58) is [+log sub], the logical subject of the predicate that *paar-si*- 'take care of' heads, *anut*- 'man' in (4.56b), will correspond to the SUB of the VP it heads at s structure and thus will appear in the absolutive case and trigger (intransitive) verb agreement on the derived intransitive verb. The logical object of the derived antipassive in (4.56b) satisfies principle M by corresponding to an indirect argument of the verb at s structure, assigned its syntactic role by the instrumental case specified in the lexical entry of the derived verb. The l-s and s structures for the antipassive in (4.56b) are displayed in (4.59a) and (4.59b) respectively.[19]

(4.59)

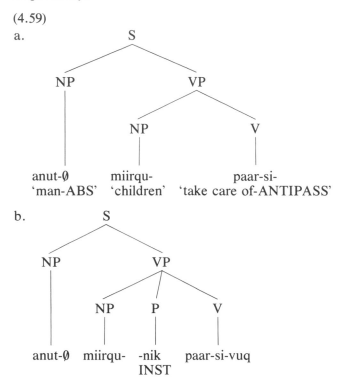

a.

```
                    S
          _____
        NP              VP
        |          _____
        |         NP        V
        |         |         |
      anut-0    miirqu-   paar-si-
     'man-ABS' 'children' 'take care of-ANTIPASS'
```

b.

```
            S
      _____
    NP          VP
    |       _____
    |      NP   P    V
    |      |    |    |
  anut-0 miirqu- -nik paar-si-vuq
                 INST
```

4.3. Lexical Reflexivization

Many languages include special intransitive verb forms with reflexive meaning. For example, Albanian transitive verbs have intransitive counterparts, with their own inflectional paradigm, which are interpreted as reflexive (Hubbard 1979). Compare the Albanian transitive verb *laj* 'wash' in (4.60a) with the corresponding intransitive verb *lahem* 'wash' in (4.60b) (the citation form of an Albanian verb is the first person singular present indicative).[20]

(4.60)

a. Agimi lan veten.
   Agim wash-3sg self
   'Agim washes himself.'

b. Agimi lahet.
   Agim wash-3sg
   'Agim washes himself.'

The subject of the reflexive verb form, *Agimi* in (4.60b), is interpreted as bearing the semantic roles borne by both the subject and the object of its transitive counterpart. While *Agimi* is the washer and *veten* 'self' the washed argument in (4.60a), *Agimi* is interpreted as both washer and washed in (4.60b).

Languages employ a variety of morphological devices to create reflexive verb forms. In Albanian no consistent morphological relation between the reflexive and nonreflexive forms of a verb spans the entire inflectional paradigm. Some languages simply employ a general intransitive version of a verb as the reflexive. Whereas Greenlandic Eskimo transitive verbs agree with both subject and object, intransitive verbs agree with the subject alone (see section 4.2; Greenlandic reflexives are discussed in chapter 6). Attaching intransitive agreement suffixes to a logically transitive verb usually yields a reflexive verb in Greenlandic, as shown in (4.61) from Sadock (1980).

(4.61)
Piniartoq toquppoq.
hunter-ABS kill-IND3sg
'The hunter killed himself.'

Dyirbal, an Australian language (whose lexical reflexive forms will also be discussed in chapter 6), uses a morpheme with the properties of a standard derivational affix to form a reflexive verb from a transitive verb root.

Many languages add a clitic to a transitive verb to derive the reflexive form. Examples of clitic-formed lexical reflexives from French and Russian are found in (4.62) and (4.63).

(4.62)
Les enfants se lavent maintenant.
the children SELF wash now
'The children are washing themselves now.'

(4.63)
Deti mojuts'a teper'.
children wash-PRES3pl-SELF now
'The children are washing themselves now.'

The French reflexive verb is formed with a preverbal reflexive clitic, *se* in the example. The Russian reflexive is derived with the postverbal clitic *-s'a*. I am using morphological criteria to identify the French and Russian reflexive morphemes as clitics; they appear outside derivational and inflectional morphology.

Regardless of the particular morphological means a language uses to relate the reflexive and nonreflexive (transitive) forms of a verb, if the relation is mediated by affixation, the present theory permits only two analyses of lexical reflexive verbs like those in (4.60b) and (4.61)–(4.63). On one analysis the reflexive affix is an s structure OBJ of the root verb. This first analysis amounts to treating the reflexive affix as one would treat pronominal object clitics in a language like French, and may therefore be dubbed the clitic analysis. The second or nonclitic analysis of reflexives requires that the reflexive verb be [−transitive]. Although the theory allows these two analyses, in languages in which one can argue for one or the other, the nonclitic analysis always proves correct. Even French, which employs pronominal object clitics that look just like the reflexive morpheme, shows clear evidence that the nonclitic analysis is appropriate for its reflexive verb forms.

If the Albanian nonreflexive and reflexive verbs *laj, lahem* 'wash' in (4.60) are to be related by affixation, they must share a P-A structure, presumably that in (4.64).

(4.64)
laj, lahem 'wash' (*patient*)

Note that *Agimi* in (4.60b) is interpreted as bearing both the agent (washer) and patient (washed) roles. But constraints on the structural representation of l-s structures prohibit a single l-s constituent from serving as both logical object of a verb and logical subject of the predicate that the verb produces. Therefore, *Agimi* may not be both the logical object and the logical subject in (4.60b), and either the logical object or the logical subject semantic role must be assigned to some other constituent. There are two possibilities: either *Agimi* is the logical object of *lahem* 'wash' in (4.60b) or it is the logical subject of the predicate that *lahem* produces. If *Agimi* is the logical object, the theory demands the nonclitic analysis of the lexical reflexive verb; if *Agimi* is the logical subject, the theory demands the clitic analysis.

Consider first the case in which *Agimi* serves as logical object to *lahem*. Since *Agimi* is the SUB of (4.60b) and the logical object of a verb corresponds to the SUB of the VP that the verb heads only if the verb is [−log sub], the lexical reflexive *lahem* must be [−log sub]. Since in Albanian the logical object of the reflexive verb may not correspond to its OBJ, *lahem* must also be [−transitive]. One may conclude that the lexical reflexive verb, like the passive, is [−log sub], [−transitive]. Since reflexive verbs are derived from [+log sub], [+transitive] verbs like *laj* 'wash' in (4.60a) via affixation, the reflexive affix REFL must carry the features [−log sub], [−transitive].[21]

By identifying *Agimi* as the logical object of *lahem* 'wash' in (4.60b), I have accounted for the interpretation of the subject of the reflexive verb as the patient. What remains to be explained is how *Agimi* is also interpreted as the agent of the reflexive verb. Since the agent role may not be assigned to *Agimi* directly at l-s structure, the agent role must be assigned to some constituent that is interpreted as coreferent with *Agimi,* that is, to some reflexive element that picks up *Agimi* as its antecedent. But where is the reflexive element in (4.60b)?

I am assuming that the reflexive verb form is derived from an active transitive verb via affixation, and I have determined that the reflexive affix REFL must carry the features [−log sub], [−transitive]. Although it is impossible to point out any piece of the reflexive Albanian verb as REFL throughout most of the inflectional paradigm (but see (4.75b)), my assumptions force me to postulate the existence of such a morpheme. It is the affix carrying the features [−log sub], [−transitive] that is assigned the logical subject role in a reflexive sentence like (4.60b). More properly, REFL must carry the features of a reflexive pronoun, and these features are assigned the logical subject role.

In addition to carrying the features [−log sub], [−transitive] and the features of a reflexive pronoun, the reflexive affix REFL must, on this nonclitic analysis, ensure that its reflexive pronoun features are assigned the semantic role of the logical subject of the sentence headed by the reflexive verb. REFL may accomplish this by carrying the semantic role assigning features and argument structure of English *by* (see section 4.1.1.2). Features of REFL, as a modifier creator, will form a modifier M with REFL's pronoun features as shown in (4.65). REFL's modifier-producing features, like the preposition *by,* assign to the reflexive pronoun features the role assigned by the predicate that the modifier M modifies—VP2 in (4.65). The modifier-producing features then apply the predicate (VP2) to the reflexive pronoun to derive a degenerate predicate, VP1 in (4.65). The proposed l-s structure for (4.60b) on the nonclitic analysis of reflexives is shown in (4.65).

(4.65)

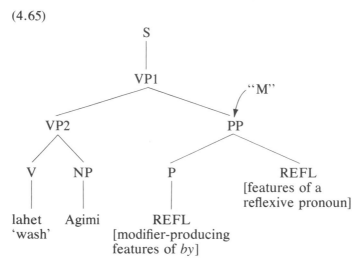

Since the REFL affix and root verb are not distinct phonological constituents, they must appear as a single constituent in surface structure. So the reflexive affix REFL must merge with the root verb somewhere between l-s and surface structure or at surface structure (on morphological merger, see chapter 7). Merger of independent l-s constituents may take place at l-s, s, or surface structure. Therefore *lahet* and REFL in (4.65) may in principle form a single l-s constituent, or a single s structure constituent, or two s structure constituents, and so on. However, if REFL merges with the root verb at l-s structure, its reflexive pronoun features could not conform to the binding theory, and the antecedent–anaphor relation between REFL's reflexive pronoun features and the SUB of the reflexive verb could not be properly established. The model of grammar I have been assuming states that antecedent–anaphor relations are established (or checked) at s structure; that is, the binding theory for anaphors applies at s structure.[22] Therefore, for the binding theory to connect Agimi and REFL, *lahet* and REFL must remain distinct at least at s structure. An s structure corresponding to (4.65) should look something like (4.66).

(4.66)

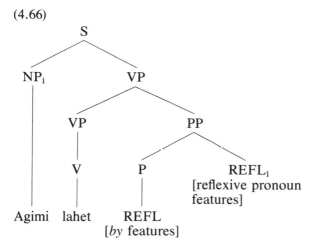

Agimi lahet   REFL
          [*by* features]

The REFL affix and root verb merge at s or surface structure, expressing the modifier-modifiee relation between the PP and the lower VP in
(4.66) (see chapter 7) to yield the surface structure in (4.67).

(4.67)

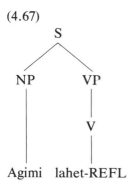

Agimi lahet-REFL

To review the nonclitic analysis of lexical reflexives: The reflexive
affix REFL carries the features [−log sub], [−transitive] plus the
modifier-producing features of English *by* and the features of a reflexive
pronoun. The *by* features of REFL assign to its reflexive pronoun features the logical subject semantic role. The SUB of the reflexive verb
serves as antecedent for REFL's reflexive pronoun features at s structure, and the root verb and REFL merge at or before surface structure.

Technically, one may assume that the *by* and reflexive pronoun features of REFL are borne by an affix (or affixes) with its own lexical
entry. Such an affix would subcategorize to attach to the [−log sub],

[−transitive] REFL affix. If this affix lacks surface structure features, it must attach to REFL before surface structure. Recall that each syntactic representation is, in effect, independently generated with items from the lexicon. If a morpheme lacks surface structure features, it may not be inserted into a surface structure representation. To put it differently, each lexical entry should be seen as a set of mapping rules, taking l-s to s structure features and s to surface structure features. If an item contains no mapping specifications between its s structure features and any surface structure features, it must merge with some other morpheme at s structure since it cannot map to surface structure independently. The *by* and reflexive pronoun features are carried by an affix (or affixes) that contains no mapping specifications between s and surface structure features.

The theory demands the nonclitic analysis of lexical reflexives on the assumption that the SUB of the VP that the lexical reflexive verb heads corresponds to its logical object. Suppose instead that the verb's SUB corresponds to the logical subject of the predicate that it produces, that is, that *Agimi* in (4.60b) is the logical subject of the sentence at l-s structure. Since *Agimi* is interpreted as the patient as well as the agent of 'wash' but cannot be assigned both roles at l-s structure, the verb in (4.60b) must assign the patient role to some constituent that is interpreted as coreferent with *Agimi*. The only constituent available to serve this function in (4.60b) is the reflexive affix REFL, so REFL must bear the features of a reflexive pronoun and serve as logical object to the lexical reflexive verb, as shown in the l-s structure for (4.60b) given in (4.68).

(4.68)

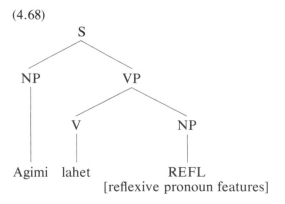

Recall that the binding theory, which establishes antecedent–anaphor relations, applies at s structure. In order for *Agimi* to bind the reflexive pronoun features of REFL in (4.60b), REFL and *lahet* must remain separate constituents at some stage of s structure. If REFL is a distinct constituent at s structure it must be head-Governed by *lahet* to satisfy principle M. Since *lahet* is [+log sub], REFL must be the OBJ of *lahet* at s structure and *lahet* must be [+transitive]. The s structure corresponding to (4.68) will look exactly like (4.68), with the exception that the subject and object will be coindexed to indicate the antecedent–anaphor relation that holds between them. On the clitic analysis of lexical reflexivization, the surface structure of sentence (4.60b) would be identical to the surface structure of the sentence on the nonclitic analysis, shown in (4.67). On the clitic analysis, the merger of the root verb and REFL expresses the direct grammatical object relation between these constituents.

Although the theory allows two analyses of reflexive verbs in principle, the clitic and nonclitic analyses, all the languages I have examined show evidence that they employ the nonclitic analysis. Recall that one major difference between the two analyses is whether or not the reflexive verb is [+transitive]; the reflexive is [+transitive] on the clitic analysis but [−transitive] on the nonclitic analysis. Grimshaw (1981) presents data from French to show that the French reflexive verb is [−transitive]. Evidence for the nonclitic analysis of French, Albanian, and Icelandic reflexives is presented below. The question remains why languages do not choose the clitic analysis of reflexive verbs made available by the theory of grammar.

One answer to this question, which may be rejected, is that the theory should rule out the clitic analysis of reflexives in principle. An analysis parallel to the clitic analysis of reflexives is required for nonreflexive pronominal object clitics in languages like French. As Grimshaw (1981) shows, French verbs with nonreflexive object clitics, unlike reflexive verbs, behave like [+transitive] verbs. One of Grimshaw's arguments derives from the behavior of French verbs embedded under the causative verb *faire*. In (4.69a) a French verb is preceded by a pronominal object clitic; (4.69b) contains a parallel reflexive verb form.

(4.69)

a. Jean l'a tué.
   John OBJclitic'PAST kill
   'John killed him.'

b. Jean s'est tué.
   John REFL'PAST kill
   'John killed himself.'

When clauses are embedded under the French causative *faire* 'make,' the logical subject of the embedded clause generally appears either as a bare NP complement to the embedded verb, as in Grimshaw's example (4.70a), or in a prepositional phrase headed by *à,* as in her (4.70b). Although complications arise unrelated to the present argument, the generalization governing the choice of expression for the lower subject in French causative constructions with *faire* is that the embedded subject appears as an unmarked complement when the head of the embedded clause is [−transitive] but is preceded by *à* when the head verb is [+transitive].

(4.70)

a. J'ai fait partir {Jean, *à Jean}.
   I'PAST make leave {John, at John}
   'I made John leave.'

b. Il fera boire un peu de vin {à son enfant, *son enfant}.
   he make-FUT drink a little of wine {at his child, his child}
   'He will make his child drink a little wine.'

Although a verb with a pronominal object clitic behaves like a transitive verb in the causative construction (compare (4.71a) with (4.70)), a reflexive verb behaves like an intransitive when embedded under *faire* (see (4.71b)).

(4.71)

a. La crainte du scandale l'a fait tuer {au juge, *le juge}.
   'Fear of scandal made the judge kill him.'

b. La crainte du scandale a fait se tuer {le frère du juge, *au frère du juge}.
   'Fear of scandal made the judge's brother kill himself.'

The behavior of nonreflexive preverbal object clitics in French indicates that they should be treated as OBJs of transitive verbs; that is, verbs with object clitics must be analyzed essentially as I have analyzed reflexive verbs on the clitic analysis. There is no principled way to prevent object clitics like that in (4.69a) from bearing in some language the reflexive pronoun features of a reflexive clitic like that in (4.69b). Thus one cannot rule out the clitic analysis of reflexive verbs in principle.

Nevertheless, some principle apparently leads speakers to hypothesize the nonclitic analysis of reflexive verbs first, choosing the clitic analysis only in the face of data inconsistent with the nonclitic analysis. French speakers even employ the nonclitic analysis when reflexive verbs look identical to verbs with preverbal object clitics in their language, where these latter verbs require a clitic analysis. Reflexive verb forms in many languages, including Russian and Icelandic, derive historically from combinations of verb plus an independent reflexive pronominal element. Some principle causes these combinations to be reanalyzed as combinations of a verb plus a [−log sub], [−transitive]—nonclitic—REFL affix. Although I could speculate on what this principle might be, I have no evidence for any of my speculations and will leave open here the problem of the preference for the nonclitic analysis.

The present nonclitic analysis of lexical reflexive verbs should be contrasted with the nonclitic analyses usually found in the literature. Since the subject of intransitive *lahem* 'wash' in (4.60b) bears the patient role, the usual approach to a lexical reflexive like *lahem* has been to assume that the patient role of its transitive counterpart is somehow absorbed into the semantics of the reflexive verb. So instead of assigning the washer role to its subject, as does the predicate produced by transitive *laj* 'wash,' the predicate produced by intransitive *lahem* would assign the self-washer role. This analysis of lexical reflexives could be implemented by postulating some lexical rule of reflexive verb formation that takes the P-A structure of *laj* in (4.72a) and yields that shown for *lahem* in (4.72b).

(4.72)
a. *laj* 'wash' (*patient*) →
b. *lahem* 'self-wash' (∅)

The predicate produced by the P-A structure in (4.72b) assigns the self-washer role to its subject. Since it changes the P-A structure and semantic role assigning properties of a verb, the operation schematized in (4.72) could not be mediated by affixation in the present theory, which does not contain the machinery necessary to state rules like

(4.72) as any sort of syntactic or lexical rule. The nonclitic analysis of reflexive verbs forced by the present verb is the mirror image of the usual analyses schematized in (4.72). Instead of absorbing the semantic role of the logical object into the verb, this analysis in essence absorbs the semantic role of the logical subject—the reflexive affix bears this role and attaches to the verb.

Since the nonclitic analysis is forced by the present theory (for [−transitive] reflexive verbs), evidence in favor of the analysis should be considered support for the theory over theories that allow any but the clitic and nonclitic analyses I have described. Two pieces of striking evidence confirm the present nonclitic analysis of reflexives, particularly in contrast to the nonclitic analysis schematized in (4.72) (see chapter 6 on ergativity for further support).

The first piece of evidence comes from the well-known fact that in many languages the lexical reflexive verb form is homophonous with the passive verb form. The Albanian reflexive sentence (4.60b) has a passive ('Agim is washed') as well as a reflexive interpretation. Consider also the sentences in (4.73), which are ambiguous between reflexive and passive readings.

(4.73)
a. I burgosuri lahet dy herë në javë.
   the prisoner wash-REFL-3sg two times in week
   'The prisoner washes himself twice a week.'
   'The prisoner is washed twice a week.'

b. Prostitutat u veshen perpara darkës.
   the prostitutes REFL dress before dinner-the
   'The prostitutes were dressed before dinner.'
   'The prostitutes dressed themselves before dinner.'

In (4.73b), the REFL affix shows up as the preverbal clitic, *u*. The form *veshen* means 'they dressed (transitive)' while *u veshen* means 'they were dressed' or 'they dressed themselves.'[23]

The present theory leads one to expect a homophony between reflexive and passive verb forms because the reflexive affix carries the same features carried by the passive affix ([−log sub], [−transitive]). Of course, the reflexive morpheme may also carry features that dictate the assignment of the logical subject semantic role. (I suggested earlier that these other features might best be seen as independent affixes that are subcategorized to attach to REFL.) A single morpheme may serve for both the reflexive and passive affixes in a language like Albanian if the features dealing with the assignment of the logical subject role are made optional in the lexical entry of the reflexive/passive affix.

The homophony between lexical reflexive and passive verb forms illustrated in Albanian is widespread cross-linguistically, appearing in French (Grimshaw 1981),[24] Eskimo (see chapter 6), Dyirbal (Dixon 1972 and chapter 6), and Lardil (Klokeid 1976), among other languages. Note that the alternative nonclitic analysis of lexical reflexive formation that postulates the absorption into the semantics of a verb of the logical object semantic role offers no immediate explanation for the homophony between lexical reflexive and passive verb forms. This homophony is also a mystery on any clitic analysis of reflexives.

Icelandic reflexive verbs provide further support for the present nonclitic analysis of lexical reflexivization, particularly over the hypothesis that reflexivization involves the absorption of the logical object semantic role into the reflexive verb. Consider a raising to object verb in Icelandic such as *telja* 'believe,' which is the main verb of the matrix sentence in (4.74). Recall from chapter 3 that a raising to object verb takes modifier and, in the marked case, predicate arguments and is [+log sub], [+transitive].

(4.74)
Þeir telja Maríu hafa skrifað ritgerðina.
they believe Mary-ACC to-have written thesis
'They believe Mary to have written her thesis.'

Icelandic includes a verb form, called the "middle" in the literature, which is generally ambiguous between passive and reflexive interpretations. Verbs in the middle end in the clitic *-st,* which is a descendent of a reflexive pronoun in Old Icelandic (sentences (4.75) are from Valfells 1970).

(4.75)
a. Hann klœddist.
       dressed-REFL
   'He dressed himself.'

b. Keisarinn klœddist nýjum fötum.
       dressed-REFL
   'The Emperor was dressed in new clothes.'

On my account, the reflexive morpheme *-st* must carry the features [−log sub], [−transitive] plus the features that assign it, as a reflexive pronoun, the semantic role of the logical subject. Recall that adding the features [−log sub], [−transitive] to a raising to object verb creates a raising to subject verb (see section 4.1.1.3). If -*st* is added to *telja* 'believe,' then, one expects to derive a raising to subject verb whose subject will be interpreted as the believer by virtue of being the antecedent of a reflexive element assigned this role. In fact, these expectations are borne out, as shown in (4.76).

(4.76)
Hann telst vera sterkur.
he-NOM believe-REFL to-be strong-NOM
a. 'He believes himself to be strong.'
b. 'He is believed to be strong.'

The subject of *telst* in (4.76), *hann* 'he,' bears the strong role by virtue of serving as syntactic role assignee of the lower verb phrase. It is interpreted as the believer because it serves as antecedent for the reflexive pronoun features of the reflexive affix, which are assigned the role of the logical subject of the upper clause. Since middle voice verbs generally have passive as well as reflexive interpretations, in addition to its reflexive reading sentence (4.76) has the passive reading indicated in (4.76b).

The subject of (4.76) in its (a) reading bears the semantic roles of the logical subject of *telja* 'believe' and of the logical subject of the lower predicate or modifier, *sterkur* 'strong.' If lexical reflexivization absorbed the semantic role of the logical object into the semantics of a verb, reflexivization could not derive the lexical reflexive verb form in (4.76). The semantic role of the subject of a complement to a raising verb obviously does not appear within the lexical entry of the raising verb and therefore cannot be involved in a lexical rule applying to the raising verb. In contrast to an approach that implicates the logical object semantic role, the analysis of lexical reflexivization that follows from the theory of this book makes exactly the correct prediction about the reflexive form of a raising to object verb, as was demonstrated in (4.75) and (4.76).

An alternative analysis of the Icelandic middle corresponding to the clitic analysis will account for sentence (4.76) in its reflexive reading but must be rejected on independent grounds. If -*st* were a reflexive pronoun object clitic, one could provide a superficially correct analysis for sentences like (4.76) repeated as (4.77b). On the clitic analysis of -*st*, (4.77b) would be syntactically parallel to (4.77a) but with the pronominal object cliticized to the matrix verb.

(4.77)

a. Hann telur sig vera sterkan/*sterkur.
   he-NOM believes himself-ACC to-be strong-ACC/*strong-NOM
   'He believes himself to be strong.'

b. Hann telst vera sterkur/*sterkan.
   he-NOM believe-REFL to-be strong-NOM/*strong-ACC
   'He believes himself to be strong.'

Since the objects of raising to object verbs are the syntactic role assignees of their complement predicates, -*st* considered as a reflexive object clitic would bear the semantic role of the lower clause subject in (4.77b), as required. Since the subject of the higher verb would serve as antecedent for -*st* as a reflexive object clitic, it would be properly interpreted as both the believer and the one who is strong.

Andrews (1981) provides conclusive evidence against this sort of clitic analysis of Icelandic middle verbs. This evidence works against any clitic analysis of reflexive verbs in Icelandic, including the clitic analysis allowed by the present theory. In raising to object constructions with transitive verbs like *telja* 'believe,' a predicate adjective in the embedded clause agrees in case with its subject, which is the object of the raising verb. In (4.77a), for example, the predicate adjective *sterkan* 'strong-ACC' must appear in the accusative in agreement with its subject, *vera* 'himself-ACC.' If -*st* were simply a reflexive object clitic, one would expect the predicate adjective embedded under the middle *teljast* 'believe-REFL' to bear accusative case in agreement with the pronominal object clitic -*st* that serves as its subject. Under the clitic analysis of -*st*, (4.77a) and (4.77b) share essentially the same syntactic structure. However, as shown in (4.77b), the adjective embedded under the middle *teljast* must appear in the nominative, agreeing with the subject of *teljast*. Andrews demonstrates that this adjective agrees in case with the subject of *teljast* regardless of the case of the subject. Agreement of the predicate adjective with the subject of *teljast* is what one would expect if, as predicted by the present theory, *teljast* were a raising to subject verb. Since it cannot distinguish (4.77a) and (4.77b) properly, the clitic analysis of (4.77b) must be rejected (see Andrews 1981 for a more thorough version of this argument against the clitic analysis).

Chapter 5

Alternations in the Expression of Arguments Not Mediated by Affixation

In chapter 4 I discussed alternations in the expression of a verb's semantic dependents—the passive and antipassive alternations—that share three crucial properties. First, the alternations do not involve alternations in the argument structures or semantic role assigning features of the verbs exhibiting them. Second, the alternations are mediated by affixation alone; attributing a set of features to an affix completely accounts for the expression of a verb's semantic dependents when the verb occurs with the affix as opposed to their expression when the verb occurs without the affix. Third, the alternations are highly productive, involving virtually all verbs compatible with the features of the affixes that mediate the alternations.

This chapter will treat alternations in the expression of a verb's semantic dependents that share none of these three properties. First, they may involve alternations in the argument structure or semantic role assigning features of the verbs exhibiting them. Second, the alternations are not mediated by affixation alone, in the sense that no affix may be considered to carry the features necessary to completely explain the observed properties of the alternations. And third, they are restricted to a limited set of verbs in the language, a set with identifiable semantic coherence. The theory described in this book explains the connections among the properties of the alternations to be discussed in this chapter. In particular, the theory prohibits an alternation that involves a difference in argument structure or semantic role assigning properties from being mediated solely by affixation. The mechanisms left open by the theory to account for such alternations suggest a reason for their limited productivity.

5.1. Alternations in Semantic Role Assigning Properties: Dative Shift

Much attention has been given in the transformational literature to the relation between sentences like (5.1a,b) and to that between sentences like (5.2a,b).

(5.1)
a. Elmer gave a porcupine to Hortense.
b. Elmer gave Hortense a porcupine.

(5.2)
a. Elmer baked a cake for Hortense.
b. Elmer baked Hortense a cake.

Some languages exhibit alternations in the expression of a verb's arguments superficially similar to these, in which the second member of each pair contains a verb marked with an affix absent from the verb in the first member. Consider, for example, the following Chichewa sentences from Trithart (1977, p. 37).

(5.3)
a. Cátherine a-ná-(yí-)phik-a n-síma.
   Catherine$_i$ she$_i$-PAST-(it$_j$)-cook-INDIC nsima$_j$
   'Catherine cooked nsima.'
b. Cátherine a-ná-(wá-)phik-ir-a ǎ-ná n-síma.
   Catherine$_i$ she$_i$-PAST-(them$_j$-)cook-APPLIED-INDIC children$_j$
   nsima
   'Catherine cooked the children nsima.'

The "applied" affix on the verb in (5.3b) signals the presence in the sentence of an NP unmarked by case or preposition that bears the benefactive role (*ǎ-ná* 'children' in (5.3b)). In chapter 7 I provide an analysis of constructions like (5.3b); in section 5.1.3 I explain how they differ crucially from structures like (5.1b) or (5.2b). In this section I examine the expression of goals (see (5.1b)) and benefactives (see (5.2b)) as direct objects of morphologically simple verbs, such as English *give* and *bake*.

5.1.1. Dative Shift with Goal Arguments

I have assumed that the P-A structure of *give* is as shown in (5.4).

(5.4)
'give' (theme, goal)

The lexical entry for *give* in (5.1a) will include the information displayed in (5.5). Since *give* in (5.5) assigns the theme role and English verbs have been assumed to assign only one role in the unmarked case (see the One Role/Role Assigner principle), the goal role in (5.1a) must be assigned by something other than the verb. In English, the preposition *to* assigns the goal role associated with *give*.

(5.5)
give, V, 'give' (*theme*, goal), [+log sub], [+transitive]

In the present theory, I account for alternations in the expression of a verb's arguments like that illustrated in (5.1) by postulating an alternation in what role a verb like *give* assigns. On this account, the difference between *give* in (5.1a) and *give* in (5.1b) is that the former assigns the theme role, the latter the goal role. The lexical entry for *give* in (5.1b) would include the information in (5.6).

(5.6)
give, V, 'give' (theme, *goal*), [+log sub], [+transitive]

That the propositional content of (5.1a) and (5.1b) are identical is explained by the fact that (5.5) and (5.6) include the same P-A structure, shown in (5.4); that is, *give* names the same function from arguments to predicates in both (5.1a) and (5.1b). By the One Role/Role Assigner principle, if *give* assigns the goal role, as in (5.6), some other semantic role assigner must assign the theme role. Although English lacks a preposition to assign the theme role in most cases, I claim that the structural position [NP, VP] may assign this role.

In chapter 2 I listed structural positions and case markings along with predicates and lexical items among the semantic role assigners. A consideration of language acquisition helps explain why [NP, VP] is a likely assigner of the theme role in dative shift constructions. As argued in Marantz 1982a, children's first knowledge of language connects semantic roles directly to their expressions in a sentence. Until around the age of five, English speaking children link agents to preverbal positions, patients and themes to postverbal positions (see the discussion of Marantz 1982a in section 2.1.2). By virtue of the acquisition process, then, the usual expression of direct objects, the structural position [NP, VP], is connected in the child's linguistic knowledge with the semantic roles canonically borne by direct objects, patients and themes. The ability of the structural position [NP, VP] to assign the theme role to an argument in dative shift constructions could be a vestige of an earlier stage of language acquisition.

Of course, the canonical appearance of themes in the [NP, VP] position in English would be motivation enough within the adult grammar to allow [NP, VP] to assign the theme role in dative shift constructions. Given that structural positions may assign roles, no appeal to language acquisition is necessary to explain this property of [NP, VP]; nevertheless, the acquisition data are suggestive.

So the dative shift alternation exhibited in (5.1) results from an alternation in which of two roles verbs like *give* assign. If the verb assigns the theme role, the goal role will be assigned by the usual assigner of this role, the preposition *to* in English. If, on the other hand, the verb itself assigns the goal role, the theme role will be assigned by the usual expression of direct object, in English, the structural position [NP, VP]. In the surface structure of an English sentence, the [NP, VP] that is the OBJ of the head verb of the VP precedes an [NP, VP] that is not an OBJ of the verb, so the goal precedes the theme in (5.1b) (see Stowell 1981 for a possible explanation of this ordering in terms of an adjacency condition on abstract Case marking, which corresponds to syntactic role assignment in the present theory).

Given the assumption that the verbs in the shifted (5.1b) and the unshifted (5.1a) have the same P-A structure and the assumption that English allows verbs to assign only one semantic role in the unmarked case, the theory of this book taken with well-established facts about English actually demands the present analysis of dative shift. Since, by assumption, verbs in English assign only one semantic role, the verb in (5.1b) may assign only one role. If it assigned the theme role, it could not also assign the goal role. But nothing in sentence (5.1b) can be seen as assigning the goal role except the verb; in particular, there is no affix on the verb that could assign the goal role. Also, since the goal argument in (5.1b) does not appear in a usual expression of goals in English, the structural position of the goal argument may not assign the goal role to this argument. Therefore, the verb in (5.1b) must assign the goal role to *Hortense*. Since the canonical expression of direct objects, [NP, VP], is associated with the semantic roles canonically borne by objects, themes and patients, [NP, VP] may assign the theme role to *a porcupine* in (5.1b).

The same line of reasoning may be extended to double object constructions cross-linguistically, leading to a significant prediction about such constructions. A double object construction is a sentence, like

(5.1b) or (5.2b), in which two arguments of a verb are expressed as direct objects are usually expressed in the language. Suppose one of these arguments bears the theme or patient role. Given three facts about a language, those listed in (5.7), I predict that in double object constructions the argument that does not bear the theme or patient role will be the direct logical object of the main verb while the theme or patient will not be a logical object of the verb.[1]

(5.7)
a. The language allows a verb to assign only one semantic role in the unmarked case.
b. The main verb of the double object construction is underived (morphologically simple).
c. There is no independent reason to believe that the usual expression of direct objects in the language may assign the semantic role borne by the argument that is not the theme or patient.

I have assumed that it is the unmarked case for a language to allow its underived verbs to assign only one semantic role (the One Role/Role Assigner principle). If the language is marked, allowing verbs to assign two roles, but facts (5.7b,c) hold, I still predict that the non-theme/patient argument will be a logical object of the verb, although the theme/patient argument may also be an object—see chapter 7 for a discussion of such marked languages. In chapter 7 I also discuss double object constructions with morphologically derived verbs. If the main verb in a double object construction were morphologically complex, the affix on the verb could assign the non-theme/patient role. As for (5.7c), if the usual expression of direct objects in a language were known to assign the non-theme/patient role of a double object construction independent of such constructions, the theme/patient role in the double object constructions of this language could be assigned by the verb while the usual expression of direct objects assigns the non-theme/patient role. For example, if the goal role were assigned by [NP, VP] in English with verbs of motion, my analysis of (5.1b) would not be forced by the theory. That is, if we said *Elmer went the store* for *Elmer went to the store*, the position [NP, VP] could be analyzed as assigning the goal role in (5.1b).

In a double object construction of a language for which (5.7) holds, the main verb must assign the semantic role to the argument that does not bear the theme/patient role and not to the theme/patient argument. If the verb did assign the theme/patient role to an argument, the other argument would not receive its semantic role. It could not receive its role from the verb, since, by (5.7a), the verb assigns only one role. It could not receive its role from an affix on the verb since, by (5.7b), the verb is underived (bears no affix). And it could not receive its role from its surface structure position because it is expressed as objects usually are and, by (5.7c), the usual expression of objects does not assign the role it bears.

So the verb must assign a role to the argument that does not bear the theme/patient role. If the verb assigns this role, from (5.7a) it follows that it cannot also assign the theme/patient role. So the usual surface structure expression of objects in the language must assign the theme/patient role. Thus my theory predicts a lexical entry like (5.8) for the main verb of a double object construction in a language meeting the stated conditions.

(5.8)
'verb' (theme/patient, *semantic role*)

If the verb in (5.8) is active ([+log sub], [+transitive]), the italicized semantic role in (5.8) will, by the usual reasoning from principle M, be borne by the s structure OBJ. If the verb is passive ([−log sub], [−transitive]), the italicized semantic role will be borne by the SUB. Since the theme/patient role is not assigned by the verb in (5.8), its bearer is an indirect semantic argument and will not correspond to the OBJ or SUB of the verb (see section 2.2.3.2). Thus the constituent bearing the theme/patient role should never exhibit direct object or subject properties.

The prediction that the present theory makes about double object constructions is confirmed in a variety of languages. Two clear examples illustrate the prediction, one from Chi-Mwi:ni (Kisseberth and Abasheikh 1977) and one from Yindjibarndi (Wordick 1979).[2]

Chi-Mwi:ni, sometimes considered a dialect of Swahili, is a Bantu language spoken in the city of Brava in Somalia. The basic structure of a Chi-Mwi:ni sentence may be represented as in (5.9), where the first NP is the subject of the sentence.

(5.9)
$_S$[(NP) $_{VP}$[V (NP) (NP) (PP*)]]

The NPs in (5.9) appear entirely without overt case marking. The verb contains an obligatory subject prefix (SP) indicating the noun class of the subject NP (noun classes—"multiple genders"—are a characteristic feature of Bantu languages). An object prefix (OP) indicating the noun class of one of the postverbal NPs optionally follows the SP within the verb. (I will return to the question of which postverbal NP controls the OP in the verb.) A partial representation of the internal structure of the Chi-Mwi:ni verb is given in (5.10).

(5.10)
$_V[SP-(OP)-V_{ROOT} \ldots]$

Sentence (5.11) is a typical Chi-Mwi:ni double object sentence headed by an underived verb. The OP in (5.11) agrees with the goal, *chiga:ri* 'cart.'

(5.11)
Ałi 0-(sh)-pashiłe chiga:ri o:liyo.
Ali SP-(OP)-applied cart oil
'Ali applied oil to the cart.'

The present theory predicts that in a sentence like (5.11) only the non-theme, *chiga:ri* 'cart,' and not the theme, *o:liyo* 'oil,' can be the logical object of the verb. As expected, if the verb in (5.11) is passivized, only the goal may serve as the subject of the passive verb.

(5.12)
a. Chiga:ri sh-pashila o:liyo.
    cart SP-applyPASS oil
    'The cart was oiled.'

b. *O:liyo i-pashila chiga:ri.
    oil SP-applyPASS cart
    'Oil was applied to the cart.'

There is every reason to believe that the OP in a Chi-Mwi:ni sentence agrees with the OBJ of a transitive verb and only with the object. In general, an argument that controls the OP on an active verb and only such argument may be the subject of the verb's passive counterpart. As expected, only the goal, *chiga:ri* 'cart' in sentence (5.11), may control the OP on the verb.

An interesting feature of Chi-Mwi:ni double object sentences in contrast to their English counterparts is that the order of the postverbal NPs is not fixed. In double object sentences headed by an underived verb, if one postverbal argument is animate and the other inanimate, the animate argument usually precedes the inanimate. When both are inanimate, however, the order of arguments after the verb is free. Thus sentence (5.13) is synonymous with (5.11).

(5.13)
Ałi Ø-(sh)-pashiłe o:liyo chiga:ri.
Ali SP-(OP)-applied oil cart
'Ali applied oil to the cart.'

The OP on the verb in (5.13), like that in (5.11), must agree with the goal, not the theme. And, of course, only (5.12a), not (5.12b), is grammatical as the passive counterpart to (5.13). Neither (5.11) nor (5.13) is marked in any way, according to Kisseberth and Abasheikh; both sentences receive normal intonation and neither has a topicalized reading.

The fact is that only one of the postverbal NPs in a Chi-Mwi:ni double object construction headed by an underived verb exhibits object behavior—controls the OP on the verb and corresponds to the SUB of the passive of the verb. Moreover, word order in general does not indicate which NP it will be. The only way to distinguish the postverbal NPs in sentences like (5.11) and (5.13) is on the basis of the semantic roles that they bear, and the theory I have outlined correctly predicts which NP is the OBJ on this basis.[3]

Unlike most of its neighbors in Australia, Yindjibarndi, a native Australian language described by Wordick (1979), is transparently nominative-accusative (see chapter 6 on nominative-accusative vs. ergative languages). The subjects of transitive and intransitive sentences alike fall into the nominative case (i.e., are unmarked for case), and the object of a transitive verb falls into the objective (accusative) case. Yindjibarndi word order is as free as that in Warlpiri (see Nash 1980), with any ordering of at least the major constituents of a simple sentence being equally acceptable and unmarked.

According to Wordick,

To derive a passive in Yindjibarndi, one takes the subject of the sentence, which is in the nominative case, and puts it into the instrumental case. The object of the verb, which is usually in the objective case, goes into the nominative case. Finally, a special intransitive verbalizer *-nguli-* is attached to the stem of the transitive verb, which is then reinflected. (Wordick 1979)

(5.14)
a. Ngaarta thuwayina pattyarriu.
   man spear-PAST euro-OBJ
   'The man speared the euro.'

b. Ngaartalu thuwayingulinha pattyarri.
   man-INST spear-PASS-PAST euro
   'The euro got speared by the man.'

Passivization, Wordick makes clear, applies to any transitive verb, by which he means a verb taking an argument in the objective case, regardless of the semantic role borne by the verb's object. For example, the verb meaning 'to go up' in Yindjibarndi puts its locative argument in the objective case and thus will passivize.

(5.15)
a. Ngayi karpayi purpaau.
   I go up rise-OBJ
   'I will go up the rise.'
b. Ngayhulu kapangulii purpaa.
   me-INST go up-PASS rise
   'The rise will be gone up by me.'

Although apparently any transitive verb will passivize in Yindjibarndi, "intransitive verbs will definitely not undergo the passive transformation" (Wordick 1979). From the data that Wordick provides, one may conclude that the Yindjibarndi passive morpheme, *-nguli-*, has the same features as the English passive morpheme, *-en* — [−log sub], [−transitive]. The [−transitive] feature carried by a passive affix prevents it from attaching to [−transitive] roots.

The Yindjibarndi verb meaning 'give' appears in double object constructions, with both its goal and theme arguments in the objective case.

(5.16)
Ngaarta yungkunha ngayu murlayi.
man give-PAST me-OBJ meat-OBJ
'The man gave me the meat.'

The ordering of the agent, theme, and goal in a sentence like (5.16) is completely free. But, "when a verb has two objects, a direct [theme] and an indirect one [goal], . . . only the indirect object can be shifted into the nominative case [in passives]. The direct object must remain in the objective case" (Wordick 1979).

(5.17)

a. Ngayi yungkungulinha murlayi ngaartaly.
    I give-PASS-PAST meat-OBJ man-INST
    'I was given the meat by the man.'

b. *Murla yungkungulinha ngayu ngaartalu.
    meat give-PASS-PAST me-OBJ man-INST
    'The meat was given me by the man.'

Since the OBJ of an active transitive verb corresponds to the SUB of its passive intransitive form, the sentences in (5.17) indicate that only the goal argument in Yindjibarndi double object constructions is an OBJ, as predicted by the theory. Again, word order and case marking cannot determine which NP in sentences like (5.16) is the OBJ; the theme and goal arguments in such sentences are indistinguishable by any criterion except that of which semantic roles they bear. And the theory tells us which argument must be the OBJ on the basis of their semantic roles.[4]

5.1.2. Dative Shift with Benefactives

Consider now the alternation illustrated in (5.2), which involves a benefactive NP. Within the present theory, the required analysis of the benefactive alternation in (5.2) is essentially the same as that described for the dative shift alternation in (5.1). The main difference between the alternations lies in the fact that, although *give* and related verbs (*hand, throw*, etc.) may be argued to include a slot for a goal argument in their P-A structures, there is little reason to believe that a benefactive slot appears in the P-A structures of verbs like *bake*. The activity of baking does not seem to imply a benefactive any more than any other creative activity does. If *bake* does not include the benefactive within its P-A structure, its lexical entry will contain the information in (5.18).

(5.18)

bake, V, 'bake' (*patient*), [+log sub], [+transitive]

Since the structural position [NP, VP] cannot be expected to assign the benefactive role in (5.2b) and since no affix appears on *bake* in this sentence to assign this role, *bake* itself must assign the benefactive role to *Hortense*. Because English verbs assign only one role in the unmarked case and *bake* assigns the benefactive role in (5.2b), the verb cannot also assign the patient role in this sentence. But, the structural position [NP, VP], the canonical expression of patients in English, may assign the patient role to *cake* in the double object construction (5.2b).

Although sentences (5.2) share propositional content, (5.2a) contains an argument taking constituent not found in (5.2b), the preposition *for*. There is no reason to believe that the *bake* in (5.2a) has a different P-A structure from the *bake* in (5.2b), yet (5.2b) includes a benefactive argument without a benefactive argument taking item. To account for the shared propositional content between (5.2a) and (5.2b), the argument structure of the preposition *for* may be embedded within the lexical entry of the *bake* in (5.2b), creating lexical entry (5.19).

(5.19)
bake, V, ('bake' (patient) 'for' (*benefactive*))

The parentheses around the P-A structure 'bake' and the modifier-argument structure 'for' are meant to indicate that *bake* applies the modifiers that the 'for' function produces to the predicates that the 'bake' function produces to yield new predicates. Note that (5.19) embeds the P-A structure in (5.18), thereby satisfying the natural principle that related verbs will share P-A structures, all other things being equal.

Just as was the case with the dative shift alternation in (5.1), the benefactive alternation (5.2) results from an alternation in which of two semantic roles a verb assigns. When the verb assigns the patient role, as in (5.2a), the preposition *for* must be used to assign the benefactive role. When the verb assigns the benefactive role, as in (5.2b), the structural position [NP, VP] assigns the patient role. So the benefactive, *Hortense,* in (5.2b) must be the OBJ of *bake* while the patient NP, *a cake,* is merely an indirect syntactic argument of the verb.

5.1.3. The Status of the Dative Shift Alternations
I have claimed that verbs like *give* and *bake* have two related lexical entries that differ essentially in which semantic role the verb assigns. The question arises of what, if anything, connects lexical entry (5.5) with lexical entry (5.6), or lexical entry (5.18) with lexical entry (5.19), other than the fact that the entries share P-A structures and all phonological features. Recall that affixation may not change a verb's semantic role assigning properties; affixation affects a root only through the mechanism of feature percolation. Thus, while an affix may itself assign a semantic role, or not, it cannot stop a root from assigning a role or add a semantic role assigning feature directly to a root. If an item assigns a semantic role, it will be an independent semantic role assigning

constituent at l-s structure regardless of the affixes that might be attached to it. Therefore, the dative shift alternations in (5.1) and (5.2) cannot be mediated by a lexical rule in the narrow sense of an affixation or word formation process.

In fact, no overt morphological affix mediates the dative shift alternations in English (and no overt affix appears in the Chi-Mwi:ni and Yindjibarndi double object constructions). Although the theory prohibits relating (5.5) to (5.6) or (5.18) to (5.19) via affixation, clearly the relations between these entries generalize to more than one or two verbs. Speakers know some relation exists between (5.5) and (5.6) and between (5.18) and (5.19) and are able to extend these relations to other verbs. One may suppose that speakers generalize the relations indicated in (5.20) by analogy to verbs similar to *give* and *bake*.

(5.20)
a. *give,* 'give' (*theme,* goal) ~ 'give' (theme, *goal*)
b. *bake,* 'bake' (*patient*) ~ ('bake' (patient) 'for' (*benefactive*))

Although one might argue that I am begging the question as to the nature of the dative shift alternations by making a vague reference to generalization by analogy, I think the evidence strongly suggests that the alternations in (5.20) are extended to new verbs in a manner best described as analogical extension. In the analogical extension of the relation A:B, one takes a C similar to A or B in features relevant to the relation and solves for X in A:B as C:X, or A:B as X:C. One may suppose that speakers are extremely conservative in their generalizations by analogy (see Baker 1979), requiring their C's to share most syntactic and semantic features with A or B. The closer the semantics of a verb to that of the canonical verbs exhibiting an alternation like those in (5.20), the more likely it is that a speaker will extend the alternation to that verb. Despite notorious examples of verbs taking theme and goal arguments that, for most speakers, do not allow dative shift (*donate* is the most widely quoted example), any verb that, like *hand,* means to direct something with a body part will exhibit the dative shift alternation. Speakers might find the sentence, *Elmer donated the library several books on porcupines,* ungrammatical, but as soon as they accept the verb *to shin,* meaning 'to kick with the shin,' they will allow *Elmer shinned me the ball during soccer practice.* Similarly, any verb meaning 'to create a food item in some specific manner' will exhibit the alternation in (5.20b). A speaker who accepts *He microwaved a potato for me* will allow *He microwaved me a potato in two seconds flat.*

Although the theory has nothing to say about the possibility of generalizing by analogy an alternation like those shown in (5.20) once it is recognized as an alternation by a speaker, the theory does set severe limits on the generalization of the particular alternations in (5.20). Recall that the theme role in (5.1b) and the patient role in (5.2b) are assigned by the structural position [NP, VP]. Recall also that "theme" and "patient" are really names for classes of semantic roles and that items assign specific semantic roles, not classes of roles. If the structural position [NP, VP] assigns the theme role that *give* also may assign, this is a particular theme role, one that may be associated only with a small set of verbs, perhaps only those that describe a transference of possession. Similarly, the patient role assigned by [NP, VP] is that associated with *bake* and is probably limited to verbs of creation. An English verb may appear in a dative shifted construction like (5.1b) and (5.2b) only if the role that it assigns in the nonshifted constructions like (5.1a) and (5.2a) may be assigned by [NP, VP]. Since morphologically unmarked alternations like those in (5.20) do not involve the addition of a semantic role assigner to the verb, the class of verbs to which the alternations may extend is limited by the range of roles that the structural position [NP, VP] assigns.

On the other hand, alternations in other languages superficially similar to (5.1) and (5.2) that do involve the addition of a morpheme to a verb should extend to most verbs in the languages. Consider the Chichewa benefactive construction illustrated in (5.3) at the beginning of this section. As will be explained in chapter 7, the "applied" affix, *-ir-*, in (5.3b) assigns the benefactive role and carries the argument structure of English *for*. Consequently, the verb in (5.3b) is free to assign the same role that it assigns in (5.3a) and may be given precisely the same P-A structure as the verb in (5.3a). As shown in chapter 7, one may attribute to the applied affix *-ir-* all the features necessary to account for the syntax of the derived verb in (5.3b), assuming that the affix merely attaches to the verb that appears in (5.3a). Since it does not rely on a structural position or on case marking to assign a role usually assigned by a verb, the Chichewa benefactive construction in (5.3b), unlike the English benefactive construction in (5.2b), should be extended to verbs regardless of the roles that they assign in their underived form. Affixation alone accounts for the Chichewa benefactive construction; no generalization by analogy is required to extend it to a new verb. In fact, benefactive alternations like the Chichewa, which are mediated by affixation, extend to a great many more verbs than benefactive alternations like the English, which involve no addition of morphemes.

In the case of an alternation like the dative shift alternation in English, one must ask which verbs may exhibit it. The expectation for any given verb is that it will not show the alternation. A verb that does in fact participate must be seen as closely similar to the canonical verbs that do. In the case of the applied verb constructions, one must ask which verbs do not exhibit the alternation. The expectation for a verb is that it will show the alternation. If it does not, there should be some reason why not. For example, the verb may not be compatible with a benefactive reading.

5.2. Alternations in Argument Structures

Having analyzed alternations in the expression of a verb's semantic dependents that involve alternations in a verb's semantic role assigning features, I now turn to alternations that seem to implicate changes in the verb's argument structure. Examples of the sorts of alternation to be considered are found in (5.21)–(5.23).

(5.21)
a. Elmer broke the porcupine cage.
b. The porcupine cage broke.

(5.22)
a. Elmer hung the porcupine cage in the window.
b. The porcupine cage hung in the window.

(5.23)
a. Elmer ate mock porcupine pie late last night.
b. Elmer ate late last night.

Sentences (5.21b) and (5.22b) display two sorts of anticausatives—the inchoative in (5.21b) and the stative in (5.22b). Sentence (5.23b) exemplifies what is sometimes called indefinite object deletion. I treat anticausatives in 5.2.1 and indefinite object deletion constructions in 5.2.2.

5.2.1. Anticausatives
Consider sentences (5.21)–(5.22). In the (a) sentences, *Elmer* is a sort of causer; in (5.21a) he causes the porcupine cage to break and in (5.22a) he causes the cage to hang in the window. Unlike the (a) sentences, the (b) sentences hold no causative implications; (5.21b) does

not imply that someone broke the porcupine cage, nor does (5.22b) imply that someone hung the cage in the window. Compare sentences (5.21b) and (5.22b) with the passives in (5.24), where the passive participles are intended to have their verbal, rather than their adjectival (stative), interpretations.

(5.24)
a. The porcupine cage was broken.
b. The porcupine cage was hung in the window.

In contrast to (5.21b) and (5.22b), sentence (5.24a) does imply that someone or something broke the cage, sentence (5.24b) that someone or something hung the cage in the window. The predicates that *break* and *hang* produce in (5.21a), (5.22a) and (5.24) must assign causer roles. Because no causers or causation are implied by (5.21b) and (5.22b), *break* and *hang* must not yield causer assigning predicates in these sentences.

One may suppose that the lexical entries for *break* and *hang* in (5.21a) and (5.22a) contain the information in (5.25a) and (5.25b) respectively.

(5.25)
a. 'break 1' (*patient*), [+log sub], [+transitive]
b. 'hang 1' (*theme*), [+log sub], [+transitive]

Since English generally has verbs assign theme/patient roles, it is reasonable to assume that the lexical entries of *break* and *hang* in (5.21b) and (5.22b) contain the information in (5.26).[5]

(5.26)
a. 'break 2' (*patient*), [−log sub], [−transitive]
b. 'hang 2' (*theme*), [−log sub], [−transitive]

The argument structures in (5.25) and (5.26) differ crucially in that the predicates produced by the P-A structures in (5.25) assign causer roles whereas the predicates produced by the P-A structures in (5.26) assign no roles at all.[6] Inasmuch as affixes do not affect the argument structures of roots to which they attach, no affixation process could relate the verb in (5.25a) to that in (5.26a) or the verb in (5.25b) to that in (5.26b). Nevertheless, the *break* in (5.25a) is clearly related to the *break* in (5.26a), the *hang* in (5.25b) to the *hang* in (5.26b). How should these relations be expressed in the lexicon?

In the lexical entry of each verb exhibiting the anticausative alternation I assume that there are two subentries, one for the transitive alternate, one for the anticausative. An example entry is shown in (5.27).

(5.27)

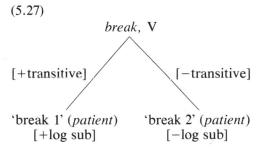

'break 1' (*patient*)   'break 2' (*patient*)
  [+log sub]   [−log sub]

The semantic relation between the transitive (V1) and the anticausative (V2) P-A structures within the lexical entry of a verb exhibiting the anticausative alternation is informally stated in (5.28). The biconditional in (5.28) is inadequate as a characterization of the semantics of the transitive verb because it does not capture the direct causative implications of the transitive alternate in an anticausative alternation (see Shibatani 1976b for a discussion of types of causation). The periphrastic "cause to V" incorrectly implies indirect causation.

(5.28)
Anticausative alternation:
for V1 = transitive alternate and V2 = anticausative, X V1 Y iff X cause Y to V2

If V2 is a stative verb, like *hang,* V2 is known as the stative of V. If V2 is a punctual verb, like *break,* V2 is known as the inchoative of V (see Bresnan 1980). In some manner speakers of English extend the branching lexical entry of verbs like *break* and *hang* to verbs that they consider similar in semantics to these verbs. As with the dative shift alternations, analogical generalization, although imprecisely characterized here, seems a reasonable mechanism for the extension of the anticausative alternation.

Since the present theory prohibits affixation alone from mediating the anticausative alternation, one expects differences between the anticausative alternation and alternations associated with productive affixation processes. Unlike passivization, for example, the anticausative alternation is limited cross-linguistically to a restricted class of verbs with some semantic coherence. Furthermore, the core members of this class are synonymous from language to language. That is, the verbs meaning 'break,' 'hang,' 'open,' and 'close,' for example, are more likely than not to exhibit the alternation in any given language. If the anticausative alternation is generalized by analogy from a few core examples, as hypothesized, and not created by a productive lexical rule, as prohibited by the theory, one would expect the alternation to be restricted to a semantically coherent class of verbs.

Consistent with the present theory is the fact that the anticausative alternation is never mediated by an anticausative morpheme. That is not to say that an affix does not appear on either the transitive or anticausative alternate in any language; many languages (e.g., French, Russian, Dyirbal) take the transitive alternate as morphologically simple and place an affix on the anticausative alternate, while some languages (e.g., Japanese,[7] Navajo) take the anticausative as morphologically simple and place an affix on the transitive alternate. Nevertheless, the affix that appears on one or the other alternate of the verbs participating in the anticausative alternation is not limited to the anticausative alternation in a language and therefore should not be considered an anticausative affix. Rather, the affix may be seen as carrying the features [−log sub] or [−transitive] or both when it appears on the anticausative alternate, or the feature [+transitive] when it appears on the transitive alternate, because the affix carries these features in unrelated constructions in the language.

If anticausativization were an affixation process similar, say, to passivization, one would expect most verbs with causative meaning in a language to exhibit the anticausative alternation and one would expect at least some languages to employ a special affix specific to the alternation. In addition, one would expect that if languages used an overt affix to signal the alternation, this affix would always be attached to the same form cross-linguistically, always to the [+transitive] or to the [−transitive] alternate. Since anticausativization is never productive and never mediated by an alternation-specific affix, a theory of grammar should not treat anticausativization as an affixation process. A theory, like the theory of this book, that rules out an analysis of anticausativization as an affixation process derives support from the behavior of anticausative alternations cross-linguistically.

Although no language I have examined employs an anticausative morpheme to mediate the anticausative alternation, languages do exploit a variety of devices, including affixation, to distinguish the [+transitive] alternate from the [−transitive] alternate in a lexical entry like (5.27). Some languages simply use the unmarked transitive form of a verb for the transitive alternate and the unmarked intransitive form for the anticausative alternate. English is an example of such a language in which the unmarked transitive and intransitive forms of a verb are homophonous.

(5.29)

a. inchoative: *break*
   Elmer broke the porcupine cage.
   The porcupine cage broke.

b. stative: *hang*
   Elmer hung the porcupine cage in the window.
   The porcupine cage hung in the window.

In some Eskimo languages a canonical transitive verb agrees with both the subject and object of a sentence, a canonical intransitive verb with the subject alone. The transitive conjugation of verbs like 'break' and 'lose' is used for the transitive member of the anticausative alternation, the intransitive conjugation for the anticausative alternate. The data in (5.30) are from Alaskan Yup'ik (see Reed et al. 1977).

(5.30)

a. inchoative: *kuve-* 'spill'
   Kuv'uq. 'It spills'
   spill-3sg
   Kuvaa. 'He spills it.'
   spill-3sg3sg

b. stative: *tamar-* 'lose'
   Tamartuq. 'It is lost.'
   lose-3sg
   Tamaraa. 'He loses it.'
   lose-3sg3sg

The unmarked intransitive form of verbs exhibiting the anticausative alternation is used for the anticausative alternate in the Eskimo dialects, like Alaskan Yup'ik, in which the intransitive form of a transitive verb usually agrees with the agent argument, not the patient or theme as in (5.30). A paradigm transitive-intransitive pair from Yup'ik is illustrated in (5.31).

(5.31)
amar- 'backpack'
Amartuq. 'He backpacks (something).'
backpack-3sg
Amaraa. 'He backpacks it.'
backpack-3sg3sg

Note that the intransitive verb in (5.31) agrees with the agent while the intransitives in (5.30) agree with the patient or theme. It seems that, if a language has some general means to mark the intransitive counterpart of a transitive verb, the anticausative alternate will be marked by these means regardless of the canonical use for the intransitive forms in the language. The notation in (5.27) is an attempt to capture this generalization by making the transitive and anticausative alternates in an anticausative alternation the transitive and intransitive versions of a single verb. Intransitive morphology leads to the [−transitive] branch of lexical entries like (5.27), transitive morphology to the [+transitive] branch.

In many languages, a marked intransitive form of the verb, usually the passive and/or reflexive form, is used for the anticausative alternate in an anticausative alternation. Examples from Russian, French, and Albanian are found in (5.32)–(5.34). In all these languages, reflexive morphology marks the anticausative. As described in chapter 4, the Albanian reflexive and passive forms are homophonous. Many Russian and French reflexive forms also have passive interpretations.

(5.32)
Russian: a. inchoative: *otkryt'* 'open'
                Boris otkryl dver'.
                Boris open-PAST door
                'Boris opened the door.'
                Dver' otkryls'a.
                door open-PAST-REFL
                'The door opened.'

             b. stative: *naxodit'* 'find'
                Oni nashli shkolu v gorode.
                they found school-ACC in city
                'They found the school in the city.'
                Shkola naxodits'a v gorode.
                school-NOM find-REFL in city
                'The school is located in the city.'

(5.33)

French: a. inchoative: *casser* 'break'
                 Jean a cassé le verre.
                 'John broke the glass.'
                 Le verre s'est cassé.
                 the glass REFL'PAST break
                 'The glass broke.'

                 b. stative: *trouver* 'find'
                 Jean a trouvé l'école dans la cité.
                 'John found the school in the city.'
                 L'école se trouve dans la cité.
                 the school REFL find in the city
                 'The school is located in the city.'

(5.34)

Albanian: a. inchoative
                 Dega u thye gjatë stuhisë.
                 branch the breakREFL-3sg during storm-the
                 'The branch broke during the storm.'

                 b. stative
                 Mollat varen në permët.
                 apple-the hangREFL-3sg on trees-the
                 'The apples hang on the trees.'

The reflexive and/or passive morphology on the anticausative verbs in French, Russian, Albanian, and other languages may be seen as carrying the features [−log sub], [−transitive]—features the morphology carries in its reflexive and/or passive use.

   Like Albanian (see chapter 4), Dyirbal, an Australian language described by Dixon (1972), uses the reflexive verb as a sort of passive (see section 6.3 for a detailed analysis of this "false reflexive" construction). Unlike Albanian, the subject of the Dyirbal reflexive verb in its passive use is the agent of the transitive root, not the patient or theme.

(5.35)

a. bala yugu baŋgul yaṛaŋgu buyban.
   stick-ABS man-ERG hides
   'Man hides stick.'

b. bayi yaṛa buybayiriɲu.
   man-ABS hides-REFL
   'Man hides himself' or 'Man hides (something).'

There is a dialect of Dyirbal called *Dyalŋuy*, or the "mother-in-law language," which is spoken in the presence of certain taboo relatives. This mother-in-law dialect has a much smaller vocabulary than the everyday language. In particular, where the everyday language contains morphologically unrelated verbs for members of certain transitive-anticausative pairs, the mother-in-law language takes the transitive verb as morphologically simple and forms the anticausative through affixation of the reflexive morpheme onto the transitive root. Transitive-anticausative pairs from the mother-in-law language are illustrated in (5.36).

(5.36)
dindan 'stand up'
a. balan bangul dindan.
   she-ABS he-ERG stands up
   'He stands her up.'

b. balan dindariɲu.
   she-ABS stand up-REFL
   'She rises.'

yilwun 'take out'
a. balan bangul yilwun.
   she-ABS he-ERG takes out
   'He takes her out.'

b. balan yilwuriɲu.
   she-ABS come out-REFL
   'She comes out.'

Compare the use of the reflexive forms for anticausatives in (5.36) with the productive use of the reflexive to allow the suppression of the theme/patient argument of a verb, as illustrated in sentences (5.37), also from the mother-in-law language. (In chapter 6 I explain why the (b) forms in (5.37) are actually passives.)

(5.37)
wuyuban 'talk'
a. balan bangul wuyuban.
   she-ABS he-ERG tells
   'He tells her.'

b. bayi wuyubarinu.
   he-ABS talks-REFL
   'He talks.'

gaɲɖaman 'follow'

a. balan bangul gaɲɖaman.
    she-ABS he-ERG follows
    'He follows her.'

b. bayi gaɲɖamariɲu.
    he-ABS follows-REFL
    'He follows (someone or something).'

What is striking about the use of the reflexive morpheme in the Dyirbal mother-in-law language to mark the anticausative is that the reflexive form, when not a true reflexive, is regularly employed when the agent of a transitive verb is the subject of the derived intransitive verb—see (5.37). In the anticausative, the theme/patient is the subject of the morphologically derived intransitive—see (5.36).

The widespread use of some [−transitive] or [−log sub], [−transitive] affix to mark the anticausative member of an anticausative alternation suggests a principle to the effect that, given a branching lexical entry like (5.27) with [alpha F] and [−alpha F] branches, attaching an [alpha F] affix to the alternate on the [−alpha F] branch yields the alternate on the [alpha F] branch and not the form expected from the productive use of the affix. For example, adding the reflexive *-s'a* affix to a Russian verb like *otkryt'* 'open' produces not a reflexive verb but rather the anticausative (i.e., [−transitive]) alternate in a branching lexical entry like (5.38), which appears in (5.32a).

(5.38)

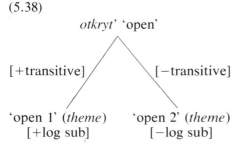

The reflexive affix carries the features [−log sub], [−transitive] and so leads down the right branch in entry (5.38).

If the anticausative alternation is truly best represented by branching lexical entries like (5.38), with affixation in such alternations, when present, merely choosing one branch in the lexical entry over the other, then one might expect some languages to take the [−transitive] or anticausative alternate as morphologically basic and add a [+transitive] affix to this form to yield the verb on the [+transitive] branch of an entry like (5.38). Since both transitive and anticausative alternates are basic (underived) verbs, it should be arbitrary which is chosen as morphologically basic. Although most of the languages I have examined take the transitive form in an anticausative alternation as morphologically basic, according to Miyagawa (1980) Japanese and Navajo take the other option, marking the transitive alternate with a [+transitive] morpheme. The reader is referred to Miyagawa (1980) for an extensive discussion of languages in which a [+transitive] morpheme is used to signal the [+transitive] member of an anticausative alternation. Here I will quickly review some of the relevant facts from Japanese.

Japanese includes a causative affix *-sas,* which Miyagawa argues must be distinguished from the causative *-sase* to be discussed in chapter 7. When *-sas* attaches to certain intransitive verbs (such as *odorok* 'be surprised'), the result is not a causative verb that one could paraphrase as 'cause to V' (e.g., 'cause to be surprised') but rather the transitive member of an anticausative alternation—for example, the direct causative *odorak-as* 'surprise' shown in (5.39a).

(5.39)
a. Eigo kantoku ga zyoyuu o odorok-asi-ta.
   director NOM actress ACC surprise-CAUSE-PAST
   'The movie director surprised the actress.'

b. Eigo kantoku ga zyoyuu o odorok-ase-ta.
   director NOM actress ACC surprise-CAUSE-PAST
   'The movie director made the actress be surprised (at something).'

Compare the verb *odorok-as* 'surprise-CAUSE' in (5.39a), formed with the causative *-sas,* to the derived causative *odorok-ase* in (5.39b), formed with *-sase.* Only the latter has the predictable semantics of a derived causative in Japanese.

When the probable transitive counterpart of an intransitive anticausative verb exists as a morphologically unrelated morpheme in Japanese, the addition of *-sas* to this verb produces a normal derived causative with predictable semantics. For example, intransitive *agar* 'rise' corresponds to morphologically unrelated *age* 'raise.' Adding *-sas* to *agar* 'rise' produces the derived causative *agar-as* 'cause to rise' in (5.40). Since the transitive *age* 'raise' exists independently in the language, *agar-as* will not mean 'raise.'

(5.40)

Taroo ga Hanako o butai agar-asi-ta.

'Taro made Hanako rise (get) on stage.'

The causative affix is [+transitive] cross-linguistically. In (5.40), for example, -*sas* creates a transitive verb, *agar-as* 'cause to rise,' from intransitive *agar* 'rise.' In (5.41) I give the lexical entry for the anticausative pair, *odorok, odorok-as* 'surprise.'

(5.41)

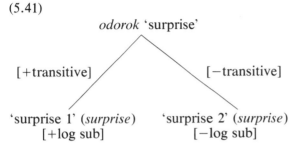

odorok 'surprise'

[+transitive]   [−transitive]

'surprise 1' (*surprise*)   'surprise 2' (*surprise*)
   [+log sub]   [−log sub]

The affixation of the [+transitive] -*sas* to [−transitive] *odorok* yields the verb on the [+transitive] branch inside the branching entry (5.41) rather than the derived causative, 'cause to be surprised.' This behavior of -*sas* accords with the previously suggested principle that might govern the effects of adding an [alpha F] morpheme to a verb whose lexical entry contains [alpha F] and [−alpha F] branches.

Since the theory prohibits deriving either verb in an anticausative alternation from the other, the present analysis of the anticausative alternation demands that both the transitive and anticausative alternates be basic verbs with basic P-A structures. Whatever requirements a language places on the construction of the P-A structures of basic verbs should thus apply to the P-A structures of both alternates. For example, if a language includes a generalization to the effect that patient and theme arguments serve as input to P-A structures, then the anticausative verbs should have unaccusative P-A structures (see sections 2.1.2 and 4.1.3), such that the patient/theme arguments appear within the P-A structure and the predicates produced by the P-A structure assign no semantic roles—see (5.42).

(5.42)

anticausative *break*: 'break' (*patient*) [−log sub], [−transitive]

We saw in section 4.1.3 that impersonal passivization (or any passivization) will not apply to unaccusative verbs. The passive affix carries the feature [−log sub], as does an unaccusative verb. The NVAP (4.9) prevents an affix like the passive morpheme with a [−log sub] feature from attaching to a [−log sub] root, thereby ruling out the (impersonal) passivization of unaccusative verbs. In languages like Dutch (see Perlmutter 1978b) anticausative verbs do not undergo impersonal passivization, confirming the hypothesis that they have P-A structures similar to that given for *break* in (5.42): unaccusative P-A structures.

Suppose a language has no basic unaccusative verbs; that is, suppose the language demands that the predicates that a basic P-A structure produces assign a semantic role, if possible, in the unmarked case. Since anticausatives must be underived verbs in the present theory, I predict that anticausatives will not be unaccusatives in such a language, and thus should undergo impersonal passivization. Arguing against the 1-Advancement Exclusiveness Law of Relational Grammar, Ostler (1979) demonstrates that most Sanskrit intransitive verbs, including anticausatives, can undergo impersonal passivization. Ostler's evidence suggests that there are no basic unaccusative verbs in Sanskrit. If most intransitive verbs are [+log sub] in Sanskrit, the passive morpheme will be able to attach to them (see section 4.1.3). The hypothesis that Sanskrit demands basic verbs to be [+log sub], if possible, taken with the consequence of the present theory that anticausative verbs must be underived, makes the correct prediction about an interesting set of Sanskrit facts reported by Ostler (1979).

The displaced subject (*by* object) of a Sanskrit passive, be it personal (5.43b) or impersonal (5.43d), appears in the instrumental case.

(5.43)
a. caitrah kusu-lam abhinat.
    Chaitra-NOM grain holder-ACC broke-3sg
    'Chaitra broke the grain holder.'

b. caitrena kusu-lo 'bhidyata.
    Chaitra-INST grain holder-NOM break-PASS-PAST
    'The grain holder was broken by Chaitra.'

c. aham a-se.
    I-NOM sit-1sg
    'I sit.'

d. maya- a-syate.
    I-INST sit-PASS
    'It is sat by me.'

Sanskrit uses passive morphology to mark the anticausative member of an anticausative alternation, as in (5.44), which should be compared to (5.43b).

(5.44)
(svayameva) kusu-lo 'bhidyata.
(of-itself) grain holder-NOM break-PASS-PAST
'The grain holder broke (of its own accord).'

In this anticausative use, *abhidyata* 'break-PASS-PAST' is incompatible with an instrumental agent phrase.

Since, ex hypothesis, underived Sanskrit verbs are [+log sub], and since the anticausative must be underived in the present theory, the anticausative in (5.44) should be the [−transitive] branch of a lexical entry something like (5.45).

(5.45)

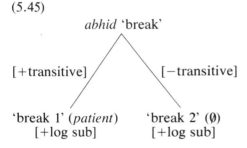

abhid 'break'

[+transitive]   [−transitive]

'break 1' (*patient*)   'break 2' (∅)
   [+log sub]   [+log sub]

Compare (5.45) with (5.38) from Russian and (5.41) from Japanese, languages in which basic verbs may be unaccusative.

Since it is [+log sub], nothing should prevent anticausative 'break,' the right branch in (5.45), from undergoing impersonal passivization in Sanskrit. In fact, there is every indication that it does.

(5.46)
(svayameva) kusu-lena abhidyata.
(of-itself) grain holder-INST break-PASS-PAST
'The grain holder broke of its own accord.'

Although only a single passive morpheme appears on the verb in (5.46), the instrumental case on 'grain holder' indicates that the verb is the (impersonal) passive version of the anticausative verb in (5.44); compare (5.46) with (5.43d). It is not uncommon for a language to use a single instance of a morpheme in situations in which the syntax calls for two. For example, Ostler (1979) notes that the causative formed from a derived causative verb in Sanskrit contains only a single causative morpheme and is thus homophonous with the simple derived causative verb, although the causative of a causative should contain two causative morphemes. Acting as the passive of the verb in (5.44), *abhidyata* in (5.46) should bear two passive morphemes, the second morpheme carrying the feature [−log sub]. The absence of a second passive morpheme, however, is not good evidence that the verb in (5.46) is not the passive of the verb in (5.44).

Now (5.44), without the material in parentheses, is ambiguous between the anticausative and the personal passive; it could also mean 'The grain holder was broken (by someone unspecified).' A derived personal passive is not, of course, a basic verb. The lexical entry of *passive* 'break' in Sanskrit is shown in (5.47).

(5.47)
abhidyata, V, 'break 1' (*patient*), [−log sub], [−transitive]

Compare (5.47) with the [−transitive] (anticausative) branch of entry (5.45). Unlike anticausative 'break,' passive 'break,' being [−log sub], should not undergo impersonal passivization (see section 4.1.3). Thus, although (5.44) is ambiguous between the passive of transitive 'break' and the anticausative, (5.46) should have only the reading of the impersonal passive of the anticausative, not that of the impersonal passive of the passive. This is precisely what Ostler reports: (5.46) is incompatible with an agent phrase and implies no breaker. So the 'break' in (5.46) must have the anticausative P-A structure 'break 2' in (5.45), not the transitive P-A structure 'break 1.' The Sanskrit data provide a clear contrast between alternations mediated by productive affixation processes, like the passive alternation, and alternations between basic verbs, like the anticausative alternation.

5.2.2. Indefinite Object Deletion
Consider now the alternation illustrated in (5.23). Some transitive verbs, like *eat,* appear freely without an object in English while others, like *lock,* do not.

(5.48)
a.   Elmer locked the porcupine cage late last night.
b.   *Elmer locked late last night.

It is an interesting and important problem to characterize the transitive verbs that permit indefinite object deletion—that may appear without an overt object, as in (5.23b)—but an investigation of this issue would lead beyond the central topics of this book (see Saksena 1980 for a possible solution). What is important to emphasize here about alternations like (5.23) is that the present theory prohibits a language from deriving the *eat* in (5.23b) from that in (5.23a), or the *eat* in (5.23a) from that in (5.23b), by simple affixation.

Suppose verbs like *eat* have branching lexical entries like that in (5.49).

(5.49)

$$
\begin{array}{ccc}
& eat\ \lfloor+\text{log sub}\rfloor & \\
& \diagup\ \diagdown & \\
[+\text{transitive}] & & [-\text{transitive}] \\
\diagup & & \diagdown \\
\text{'eat 1' } (patient) & & \text{'eat 2' } (\emptyset)
\end{array}
$$

The relation between 'eat 1' and 'eat 2' is informally stated in (5.50).

(5.50)
The indefinite object deletion alternation:
for V1 = transitive, V2 = intransitive, X V2 iff X V1 something unspecified

Since the relation between the verbs on the two branches in (5.49) involves a change in P-A structure and in semantic role assigning features, the relation could not be mediated by affixation alone in the present theory.[8]

As was the case with the anticausative alternation, the indefinite object deletion (or iod) alternation illustrated in (5.48) clearly differs from alternations like the passive that are mediated by a productive affixation process. The iod alternation is limited to a restricted set of verbs cross-linguistically, and the iod set in a given language seems to have some semantic coherence. The translations of the verbs in the iod set from one language are quite likely to fall into the iod set for another. The core verbs that exhibit the iod alternation in language after language are the so-called ingestives, for example, 'eat,' 'drink,' and 'learn.' The restriction of the iod alternation to a limited set of verbs with semantic coherence is what one expects if, as demanded by the present theory, the alternation is created not by a productive lexical rule but by generalization by analogy with certain core verbs exhibiting the alternation.

In harmony with the impossibility of mediating the iod alternation with affixation alone in the present theory, no language I have encountered contains an indefinite object deleting suffix.[9] Many languages resemble English in employing the unmarked intransitive form of a verb for the indefinite object deleting alternate. In English, intransitive and transitive forms are homophonous. Eskimo transitive verbs agree with both subject and object while Eskimo intransitives agree with a single constituent. Eskimo dialects use the unmarked intransitive verb form for the indefinite object deleting alternate in an iod alternation. This generalization holds even in dialects like Greenlandic Eskimo in which the unmarked intransitive form of a transitive verb regularly agrees with the theme or patient of its transitive counterpart, not the agent.

Many basically transitive verbs [in Greenlandic], but by no means all, can be used directly as formal intransitives just by affixing intransitive agreement morphemes. In many cases where the English counterpart is an object-deleting verb, the Greenlandic intransitive thus formed has roughly the meaning of the corresponding English intransitive. The agent in such an intransitive construction is in the absolutive case, and the verb is marked for agreement with it. The patient, if it is expressed, is in the instrumental case, and is not cross-referenced on the verb. (Sadock 1980, pp. 304–305)

(5.51)
Neqi nerivara.
meat-ABS eat-INDIC-1sg3sg
'I ate the meat.'

(5.52)
Neqimik nerivunga.
meat-INST eat-INDIC-1sg
'I ate meat.'

. . . At least in the older language, other inherently transitive verbs acquired a passive sense when used with intransitive verb endings. The verb in such usages agrees only with the patient. (Sadock 1980, p. 305)

(5.53)
Piniartoq toquppaa.
hunter-ABS kill-INDIC-3sg3sg
'He killed the hunter.'

(5.54)
Piniartoq toquppoq.
hunter-ABS kill-INDIC-3sg
'The hunter was killed.'

As Sadock points out, the intransitive form of a Greenlandic transitive verb is usually the passive; it carries the feature [−log sub] as well as the feature [−transitive]. In the case of transitive verbs like 'eat,' however, the intransitive version is simply [−transitive], not [−log sub]. If a verb has a branching lexical entry like (5.49), then, it seems that the intransitive form of the verb will be simply the [−transitive] branch regardless of what usually occurs when the feature [−transitive] is added to a transitive verb in the language. This follows from the principle that, given a branching lexical entry like (5.49) with [alpha F] and [−alpha F] branches, attaching an [alpha F] affix to the alternate on the [−alpha F] branch yields the alternate on the [alpha F] branch and not the form expected from the productive use of the affix.[10]

Chapter 6
The Ergative Parameter

Within the present theory it is an arbitrary fact about English that verbs usually assign theme and patient roles whereas predicates assign agent roles (see section 2.1.2). Although, I have claimed, languages must include generalizations over classes of semantic roles as to which are assigned to P-A structure-internal arguments and which are assigned to logical subjects, a language may choose between the generalizations in (6.1a) and those in (6.1b) for verbs that are associated both with an agent and with a theme or patient.

(6.1)
a. agent roles   — assigned by predicates
   theme/patient roles — assigned by verbs
b. agent roles   — assigned by verbs
   theme/patient roles — assigned by predicates

Languages choosing the (a) generalizations are called nominative-accusative languages; languages choosing the (b) generalizations are called ergative.[1] At this point in the exposition of the present theory, it is possible to demonstrate that ergative languages, as just defined, exist. The theory predicts several crucial differences between nominative-accusative and ergative languages, some of which are readily tested with data available in the literature. On the basis of these predictions, one may tentatively conclude that Dyirbal, an Australian language discussed in Dixon 1972, and Central Arctic Eskimo (Johnson 1980) are truly ergative.

Before turning to Dyirbal and Eskimo, I should clear up some terminological confusions surrounding ergative languages. On the definitions just given, many of the languages called ergative in the literature turn out to be nominative-accusative. These languages distribute case marking in such a way that, for the most part, the correspondence between semantic roles and case marking matches that for a true ergative language. Table 6.1 indicates the correspondences among semantic roles, grammatical relations, and case marking for the various sorts of languages under discussion.

In Table 6.1 NOM (nominative) is the case of the subject of an intransitive (tensed, matrix) verb; ACC (accusative) is the case of either the SUB or the OBJ of a transitive verb—whichever case is not identical to the nominative case in the language. Nominative case is generally unmarked; that is, it is phonologically null. Nominative case in an ergative language exhibiting type A case marking or in a nominative-accusative language exhibiting type B case marking is generally called absolutive (ABS) in the literature. Accusative case in these languages is called ergative (ERG). It is the nominative-accusative type B case marking languages that are usually identified as ergative. In fact, Mel'čuk (1979) explicitly defines ergative languages as those I have identified as nominative-accusative with type B case marking.

Many languages employ both the A and B case marking paradigms, with the choice between the two conditioned by context or by the character of the NP to be case marked. For example, a language may exhibit type A case marking in main clauses but type B in certain sorts of subordinate clauses. Or nonpronominal noun phrases might show type A case marking while personal pronouns show type B case marking (as seems to be the case in Dyirbal, an ergative language). Languages that use both types of case marking displayed in Table 6.1 are said to have "split ergative" case marking (see Silverstein 1976 and DeLancey 1981 on split ergativity).

Previous investigators (see, in particular, Dixon 1972 and Mel'čuk 1979) have attempted to show that Dyirbal, among other languages, is truly ergative—that is, that the sole syntactic dependent of an intransitive verb and the theme or patient of a transitive verb are syntactic subjects. The methodology employed by these linguists is to demonstrate that the sole argument of the intransitive verb and the theme/patient of the transitive verb both exhibit subject properties. Readers of previous proofs of ergativity were, therefore, persuaded that ergative languages exist to the extent that they believed the properties identified as subject properties must necessarily single out subjects.

Consider the phenomenon of "topic chaining" in Dyirbal (see Dixon 1972), which has sometimes been considered evidence for Dyirbal's ergativity. For purposes of discussion, I call the class including subjects

Table 6.1
Correspondences Among Semantic Roles, Grammatical Relations, and Case Marking

a. Semantic Roles and Grammatical Relations

Roles	Nominative-Accusative languages	Ergative languages
agent	SUB of [+transitive], [+log sub] verb	OBJ of [+transitive], [+log sub] verb
patient/theme	OBJ of [+transitive], [+log sub] verb	SUB of [+transitive], [+log sub] verb

b. Grammatical Relations and Case Marking

	Nominative-Accusative Languages		Ergative Languages	
	A	B	A	B
SUB of [−transitive] verb	NOM	NOM (ABS)	NOM (ABS)	NOM
SUB of [+transitive] verb	NOM	ACC (ERG)	NOM (ABS)	ACC
OBJ of [+transitive] verb	ACC	NOM (ABS)	ACC (ERG)	NOM

of intransitive verbs and the theme/patient arguments of transitive verbs the "absolute NPs" in Dyirbal (owing to Dyirbal's split ergative case marking, the members of this class will not always be case marked in the absolutive). A series of Dyirbal sentences may be conjoined in a topic chain if, roughly, the absolutive NPs in the sentences are all coreferent. Only the absolutive NP in the first sentence of a topic chain actually shows up overtly in the chain; the remaining topics are phonologically null. Since topic chains resemble control constructions in English (see chapter 3), and only subjects in English are controlled, one might argue that the conditions on the Dyirbal topic chain construction indicate that Dyirbal absolutive NPs are subjects and that therefore Dyirbal is ergative. Nevertheless, the present theory does not demand that the coreferent NPs in constructions like the Dyirbal topic chain be restricted to subjects. The theory does make specific demands about structures of control, but the Dyirbal topic chain only superficially resembles such structures.

In fact, Dixon (1977) reports that Yidin, a language closely related to Dyirbal, exhibits a (coordination) construction similar to the topic chain in which the condition on coreference must be stated in terms of case marking, not grammatical relations.[2] The topics of the Yidin topic chain are the morphologically unmarked NPs. Because of split ergative case marking in Yidin, the morphologically unmarked NPs do not form a homogeneous class defined in grammatical relational terms. As evidenced in Yidin, a rule creating topic chain constructions need not necessarily pick out subjects. Therefore, that Dyirbal topic chains implicate absolutive NPs cannot serve as conclusive evidence that Dyirbal is ergative.

The theory presented in this book makes specific predictions about ergative languages and about differences one should observe between ergative and nominative-accusative languages. For example, since the theory requires that an s structure SUB be the PRO in control constructions such as English *Elmer persuaded Hortense [PRO to buy a green porcupine]*, it predicts that the theme/patient argument of a [+log sub], [+transitive] verb associated with an agent and a theme or patient should be the PRO in such control constructions in an ergative language. In contrast, the agent argument of transitive verbs in nominative-accusative languages is the PRO in control constructions. Unfortunately, the good candidates for ergative languages for which I have data do not exhibit clear cases of control constructions in which this prediction might be tested. There are data relevant to other predictions of the theory concerning ergative languages, however. I shall exploit these data to demonstrate that Dyirbal and Central Arctic Eskimo are truly ergative.[3]

6.1. Passive in Ergative Languages

The passive form in a true ergative language has often been called the antipassive. In chapter 4, I defined passivization as the addition to a verb of a [−log sub] affix and antipassivization as the addition of a [−transitive] affix unmarked for the feature [±log sub]. As shown in (6.2) and (6.3), passivization in a true ergative language with type A case marking looks like antipassivization in a nominative-accusative language with type B case marking, as far as its effects on the correspondence between semantic roles and case marking are concerned. In both ergative type A passivization and nominative-accusative type B antipassivization, the ergative marked NP of the transitive verb form, usually the agent, corresponds to the absolutive marked NP of the derived intransitive, and the absolutive NP of the transitive, usually a theme or patient, corresponds to an oblique NP complement to the intransitive. In (6.2) I provide a schematic diagram of the effects of antipassivization on the association of semantic roles and surface cases in a nominative-accusative language with type B case marking. (See section 4.2 for a more complete description of antipassivization in such a language, Greenlandic Eskimo.)

(6.2)
Antipassivization in a nominative-accusative type B language
a. active ([+log sub], [+transitive]) verb

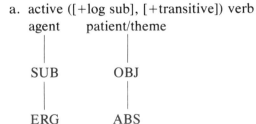

agent   patient/theme

SUB   OBJ

ERG   ABS

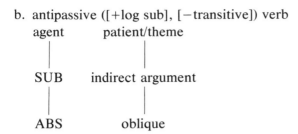

b. antipassive ([+log sub], [−transitive]) verb

agent	patient/theme
SUB	indirect argument
ABS	oblique

In (6.3) is a schematic diagram of the effects of passivization on the association of semantic roles and surface cases in an ergative language with type A case marking.

(6.3)
Passivization in an ergative type A language
a. active ([+log sub], [+transitive]) verb

agent	patient/theme
OBJ	SUB
ERG	ABS

b. passive ([−log sub], [−transitive]) verb

agent	patient/theme
SUB	indirect argument
ABS	oblique

From the correspondences in (6.2) and (6.3) it should be clear that the fact that a verb form in a given language can be analyzed as a passive under the assumption that the language is ergative does not provide evidence that the language is in fact ergative. The verb form could be an antipassive and the language in question a nominative-accusative type B language. Although it provides no evidence for the existence of ergative languages, I will run through an analysis of passivization in Dyirbal and Central Arctic Eskimo on the assumption that these languages are ergative. The exercise illustrates what it means to be ergative and presents some constructions crucial to later sections.

Consider the Central Arctic Eskimo (hereafter, Arctic) verb *kapi-* 'stab' and the Dyirbal verb *ḍurgay* 'spear.' If Arctic and Dyirbal are ergative, these verbs should have the P-A structures shown in (6.4).

(6.4)

a. Arctic: *kapi-* 'stab' (*agent*)

b. Dyirbal: *ḍurgay* 'spear' (*agent*)

The predicates produced by the P-A structures in (6.4) assign patient roles. The active transitive forms of the verbs in (6.4) appear in sentences (6.5) and (6.6). Note that the transitive Arctic verb agrees with both its subject and its object in person and number.

(6.5)

Arctic: Piruutisi-up Siisa-∅ kapi-vaa.
           Brutus-ERG Caesar-ABS stab-3sg3sg
           'Brutus stabbed Caesar.'

(6.6)

Dyirbal: bayi bargan baŋgul yaṛaŋgu ḍurgaɲu.
         wallaby-ABS man-ERG spear
         'Man is spearing wallaby.'

Since the verbs in (6.5) and (6.6) are [+log sub], [+transitive], their logical objects, which are assigned agent roles, will correspond to grammatical OBJs. The OBJs are marked ergative (accusative); the subjects bear patient roles and are marked absolutive (nominative)—see Table 6.1.

If the verbs in (6.5) and (6.6) are passivized, by adding *-si-* in Arctic and *-ŋay-* in Dyirbal, their logical objects (agents) should correspond to grammatical SUBs and show up in the absolutive case. Both Arctic and Dyirbal exploit case markings to serve the function in these languages that *by* serves in English. In Arctic this is the comitative, in Dyirbal the instrumental or dative (see Dixon 1972, p. 66, for a discussion of the differences between these two case markings in the *-ŋay-* construction). Passive sentences corresponding to the actives in (6.5) and (6.6) are found in (6.7) and (6.8). Note that the agents appear in the absolutive case, the patients in the comitative (Arctic) or dative or instrumental (Dyirbal). Note also that the passive form of the Arctic verb, being intransitive, agrees only with its subject, which appears in the absolutive.

(6.7)

Arctic: Piruutisi-∅ Siisa-mik kapi-si-vuq.
           Brutus-ABS Caesar-COM stab-PASS-IND3sg
           'Brutus stabbed Caesar.'

(6.8)

Dyirbal: bayi yaɽa {bagul bargangu, baŋgul bargandu} ḍurganaɲu.
           man-ABS {wallaby-DAT, wallaby-INST} spear-PASS
           'Man is spearing wallaby.'

6.2. Dative Shift in Ergative Languages

A dative shifted construction may be characterized as a sentence containing a theme or patient and another argument, not bearing a theme or patient role, that appears in the usual expression of themes or patients in the language. In nominative-accusative languages, whose theme and patient roles are canonically assigned to direct objects, dative shifted constructions contain non-theme/patient arguments expressed in the way direct objects are usually expressed. I argued in chapter 5 that given certain assumptions, these non-theme/patient arguments must, in fact, be OBJs. Because theme and patient roles are canonically assigned to subjects in ergative languages, expressing, say, a goal in the way that themes and patients are usually expressed in these languages involves putting the goal in the case and/or structural position of a subject.

Consider the dative shift alternations in Arctic and Dyirbal illustrated in (6.9) and (6.10).

(6.9)

Arctic: a. anguti-up titiraut nutarar-mut tuni-vaa.
             man-ERG pencil-ABS child-ALL give-IND3sg3sg
             'The man gave a pencil to the child.'

          b. anguti-up titirauti-mik nutaraq tuni-vaa.
             man-ERG pencil-COM child-ABS give-IND3sg3sg
             'The man gave the child a pencil.'

(6.10)

Dyirbal: a. balam baŋgun wugan bagul.
                  it(food)-ABS she-ERG give he-DAT
                  'She gives food to him.'

            b. bayi baŋgun baŋgum wugan.
                  him-ABS she-ERG it-INST give
                  'She gives him food.'

In the (a) sentences of (6.9) and (6.10) the theme argument is in the absolutive case and the goal argument is in the allative or dative. One may assume that the dative and allative cases assign the goal role in these sentences. The presumed P-A structures for the verbs in (6.9a) and (6.10a) are given in (6.11), with the semantic roles of the logical objects italicized.

(6.11)

a. *tuni-* 'give' (*agent,* goal)

b. *wugal* 'give' (*agent,* goal)

Since the (a) and (b) sentences in (6.9) and (6.10) have the same propositional content, there is no reason to believe that *tuni-* and *wugal* in (6.9b) and (6.10b) do not have the same P-A structures as the homophonous verbs in (6.9a) and (6.10a). Since the absolutive case cannot be argued to assign the goal role to the goal arguments in the (b) sentences, either the verb or the predicate in these sentences must assign that role. If the verbs in (6.9b, 6.10b) are to have the same P-A structures as the verbs in (6.9a, 6.10a), however, the predicates in (6.9b, 6.10b) cannot assign the goal role—the predicates produced by the P-A stuctures in (6.11) assign the theme role.

    Therefore, either the verbs in (6.9b, 6.10b) must assign the goal role or they do not have the same argument structures as the verbs in (6.9a, 6.10a) and the predicates that they produce assign the goal role. The data available from the two languages under discussion indicate that they choose different options here. For Central Arctic Eskimo, the evidence suggests that the goal argument in (6.9b) is a logical object. For Dyirbal, it seems as if an alternate argument structure is chosen for the dative shifted (6.10b), with the goal role assigned by a predicate. These options are equally valued in the present theory. As explained in chapter 5, a relation between verbs differing in argument structure has the same status in the theory as a relation between verbs differing in semantic role assigning features. Neither sort of relation may be completely accounted for by postulating a productive affixation process associating the verbs. Although the preservation of argument structure between dative shifted and nonshifted sentences accounts for the shared propositional structure between these sentences, it requires postulating an extremely marked lexical entry for the verb in the dative shifted sentence of an ergative language. Thus the option that Dyirbal appears to take avoids a marked construction, although it obscures the basic synonymy relation between dative shifted and nonshifted sentences. In both Dyirbal and Arctic, the behavior of the dative shift alternation argues for the basic ergativity of the language.

In Arctic the verb in the dative shifted (6.9b) shows evidence of assigning the goal role. Nevertheless, the goal argument appears in the absolutive case, the case of subjects. If the goal argument (a logical object) is to be the syntactic SUB in (6.9b), the verb must be [−log sub], for if it were [+log sub], the theme argument (the logical subject) would be SUB. In short, the present theory demands a lexical entry for the verb in (6.9b) as shown in (6.12).

(6.12)
tuni-, V, 'give' (*agent, goal*) [−log sub], [+transitive]

The lexical entry (6.12) contains the P-A structure in (6.11a), accounting for the fact that the (a) and (b) sentences in (6.9) share propositional content. Since the agent shows up as the OBJ in (6.9b), the agent as well as the goal must be a logical object of the verb. Since the goal argument, not the agent, becomes the subject in these sentences, the agent must be specified to correspond to the s structure OBJ. If the agent were not specified to correspond to the OBJ, nothing would prevent the goal from corresponding to OBJ and the agent to SUB.

Lexical entry (6.12) is marked in three respects: First, the verb in (6.12) assigns more than one semantic role in violation of the One Role/Role Assigner principle. Second, a connection must be specified between one of the verb's logical objects and the grammatical OBJ relation. Third, the verb is [−log sub] but [+transitive]. A lexical entry like (6.12) would also be required for the English sporadic advancement constructions discussed in section 4.1.3. An example of such sporadic advancement is shown in (6.13b); the lexical entry for the verb in (6.13b) is given in (6.14).

(6.13)
a. I bought this porcupine for five dollars in 1913.
b. Five dollars bought this porcupine in 1913.

(6.14)

buy, V, 'buy' *(theme, means)* [−log sub], [+transitive]

Entry (6.14) is marked in exactly the same manner as (6.12). Note that the theme argument must be specified to correspond to the grammatical OBJ. Again, the entry in (6.14) is directly motivated if one wishes to capture the fact that the sentences in (6.13) share propositional content by providing the verbs in each sentence with identical P-A structures. A child learning Arctic or English should be led to the entries in (6.12) and (6.14) by the same general principles and considerations that lead the linguist to them. Recall from chapter 4 that the analysis of sporadic advancements in English that postulated that they involve [−log sub] verbs correctly predicted that the verb in (6.13b) will have no passive counterpart.

A dative shift construction involves the expression of a non-theme/ patient argument as themes and patients are usually expressed. Because themes and patients are assigned by predicates in ergative languages, expressing the goal argument of a verb like 'give' as themes and patients are usually expressed involves making the goal argument a subject. The only way to make the goal argument in Arctic a subject while satisfying the generalization that, all other things being equal, related verbs share P-A structures is to have the verbs in a dative shifted construction assign the goal role and to make the verbs [−log sub], as shown in (6.12). Dyirbal apparently chooses to make the goal a logical subject in dative shift constructions, assigning related verbs different argument structures but avoiding the marked lexical entry in (6.12), as I shall show. However, the analysis of the dative shift alternation I have provided for Arctic, involving entry (6.12), makes two related predictions.

First, since the verb in a dative shifted sentence like (6.9b) is [−log sub], if a constituent is to bear the theme role (the role of the logical subject), that role must be assigned by the semantic role assigner serving the function of English *by* in the language in question. That is, the theme argument should be expressed as are the displaced subjects in passive constructions. Recall that the displaced subject in an Arctic passive falls into the comitative case (see (6.7)). When the goal argument of the verb meaning 'give' is in the absolutive in Arctic, indicating that it is the subject, the theme is in the comitative case as predicted (see (6.9b)).

Second, since the verb in the dative shifted (6.9b) is [−log sub], as shown in lexical entry (6.12), I predict that the passive affix should not attach to this verb (see section 4.1.3). In fact, there is good evidence that sentence (6.9b) has no passive counterpart in Arctic, evidence to be examined shortly.

If Dyirbal expresses goals in dative shift constructions as themes are usually expressed by making the goals logical subjects, the lexical entry for the Dyribal verb in (6.10b) should look like (6.15).

(6.15)
wugal, V, 'give' (*agent,* theme), [+log sub], [+transitive]

The predicates produced by the P-A structure in (6.15) assign goal roles. Although the theme falls into the instrumental case in (6.10b), one of the cases used for the displaced subject in a Dyirbal passive construction, Dixon (personal communication) has uncovered strong evidence that the theme in (6.10b) should not be analyzed as the Dyirbal equivalent of a *by*-object, that is, as an argument assigned its role by the predicate. Dixon points out that the theme appears in the instrumental with *wugal* even in dialects (and in certain constructions in all dialects) that normally must put the displaced subject in a passive in the dative, not the instrumental case. Therefore, the instrumental in (6.10b) is simply assigning the theme role, perhaps because instrumentals and themes are semantically close in certain situations, as the English sentences in (6.16) might suggest, or perhaps for other Dyirbal-internal reasons.

(6.16)
a. Elmer filled the glass with water.
b. Hortense loaded hay onto the wagon.
c. Hortense loaded the wagon with hay.

In any case, the data indicate that (6.15) is an appropriate lexical entry for the dative shifted Dyirbal verb. Note that if (6.15) is the correct entry, it should be possible to passivize the dative shifted Dyirbal verb in (6.10b), unlike the [−log sub] dative shifted Arctic verb in (6.9b). Dixon (personal communication) points out that the passive in (6.17) should be considered the passive version of the dative shifted construction in (6.10b).

(6.17)
. . . yuɾiŋgu ɾulguŋgu wugalɲaygu bagul ɲalŋgagu.
. . . kangaroo-INST heart-INST give-PASS-PURP there-DAT child-DAT
'. . . in order that he [not specified in sentence] might give a kangaroo's heart to the child.'

In order for (6.17) to include the passive of the non-dative-shifted verb in (6.10a), one would have to analyze the instrumental in (6.17) as the displaced subject marking. But Dixon reports that sentences like (6.17) occur in dialects and in constructions that do not allow instrumental for the displaced subject. In particular, Dixon notes that when a passive verb appears in the purposive, as in (6.17), the logical subject may not show up in the instrumental. Therefore, 'the child' in (6.17), not 'a kangaroo's heart,' must be the displaced subject of the passive.

If Arctic and Dyirbal were nominative-accusative languages with type B case marking, one would expect double absolutive constructions with the verbs meaning 'give' just as double object constructions appear in English and Chi-Mwi:ni and double accusative constructions appear in Yindjibarndi (see chapter 5). On the nominative-accusative analysis of Arctic and Dyribal, the verbs in the (a) sentences of (6.9) and (6.10) would include (6.18) in their lexical entries.

(6.18)
a. Arctic: *tuni-* 'give' (*theme,* goal)
b. Dyirbal: *wugal* 'give' (*theme,* goal)

If the verbs *tuni-* and *wugal* in (6.18) assigned goal roles instead of theme roles, the usual expression of themes (absolutive case) would be expected to assign the theme roles. The verbs in the (b) sentences of (6.9, 6.10) would then be expected to include (6.19) in their lexical entries.

(6.19)
a. Arctic: *tuni-* 'give' (theme, *goal*)
b. Dyirbal: *wugal* 'give' (theme, *goal*)

If (6.19) were included in the lexical entries for the verbs in (6.9b, 6.10b), as required on the hypothesis that Arctic and Dyirbal are nominative-accusative, one would wrongly expect both the theme and goal arguments in (6.9b, 6.10b) to appear in the absolutive—the theme arguments because they would be assigned their semantic roles by absolutive case, the goal arguments because they would be OBJs. On the other hand, the hypothesis that Arctic and Dyirbal are ergative either correctly predicts (in Arctic) or is consistent with (in Dyirbal) the case marking on the themes in (6.9b, 6.10b).

As just explained, a nominative-accusative language with type B case marking would be expected to show double absolutive constructions with 'give.' The existence of a nominative-accusative type B language with double absolutive constructions would demonstrate that the failure of Arctic and Dyirbal to exhibit such constructions is unrelated to ergative case marking, that is, to the marking of themes and patients of transitive verbs in the same manner as subjects of intransitive verbs. Donaldson (1980) provides conclusive evidence that Ngiyambaa, an Australian language, is, in my terms, nominative-accusative with type B case marking. The agent NP of a transitive clause, marked ergative in main clauses (if nonpronominal), and the absolutive NP of an intransitive clause become PRO in a variety of control constructions in Ngiyambaa (Donaldson 1980, pp. 280–281). This fact indicates that the agent in a transitive clause and the absolutive in an intransitive are SUBs in the technical sense (see chapter 3). Since the agent of a transitive Ngiyambaa sentence appears in the ergative case, the theme or patient in the absolutive, it should be clear from Table 6.1 that the behavior of Ngiyambaa's control constructions show that it is indeed a nominative-accusative language with type B case marking. And, as expected, both the theme and the goal arguments of the verb meaning 'give' appear in the absolutive in a dative shifted construction.

(6.20)
guya=ndu bura:y ŋu-nhi.
fish-ABS=you-NOM child-ABS give-PAST
'You gave a child fish.'

(The agent (SUB) in (6.20) appears in the nominative case because Ngiyambaa actually exhibits a split case marking system. Second person pronouns display the type A pattern in Table 6.1, while nonpronominal NPs use type B case marking. Pronouns may appear as clitics, as exemplified in (6.20).)

   In addition to predicting the case marking on the theme in a dative shifted construction, my analysis of Arctic dative shift predicts that the verbs heading the dative shifted sentences like (6.9b) should not passivize. Recall that a morphological principle—the NVAP—prevents the passive morpheme from attaching to a [−log sub] verb. Since my analysis of Arctic gives the verb in (6.9b) the [−log sub] feature, as shown in (6.12), it predicts that this verb should have no passive version. It is difficult to demonstrate that this prediction is correct because, in the present theory, even if the passive morpheme could attach to the verb in (6.9b), the derived verb could not head a grammatical sentence. Consider the result of adding the passive morpheme to the verb in (6.12).

(6.21)

tuni-si, V, 'give' (*agent, goal*), [−log sub], [−transitive]

Since the verb in (6.21) is [−transitive], the two logical objects in an l-s structure containing this verb would compete for SUB status in the corresponding s structure. The loser would violate principle M since its s structure counterpart would not be head-Governed by the passive verb. As a result, there is no ungrammatical sentence I can use to confirm the prediction that the verb in (6.10a) has no passive. Arctic *tuni-* 'give' does have a passive form, which appears in sentence (6.22), for example. But the verb in (6.22) is clearly the passive of (6.11a), the verb in (6.9a).

(6.22)

angut titirauti-mik nutarar-mut tuni-si-vuq.
man-ABS pencil-COM child-ALL give-PASS-IND3sg
'The man gave a pencil to the child.'

Although it is impossible to provide ungrammatical sentences to confirm the prediction that (6.10a) has no passive counterpart, the prediction may be used to support the hypothesis that Arctic is ergative over the hypothesis that it is nominative-accusative with type B case marking. The hypothesis that Arctic is nominative-accusative would predict that *tuni-* 'give' in (6.10a) should have a *-si-* form, and the sentences that this alternate hypothesis predicts should be grammatical are known to be ungrammatical.

Consider a nominative-accusative analysis of Arctic. What I have called passivization in Arctic on the ergative analysis would be considered antipassivization on the nominative-accusative analysis; that is, the morpheme *-si-* would carry only the feature [−transitive] and would provide the comitative case to assign syntactic roles to the logical objects of the verbs to which it attaches (see section 4.2).

Recall the supposed active-passive pair of Arctic sentences, repeated here as (6.23). In (6.23b) I gloss the *-si-* form as appropriate for the nominative-accusative analysis of Arctic.

(6.23)

a. Piruutisi-up Siisa kapi-vaa.
   Brutus-ERG Caesar-ABS stab-IND3sg3sg
   'Brutus stabbed Caesar.'

b. Piruutisi Siisa-mik kapi-si-vuq.
   Brutus-ABS Caesar-COM stab-ANTIPASS-IND3sg
   'Brutus stabbed Caesar.'

On a nominative-accusative analysis, *Piruutisi* 'Brutus' is the subject of
(6.23a) and *Siisa* 'Caesar' the object. Antipassivization leaves *Piruutisi*
as the subject of the derived intransitive verb in (6.23b), but *Siisa* becomes an oblique argument of the verb. *Piruutisi* bears ergative case in
(6.23a) as the subject of a transitive verb, absolutive case in (6.23b) as
the subject of an intransitive.

The lexical entry for *tuni-* 'give' in (6.9a) would include the information in (6.24a) on a nominative-accusative analysis, and the entry for
tuni- 'give' in the dative shifted (6.9b) would include the information in
(6.24b).[4]

(6.24)
a. *tuni-*, V, 'give' (*theme,* goal), [+log sub], [+transitive]
b. *tuni-*, V, 'give' (theme, *goal*), [+log sub], [+transitive]

Now there is absolutely no reason why *-si-,* analyzed as an antipassive
affix, should not attach to the verb in (6.24b), yielding a verb that
should occur in sentence (6.25).

(6.25)
*angut titirauti-mik nutarar-mik tuni-si-vuq.
 man-ABS pencil-COM child-COM give-ANTIPASS-IND3sg
 'The man gave a pencil to the child.'

But (6.25) is ungrammatical. In short, the ergative analysis of Arctic
predicts that *-si-* should not attach to the verb in (6.9b). On the other
hand, the nominative-accusative analysis predicts that *-si-* will attach to
the verb in (6.9b), yielding the verb in (6.25). The ungrammaticality of
(6.25) thus supports the ergative over the nominative-accusative analysis of Arctic.[5]

6.3. Lexical Reflexives in Ergative Languages

Perhaps the most convincing demonstration of the existence of ergative
languages derives from a prediction the present theory makes about
lexical reflexive forms in these languages. Recall that the theory predicts a homophony between the reflexive and passive forms of a verb.
Since the patient or theme of a transitive verb is the subject of the
passive of this verb in a nominative-accusative language, this predic-

tion leads to the expectation that a sentence meaning 'He washes himself' will mean also 'He is washed' (see discussion of lexical reflexives in section 4.3). In contrast, since the agent of a transitive verb is the subject of the passive form of the verb in an ergative language (see the passives in (6.7) and (6.8)), one expects a sentence meaning 'He washes himself' to mean also 'He washes (something unspecified)' in such a language. This prediction about reflexive forms in ergative languages is confirmed directly in Dyirbal, indirectly in Arctic.

The Dyirbal affix -riy- (which has various allomorphs), is used to form the reflexive of a transitive verb. Example (6.26a) is a simple transitive Dyirbal sentence containing *buybal* 'hide.' The reflexive form of *buybal* heads the sentence in (6.26b).

(6.26)
a. bala yugu baŋgul yaṟaŋgu buyban.
    stick-ABS man-ERG hides
    'Man hides stick.'

b. bayi yaṟa buybayirɲu.
    man-ABS hides-REFL
    'Man hides himself' or 'Man hides (something).'

According to the (nonclitic) analysis of lexical reflexives supported in chapter 4, the verb in (6.26a) should have a lexical entry like (6.27a), the verb in (6.26b) an entry containing at least the information in (6.27b).

(6.27)
a. *buybal,* V, 'hide' (*agent*), [+log sub], [+transitive]
b. *buybayiriy* (=*buybal*+REFL), V, 'hide' (*agent*), [−log sub],
    [−transitive], ('by' (reflexive-pronoun-features), etc.)

Suppose one inserts the verb in (6.27b) into sentence (6.26b) and chooses to take the features in parentheses, the specifically reflexive features (recall the suggestion in chapter 4 that these features may actually belong to independent affixes). The *by* features of the REFL affix in (6.27b) will assign the role of the logical subject—the hid role—to its reflexive pronoun features. Since the verb in (6.27b) is [−log sub], [−transitive], the logical object, which is assigned the agent role, will correspond to the syntactic SUB and serve as antecedent for the reflexive pronoun features of REFL. The SUB will thus be interpreted as both the hider and the hid, yielding the reflexive interpretation of (6.26b), 'The man hides himself.'

As noted in (6.26b), the Dyirbal reflexive verb form also has a passive reading. This results when one inserts the verb in (6.27b) into sentence (6.26b) without choosing the reflexive features in parentheses. Since the derived verb in (6.27b) is [−log sub], [−transitive] in this case as well, the logical object, the agent argument, corresponds to the SUB of the sentence. Without the features in parentheses in (6.27b), the derived verb does not assign the logical subject (hid) role to reflexive pronoun features. Thus the subject of sentence (6.26b) is interpreted as the agent only in this case, and the sentence means 'The man hides (something unspecified).' As predicted by the hypothesis that Dyirbal is truly ergative, then, a reflexive sentence like (6.27b), in addition to its reflexive reading, has the interpretation 'The man hides something' and not 'The man is hid.'

Dixon (1972) calls the nonreflexive use of the reflexive verb form the false reflexive. As Dixon is careful to point out (p. 91), the false reflexive has the same syntax as the -ŋay- verb form, which I have identified as the passive. Compare the active and false reflexive pair in (6.28) with the active and passive pair in (6.29).

(6.28)
a. balam wuḍu baŋgul yaṛaŋgu ḍaŋgaɲu.
   fruit-ABS man-ERG eat
   'The man is eating fruit.'

b. bayi yaṛa ḍaŋgaymariɲu (bagum wuḍugu).
   man-ABS eat-REFL (fruit-DAT)
   'The man is eating (fruit).'

(6.29)
a. bayi bargan baŋgul yaṛaŋgu ḍurgaɲu.
   wallaby-ABS man-ERG spear
   'Man is spearing wallaby.'

b. bayi yaṛa bagul bargangu ḍurganaɲu.
   man-ABS wallaby-DAT spear-PASS
   'Man is spearing wallaby.'

Note that the subjects in the active sentences of (6.28) and (6.29), marked absolutive, correspond to a dative marked noun phrase in the (b) sentences. Dixon remarks that, just as in a -ŋay- construction, the instrumental may also be used to mark the displaced subject of a false reflexive. The objects, marked ergative, in the (a) sentences correspond to the subjects, marked absolutive, of the (b) sentences. If the dative noun phrase is left out of the false reflexive in (6.28b), it may be interpreted as a true reflexive, meaning 'The man is eating himself,' say, chewing on a finger.

In Central Arctic Eskimo, the reflexive pronouns have neither ergative nor absolutive forms. Therefore, one cannot say something that would be glossed 'I saw myself' (or 'I myself saw'), with 'I' in the absolutive and 'self' in the ergative, or with 'self' in the absolutive and 'I' in the ergative. To form the reflexive with a transitive verb, one uses the unmarked intransitive form of the transitive verb; that is, one conjugates the verb with an ending that agrees with one NP only. In addition, one uses a reflexive pronoun in the comitative. The examples in (6.30) are adapted from Johnson (personal communication).

(6.30)
a. uvamnik taku-vunga.
   myself-COM see-IND1sg
   'I see myself.'

b. angut ingminik kapi-vuq.
   man-ABS himself-COM stab-IND3sg
   'The man stabbed himself.'

Now the unmarked intransitive form of a verb in Arctic, if one is possible outside the reflexive construction, is generally used for the passive (but see section 6.4). An example of this passive use for an unmarked intransitive is given in (6.31a); a reflexive is shown in (6.31b) for comparison.

(6.31)
a. angut arnar-mik taku-vuq.
   man-ABS woman-COM see-IND3sg
   'The man sees the woman.'

b. angut ingminik taku-vuq.
   man-ABS himself-COM see-IND3sg
   'The man sees himself.'

It should be clear from a comparison of (6.31a) and (6.31b) that, just as in Dyirbal, the passive and reflexive constructions have the same syntax in Arctic. As in Dyirbal, the subject of the reflexive verb form, in the absolutive, corresponds to the agent of the passive constructions, not to the patient or the theme as would be expected for a nominative-accusative language. Lexical reflexivization in Arctic, as in all languages that use the nonclitic analysis of chapter 4, involves the attachment of the features [−log sub], [−transitive] to a transitive verb and the assignment of the semantic role of the predicate produced by the verb to a reflexive element. In Arctic, unlike the other languages examined, the reflexive element is phonologically realized distinct from the reflexive affix—as a reflexive pronoun in the comitative case. The comitative case assigns the roles of predicates in Arctic passive sentences.

The remarkable support that the Arctic reflexive construction offers the present analysis of lexical reflexives and ergative languages becomes clearer when Central Arctic Eskimo is compared with Greenlandic Eskimo, a related language discussed in Sadock (1980), Woodbury (1977a,b), and Swadesh (1944) (see also the discussion of Greenlandic in section 4.2). Greenlandic resembles Arctic very closely. Like Arctic, it marks the agents of transitive verbs ergative and the patients or themes absolutive; therefore, it is either a true ergative language or a nominative-accusative language with type B case marking. According to Sadock (1980) and the other sources cited, however, the absolutive NP of the unmarked intransitive form of a Greenlandic verb usually corresponds to the absolutive NP of its transitive counterpart, not to the ergative NP as in Arctic (but see section 6.4).[6]

(6.32)
Greenlandic Eskimo (from Sadock 1980):
a. Piniartoq toquppaa.
   hunter-ABS kill-IND3sg3sg
   'He killed the hunter.'

b. Piniartoq toquppoq.
   hunter-ABS kill-IND3sg
   'The hunter was killed.'

The difference between Arctic and Greenlandic unmarked intransitives is clearly displayed in (6.33). The subject of the unmarked intransitive form of *taku-* 'see' is the seer in Arctic but the seen in Greenlandic.

(6.33)
Arctic:
a. angut taku-vuq.
   man-ABS see-IND3sg
   'The man sees (something).'

Greenlandic (from Woodbury 1977a, (45)):
b. Tigianaq taku-vuq.
   fox-ABS see-IND3sg
   'The fox was seen.'

The unmarked intransitive form of a verb in Greenlandic may be used for the reflexive. Unlike Arctic, Greenlandic does not require a reflexive pronoun in reflexive constructions with the unmarked intransitive verb.

(6.34)
Piniartoq toquppoq.
hunter-ABS kill-IND3sg
'The hunter was killed' or 'The hunter killed himself.'

Since sentence (6.34) meaning 'The hunter killed himself' may also mean 'The hunter was killed' in Greenlandic, this dialect of Eskimo proves to be a nominative-accusative language with type B case marking. The present theory predicts that the reflexive will be synonymous with the passive in any language. If (6.34) is a passive, then its subject (the patient argument) must be the logical object of the verb. But if the patient arguments of verbs like *toqupp-* 'kill' are logical objects in Greenlandic, the language is nominative-accusative (see Table 6.1).

Although a reflexive pronoun is not obligatory in Greenlandic reflexive constructions, a reflexive pronoun in the allative may cooccur with reflexive verbs.

(6.35)
Piniartoq imminut toquppoq.
hunter-ABS self-ALL kill-IND3sg
'The hunter killed himself.'

If my analysis of lexical reflexivization is correct, the allative should be the case that serves the *by* function in Greenlandic, that marks the displaced subject in passive constructions. The reflexive verb in (6.35) itself should be [−log sub], so the predicate that it heads will not assign the logical subject role, and an item with the properties of English *by* is required in (6.35) to assign this role to the reflexive pronoun. In fact, as Woodbury (1977a) reports, the allative is one of the cases in which the displaced subject of a passive may appear. (The Greenlandic passive morpheme *-tau-* in (6.36) is discussed in section 4.2.)

(6.36)

Greenlandic (from Woodbury 1977a, p. 324):

a. Anut-ip arnaq taku-vaa.
    man-ERG woman-ABS see-IND3sg3sg
    'The man saw the woman.'

b. Arnaq anuti-mut taku-tau-puq.
    woman-ABS man-ALL see-PASS-IND3sg
    'The woman was seen by the man.'

The predicted differences between reflexive constructions in nominative-accusative and ergative languages are clearly illustrated in (6.37) and (6.38), which contain passives (6.37) and reflexives (6.38) from Arctic and Greenlandic.

(6.37)

a. Central Arctic passive:
    angut arnar-mik taku-vuq.
    man-ABS woman-COM see-IND3sg
    'The man sees the woman.'

b. Greenlandic passive:
    Arnaq anuti-mut taku-tau-puq.
    woman-ABS man-ALL see-PASS-IND3sg
    'The woman was seen by the man.'

(6.38)

a. Central Arctic reflexive:
    angut ingminik taku-vuq.
    man-ABS self-COM scc-IND3sg
    'The man sees himself.'

b. Greenlandic reflexive:
    Anut inmi-nut taku-vuq
    man-ABS self-ALL see-IND3sg
    'The man saw himself.'

It should be clear from a comparison of the passives and reflexives in (6.37) and (6.38) that the subject of an Arctic reflexive bears the agent role, while the subject of a Greenlandic reflexive bears the patient or theme role (for verbs that are associated with an agent and a theme or patient). Since my analysis of lexical reflexives makes the logical object the grammatical subject of a reflexive verb form, I conclude that the seer is the logical object of Arctic *taku-* 'see' while the seen is the logical object of Greenlandic *taku-* 'see'—that is, Arctic is ergative, Greenlandic nominative-accusative.

6.4. Unmarked Intransitive Forms of Eskimo Transitive Verbs

I must qualify here the generalization that the unmarked intransitive forms of Arctic and Greenlandic transitive verbs are the passive ([−log sub], [−transitive]) counterparts of their transitive forms. Eskimo transitive verbs may be divided into at least five different classes on the basis of the relation between their transitive and unmarked intransitive forms (see Woodbury 1977b); the generalization concerning intransitives and passives holds for only one of these classes. As far as I have been able to discover, cognate verbs in the various Eskimo dialects generally fall into the same classes regardless of whether the dialects would be considered nominative-accusative or ergative in the present theory.

First, some transitive verbs have no unmarked intransitive forms— outside the reflexive construction, at least. (Johnson (personal communication) reports that the intransitive conjugation of the Arctic verbs in this class appear in the reflexive construction illustrated in (6.30).)

Second, the intransitive forms of some transitive verbs have an inchoative or a stative reading. Inchoatives and statives were discussed in section 5.2.1. An inchoative of a basic transitive verb like English *break* is an intransitive verb that lacks the causative implications of its transitive counterpart. Compare transitive *break* in *Elmer broke the glass* with intransitive, inchoative *break* in *The glass broke*. The stative of a verb like English *hang* is an intransitive verb that lacks the causative and punctual implications of its transitive counterpart. Compare transitive *hang* in *Elmer hung the clothes out to dry* with intransitive, stative *hang* in *The clothes are hanging out to dry*. The English glosses of the Eskimo verbs in this class often show inchoatives and statives as their unmarked intransitive counterparts. The examples of this class in (6.39) are from Alaskan Yup'ik (Reed et al., 1977), which is closely related to Arctic.

(6.39)

Transitive:	Intransitive:
a. Tamaraa.	a. Tamaruq.
'He (ERG) loses it (ABS)'	'It (ABS) is lost.' stative
b. Kuvaa.	b. Kuv'uq.
'He (ERG) spills it (ABS).'	'It (ABS) spills.' inchoative

In chapter 5 I explained why the unmarked intransitive forms of transitive verbs like 'lose,' 'hang,' 'spill,' 'break,' 'open,' in a language should be expected to serve as their stative or inchoative counterparts regardless of whether the language is nominative-accusative or ergative.

The third class of Eskimo transitive verbs corresponds to the indefinite object deleting verbs of English (e.g., *eat*). As Sadock remarks about Greenlandic, "In many instances where the English counterpart is an object-deleting verb, the Greenlandic intransitive formed [by changing from transitive to intransitive agreement suffixes] has roughly the meaning of the corresponding English intransitive" (1980, pp. 304–305).

(6.40)

a. Neqi nerivaa.
meat-ABS eat-IND1sg3sg
'I ate the meat.'

b. Nerivunga.
eat-IND1sg
'I ate (something).'

Indefinite object deletion was discussed in section 5.2.2, where I explained why the unmarked intransitive form of verbs like 'eat' in a language might have the eater as subject regardless of whether the language is nominative-accusative or ergative.

A fourth class of Eskimo transitive verbs (described in Woodbury 1977b) should be analyzed as derived from their unmarked intransitive counterparts. Some Greenlandic examples are given in (6.41) (I have no evidence that this class exists in the other Eskimo dialects).

(6.41)

Transitive:	Intransitive:
a. Tikipaa.	a. Tikippuq.
'He (ERG) has come to it.'	'He (ABS) has come.'
b. Analavaa.	b. Analavuq.
'He (ERG) walks through it.'	'He (ABS) walks around.'

For many verbs of this class, the unmarked intransitive form is a verb of motion; the extra argument of the transitive verb indicates a direction.[7] In the present theory, the sort of alternation exhibited in (6.41) is analyzed as the result of morphological merger, to be discussed in chapter 7.

Again, cognate transitive verbs in the various Eskimo dialects more or less fall into the same classes regardless of whether one would identify them as nominative-accusative or ergative on independent grounds. For example, the subject of intransitive 'eat' in all dialects will be the eater, the subject of intransitive 'lose' the thing lost.

Removing these four classes of basic transitive verbs from the transitive verbs of an Eskimo dialect leaves a fifth, residual, class. It is for this fifth class that the generalization that the unmarked intransitive form of a transitive verb serves as the passive is supposed to hold. Cognate unmarked intransitive verbs from this class should therefore exhibit the distinction between passivization in a nominative-accusative Eskimo dialect like Greenlandic and passivization in an ergative dialect like Arctic as to which semantic role is borne by the subject of the passive verb. This distinction was illustrated in (6.33).

6.5. On the Scarcity of Ergative Languages

Any account of ergativity that claims that universal grammar does not treat either nominative-accusative or ergative languages as marked, or unexpected, must face the clear fact that the number of true ergative languages in the world is extremely small in comparison with the number of nominative-accusative languages. An explanation for this fact should presumably be related to an explanation for split-ergativity (see Silverstein 1976 and DeLancey 1981). In order to find out why certain case marking patterns are preferred over others, it is necessary to discover what functions case marking serves in addition to expressing grammatical relations. For example, case marking that expresses grammatical relations overlaps with case marking employed to indicate topics and foci. Inasmuch as pronouns are most often used to point to a previously mentioned or understood entity, topicality and focus directly implicate the pronominal system of a language. A split-ergative system often splits between the pronouns and nonpronominal NPs or within the pronominal system. Such considerations indicate the complexity of the issues at stake if the problem of the scarcity of ergative languages were to be seriously addressed here.

Suppose children most often make themselves the topic of discourse (the me-first principle) and suppose they most often talk about things they are actively doing, both logically transitive things, like hitting, and logically intransitive things, like running. If topicality is associated with the subject relation in a language, then the child will have reason to associate the subject relation with agents of both transitive and intransitive verbs, hypothesizing that the language he is learning is nominative-accusative. Thus if topicality is associated with subjecthood, the acquisition process may make ergative languages more marked than nominative-accusative ones. The Surface Appearance principle (2.86) ties topicality to the subject relation. This principle implies that the subject is the easiest nominal in a sentence to leave out—have phonologically null—when it is understood as coreferent with the topic of discourse. The phonologically null topic may pick up its antecedent in the next higher clause—the case of controlled PRO (see 3.2.1)—or in discourse—the case of noncontrol PRO in English. I do not think there is yet any empirical support for this particular acquisition-based account of the markedness of ergative languages, but I believe it is the sort of account linguists should be looking for.

Chapter 7

Affix-Mediated Alternations in the Expression of Arguments II: Morphological Merger

I have assumed that a general principle governs morphemes with semantic role assigning features or argument structures:

(7.1)
Principle:
If a lexical item assigns a semantic role or has an argument structure, it is an independent constituent at l-s structure.

Since they carry argument structures, by principle (7.1) the affixes to be discussed in this chapter must appear as independent items in the list of constituents and relations that constitute l-s structure. What it means to say that a morpheme is an affix is that it constitutes part of a derived word (in a loose sense of "word") at some level of syntactic analysis. I have assumed that each level of syntactic analysis is independently generated, in an important sense. Lexical insertion takes place at every level of syntax. From these principles and assumptions one may draw two important conclusions. First, since an affix with an argument structure must be independent at some level of analysis yet form part of a derived word at some other level, the affixes under discussion must, in effect, merge with a root or stem at some point in the syntactic analysis of a sentence. Second, since lexical insertion takes place at every level of structure, all affixation, including the merger under discussion here, must take place in the lexicon, which is the source of constituents for lexical insertion.

Therefore, the answer to Anderson's (1982) question "Where's morphology?" is both that morphology is everywhere in syntax—two (lexical) constituents at any level of syntactic analysis may correspond to a single derived constituent at the next level—and that morphology is restricted to the lexicon—all affixation is lexical. The results of affixation, derived words, are inserted at some level of syntactic analysis.

In contrast to the approach taken in the earlier draft of the present work, I assume here that morphological merger—the correspondence of two lexical items in one syntactic representation with a single constituent in another representation—takes place at a single level of analysis rather than between levels. That is, merger relates lists of constituents and relations at l-s, s, or surface structure; it does not interact in the mapping between levels of syntactic analysis. Schematically, the effects of morphological merger may be visualized as in (7.2).

Each of the levels of syntactic analysis discussed in the previous chapters is given a complex internal structure by the effects of morphological merger. A particular list of constituents and relations, shown in the left-hand column of (7.2), is mapped onto a list from the previous level of analysis, if there is one, that is, if the level of analysis in question is s or surface structure. This list has some constituent structure representation, which must meet whatever constraints hold of constituent structure representations. Morphological merger may map this list onto another list, which is also subject to mapping by merger. A list of constituents and relations that is related to the initial list via a chain of mergers is mapped onto the initial list of constituents and relations for the next level of analysis, if there is such a level.

Morphological merger, which relates lists of constituents and relations as shown in (7.2), could be seen as a type of transformational mapping. Unlike the mappings between syntactic levels, the mappings determined by merger relate structures of the same sort: the same vocabulary is found in each of the lists of constituents and relations displayed in (7.2). The mappings between syntactic levels—for example, between l-s and s structure—are strictly nontransformational in that they relate objects of different ontological types.

One general principle describes and constrains morphological merger. The insight behind this principle is that the affixation of morphemes with independent argument structures is a way of expressing relations. For example, when a language uses an affix in a derived causative construction, the affixation of the causative affix to a root verb expresses a relation that a language like English expresses syntactically by placing a causative verb like *make* in front of a phrase, a phrase headed by the verb that would serve as the stem for derived causative formation in a language like Japanese. I state the merger principle as in (7.3).

(7.2)

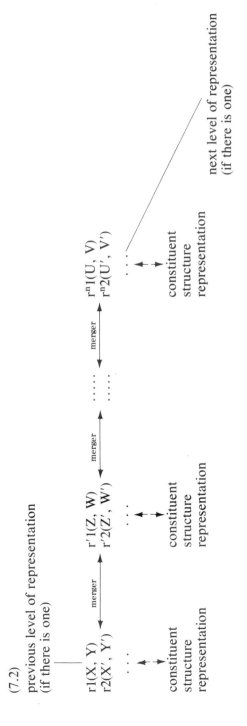

(7.3)

The Merger Principle:

The merger of X and Y at level L expresses all relations between X and/or phrases headed by X and Y and/or phrases headed by Y at L. "Express" means that the merger relates a list of constituents and relations at L containing the relation(s) between constituents headed by X and constituents headed by Y to a list of constituents and relations at L lacking all such relations.

In the current theory, semantic relations are generally expressed by projecting (corresponding) to s structure relations, which project to surface structure relations, which in turn are realized in the surface constituent structure tree. By removing relations from a given level of analysis, morphological merger stops the projection of these relations to the next level. Where the relations would generally be expressed by some aspect of the surface structure tree, after merger they are expressed solely by the merger: by the affixation relation between two morphemes.

Although the Merger principle (7.3) expresses the results of morphological merger as a mapping principle between lists of constituents and relations at a given level of syntactic analysis, it does not sufficiently define the mapping involved. Call the phrases whose relations are expressed by the merger of X and Y "X-h" and "Y-h" for "X-*headed*" and "Y-*headed*" constituent. In the limiting case, X-h will be X, Y-h will be Y. Call the list of constituents and relations containing X and Y as independent items "LIST" and the corresponding list containing X and Y as a derived word, X+Y, "LIST'." The Merger principle constrains the mapping between LIST and LIST', but the grammar must also say something explicit about the correspondence between the relations in LIST and LIST' borne by constituents that stand between X and X-h and between Y and Y-h in the constituent structure representation of LIST.

To take a concrete though hypothetical example, suppose the English verb *understand* were productively derived by affixing a prefix with the lexical entry of the preposition *under* to the verb root *stand*. A sentence like (7.4a) would then be roughly synonymous with sentence (7.4b).

(7.4)

a. Elmer stood under the porcupine.

b. Elmer understood the porcupine.

With this assumption, the prefix *under-* and the root *stand* would have the lexical entries in (7.5).

(7.5)
a. *under-*, 'under' (*locative*), [+transitive]
b. *stand*, 'stand' (∅), [+log sub], [−transitive]

The l-s structure for sentence (7.4b) would look something like (7.6).

(7.6)

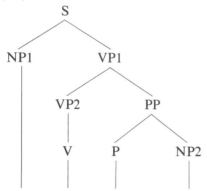

Elmer   stood   under-   the porcupine

I assume that the preposition *under* and its hypothetical prefixal counterpart *under-* produce a predicate modifier.

The list of constituents and relations represented in (7.6) includes the constituents and relations in (7.7).

(7.7)
arg(VP1, NP1)   role(VP1, NP1)   arg(PP, VP2)
arg(P, NP2)   role(P, NP2)

Call the list in (7.7) LIST. Merger of *stand* and *under-* at l-s structure will map LIST onto LIST′, containing the derived verb *understand,* which is P+V. Since *under-* heads PP and *stand* heads VP2, the Merger principle determines that the merger of these constituents will express the relation between PP and VP2—arg(PP, VP2)—and thus that LIST′ will lack this relation. What the Merger principle does not determine is what happens to relations arg(P, NP2) and role(P, NP2) at LIST′.

The principle in (7.8) formalizes the force of the Merger principle in (7.3) to further constrain the mapping between LIST and LIST′ in cases of merger.

(7.8)

The Merger Principle (revised):

When X and Y merge, the argument structure of the derived word X+Y is the argument structure of X applied to the argument structure of Y, or to Y itself, or the argument structure of Y applied to the argument structure of X, or to X itself. Where the merger of X and Y expresses the relation(s) between X-h and Y-h (constituents headed by X and Y respectively), the LIST' relations corresponding to LIST relations borne by X and Y and constituents between X and X h and between Y and Y-h in constituent structure are determined by examining the internal structure of the derived word X+Y.

The internal structure of the derived word in the hypothetical English example is shown in (7.9).

(7.9)

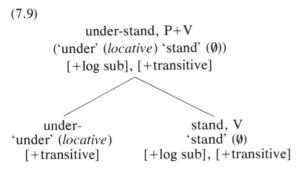

                under-stand, P+V
        ('under' (*locative*) 'stand' (∅))
            [+log sub], [+transitive]

        under-   stand, V
'under' (*locative*)   'stand' (∅)
    [+transitive]   [+log sub], [+transitive]

In accordance with the revised Merger principle, the argument structure of the derived verb *understand* is the argument structure of the affix applied to the argument structure of the root verb. That is, the derived word takes in arguments to form the predicate formed by *stand*'s P-A structure and the predicate modifier formed by *under-*'s argument structure. It applies the modifier to the predicate to derive a predicate. Thus the argument structure of the derived verb is a P-A structure; it takes in arguments to form predicates.

The feature percolation conventions described in the introduction to chapter 4 operate to determine the remaining features of the derived verb in (7.9). In particular, the features of an affix take precedence over the features of a stem in determining the features of a derived word. Thus the semantic role assigning feature of the prefix *under-* (it assigns a locative role) percolates to become a semantic role assigning feature of the derived verb *understand*. This is indicated by italicizing the locative role in the P-A structure of the derived verb in (7.9). In the case of semantic role assigning features, no feature of the root verb competes with features of the prefix in percolation, but the prefix is [+transitive], the stem verb [−transitive]. According to the conventions, then, the derived verb should be [+transitive], in agreement with the affix.

Note that in the present theory the affixation schematized in (7.9) takes place in the lexicon. Both the LIST containing the root verb and prefix as separate constituents and the LIST′ containing the derived verb *under-stand* are independently generated with items from the lexicon. The principles of morphological merger merely constrain the mapping between LIST and LIST′. Thus, although it may be involved in the syntax, in the mapping between syntactic representations, affixation is restricted to the lexicon.

Having determined the internal structure of the derived verb in (7.9), I am ready to apply the Merger principle to LIST (7.7) to determine the contents of LIST′. First, since the argument structure of the derived verb is simply the combination of the argument structures of the constituent morphemes, all the arguments of the merging constituents in LIST should correspond to arguments of the derived verb in LIST′. Since only the prefix takes arguments, arg(P, NP2) should correspond to arg(P+V, NP2). As for role assigning relations, since the role assigning feature of the prefix becomes a feature of the derived verb via feature percolation, role(P, NP2) should correspond to role(P+V, NP2).

These considerations cover all the relations on LIST except those involving VP1. An examination of constituent structure (7.6) reveals that VP1 is simply the result of applying the predicate modifier formed by P to the predicate formed by V. According to the Merger principle, the derived verb *understood* itself will apply the predicate modifier formed by P to the predicate formed by V. Thus the principles of merger determine that the constituent corresponding to VP1 in (7.6) and (7.7) will be the predicate headed by the derived verb P+V, and any relations borne by VP1 in LIST should be borne by this predicate in LIST′. The merger principles yield the LIST′ in (7.10) with the corresponding constituent structure representation in (7.11).

(7.10)
arg(VP1, NP1)   role(VP1, NP1)   arg(P+V, NP2)
role(P+V, NP2)

(7.11)

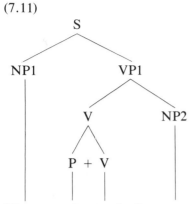

Elmer   understood   the porcupine

The principles of merger imply the following four-step procedure for mechanically transforming any LIST into the corresponding LIST', for a LIST and LIST' at l-s or s structure. Consider the merger of X and Y expressing relation(s) between X-h and Y-h, constituents headed by X and Y respectively, or X and Y themselves. LIST is the list of constituents and relations containing X and Y as independent items; LIST' is the list of constituents and relations containing the derived (merged) X+Y. To derive LIST' mechanically from LIST:

I. Cross out any relations between X-h and Y-h. These are expressed by the merger.

II. If any constituents structurally between X-h and X and/or between Y-h and Y—or X and/or Y themselves—are argument takers in arg/ ARG(A, B) relations in LIST, change these LIST argument takers to X+Y to derive arg/ARG(X+Y, B) relations for LIST'. This mechanically encodes the fact that the argument structure of X+Y is the argument structure of X applied to the argument structure of Y or to Y itself, or vice versa.

III. For role/ROLE(X, A) and role/ROLE(Y, B) relations in LIST, change X and/or Y to X+Y to derive relations for LIST' when the role assigning features of these constituents percolate to become features of X+Y.

There is one situation for which the merger principles offer no clear guide. Consider a role assigner, either semantic or syntactic, that lies structurally between X-h and X or Y-h and Y. This would be a phrasal role assigner. As such, its role assigning features are not lexical features and would not percolate within a derived word. I will show in sections 7.1.2 and 7.2 that the derived word X+Y must in some sense be seen as assigning the roles of such phrasal role assigners in some situations. In just this case where the proposed universal principles make no direct commandments, however, languages differ on whether or not to replace the phrasal role assigner A, where A falls between X-h and X or Y-h and Y, in the role/ROLE(A, B) relation in LIST with X+Y to create a role/ROLE(X+Y, B) relation for LIST'.

IV. Except for the situation described in the preceding paragraph, all relations from LIST not mentioned in I–III become relations of LIST' unchanged.

A few features of the proposed analysis of morphological merger should be exposed now. First, although merger is intuitively directional—X and Y merge to form X+Y—and although the mechanical procedures I–IV are explicitly directional, merger need not take place from left to right in the diagram in (7.2): distinct constituents X and Y in a list of constituents and relations to the right in (7.2) might correspond to a derived constituent X+Y to the left. Concretely, this means that, just as a single s structure constituent may correspond to two l-s constituents, a single l-s constituent may correspond to two s structure constituents. Because of standard derivational thinking—one conceives of a derivation taking an l-s structure through s to surface structure—the situation in which a single l-s item corresponds to two s structure items might be called splitting rather than merger. In any case, the principles of merger will operate identically right to left in (7.2) as well as left to right. I shall briefly discuss some situations that seem to implicate right-to-left merger (or splitting) in section 7.2.4.

Second, although the principles of merger apply clearly to l-s structure, and almost as clearly to s structure, their application to surface structure is as fuzzy as the descriptions of surface structure in chapters 2 and 3. I will discuss some cases of merger at surface structure in section 7.3, but since the analysis of surface structure in general is not well developed, the discussion must be taken as tentative. The problem of applying the principles to s structure involve the fuzziness of the notion of argument structure at this level of analysis. I will suggest a straightforward method of avoiding this problem while simultaneously sticking to the Merger principle and relying on the overarching assumption that the features of s structure are projections of the features of l-s structure.

7.1. Applied Verbs

In chapter 5 I presented an analysis of dative shift alternations like those in English that are not mediated by morphology on a verb. This section explores alternations superficially similar to dative shift but which are mediated by morphology. Consider the applied verb construction from Chi-Mwi:ni (Kisseberth and Abasheikh 1977) illustrated in (7.12b).

(7.12)
a. Hamadi Ø-sh-pishiłe cha:kuja.
   Hamadi SP-OP-cook-T/A food
   'Hamadi cooked the food.'

b. Hamadi Ø-wa-pik-il-ile wa:na cha:kuja.
   Hamadi SP-OP-cook-APPL-T/A children food
   'Hamadi cooked food for the children.'

The applied affix, -il-, in (7.12b) signals the presence in the sentence of an NP not contained within the argument structure of the verb to which it attaches. In (7.12b) this additional argument is interpreted as the benefactive. The Chi-Mwi:ni applied affix may also be used to indicate the presence of a goal NP, an instrumental NP, or an NP adversely affected by what the sentence describes (a malefactive). The analysis of applied affixes provided in this section is intended to cover affixes cross-linguistically that function like the Chi-Mwi:ni applied affix and are associated with the semantic roles listed in (7.13).

(7.13)
goals, benefactives, sources, malefactives, instrumentals

Instrumental applied affixes will be discussed in section 7.1.2; in section 7.1.1 I treat applied affixes associated with the remaining roles in (7.13). Applied affixes are also used with place, as opposed to directional, locatives (see Trithart 1977), but I have nothing to say about such locative applied verb forms in this book.

7.1.1. Applied Verbs with Goals, Benefactives, Sources, and Malefactives

7.1.1.1. Languages That Allow One Object per Verb It seems reasonable to assume that the Chi-Mwi:ni sentence (7.12b) has an l-s structure isomorphic to that of its English gloss, something like that in (7.14).

(7.14)

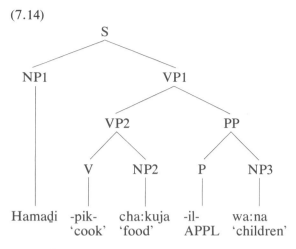

Hamaḍi -pik-   cha:kuja -il-   wa:na
        'cook' 'food'   APPL   'children'

A possible partial lexical entry for the applied (APPL) affix in its benefactive use is displayed in (7.15a). Compare this entry with that of the
English preposition *for*, given in (7.15b).[1]

(7.15)
a. *-il-*,]$_V$———, 'for' (*benefactive*), [+transitive]
b. *for*, P, 'for' (*benefactive*), [+transitive]

The essential difference between the entries in (7.15) is that *-il-* has the
morphological subcategorization feature of an affix—it attaches to the
right of verbs—whereas *for* is identified as an independent morpheme.

As a morpheme with its own argument structure, the applied affix
will be an independent constituent at l-s structure. Since the applied
affix is an affix, however, it will appear on the verbs to which it attaches
at some level of syntactic analysis. That is, at some level in the syntax,
the applied affix must merge with the root verb. The applied affixes to
be discussed in this section all seem to merge with root verbs at l-s
structure; see sections 7.1.2 and 7.2.3 for examples of merger at
s structure, section 7.3 for a discussion of merger at surface structure.

Recall that a lexical entry consists of a set of correspondences mapping between features relevant at different levels of analysis. Presumably, a morpheme that merges at level L contains among its features
relevant at L a morphological subcategorization feature specifying that
it attaches to roots or stems of a certain L category type. The morphological subcategorization feature could thereby determine the locus of
merger for a morpheme.

Suppose the Chi-Mwi:ni applied affix *-il-* in (7.15a) attaches to *-pik-* 'cook' to yield a single l-s structure verb for sentence (7.12b). The standard feature percolation principles plus the Merger principle (7.8), which determines the argument structure of derived words, predict the following internal structure for the derived verb *-pik-il-*.

(7.16)

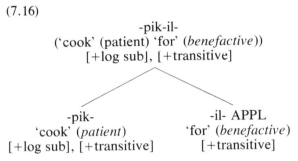

-pik-il-
('cook' (patient) 'for' (*benefactive*))
[+log sub], [+transitive]

-pik-   -il- APPL
'cook' (*patient*)   'for' (*benefactive*)
[+log sub], [+transitive]   [+transitive]

The Merger principle determines that the argument structure of the derived verb in (7.16) will be the argument structure of the applied affix applied to the argument structure of the root verb. Feature percolation determines the other features of the derived verb in (7.16). Since features of affixes take precedence over features of roots and stems in determining the features of derived words, the semantic role assigning feature of the APPL affix in (7.16) will become the feature of the applied verb, and this verb will assign the benefactive role. Assume for the moment that, consistent with the One Role/Role Assigner principle, Chi-Mwi:ni verbs assign only a single semantic role in the unmarked case (I will return to this point; see also the discussion in section 5.1.1 on Chi-Mwi:ni dative shift). If the derived verb in (7.16) assigns the benefactive role, then it cannot also assign the patient role, and the semantic role assigning property of the root in (7.16) may not percolate.

Given the l-s structure in (7.14) and the derived applied verb in (7.16), the effects of merger in l-s structure may be computed for the applied verb sentence (7.12b). Consider the list of relations encoded in (7.14):

(7.17)
a. sub(VP1, NP1)   b. mod(PP, VP2)   c. arg(V, NP2)
d. role(V, NP2)   e. arg(P, NP3)   f. role(P, NP3)

How do the principles determine the post-morphological-merger list of relations corresponding to (7.17)? First, the merger of P and V at l-s structure expresses all the relations between constituents headed by these lexical items. In the case at hand, this implies that the relation mod(PP, VP2) will not appear in the postmerger list. Next, since the argument structure of the derived applied verb is a simple combination of the argument structures of its constituent parts, all arguments of P and V will be arguments of V+P in the derived list. Thus, corresponding to arg(V, NP2) and arg(P, NP3) will be arg(V+P, NP2) and arg(V+P, NP3). The internal structure of the derived verb V+P shows that it takes over the role assigning properties of P but not of V. Thus role(P, NP3) will correspond to role(V+P, NP3) but role(V, NP2) will correspond to role(V, NP2). Finally, VP1 is simply the result of applying the modifier produced by P to the predicate produced by V. Since this application is performed within the derived verb, VP1 will correspond to the predicate headed by V+P in the postmerger list of relations.

Retaining the label VP1 for this predicate, I derive the postmerger list of relations shown in (7.18), with the corresponding constituent structure representation in (7.19).

(7.18)

a. sub(VP1, NP1)   b. arg(V+P, NP2)   c. arg(V+P, NP3)
d. role(V+P, NP3)   e. role(V, NP2)

(7.19)

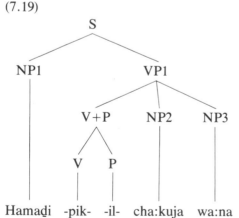

Hamaḍi -pik- -il- cha:kuja wa:na

Note that the definition of sisterhood in (2.36) identifies V and NP2 as sisters in (7.19). Thus the role(X, Y) relation between V and NP2 is correctly represented in this structure.

The reader should verify that the mechanical procedures listed in I–IV correctly relate the list in (7.17) to the list in (7.18).

In applied verb merger, then, the direct argument of the applied affix becomes the direct argument of the applied verb and the direct argument of the root verb becomes an indirect argument of the applied verb. This state of affairs is a direct result of the feature percolation conventions and the assumption that verbs in Chi-Mwi:ni, whether simple or derived, may assign only one semantic role each.

My analysis of (7.12b) automatically accounts for many features of the applied verb construction in Chi-Mwi:ni. On this analysis, only the benefactive NP in (7.12b) may be the OBJ of the derived verb. As shown in chapter 2, only direct l-s arguments of verbs, not indirect arguments, may correspond to syntactic direct objects (OBJs). Kisseberth and Abasheikh (1977) demonstrate that only the NP that depends on the applied affix, the benefactive NP in (7.12b), displays direct object behavior in Chi-Mwi:ni;[2] in particular, only the benefactive NP *wa:na* may control the object prefix (OP).

(7.20)
*Hamadi Ø-sh-pik-il-ile wa:na cha:kuja.
  Hamadi SP-OP$_i$-cook-APPL-T/A children food$_i$
  'Hamadi cooked food for the children.'

Sentence (7.20) is ungrammatical because the OP agrees with *cha:kuja* 'food' and not with the benefactive NP, as it does in (7.12b). Only the benefactive NP in (7.20) is the OBJ of the derived verb, and the OP on a verb must agree with its OBJ.

Also, only the applied object (the logical object of the applied affix) may show up as the subject of VPs headed by the passives of Chi-Mwi:ni applied benefactive verbs, as illustrated in (7.21) and (7.22).

(7.21)
  Wa:na wa-pik-il-ila cha:kuja na Hamadi.
  children SP-cookPASS-APPL-T/A food by Hamadi
  'The children had food cooked for them by Hamadi.'

(7.22)
*Cha:kuja sh-pik-il-ila wa:na na Hamadi.
  'Food was cooked for the children by Hamadi.'

Since the s structure counterpart to the logical object of the root verb in an applied verb construction (*cha:kuja* 'food' in these examples) must be head-Governed by the root verb itself and since the root verb does not head a VP at s structure, the root object may not correspond to a subject under passivization on my analysis.

In addition to predicting which of the postverbal NPs in (7.12b) will exhibit object behavior, my analysis accounts for the expression of the logical object of -*pik*- 'cook' as an [NP, VP]. Chi-Mwi:ni expresses the syntactic role assignee of a verb as an [NP, VP] and allows more than one [NP, VP] per surface structure VP. Since the logical object of -*pik*- 'cook' in (7.12b), *cha:kuja* 'food,' must also receive its syntactic role from -*pik*- at s structure, the analysis correctly expects it to appear in the position of syntactic role assignees of verbs: as an [NP, VP].

In Chi-Mwi:ni the applied affix may attach to intransitive as well as transitive verbs. Abasheikh (1979) provides an example of this, (7.23), in which the applied affix assigns the directional goal semantic role.

(7.23)
Muti u-m-tuluk-il-ile mwa:limu.
tree SP-OP-fall-APPL-T/A teacher
'The tree fell on the teacher.'

The internal structure of the applied verb in (7.23) is displayed in (7.24).

(7.24)

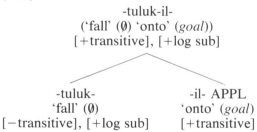

-tuluk-il-
('fall' (∅) 'onto' (*goal*))
[+transitive], [+log sub]

-tuluk-   -il- APPL
'fall' (∅)   'onto' (*goal*)
[−transitive], [+log sub]   [+transitive]

Since the features of an affix take precedence over the features of a root in percolation, the derived verb in (7.24) will be [+transitive] and may be seen as assigning the goal role. The reader should be able to complete the analysis of sentence (7.23) following the principles set forth in this chapter. The goal in (7.24) is identified as the OBJ of the derived verb and, in fact, exhibits OBJ behavior, as Abasheikh (1979) notes.[3]

Since it transitivizes an otherwise intransitive verb in (7.23), the Chi-Mwi:ni applied affix is clearly [+transitive]. Suppose there were a language whose applied affix differed crucially from Chi-Mwi:ni's in being unmarked for transitivity. The behavior that the theory predicts for the resulting applied verb constructions is exemplified in Bahasa Indonesia, a Western Austronesian language described in Chung (1976). The superficial syntax of Bahasa Indonesia is virtually the same as that found in Chi-Mwi:ni. Bahasa Indonesia is an SVO language whose subjects and objects are unmarked by case or adposition. The applied affix, -*kan*-, assigns the goal and benefactive roles. Some applied verb constructions are illustrated in (7.25b) and (7.25d) (TRANS is a transitivity marker).

(7.25)

a. Saja mem-bawa surat itu kepada Ali.
   I TRANS-bring letter the to Ali
   'I brought the letter to Ali.'

b. Saja mem-bawa-kan Ali surat itu.
   I TRANS-bring-APPL Ali letter the
   'I brought Ali the letter.'

c. Mereka men-dapat suatu perkerdjaan untuk anak-ku.
   they TRANS-find a job for child-my
   'They found a job for my daughter.'

d. Mereka men-dapat-kan anak-ku suatu perkerdjaan.
   they TRANS-find-APPL child-my a job
   'They found my daughter a job.'

On the hypothesis that -*kan*- is unmarked for transitivity, the internal structure of the applied verb in (7.25d) would look something like (7.26).

(7.26)

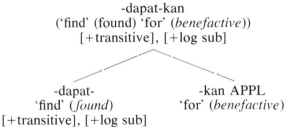

-dapat-kan
('find' (found) 'for' (*benefactive*))
[+transitive], [+log sub]

-dapat-   -kan APPL
'find' (*found*)   'for' (*benefactive*)
[+transitive], [+log sub]

Since the suffix in (7.26) is unmarked for transitivity, the morphological percolation conventions demand that the transitivity feature of the root, [+transitive], percolate to become the transitivity feature of the derived verb. The analysis of (7.25d) exactly parallels that for the Chi-Mwi:ni sentence in (7.12b) (compare the derived verbs in (7.26) and in (7.16)). As in the Chi-Mwi:ni sentence, I predict that only the benefactive NP in (7.25d) may be the OBJ of the derived verb or the SUB of the VP that this verb heads, because only the applied object (the benefactive) not the root object (the found argument) is a direct l-s argument of the derived verb. Chung (1976) demonstrates that only the benefactive NP in a benefactive applied verb construction may passivize, as predicted.

(7.27)

a. Orang itu me-masak-kan perempuan itu ikan.
    man the TRANS-cook-APPL woman the fish
    'The man cooked fish for the woman.'

b. Perempuan itu di-masak-kan ikan oleh orang itu.
    woman the PASS-cook-APPL fish by man the
    'The woman was cooked fish by the man.'

c. *Ikan di-masak-kan perempuan itu oleh orang itu.
    fish PASS-cook-APPL woman the by man the
    'A fish was cooked for the woman by the man.'

As explained in connection with the Chi-Mwi:ni applied verb construction, since the applied object but not the root object is the direct argument of the applied verb, only the applied object should correspond to the subject of the passive of an applied verb. Thus I predict the data in (7.27).

Just like Chi-Mwi:ni, Bahasa Indonesia expresses the syntactic role assignee of a verb as an [NP, VP] and allows more than one [NP, VP] per surface structure VP. As expected on the present analysis, since it is the syntactic role assignee of the root verb in (7.25d), the logical object of -dapat- 'find' (*suatu perkerdjaan* 'a job') appears as [NP, VP].

Suppose -*kan* is attached to an *in*transitive verb, as shown schematically in (7.28).

(7.28)

$$
\begin{array}{c}
\text{V-kan} \\
\text{('verb' ($\emptyset$) 'for' (\textit{benefactive}))} \\
\text{[$-$transitive], [$+$log sub]}
\end{array}
$$

$$
\begin{array}{cc}
\text{V} & \text{-kan APPL} \\
\text{'verb' ($\emptyset$)} & \text{'for' (\textit{benefactive})} \\
\text{[$-$transitive], [$+$log sub]} &
\end{array}
$$

Since the derived verb in (7.28) inherits the semantic role assigning properties of the affix -*kan*, the applied object will be the direct logical object of the derived applied verb in a sentence containing V-*kan*. But because the applied affix is unmarked for transitivity, the [−transitive] feature of the verb root in (7.28) percolates to become the transitivity feature of the derived verb. Now by principle M (chapter 2), the derived applied verb in (7.28) will have to head-Govern the s structure counterpart of the applied object. Since the verb is [+log sub], the applied object cannot correspond to the subject of the VP that the applied verb heads. Since the verb is [−transitive], the applied object cannot correspond to the OBJ of the verb. Unless Bahasa Indonesia provides some s structure constituent that might assign a syntactic role to the s structure counterpart of a logical object, the applied object may not correspond to an indirect argument of the applied verb at s structure. Thus the s structure counterpart of the logical object of *-kan* will violate principle M when *-kan* attaches to intransitive verbs. In fact, as Chung (1976) notes, *-kan* may not attach to intransitive verbs in Bahasa Indonesia, confirming the hypothesis that the applied affix *-kan* is unmarked for transitivity.

7.1.1.2. Languages that Allow More than One Object per Verb   The present theory provides an analysis for applied verb constructions in Chi-Mwi:ni and Bahasa Indonesia under the assumption that these languages allow a verb to assign only one semantic role in the unmarked case (and only one syntactic role). It was assumed that the limit of one logical object and one grammatical OBJ per verb represents the unmarked case cross-linguistically—see the One Role/Role Assigner principle. If linguists or children are to hypothesize that a language allows verbs more than one object, then they must have strong positive evidence that sentences in the language contain two or more objects in a single clause. As Kisseberth and Abasheikh (1977) demonstrate, only one NP in a Chi-Mwi:ni sentence will display object properties, even in double object constructions like those discussed in section 5.1. Only one NP per Chi-Mwi:ni verb will passivize and/or control the object prefix (OP), for example. Chung (1976) presents similar evidence for Bahasa Indonesia. Since there is no reason to believe that a verb in Chi-Mwi:ni or Bahasa Indonesia may take more than one object, the theory says that these languages restrict verbs to one object each.

Nevertheless, some Bantu languages superficially similar to Chi-Mwi:ni provide direct positive evidence that they allow more than one logical and grammatical object per verb. Kimenyi (1980) demonstrates that both arguments in a Kinyarwanda double object construction with *-haa-* 'give,' like that in (7.29a), exhibit object properties. For example,

either the theme or goal of *-haa-* may correspond to the SUB of the VP
headed by *-haa-*'s passive form, *-haa-w-*, as shown in (7.29b,c).

(7.29)

a. Umugabo y-a-haa-ye umugóre igitabo.
   man SP-PAST-give-ASP woman book
   'The man gave the woman the book.'

b. Igitabo cy-a-haa-w-e umugóre n'ûmugabo.
   book SP-PAST-give-PASS-ASP woman by-man
   'The book was given to the woman by the man.'

c. Umugóre y-a-haa-w-e igitabo n'ûmugabo.
   woman SP-PAST-give-PASS-ASP book by-man
   'The woman was given the book by the man.'

Compare the sentences in (7.29) with the Chi-Mwi:ni sentences (7.30).

(7.30)

a. Ni-m-pełe Ja:ma kujá.
   SP(='I')-OP-gave Jama food
   'I gave Jama food.'

b. *Kuja i-pela Ja:ma na: mi.
   food SP-gavePASS food by me
   'Food was given to Jama by me.'

c. Ja:ma Ø-pela: kuja na: mi.
   Jama SP-gavePASS food by me
   'Jama was given food by me.'

In contrast to the situation in Kinyarwanda, only the goal argument in
a Chi-Mwi:ni double object construction with 'give' may passivize
and, Kisseberth and Abasheikh (1977) claim, display other object
properties.

   Kimenyi (1980) provides evidence that a Kinyarwanda verb may
actually have more than two objects. Assume that in languages that
allow a verb more than one OBJ—that is, in languages that allow verbs
to assign more than one syntactic role—transitivity is a multivalued
feature. Intransitive verbs will be [0 transitive], verbs taking one OBJ
will be [+1 transitive], verbs taking two OBJs will be [+2 transitive],
and so on. The passive morpheme in such a language will carry the
features [−log sub], [−1 transitive]. I will amend the feature percolation conventions for multivalued features such that all such features in
every constituent part of a derived word percolate and add together to

determine the value of the feature for the derived word. For example, attaching the passive morpheme to a [+2 transitive] verb like -*haa*- in (7.29a) will yield a [+1 transitive] verb, the verb in (7.29b,c). As Kimenyi (1980) provides evidence that the postverbal NPs in the passives of [+2 transitive] verbs (e.g., *umugóre* 'woman' in (7.29b) and *igitabo* 'book' in (7.29c)) exhibit the same object properties that they exhibit in the active counterparts of these sentences, it seems correct to say that the passive verbs in (7.29b,c) are [+1 transitive], that is, that they take an OBJ.

The available evidence points to a partial lexical entry for Kinyarwanda -*haa*- 'give' like that in (7.31).

(7.31)
-*haa*-, 'give' (*theme, goal*), [+2 transitive], [+log sub]

In order for both the theme and goal arguments of -*haa*- to be OBJs of the verb, the verb must assign both the theme and goal roles—recall that only direct semantic arguments of verbs correspond to direct objects at s structure. A partial lexical entry for the passive of -*haa*- 'give,' the verb in (7.29b,c), is shown in (7.32).

(7.32)
-*haa-w*-, 'give' (*theme, goal*), [+1 transitive], [−log sub]

Since the verb in (7.32) assigns only one syntactic role, only one of its logical objects may correspond to a grammatical OBJ; the other will satisfy principle M by corresponding to the SUB of the VP headed by the passive verb. Which logical object becomes the OBJ and which the SUB is not specified within the lexical entry in (7.32), and, as shown in (7.29b,c), both possibilities are realized.

Given that Kinyarwanda allows a verb to assign more than one semantic role in the unmarked case, the present theory makes the correct predictions about the grammatical relations borne by arguments in Kinyarwanda applied verb constructions. Consider the benefactive applied affix -*ir*- in Kinyarwanda. The lexical entry for -*ir*- in its benefactive use is shown in (7.33). Some benefactive applied verbs appear in (7.34).

(7.33)
-*ir*-, 'for' (*benefactive*), [+1 transitive]

(7.34)

a. Umugóre a-rá-kor-er-a umugabo.
   woman SP-PRES-work-APPL-ASP man
   'The woman is working for the man.'

b. Umukoôbwa a-ra-som-er-a umuhuûgu igitabo.
   girl SP-PRES-read-APPL-ASP boy book
   'The girl is reading a book for the boy.'

The internal structure of the verb in (7.34b) is shown in (7.35).

(7.35)

$$
\begin{array}{c}
\text{-som-er-} \\
\text{('read' } (read) \text{ 'for' } (benefactive)) \\
[+\log \text{ sub}], [+2 \text{ transitive}]
\end{array}
$$

$$
\begin{array}{cc}
\text{-som-} & \text{-ir-} \\
\text{'read' } (read) & \text{'for' } (benefactive) \\
[+\log \text{ sub}], [+1 \text{ transitive}] & [+1 \text{ transitive}]
\end{array}
$$

Since a Kinyarwanda verb may assign more than one semantic role, the derived verb in (7.35) may inherit the semantic role assigning properties of both affix and root. Semantic role assigning properties, like argument structures but unlike grammatical features such as [± log sub], should not be seen as something for which a lexical item is either specified or not, such that if the item is specified for the features, it cannot inherit them. A constituent specified for [± log sub] may not inherit a value for this feature. On the other hand, a constituent with semantic role assigning properties may inherit other semantic role assigning properties as long as this inheritence does not violate independent constraints, either language specific or universal.

So the derived applied verb in (7.35) will assign both the read and the benefactive roles. The values of the transitivity feature from both the root and the applied affix in (7.35) will add together to yield a [+2 transitive] value for the derived applied verb. Since the derived verb -som-er- will take both the root and the applied objects as direct semantic arguments and since the verb is [+2 transitive], both the root and applied objects may correspond to grammatical direct objects of the derived verb. Kimenyi demonstrates that both these constituents display all the OBJ properties he was able to uncover in Kinyarwanda. Furthermore, since both the root and applied objects are direct l-s arguments of the applied verb, both may correspond to the SUB of the

VP headed by the applied verb in passive constructions. This is confirmed in (7.36).

(7.36)
a. Umuhuûnga a-ra-andik-ir-a umukoôbwa íbárúwa.
   boy SP-PRES-write-APPL-ASP girl letter
   'The boy is writing the letter for the girl.'

b. Íbárúwa i-ra-andik-ir-w-a umukoôbwa n'ûmuhuûngu.
   letter SP-PRES-write-APPL-PASS-ASP girl by-boy
   'The letter is written for the girl by the boy.'

c. Umukoôbwa a-ra-andik-ir-w-a íbárúwa n'ûmuhuûngu.
   girl SP-PRES-write-APPL-PASS-ASP letter by-boy
   'The girl is having the letter written for her by the boy.'

The sentences in (7.36) should be compared with sentences (7.12b) and (7.21, 7.22) from Chi-Mwi:ni and sentences (7.27) from Bahasa Indonesia, languages I have claimed restrict verbs to one OBJ each.

That the Kinyarwanda benefactive affix attaches to [0 transitive] stems like -kor- 'work' in (7.34a) is further evidence that it is indeed [+1 transitive] and not unmarked for transitivity. Recall that an applied affix unmarked for transitivity, like -kan in Bahasa Indonesia, cannot attach to intransitive stems without causing a violation of principle M in sentences containing the resulting derived verb.

The simple hypothesis that Chi-Mwi:ni restricts verbs to one logical and grammatical object whereas Kinyarwanda allows more than one object per verb accounts for differences between these languages in the behavior of applied verb constructions (and double object constructions without derived verbs). In section 7.2.3, I show that the hypothesis that Kinyarwanda allows a verb to be multiply transitive makes correct predictions for causative constructions as well. The arguments for multiple transitivity could be repeated with data from Kimeru (Hodges 1977) and Chichewa (Trithart 1977), among other Bantu languages. I will argue in section 7.2 that Japanese also allows more than one OBJ per verb.

7.1.2. Instrumental Applied Verbs
Since it is forced by the theory, the analysis I have provided for applied verb constructions should extend to all such constructions cross-linguistically. For the semantic roles involved in the applied verb constructions discussed in the last section, all the evidence I have uncovered supports the analysis (see, e.g., Thomas-Flinders 1982 on

Maricopa and Nichols 1982 on Indo-European applied verb constructions). In many languages, however, applied verb constructions that
involve instrumentals behave differently from other applied verb sentences. Fula, a Niger-Congo language described by Sylla (1979) is one
such language. The Fula benefactive applied verbs behave just like
their counterparts in Chi-Mwi:ni. When a benefactive applied affix is
attached to a transitive root, for example, the benefactive NP but not
the logical object of the root verb becomes the direct 1-s argument of
the derived applied verb, as evidenced by the fact that only the benefactive may passivize.

(7.37)
a. Takko def-an-ii sukaaɓe ɓe gertogal.
    Takko cook-APPL-PAST children Det chicken
    'Takko cooked the chicken for the children.'

b. Sukaaɓe ɓe ndef-an-aama gertogal.
    children Det cook-APPL-PAST/PASS chicken
    'The children had a chicken cooked for them.'

c. *Gertogal def-an-aama sukaaɓe ɓe.
    chicken cook-APPL-PAST/PASS children Det
    'Chicken was cooked for the children.'

Compare sentences (7.37) with (7.12b) and (7.21, 7.22) from Chi-
Mwi:ni.
    When the Fula instrumental applied affix -r- is attached to an in-
transitive verb, the instrumental NP takes on the properties of the logical object of the instrumental applied verb. It passivizes, for example.

(7.38)·
a. Mi am-ii.
    I dance-PAST
    'I danced.'

b. Mi am-r-ii paɗe.
    I dance-INST-PAST shoes
    'I danced with shoes.'

c. Paɗe hgam-r-aama.
    shoes dance-INST-PAST/PASS
    'Shoes were danced with.'

When the instrumental applied affix attaches to a transitive verb, on the
other hand, it is the logical object of the root verb and not the instru-

mental NP that behaves as if it were the logical object of the instrumental applied verb.

(7.39)

a. Aali tay-ii lekki.
   Aali cut-PAST tree
   'Aali cut the tree.'

b. Aali tay-r-ii lekki jammbere.
   Aali cut-INST-PAST tree axe
   'Aali cut the tree with an axe.'

c. Lekki tay-r-aama jammbere.
   tree cut-INST-PAST/PASS axe
   'A tree was cut with an axe.'

d. *Jammbere tay-r-aama lekki.
   axe cut-INST-PAST/PASS tree
   'An axe was used to cut a tree.'

Compare sentences (7.39c,d) with sentences (7.37). In the Fula benefactive applied verb construction with a transitive root verb, the applied object (the benefactive argument) is the logical object of the derived applied verb.

Chichewa (Trithart 1977) also displays an instrumental applied verb with unusual properties. A combination of the causative affix, -ts-, and the passive affix, -dw-, indicates that an instrumental NP is the subject of the sentence headed by the verb to which the affixes attach. These two morphemes may attach to an intransitive or transitive verb as in (7.40a) and (7.40b).

(7.40)

a. Khásu lí-ma-(li-)lim-its-ídw-a (ndí Jóni).
   hoe$_i$ it$_i$-HABIT-(it$_i$-)farm-CAUSE-PASS-INDIC (by John)
   'The hoe is farmed with (by John).'

b. Khásu lí-ma-(li-)lim-its-ídw-a chí-manga (ndí Jóni).
   hoe$_i$ it$_i$-HABIT-(it$_i$-)farm-CAUSE-PASS-INDIC corn (by John)
   'The hoe is used to farm corn with (by John).'

For present purposes, the important property of this instrumental applied verb construction in Chichewa is that the causative affix alone may not indicate that an instrumental argument is a postverbal NP or object. Without the passive affix, -dw-, the causative affix has no instrumental implications, as shown in (7.41), where the sentences are ungrammatical because they block both the instrumental and the causative readings. They block the instrumental reading because this reading is reserved for sentences containing the passive affix; they block the causative reading because the Chichewa causative construction requires an animate causee. If possible with a causative reading, (7.41a) would mean 'John caused the pen to write.'

(7.41)

a. *Jóni á-ma-(yi-)lemb-éts-a pêni.

John$_i$ he$_i$-HABIT-(it$_j$-)write-CAUSE-INDIC pen$_j$

'John writes with a pen.'

b. *Jóni a-ná-(yí-)lemb-ets-a pêni dz-íná lá-ké.

John$_i$ he$_i$-PAST-(it$_j$-)write-CAUSE-INDIC pen$_j$ name his

'John wrote his name with a pen.'

The Bantu language Mashi (Gary 1977) has an instrumental applied verb construction with the same characteristics as the Chichewa construction just described. The instrumental affix is not homophonous with the causative in Mashi, however.

One simple assumption about the manner in which the instrumental role may be assigned predicts both the Fula and Chichewa constructions I have described and explains why they differ from the applied verb constructions discussed in section 7.1.1. This assumption is independently motivated; in fact, it was proposed by Dick Carter (personal communication) on independent grounds. Translated into the terms of the present theory, Carter claims that it is wrong to look at the preposition *with* in (7.42) as assigning some instrumental role inherently associated with the preposition.

(7.42)

Elmer unlocked the porcupine cage with a key.

Rather, a predicate produced by *unlock* assigns an instrumental role to *a key*. The idea is that the class of roles usually called instrumentals includes widely varying roles. Which member of this class a given instrumental NP will bear depends on the verb producing the predicate with which the instrumental is associated.

One may say that verbs compatible with instrumentals name two functions from arguments to predicates, one producing predicates that assign agent and related roles (e.g., experiencer), the other producing predicates that assign instrumental roles. On this view, the preposition *with* in English serves much the same function that *by* does. *With* names a function from an argument bearing an instrumental role to modifiers of predicates. *With* and its argument form a modifier that modifies a predicate, which I will call VP. *With* must indicate that its argument receives an instrumental semantic role assigned by a predicate produced by the head of VP. Similarly, *by* and its argument form a modifier that modifies a predicate VP. *By* assigns to its argument the role assigned by VP (see section 4.1.1.2).

A number of considerations support this conception of the semantics of instrumentals. First, the semantic role of an instrument does in fact vary widely, crucially depending on the verb with which the instrumental appears. Compare the roles of the instrumental NPs in (7.43).

(7.43)
a. Elmer unlocked the porcupine cage with a key.
b. Elmer examined the inscription with the magnifying glass.

In (7.43a) *a key* is an intermediary agent in the act of unlocking the porcupine cage; Elmer does something to the key, the key does something to the cage, and the cage unlocks. In (7.43b), *the magnifying glass* is an indispensable tool in Elmer's examination of the inscription, but it is not an intermediary agent in the examination. This difference is reflected syntactically in English in the contrast between (7.44a) and (7.44b), in which the subjects are intended to be interpreted as instrumentals, not (simply) agents.

(7.44)
a. A key unlocked the porcupine cage.
b. *The magnifying glass examined the inscription.

Intermediary agent instrumentals can generally serve as subjects of the verb with which they are associated in English, as in (7.44a). On the other hand, facilitating instrumentals like *the magnifying glass* in (7.43b) cannot generally serve as subjects—see (7.44b).

A second consideration that supports the view that instrumental roles are assigned by predicates, not instrumental adpositions or case, is the widespread homophony between instrumental and comitative markings. English *with*, for example, has a comitative use illustrated in (7.45).

(7.45)
Elmer ate dinner with Hortense.

It is clear from (7.45) that *Hortense* is an eater of dinner; that is, *Hortense* bears the role assigned by the predicate that the 'eat' function produces, the same role that is assigned to the logical subject of the sentence, *Elmer*. Since instrumental adpositions and case markings in their *comitative* use mark a constituent to receive a semantic role assigned by a predicate, it is reasonable to assume that the instrumental adpositions and case marking perform the same duty in their *instrumental* use.

Finally, instrumental case marking and adpositions are the most common markers of the logical subject in passive constructions cross-linguistically; they are the items most commonly used to perform the function that *by* performs in English. Since the constituent performing the *by* function marks phrases to receive the semantic role assigned by a predicate, the cross-linguistic use of the instrumental case marking and adpositions for the *by* function strongly suggests that they mark phrases to receive the semantic role assigned by a predicate in their instrumental use as well. One might suppose that the instrumental is used for the displaced subject in passives in many languages simply because of some close semantic correspondence between instrumentals and agents. But note that the instrumental case (called comitative in Central Arctic Eskimo) is used for the displaced subjects in the passives of the ergative languages discussed in chapter 6, even though the displaced subject in the passives of these languages is canonically a theme or patient rather than an agent.

If Carter's suggestion is essentially correct, the instrumental case or adposition in a language operates in much the same manner as English *by*. That is, the instrumental marking ensures that its argument receives a semantic role assigned by a predicate. Given Carter's suggestion, it is possible to interpret the semantic role assigning properties of instrumental adpositions and cases in two ways. First, one may view the adposition or case as itself assigning the instrumental role assigned by the instrumental predicate with which it is associated. On this view, the l-s structure for (7.42) would look like (7.46).

(7.46)

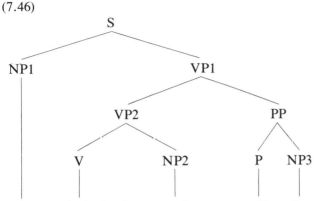

Elmer unlocked the porcupine cage with a key

The verb *unlock* in (7.46) names two functions from arguments to predicates; one function produces predicates that assign agent roles, the other produces predicates that assign instrumental roles. The preposition *with* in (7.46) assigns to *a key* the role assigned by the instrumental assigning predicate produced by *unlock*. Compare (7.46) with the l-s structure for the passive sentence (7.47), shown in (7.48).

(7.47)
The porcupine cage was unlocked by Elmer.

(7.48)

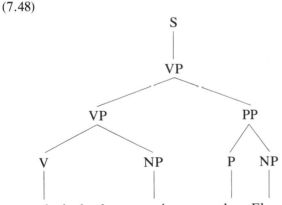

was unlocked   the porcupine cage by Elmer

The preposition *by* assigns to *Elmer* the role assigned by the agent assigning predicate that *unlock* produces.

If the instrumental applied affix is viewed as assigning an instrumental role as *with* does in (7.46), one would not expect the instrumental applied verb to behave any differently from, say, the benefactive applied verb, whose applied affix assigns the benefactive role. In some languages, instrumental applied verbs do behave like other applied verbs, indicating that these languages view the instrumental affix itself as assigning the instrumental role. Unlike the situation in sentences containing the Fula instrumental applied verbs, it is the instrumental NP that is the logical object of the Chi-Mwi:ni instrumental applied verb, regardless of whether the instrumental affix is added to intransitive or transitive verb roots. There are some complications surrounding the instrumental constructions in Chi-Mwi:ni, discussed at length by Kisseberth and Abasheikh (1977), for which I have no explanation. For the most part, however, instrumental applied verbs in Chi-Mwi:ni exhibit the same behavior as the benefactive applied verbs I have analyzed, with an instrumental NP replacing the benefactive NP. Therefore, Chi-Mwi:ni must take the first view of the semantic role assigning properties of the instrumental affix.

On the second interpretation of the assignment of the instrumental role, the instrumental adposition, case marking, or affix does not itself assign a role. Rather, it marks a constituent to receive the instrumental role, which is actually assigned directly by an instrumental predicate. The constituent structure representation of the l-s structure of sentence (7.42) would not look any different from (7.46) on this analysis. Nevertheless, the competing interpretations propose different lists of constituents and relations for the l-s structure of (7.42). Where NP3 receives its role from *with* on the first analysis (role(with, NP3)), on the second analysis NP3 actually receives its semantic role from an instrumental-assigning predicate (role($VP2_{instr}$, NP3)). Again, the verb *unlock* names two functions from arguments to predicates. One function produces predicates that assign agent roles; the other produces predicates that assign instrumental roles. On the second analysis of instrumentals, the instrumental marker effects the assignment of a role by the instrumental-assigning predicate to the argument of the instrumental marker. On this analysis, the preposition *with* has the special ability, like that of *by,* to assign the role assigned by a predicate to its argument. The preposition itself stands in the constituent structure position to represent the role assigning relation between the instrumental predicate and its argument—after all, the preposition is effecting the assignment of the role—but the actual role assigner must appear in the l-s structure, in the list of constituents and relations at this level.

To repeat, the distinction between the two analyses of instrumentals is simply whether the instrumental role assigning relation is listed as a relation between an instrumental marker, like a preposition, and the argument of this marker, or whether the relation is listed as a relation between an instrumental assigning predicate and the argument of the instrumental marker.

If one assumes that the Fula and Chichewa instrumental applied affixes effect the assignment of the instrumental role consistent with the second interpretation of instrumental assignment rather than the first interpretation, one correctly predicts the syntax of the instrumental applied verb constructions in these languages. The difference between the instrumental constructions in the two languages follows from the assumption that the instrumental applied affix merges with the root verb at l-s structure in Fula but not until s structure in Chichewa.

Consider first the Fula sentence (7.39b). Given that the instrumental affix -r- and the root verb *tayʕ-* 'cut' form a single l-s structure verb, the internal structure of the applied verb, *tayʕ-r-* in (7.39b) should look like (7.49).

(7.49)

$$tayʕ\text{-}r\text{-}$$
('cut' (*patient*) 'with' (instrumental))
[+transitive], [+log sub]

tayʕ-	*-r-*
'cut' (*patient*)	'with' (instrumental)
[+transitive], [+log sub]	[+transitive]

The essential difference between the instrumental applied verb in (7.49) and, say, the Chi-Mwi:ni benefactive applied verb in (7.16) is that the instrumental applied affix, unlike the benefactive applied affix, does not itself assign a semantic role. Therefore, it does not percolate a semantic role assigning feature in the derived verb in (7.49). Since the affix does not percolate a role assigning feature in (7.49), the root verb may percolate its feature, and the derived verb will assign the patient role.

The l-s structure of (7.39b) before merger will include the list of constituents and relations in (7.50), represented in the tree structure (7.51).

(7.50)

a. sub(VP1, NP1)   b. mod(PP, VP2)   c. role(V1, NP2)
d. arg(V1, NP2)   e. arg(P, NP3)   f. role(VP2$_{instr}$, NP3)

(7.51)

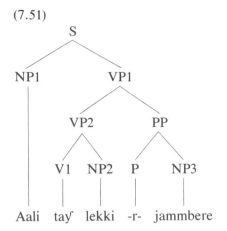

Aali   tay   lekki   -r-   jammbere

Computing the relations for the post-merger list corresponding to (7.50) is straightforward, with the exception of the postmerger counterpart to role(VP2$_{instr}$, NP3). VP2$_{instr}$ is the instrumental assigning predicate formed by V1. Merger of the instrumental applied affix with the root verb places within the argument structure of the derived verb all the compositional semantics of the modifier produced by the affix and of the predicates produced by the verb. The predicates produced by the root verb are internal to the argument structure of the derived verb. Thus the instrumental assigning predicate must be seen as internal to the derived instrumental applied verb.

Instrumental merger provides an example of a situation mentioned briefly in the introduction to this chapter. The situation arises when the merger of X and Y expresses a relation or relations between X-h, a phrase headed by X, and Y-h, a phrase headed by Y. The argument structures of X and Y, one applied to the other, become the argument structure of the derived verb X+Y; therefore, X-h and Y-h, and all phrases between X and X-h and between Y and Y-h in constituent structure, are internalized inside the argument structure of the derived verb and are no longer independent l-s constituents. The problem arises, as in the present case, when X-h, Y-h, or some phrase between X-h and X or between Y-h and Y participates in a semantic role assigning relation that the merger does not express. In the present situation, an instrumental predicate formed by the root verb is internalized inside the argument structure of the derived verb although the role assigning relation between it and the instrumental argument is not expressed by the merger.

The Merger principle does not determine what must occur in such situations; each language must decide how to handle these cases within the constraints imposed by the theory. Since the argument structure of the root verb, which will dictate the formation of the instrumental predicate, appears both with the root verb and with the derived verb in (7.49), Fula could allow either of these verbs to act as operator in the role assigning relation after merger. Since verbs in Fula assign only one role each, however, and the derived verb assigns the patient role (owing to feature percolation), only the root verb is free to stand in the role assigning relation with respect to the instrumental argument.

Given these considerations and following the Merger principle, one derives (7.52) as the postmerger list of l-s constituents and relations for sentence (7.39b). This list has the constituent structure representation in (7.53).

(7.52)
a. sub(VP1, NP1)   b. arg(V2, NP2)   c. role(V2, NP2)
d. arg(V2, NP3)   e. role(V1, NP3)

(7.53)

The l-s structure in (7.53) is precisely isomorphic to the structure for the Chi-Mwi:ni benefactive applied verb construction in (7.19). The difference, not displayed graphically, is that the applied object is the direct argument of the applied verb in the Chi-Mwi:ni benefactive construction whereas the root object is the direct argument of the applied verb in the Fula instrumental construction. This difference follows, given the considerations just mentioned, from the hypothesis that although the benefactive affix itself assigns the benefactive role in a benefactive applied verb construction, some instrumental predicate produced by the root verb assigns the instrumental role in a Fula instrumental applied verb construction. In (7.39) it is the logical object of the root verb that displays direct argument properties in a Fula instrumental applied verb construction, as predicted by this analysis.

The analysis of a Fula instrumental applied verb derived from an intransitive verb like that in (7.38b) is comparatively straightforward. The l-s structure for sentence (7.38b), repeated here as (7.54), is given in (7.55), with the corresponding constituent structure tree in (7.56).

(7.54)
Mi an-r-ii pade.
I dance-INST-PAST shoes
'I danced with shoes.'

(7.55)
a. sub(VP1, NP1)   b. mod(PP, VP2)   c. arg(P, NP2)
d. role(VP2$_{instr}$, NP2)

(7.56)

```
              S
           ⟋     ⟍
        NP1        VP1
         |       ⟋    ⟍
         |     VP2      PP
         |      |     ⟋   ⟍
         |      V1   P    NP2
         |      |    |     |
        mi     am-  -r-   pade
```

The internal structure for the derived applied instrumental verb in (7.54) is shown in (7.57).

(7.57)

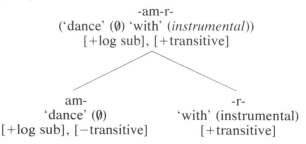

```
                        -am-r-
            ('dance' (∅) 'with' (instrumental))
                 [+log sub], [+transitive]
                ⟋                    ⟍
           am-                          -r-
        'dance' (∅)              'with' (instrumental)
   [+log sub], [−transitive]         [+transitive]
```

As in the case of instrumental applied verbs formed on transitive roots, the instrumental assigning predicate produced by the root verb in (7.54) is, so to speak, accidently internalized in the derived verb. As was the situation with (7.39b), Fula must decide for sentences like (7.54) what constituent should be seen as standing in the instrumental role assigning relation in the postmerger l-s structure. Again, both the derived verb and the verb root contain the argument structure of the verb that would produce the instrumental-assigning predicate. In the case of (7.54), however, since the derived verb inherits no role assigning features from either root or affix, it may stand in the role assigning relation with respect to the instrumental role without violating the restriction limiting verbs to one role each. In (7.38) the instrumental argument does behave like a direct semantic argument of the derived instrumental applied verb; therefore, Fula must take the derived verb as standing in the role assigning relation. In fact, Fula has no choice here. If the instrumental NP were an indirect l-s argument of the derived verb, assigned its role by the root verb, it would also have to receive a syntactic role from the root verb, as shown in section 2.2.3.2. But since the root verb is [−transitive], it could not assign a syntactic role to the instrumental NP. Therefore, the derived applied verb must assign the instrumental role in the postmerger l-s structure.

If one assumes that the Chichewa instrumental affix effects the assignment of the instrumental role in the same manner as the Fula instrumental affix, but that the Chichewa affix, unlike the Fula, merges with root verbs at s structure, it is possible to explain the peculiar aspects of the Chichewa instrumental applied verb construction presented at the beginning of this section. Recall that the instrumental argument appears as the subject of sentences containing the Chichewa instrumental applied verb and that the passive morpheme must obligatorily cooccur with the Chichewa instrumental applied affix. Consider the Chichewa sentence (7.40b). On the assumption that the Chichewa instrumental suffix -ts- effects the assignment of the instrumental role as does the Fula affix -r-, the l-s structure of (7.40b) should look like (7.58) in all relevant details.

(7.58)

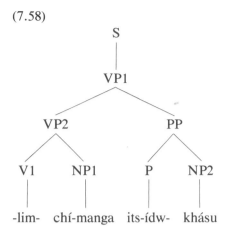

-lim- chí-manga its-ídw- khásu

Note that I have attached the passive morpheme, -*dw*-, to the instrumental applied affix -*ts*- in (7.58), respecting the order of constituents inside the Chichewa verb. The passive morpheme -*dw*- should carry the feature [−log sub] in (7.58) as it does in canonical passives like (7.60).

(7.59)
Jóni a-ná-(zí-)nyamul-a n-thóchí.
John$_i$ he$_i$-PAST-(them$_j$-)carry-INDIC bananas$_j$
'John carried the bananas.'

(7.60)
N-thóchí zi-ná-(zí-)nyamul-idw-a.
bananas$_i$ they$_i$-PAST-(they$_i$-)carry-PASS-INDIC
'The bananas were carried.'

Since the modifiers produced by the argument structure of the instrumental applied affix modify predicates to yield predicates, as in (7.58), the [−log sub] feature on the combination of instrumental applied affix and passive suffix should be interpreted to mean that the predicates resulting from the combination of the modifiers headed by these affixes and their modifiees will not take logical subjects. The relevant predicate in (7.58) is VP1, and it lacks a logical subject, as required.

The l-s relations encoded in l-s structure (7.58) are listed in (7.61).

(7.61)
a. mod(PP, VP2)   b. arg(V1, NP1)   c. role(V1, NP1)
d. arg(P, NP2)   e. role(VP2$_{instr}$, NP2)

Again, the special feature of instrumental markers is that they effect the assignment to their arguments of a role assigned by a predicate—the instrumental-assigning predicate produced by the head of the predicate that the modifiers that they head modify. Since, by hypothesis, merger of the instrumental applied affix with verb roots does not take place until s structure in Chichewa, the l-s relations in (7.61) are those that will be mapped onto surface structure.

I shall assume that Chichewa says nothing special about the mapping between l-s and s structure and that, moreover, the instrumental applied affix has no special ability at s structure similar to its power at l-s structure to effect the assignment of a semantic role to its argument by a particular predicate. Given that nothing special is going on in the mapping between l-s and s structure, the s structure counterparts of the relations in (7.61) are clearly determined, with the exception of the role($VP2_{instr}$, NP2) relation. According to principle M, NP2′, the s structure counterpart of NP2, must be head-Governed by $VP2_{instr}′$, the s structure counterpart of $VP2_{instr}$. But what is $VP2_{instr}′$? By the definition of the s structure counterpart to an l-s phrase (see section 2.2.3.1), the s structure counterpart to $VP2_{instr}$ should be the s structure phrase whose immediate head is the s structure counterpart to the immediate head of $VP2_{instr}$. The immediate head of $VP2_{instr}$ is V1—the same verb produces both the instrumental and the agent assigning predicates. Thus $VP2_{instr}′$ is simply the s structure constituent headed by V1′. But the s structure constituent headed by V1′ is also the s structure counterpart of VP2, VP2′. So $VP2_{instr}′$ and VP2′ are the same s structure constituent. Recall that when a constituent must be head-Governed by the s structure counterpart to a predicate, an s structure verb phrase, it must in the unmarked case become the subject of this verb phrase or the subject of a verb phrase that this verb phrase heads. VP2′ will not take subjects since it must serve as the syntactic modifiee to the s structure counterpart of the PP in (7.58). Therefore, NP2′ will be the s structure subject of VP1′, a verb phrase headed by VP2′.

I list in (7.62) the s structure relations mapped from the l-s relations in (7.61). The corresponding s structure tree is shown in (7.63).

(7.62)
a. MOD(PP′, VP2′) b. ARG(V1′, NP1′) c. ROLE(V1′, NP1′)
d. ARG(P′, NP2′) e. SUB(VP1′, NP2′)

(7.63)

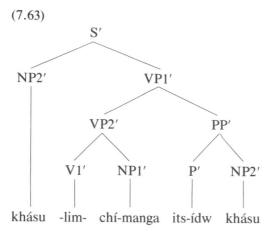

khásu   -lim-   chí-manga   its-ídw   khásu

Note that NP2′ appears in two places in s structure (7.63). As seen in
chapter 3, nothing rules out this possibility as long as the two occurrences of the same constituent are identified as the same constituent in
the mapping between l-s and s structure, a condition satisfied in this
case, or are identified by the Government Transitivity principle.

Merger of the applied affix and root verb at s structure in Chichewa
has precisely the same effects as the corresponding merger at l-s structure in Fula. The merger of V1′ and P′ in (7.63) expresses the MOD
relation between VP2′ and PP′; thus this relation is removed from the
list of constituents and relations at s structure. Although I have assumed that lexical entries do not contain syntactic argument structures
corresponding to semantic argument structures, for purposes of morphological merger the theory treats s structure argument takers as if
they possessed grammatical argument structures. It does not matter for
the principles of merger what these pseudo-argument structures are,
just that they exist. Since the (pseudo-)argument structures of V1′ and
P′ become argument structures of the derived verb V2, the grammatical
arguments of V1′ and P′ become arguments of the derived verb. Since
P′ assigns no syntactic roles but V1′ does, the syntactic role assigning
properties of V1′ percolate in the derived verb and ROLE(V1, NP1′)
will correspond to ROLE(V2, NP1′) after merger. The resulting postmerger s structure is displayed in (7.64).

(7.64)

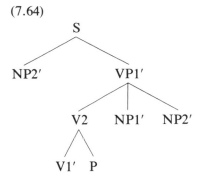

Since NP2′ is lexically Governed both by V2 and by tense/aspect in the main clause (not shown in (7.64)), the s structure in (7.64) will not map onto a well-formed surface structure. As seen in chapter 2, an NP multiply lexically Governed at s structure must appear twice at surface constituent structure, but a single surface structure constituent may not appear twice. Therefore, the NP2′ Governed by the derived verb V2 in (7.64) must merge with this verb at s structure to express the relation between the verb and NP2′. After merger, NP2′ will no longer be Governed by two lexical items at s structure. The merger of the instrumental and the derived verb shows up in the optional (object) agreement marker displayed in (7.40b), which agrees with the instrumental subject, not the root object.

The foregoing discussion has explained why the instrumental NP in Chichewa becomes the SUB of a sentence containing an instrumental applied verb. It should be clear why the passive morpheme is obligatorily used with the Chichewa instrumental applied affix -ts-. If the passive morpheme were absent from (7.58), P would not be [−log sub] and thus VP1 would be sister to some logical subject. The resulting l-s structure would look something like (7.65), with some NP3 serving as logical subject to VP1.

(7.65)

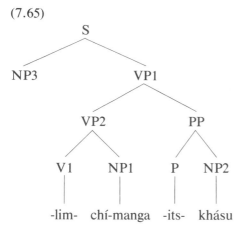

-lim- chí-manga -its- khásu

As explained above, NP2', the s structure counterpart of NP2, must be head-Governed by VP2', the s structure counterpart of VP2. Moreover, NP3', the s structure of NP3, must be head-Governed by VP1', the s structure counterpart of VP1. But I have shown that VP2' will head-Govern NP2' by virtue of the fact that VP1' Governs NP2'. Unless something very special happens, the only way in which VP2' may head-Govern anything is by having the VP it heads, VP1', Govern this constituent. Thus, both NP2' and NP3' must be Governed by VP1'— both must be SUBs of VP1'. But this is impossible. Thus the instrumental applied affix must be accompanied by the passive affix in Chichewa to supply it with the feature [−log sub], preventing a logical subject from competing with the instrumental argument for the SUBject position in the matrix clause.

Of course, this analysis of Chichewa instrumentals is based on the assumption that the instrumental applied affix cannot do at s structure what it does at l-s structure. At l-s structure, this affix effects the assignment of a semantic role by a predicate in the manner described. If it effected the assignment of a syntactic role by some verb phrase headed by the root verb of the applied verb construction in exactly the same manner at s structure, the s structure of the Chichewa instrumental construction would be isomorphic to its l-s structure. But given the assumption that the instrumental applied affix's exceptional properties are restricted to the compositional semantics, I predict several interesting aspects of the Chichewa instrumental construction, including the obligatory presence of the passive morphology, the SUB relation of the instrumental NP, and the presence of some marking to indicate that the instrumental NP is also a syntactic argument of the derived instrumental verb (the optional object-agreement marking agreeing with the instrumental subject).

7.2. Causative Constructions

Causative constructions containing morphologically derived causative verbs have received a great deal of attention in recent years (see, e.g., Aissen 1974 and Shibatani 1976a). Some examples of these constructions from Turkish (Comrie 1976) are given in (7.66).

(7.66)
a. Ali Hasan-i öl-dür-dü.
   Ali Hasan-ACC die-CAUSE-PAST
   'Ali caused Hasan to die.'

b. Dişçi mektub-u müdür-e imzala-t-ti.
   dentist letter-ACC director-DAT sign-CAUSE-PAST
   'The dentist made the director sign the letter.'

Since the term "causative construction" has been used in different ways in the literature, I should make precise the class of derived causative constructions under consideration in this section. First, the head verbs in these constructions are morphologically derived causative forms. In (7.66), for example, the causative morphemes -dür- and -t- attach to the root verbs öl- and imzala- to derive causative verbs. Second, the causative verb formation process that produces the derived causative verbs is productive. Most verbs in the language containing the causative constructions under consideration will have derived causative forms. Third, although they contain two logical clauses, the causative constructions under discussion constitute a single surface sentence. For example, although their English glosses are biclausal, the surface structures in (7.66a) and (7.66b) contain a single S (as argued in Aissen 1974). Finally, the semantics of the derived causative constructions is predictable, conveying the basic meaning 'causer cause that S.' For example, (7.66a) means 'Ali caused that Hasan died' and (7.66b) means 'The dentist caused that the director signed the letter.'

Comrie (1976) has proposed a universal analysis for this sort of causative construction. To explain Comrie's analysis, it will be useful to refer to a canonical causative sentence, that shown in (7.67).

(7.67)
Elmer made Hortense lock the porcupine cage.

I have provided an l-s structure for (7.67) in (7.68) and have labeled the constituents of (7.68) to facilitate the discussion.

(7.68)

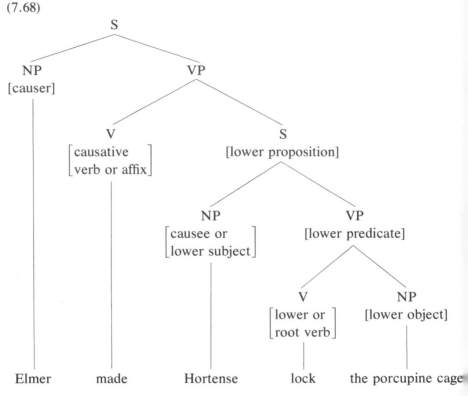

I claim that, when one abstracts away from the differences among the lexical items of particular languages, the l-s structure of derived causative constructions cross-linguistically are essentially identical to (7.68).

The account of causative constructions I shall present is also compatible with an alternative analysis of such causative constructions in which the lower predicate, in place of the lower proposition, is taken as the logical object of the causative verb or affix. This possibility deserves attention, but the issue will not figure in the following discussion.

For his analysis of derived causative constructions, Comrie (1976) introduces the relational hierarchy shown in (7.69).

(7.69)
subject - object - indirect object - other oblique position

Comrie assumes that a derived causative construction has an underlying structure similar to (7.68). He claims that the embedded subject or causee in a causative constructions is knocked out of the subject slot in the relational hierarchy (7.69) by the causer. The causee then moves down the hierarchy, occupying the first empty slot. Thus in the causative of an intransitive verb like Turkish *öl-* 'die' in (7.66a), the causee will become the direct object, since no argument of the root verb occupies this slot. In the causative of a transitive verb like *imzala-* 'sign' in (7.66b), on the other hand, the causee must travel to the indirect object position in (7.69) to find an empty slot.

From his assumptions about the formation of derived causative constructions and from the hierarchy (7.69), Comrie computes the following "paradigm case" syntax for derived causatives cross-linguistically. The paradigm case generalizations in (7.70) are supposed to hold when the derived causative verb is active.

(7.70)
a. causative of intransitive verb:
   causer—subject of derived causative verb
   causee—direct object of derived causative verb

b. causative of transitive verb:
   causer—subject of derived causative verb
   lower object—direct object of derived causative
   causee—indirect object of derived causative

The paradigm case is illustrated by the Turkish examples in (7.66), where ACC is the direct object marking and DAT the indirect object marking.

Although he provides examples of languages that seem to exemplify the paradigm case of causative constructions, Comrie (1976) also notes many languages that do not conform to the pattern in (7.70). Of particular importance to the analysis to be presented, the generalization that the causee in the causative of a transitive verb becomes the indirect object finds little cross-linguistic support. While it is possible in many languages to express the causee of a causative built on a transitive root in the same case and/or with the same adposition used to express the goal argument of verbs like 'give,' a number of considerations lead one to conclude that this fact provides little evidence that the causee becomes an indirect object in the paradigm case (7.70b).

In the first place, some languages never express the causee as goals are expressed (cf. the discussion of Malayalam in section 7.2.3). I know of no statistical study demonstrating that the causee with causatives built on transitive verbs is significantly more likely to be expressed as goals are expressed than to be expressed as, say, instrumentals are. Second, in,languages that allow a causee to be expressed as goals are, this expression is often not obligatory (see Comrie 1976). Third, Comrie cites cases of what he calls "doubling on indirect object," cases of the causee's being expressed as goals are expressed in the language in the same clause as a goal, yielding two indirect objects in a single sentence. If the causee were truly occupying the indirect object slot in the hierarchy (7.69) in the paradigm case, where indirect object has the same theoretical status as direct object, one would not expect the causee to become an indirect object in sentences already containing one, just as the causee does not (normally) become a direct object in sentences containing direct objects. A careful reading of Comrie's cross-linguistic survey of causative constructions, then, makes it clear that there is no evidence for a paradigm case in which the causee in causatives built on transitive verbs becomes an indirect object. Rather, the evidence indicates that many languages allow the causee of a transitive verb to be expressed as the goals of verbs like 'give' are expressed, whereas other languages allow this causee to be expressed as instrumentals are, and still others provide different options.

Given a set of reasonable assumptions, the principles of morphological merger outlined in this chapter explain not only the main aspects of Comrie's paradigm case causative constructions but also the existence of a major, unrecognized class of exceptions to the paradigm case, as well as phenomena Comrie does not discuss. I will assume that the causative affix or morphology in derived causative constructions has basically the same lexical entry as the English causative verb *make* — the entry displayed in (7.71).

(7.71)
'cause' (*caused*), [+log sub], [+transitive]

I assume here that the causative verbs and affixes take propositional arguments but exceptionally Govern into the s structure counterparts of these arguments at s structure.[4] On the assumption that every morpheme with its own argument structure or semantic role assigning features functions as an independent l-s constituent, the l-s structures of derived causative constructions cross-linguistically will look just like the l-s structure of the English causative in (7.68), with the causative affix replacing *make*.

Inasmuch as the causative affix in a derived causative construction appears on the root verb in surface structure, the causative affix must merge with the root verb at some level of syntactic analysis. The theory predicts that languages in which this merger takes place at l-s structure will exhibit causative constructions with the basic syntax of Comrie's paradigm case. Nevertheless, there are languages in which the merger of causative affix and root verb takes place at s structure. The syntax of causative constructions in these languages differs markedly from the syntax of the paradigm case in a manner predicted by the theory.

Within the present theory, then, one expects at least three sorts of causative constructions cross-linguistically: the English-type causative in which the causative morpheme remains a separate constituent at every level of syntactic analysis, derived causative constructions in which the causative morpheme merges with the lower verb at s structure, and the paradigm-case derived causative constructions in which this merger takes place at l-s structure. In addition, another type of causative is allowed by the possibility of splitting; the causative morpheme merges with the lower verb at l-s structure but splits from it again at s structure.

7.2.1. Causative Constructions Without Merger

In the English causative construction with *make*, no morphological merger takes place between the causative morpheme and the lower verb. On the assumption that *make* is a (noncanonical) raising verb in the sense that it exceptionally Governs into its sentential complements (see chapter 3), the s structure for sentence (7.67) should look something like (7.72).

(7.72)

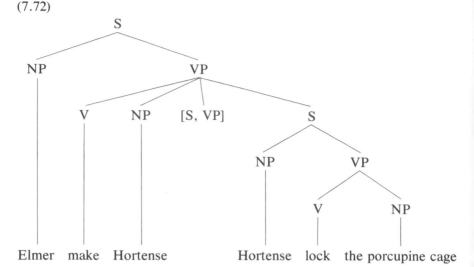

Elmer   make   Hortense   Hortense   lock   the porcupine cage

Recall that I am assuming that *make* somehow Governs into its s structure sentential complements, Governing the VP that heads this complement and therefore head-Governing the subject of this VP by the Government Transitivity principle. Recall also that English provides the structural position [X, VP] to assign syntactic roles to sentential arguments at s structure.

Certain aspects of the syntax of English causative constructions are easily inferred from (7.72) and the lexical entry of *make* in (7.71). First, adding the passive affix to the causative *make,* a raising to object morpheme, will create a raising to subject morpheme (see section 4.1.1.3). Thus the causee will be the subject of the passive form of *make,* as in (7.73a). The lower object may not become the subject of the passive form of the causative verb, of course—see (7.73b).

(7.73)
a.   Hortense was made to lock the porcupine cage.
b.   *The porcupine cage was made Hortense to lock.

The passive affix might be attached to the lower verb, however, making the lower object correspond to the SUB of the embedded clause at s structure and thus to the OBJ of the causative verb, as in (7.74).

(7.74)
Elmer made the porcupine cage be locked by Hortense.

The possible antecedent–anaphor connections in English are governed by the binding theory, which I assume to apply at s structure. According to binding theory, a lower object reflexive might have the causee as its antecedent (see (7.75b)), but the causer, falling outside the lower clause in a causative construction, may not serve as antecedent for a lower object reflexive (see (7.75c)). Of course, the causee as reflexive may take the causer as antecedent, as in (7.75a).

(7.75)
a. Elmer made himself lock the porcupine cage.
b. Elmer made Hortense help herself to the pâté.
c. *Elmer made Hortense help himself to the pâté.

7.2.2. Merger at s Structure

Consider next Chi-Mwi:ni, a language in which the causative morpheme and lower verb merge at s structure (data from Abasheikh 1979). A typical Chi-Mwi:ni causative sentence is found in (7.76).

(7.76)
Mwa:limu Ø-wa-ándik-ish-iz-e wa:na xaṭi.
teacher SP-OP-write-CAUSE-T/A children letter
'The teacher made the children write a letter.'

If the Chi-Mwi:ni causative affix -ish- has basically the same lexical entry as English *make,* containing the information displayed in (7.71), and if the merger of the affix and verb roots does not take place until s structure, the initial s structure of a Chi-Mwi:ni causative like (7.76), shown in (7.77), should look just like the s structure of an English causative like (7.67), shown in (7.72).

(7.77)

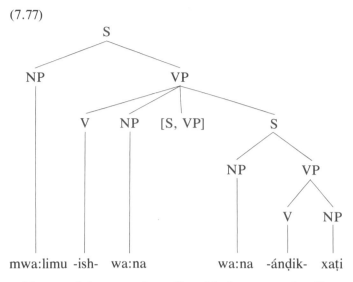

mwa:limu -ish- wa:na   wa:na -ándik- xaṭi

Merger of the causative affix with the root verb will express the syntactic argument relation between the affix and the sentence headed by the root verb. Merger at s structure is simply the syntactic counterpart of merger at l-s structure. Although lexical items do not have syntactic argument structures parallel to their semantic argument structures, one may infer an acting (pseudo) syntactic argument structure for lexical items entering into merger. Basically, I assume that the syntactic argument structure of an item reflects whatever arguments it in fact takes at s structure. Since the arguments of the subparts of a derived word all become arguments of the derived word, all the premerger argument relations held with respect to the subparts will correspond to postmerger argument relations held with respect to the derived word. The causative affix in (7.77) takes two arguments, the NP and the sentence. It also assigns a syntactic role to its nominal argument, making this constituent its direct object. The root verb takes a syntactic argument, its direct object. Following the principles of merger, then, all the arguments in the argument structures of root and affix become arguments of the derived verb—save the sentential argument, of course, since the argument relation between the affix and its sentential argument is expressed by the merger.

Feature percolation within the derived verb determines that the syntactic role assigning property of the affix takes precedence over the syntactic role assigning property of the root to become a feature of the derived verb. Since the causee is the syntactic role assignee of the

causative affix, the causee will receive its syntactic role from the derived verb and become its direct object. Since Chi-Mwi:ni verbs assign
only one role each, the derived verb cannot also assign a syntactic role
to the root object. The root object thus remains the syntactic role assignee of the root and qualifies as an indirect syntactic argument of the
derived verb.

Merger collapses the lower verb phrase in (7.77) into the derived
verb, making the lower subject an argument of the derived verb (for
technical details of this collapsing, see section 7.2.3). Since the lower
subject is identical to the direct object of the causative affix, its argument status relative to the derived verb has already been fixed. Finally,
since the lower sentence in (7.77) as the argument of the affix is internalized in the derived verb, one may say whatever one wishes about
the postmerger counterpart of the role assigning relation between the
structural position [S, VP] and the sentential argument. The postmerger s structure for (7.76) is displayed in (7.78).

(7.78)

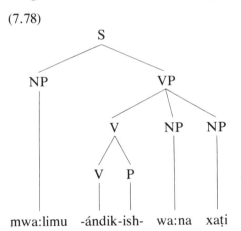

mwa:limu   -ándik-ish-   wa:na   xaṭi

Note that this s structure is isomorphic to the s structures for Chi-
Mwi:ni applied verb constructions discussed in section 7.1.1.1. As expected, the causative and applied verb constructions have precisely
parallel surface structures as well.

As was the case with the English causative construction discussed in
the last section, placing the passive morpheme on the Chi-Mwi:ni
causative morpheme, a raising to object verb, should create a raising to
subject verb. Therefore, one expects the logical subject of the lower
clause to show up as the subject of the derived causative under passivization of the causative affix, as shown in (7.79a). Of course, the lower

object may not passivize when the passive morpheme is attached to the causative affix—see (7.79b).

(7.79)
a. Wa:na wa-ándik-ish-iz-a: xaṭi na mwa:limu.
    children SP-write-CAUSE-PASS-T/A letter by teacher
    'The children were made to write a letter by the teacher.'
b. *Xaṭi a-andik-ish-iz-a wa:na na mwa:limu.
    'The letter was made to be written by the children by the teacher.'

Owing to constraints on the ordering of morphemes within the Chi-Mwi:ni verb, there is no way to passivize the lower verb in a Chi-Mwi:ni causative. The passive morpheme is always interpreted as attaching to the causative affix.

   Abasheikh (1979) demonstrates that there are severe restrictions on the distribution of and possible antecedents for the Chi-Mwi:ni reflexive pronoun *ru:hu-* 'self.' In particular, *ru:hu-* may appear only as an OBJ of a verb, as in (7.80).

(7.80)
Chi-i-um-ił-e ruhu-z-i:tu.
SP(= we)-bit-T/A ourselves
'We bit ourselves.'

Abasheikh provides convincing evidence that the restriction on the distribution of *ru:hu-* refers to the grammatical relation OBJ and not to the structural position [NP, VP] or some similar surfacy characterization of the anaphor. For example, in sentence (7.81) the benefactive 'you,' expressed as the object prefix (OP) alone, is the direct object (OBJ) of the applied verb. The postverbal NPs are indirect syntactic arguments but not OBJs of this verb (see section 7.1.1.1 on applied verb constructions).

(7.81)
Ni-xu-som-esh-ełez-e mwa:na chingere:nzá.
SP(I)-OP(you)-learn-CAUSE-APPL-T/A child English
'I taught the child English for you.'

Since *mwa:na* 'child' in (7.81), although an [NP, VP], is not the OBJ of the verb with respect to which it bears the argument relation (the derived applied verb), it may not be replaced by the reflexive *ru:hu-*, as shown in (7.82).

(7.82)
*Ni-xu-som-esh-eɫez-e ru:hu-y-a chingere:nzá.
                myself
'I taught myself English for you.'

In addition to being restricted to the OBJ relation, the reflexive *ru:hu-* must have a SUB as its antecedent, and this SUB must occur in the same s structure clause as *ru:hu-* (the latter condition is predicted by the binding conditions as applicable to English); the reader is referred to Abasheikh (1979) for evidence for these restrictions.

Given the independently established characteristics of the Chi-Mwi:ni reflexive *ru:hu-*, the present analysis of Chi-Mwi:ni causative constructions predicts that the causer, as SUB of the causative affix at s structure, can serve as antecedent for the causee, the OBJ of the causative affix, as a reflexive. The causee, as s structure SUB of the sentential complement of the causative affix, can serve as antecedent for the lower object, the OBJ of the embedded verb. But if the binding conditions apply to the initial s structure of a sentence—to the s structure that is directly associated with l-s structure—then the causer may not serve as antecedent for a lower object reflexive because the causer, although a SUB, does not appear in the same s structure clause as the lower object at this initial s structure—see (7.77). Abasheikh reports just the predicted range of data:

(7.83)
a. Mi m-pʰik-ish-iz-e ru:hu-y-a cha:kuja.
    I SP-cook-CAUSE-T/A myself food
    'I made myself cook food.'

b. Mi ni-m-big-ish-iz-e mwa:na ru:hu-y-é.
    I SP-OP-hit-CAUSE-T/A child himself
    'I made the child hit himself.'

c. *Mi ni-m-big-ish-iz-e Aɫi ru:hu-y-á.
    I SP-OP-hit-CAUSE-T/A Ali myself
    'I made Ali hit myself.'

Compare (7.83) with the English sentences (7.75). As expected, the evidence indicates that the Chi-Mwi:ni and the English causative constructions have structurally isomorphic biclausal s structures.

Chi-Mwi:ni provides striking support for the biclausal analysis of certain derived causative constructions at s structure. The surface structure of a Chi-Mwi:ni causative, schematized in (7.84), is identical to the surface structure of sentences headed by simple verbs (see section 5.1.1) and morphologically derived verbs such as the applied verbs discussed in section 7.1.1.1.

(7.84)
NP V NP (NP)

Recall that only one of the postverbal NPs in a Chi-Mwi:ni sentence may be the direct object of the main verb of the sentence. Outside of causative constructions, in no situation may *ru:hu-* 'self' appear as a postverbal [NP, VP] whose antecedent is another [NP, VP] in the same clause in a surface structure like (7.84). It is just in the case where the theory leads one to believe that two s structure clauses underlie a single surface structure clause—that is, it is just in causative constructions—that this generalization concerning the distribution of *ru:hu-* is violated (see (7.83b)).

Like Chi-Mwi:ni, other Bantu languages provide evidence that their derived causative constructions involve merger at s structure. Features of Japanese causative constructions also follow from an s structure merger analysis. Some examples of Japanese derived causatives are given in (7.85).

(7.85)
a. Taroo ga Hanako o hatarak-ase-ta.
   Taro NOM Hanako ACC work-CAUSE-PAST
   'Taro made Hanako work.'

b. Taroo ga Hanako ni hatarak-ase-ta.
   Taro NOM Hanako DAT work-CAUSE-PAST
   'Taro let Hanako work.'

c. Taroo ga Hanako ni okasi o tabe-sase-ta.
   Taro NOM Hanako DAT cake ACC eat-CAUSE-PAST
   'Taro let/made Hanako eat the cake.'

The Japanese causative affix is *-sase*. In the causative of an intransitive verb, the causee may be marked with either *o* or *ni*, the accusative and dative particles respectively. If the accusative *o* is used, the causative has a coercive reading, as indicated in (7.85a); if the dative *ni* is used, the causative is interpreted with a permissive reading, as in (7.85b).

If the Japanese causative construction, like the Chi-Mwi:ni, merges the causative *-sase* with root verbs at s structure, the initial s structures of Japanese causatives should look just like (7.72) and (7.77). As with the Chi-Mwi:ni causative construction, one expects that only the causee, not the lower object, may passivize when the passive affix, *-rare*, is attached to the causative verb. (The particle *ni* serves the same function in Japanese passives as *by* serves in English passives.) The Japanese examples in (7.86) are from Farmer (1980, p. 105).

(7.86)
a. Taroo wa Hanako ni sashimi o tabe-sase-ta.
       TOP   DAT sashimi ACC eat-CAUSE-PAST
      'Taro made Hanako eat sashimi.'
b. Hanako wa Taroo ni sashimi o tabe-sase-rare-ta.
       TOP   DAT   eat-CAUSE-PASS-PAST
      'Hanako was made to eat sashimi by Taro.'
c. *Sashimi wa Taroo ni Hanako ni tabe-sase-rare-ta.
      'Sashimi was made to be eaten by Hanako by Taro.'

Some speakers of Japanese permit the passive affix to appear between the causative affix and the root in a derived causative verb. As predicted by the present analysis, the addition of the causative affix to a derived passive root yields the causative of the passive, as shown in (7.87).

(7.87)
Mary wa Taroo o Ziroo ni home-rare-sase-ta.
                     praise-PASS-CAUSE-PAST
'Mary made Taro be praised by Ziro.'

When the causative affix and root verb are distinct s structure constituents in a causative construction, as in Chi-Mwi:ni, Japanese, and English, the causee is both the s structure SUB of the lower clause and the s structure OBJ of the causative verb, while the lower object is only the OBJ of the lower verb. In Japanese, with complications discussed at great length in the sources cited in Marantz 1981a, only subjects may be antecedents for the reflexive *zibun* 'self.' Sentence (7.88) shows that the causee in Japanese causative may serve as antecedent for *zibun*, as expected under the present analysis. Since the antecedent–*zibun* relation in Japanese is not clause bound, the causer may also serve as antecedent for a *zibun* in the lower clause of (7.88).

(7.88)
Taroo wa Hanako o zibun no kuruma kari ori-sase-ta.
                  self GEN car from come down-CAUSE-PAST
'Taro made Hanako come out of his/her car.'

My informant tells me that "object honorification" marking on the derived causative verb may indicate the esteemed status of the causee but not the lower object, supporting the claim that the causee but not the lower object is an OBJ of the derived causative verb in Japanese.

An apparent problem with this analysis of Japanese causative constructions should be mentioned here. Although I claim that it is a direct object, the causee in a Japanese causative is marked with the dative particle *ni* rather than with the accusative particle *o* in many cases. The accusative *o* is the usual marking for OBJs in Japanese. As was shown in (7.85a,b), if the lower verb is intransitive, the use of *ni* on the causee indicates a permissive or "let" causative whereas the use of *o* indicates a coercive or "make" causative. As illustrated in (7.85c), when the lower verb takes an object in *o,* the causee must be marked *ni* and the resulting causative is ambiguous between the permissive and coercive readings.

Within the present theory, I have to say that Japanese marks some direct objects with *ni* independent of the causative construction. As Kuno and others point out, some verbs require *ni* marking on their direct objects. An example is *soodan suru* 'consult' in (7.89), taken from Kuno (1973, p. 347).

(7.89)

a. John ga Mary ni soodansita.
   'John consulted Mary.'

b. Mary ga John ni soodans-(r)are-ta.
   'Mary was consulted by John.'

The passivizability of the consulted argument of *soodan suru,* illustrated in (7.89b), is, ceteris paribus, sufficient evidence that it is an OBJ in (7.89a) in the present theory. Martin (1975) also points out that the object of *soodan suru* may trigger object honorification.

Like the OBJ of *soodan suru,* the goal argument of verbs like *ataeru* 'give' is marked with *ni* in Japanese. Since either the goal or theme of *ataeru* may passivize, both should be considered direct objects in sentences with the active form of the verb.

(7.90)

From Kuno (1980, p. 103):

a. Yoshida-syusuoo ga Tanaka-tuusandaizin ni kunsyoo o ataeta.
   prime minister Yoshida NOM minister Tanaka DAT medal ACC give-PAST
   'Prime minister Yoshida awarded minister Tanaka a medal.'

b. Tanaka-tuusandaizin ga Yoshida-syusuoo ni kunsyoo o ataerareta.

$$\text{give-PASS-PAST}$$

'Minister Tanaka was awarded a medal by prime minister Yoshida.'

c. From Ostler (1980, p. 78):

Sono dorei wa Taroo ni Hanako ni ataerareta.[5]

the slave TOP Taro DAT Hanako DAT give-PASS-PAST

'The slave was given to Hanako by Taro.'

The data indicate, then, that Japanese OBJs may be marked with *ni*.

Although Japanese direct objects may bear *ni* marking, the question remains why the causee as OBJ must be marked *ni* in case the lower verb is transitive. This question divides into two parts. First, why cannot the lower object and the causee both be marked *o*? As has been discussed at length in the literature, Japanese observes a constraint that prohibits two *o* marked direct objects from appearing in the same surface clause (see Poser 1983 for a more precise formulation of this constraint). If both the causee and the lower object were marked with *o*, as in (7.91), this double *o* constraint would be violated.

(7.91)

*Taroo ga Hanako o okasi o tabe-sase-ta.

'Taro made Hanako eat the cake.'

But if the lower object must be marked *ni* for some reason—say it is the OBJ of *soodan suru,* which, as shown in (7.89a), requires *ni* marking on its OBJs—then the causee may be marked with *o*.

(7.92)

Bill wa John o Mary ni soodansaseta.

$$\text{consult-CAUSE-PAST}$$

'Bill made John consult Mary.'

Given that some constraint against two *o* marked OBJs in a surface clause prevents both the causee and lower object from receiving *o* marking in a causative construction, the question remains, why does the lower object rather than the causee receive the unique available *o* marking? I have no principled account for this phenomenon and leave the problem open for further investigation.[6]

7.2.3. Merger at l-s Structure

The next type of causative construction to be considered corresponds to Comrie's paradigm case. In the present theory, the paradigm case results from the merger of the causative affix with the root verb at l-s structure. Consider the Malayalam causatives in (7.93b) and (7.93d) (from Mohanan 1981, 1982a,b).

(7.93)

a. Kuṭṭi kaṟaññu.
   child-NOM cried
   'The child cried.'

b. acchan kuṭṭiye kaṟayiccu.
   father-NOM child-ACC cry-CAUSE-PAST
   'Father made the child cry.'

c. kuṭṭi annaye ṇuḷḷi.
   child-NOM elephant-ACC pinched
   'The child pinched an elephant.'

d. amma kuṭṭiyekkonṭə aanaye ṇuḷḷiccu.
   mother child-INST elephant-ACC pinch-CAUSE-PAST
   'Mother made the child pinch the elephant.'

In the causative of an intransitive Malayalam verb like *kaṟa* 'cry' in (7.93b), the causee normally appears in the case of direct objects, the accusative in (7.93b). When the causative affix is attached to a transitive verb as in (7.93d), however, the lower object is marked as direct objects are marked, while the causee appears with an instrumental postposition *-konṭə*. The basic syntax of the Malayalam causative constructions follows from the principles of merger described in this chapter given the assumption that Malayalam causative merger takes place at l-s structure.

On the assumption that the Malayalam causative affix *-ik'k'-* has basically the same lexical entry as the English causative *make*, that in (7.71) (except that *-ik'k'-* has the morphological subcategorization features of an affix), the l-s structure of (7.93b) should appear as in (7.94); the l-s relations encoded in (7.94) are summarized in (7.95).

(7.94)

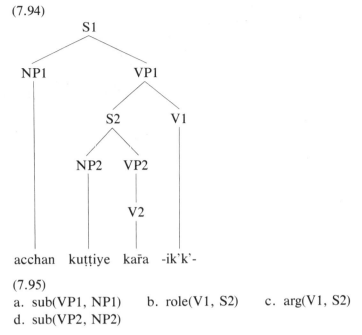

acchan   kuṭṭiye   kaṛa -ik'k'-

(7.95)
a. sub(VP1, NP1)   b. role(V1, S2)   c. arg(V1, S2)
d. sub(VP2, NP2)

To determine the list of l-s constituents and relations corresponding to the list in (7.95) after the merger of V1 and V2 (the causative affix and root verb), one must examine the internal structure of the derived causative verb *kaṛa-ik'k'-* 'cry-CAUSE.'

(7.96)

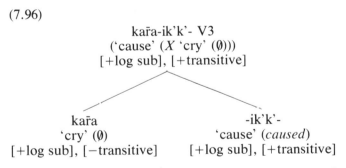

The merger of V1 and V2 at l-s structure expresses the relations between V1, the causative affix, and the proposition headed by V2. As shown in (7.96), the argument structure of the derived verb, call it V3, is the argument structure of V1 applied to the proposition consisting of the argument structure of V2 applied to some constituent. That is, the merger of V1 and V2 internalizes within the derived causative verb the propositional argument of the causative affix. Thus the subject of the lower predicate in (7.94) becomes the argument of the derived causative verb, indicated as "X" in the derived argument structure of V3 in (7.96).

Since both the root verb and the derived causative contain the argument structure of the root, either may be seen as assigning the semantic role to the subject of the predicate within the derived argument structure of V3. Where this does not violate the restriction on one semantic role assignment per verb, Malayalam allows the derived verb to assign the semantic role of the predicate. I indicate that the derived verb assigns the role of the lower predicate by italicizing the X in (7.96). Thus, through merger, the causee becomes the direct l-s object of the derived causative verb. The postmerger l-s structure for sentence (7.93b) is indicated in the list of relations in (7.97) and the corresponding constituent structure tree (7.98).

(7.97)
a. sub(V1, NP1)   b. role(V3, NP2)   c. arg(V3, NP2)

(7.98)

```
                  S1
              ╱       ╲
        NP1              VP1
         │            ╱      ╲
         │         NP2        V3
         │          │       ╱    ╲
         │          │     V2      V1
         │          │      │       │
      acchan    kuṭṭiye   kaṟa   -ik'k'-
```

Note that V3 inherits the [+transitive] feature of the causative affix, allowing it to take direct objects at s structure. Therefore, the s structure for sentence (7.93b) should look essentially the same as the l-s structure (7.98).

Unlike the causee in Chi-Mwi:ni or English, the causee in a Malayalam causative will not be a SUB at s structure unless the derived causative verb is passivized. Malayalam restricts the antecedent of the reflexive *swa-* 'self' to subjects (Mohanan 1982a). As predicted, the causee of an active causative construction may not serve as antecedent for a reflexive in Malayalam.

(7.99)
acchan kuṭṭiye swaṉtam wiiṭṭil weccə kaṟayiccu.
father-NOM child-ACC self's house at cry-CAUSE-PAST
'Father made the child cry at father's/*child's house.'

Recall that the antecedent of the Chi-Mwi:ni reflexive *ru:hu-* 'self' is also restricted to SUBs. In Chi-Mwi:ni the causee may serve as antecedent for *ru:hu-*, as shown in (7.83b). The contrast displayed in (7.83b) and (7.99) is a direct consequence of the difference between Chi-Mwi:ni and Malayalam in the locus of the merger between the causative affix and root verb.

The analysis of a Malayalam causative containing a transitive root verb is only slightly more complicated than the analysis of (7.93b). In (7.101) I display the l-s structure of (7.93d), repeated here as (7.100); the l-s relations encoded in (7.101) are listed in (7.102).

(7.100)
amma kuṭṭiyekkoṇtə aanaye ṉuḷḷiccu.
mother-NOM child-INST elephant-ACC pinch-CAUSE-PAST
'Mother made the child pinch the elephant.'

(7.101)

(7.102)
a. sub(VP1, NP1)   b. role(V1, S2)   c. arg(V1, S2)
d. arg(VP2, NP2)   e. role(VP2, NP2)   f. role(V2, NP3)
g. arg(V2, NP3)

The internal structure of the derived causative verb ṇuḷḷik'k'- 'pinch-CAUSE' is shown in (7.103).

(7.103)

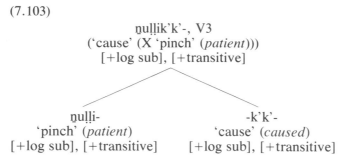

ṇuḷḷik'k'-, V3
('cause' (X 'pinch' (*patient*)))
[+log sub], [+transitive]

ṇuḷḷi-
'pinch' (*patient*)
[+log sub], [+transitive]

-k'k'-
'cause' (*caused*)
[+log sub], [+transitive]

As the merger of V1 and V2 at l-s structure expresses the relations between V1 and the proposition headed by V2, these relations will not appear in the postmerger l-s structure of sentence (7.100). The derived argument structure of the causative verb in (7.101), call it V3, is the argument structure of V1 applied to the proposition formed by the argument structure of V2 applied to some constituent, X. Merger internalizes the causee, X, into the argument structure of V3, and the causee becomes an argument of the derived causative verb. The semantic role assigning properties of the causative affix are merged into the derived verb; the role assigning relation between the affix and its propositional object is expressed by the merger. Since the affix percolates no role assigning features, the role assigning properties of the root may percolate to become the role assigning feature of the derived V3 in (7.103). As a result, the direct logical object of the root verb becomes the direct logical object of the derived causative.

Since the argument structure of the root is part of the argument structure of the derived verb in (7.103), in principle either the root or the derived verb may be seen as assigning the role of the predicate formed by this argument structure to the argument designated as X in (7.103). However, since the derived causative inherits the semantic role assigning properties of the root verb, and Malayalam allows verbs to assign only one role in the unmarked case, the root verb must assign the role to the causee. This makes the causee an indirect argument of the derived causative. The postmerger l-s structure for (7.100) is shown in (7.104) and (7.105).

(7.104)
a. sub(VP1, NP1)   b. role(V3, NP3)   c. arg(V3, NP3)
d. role(V2, NP2)   e. arg(V3, NP2)

(7.105)

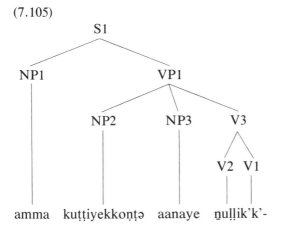

amma kuṭṭiyekkoṇṭə aanaye ṇuḷḷik'k'-

The l-s structure in (7.105) is structurally similar to the postmerger l-s structures of the applied verbs analyzed in section 7.1. In particular, compare (7.105) with the l-s structure of the Fula instrumental applied verb construction in (7.53). As in (7.53), the logical object of the root verb in (7.105) corresponds to the direct logical object of the derived verb. Since the causee NP2 receives its semantic role from a verb, V2, and should correspond to the syntactic role assignee of the verb at s structure, one would expect it to be expressed in the way syntactic role assignees of verbs are usually expressed in Malayalam, just as *jammbere* 'axe' in the Fula sentence (7.39b) is expressed as an [NP, VP] although it is not the OBJ of the main verb. Unlike Fula, however, Malayalam does not exhibit double object constructions in surface structure; it does not allow two constituents to be expressed as OBJs are usually expressed in a single surface structure clause. Malayalam chooses to express the causee in structures like (7.105) as the object of the instrumental postposition -*koṇṭə*.

Tamil is a Dravidian language very closely related to Malayalam. As far as I have been able to determine, the syntax of Tamil and Malayalam causative constructions is identical, with the following exception: where Malayalam expresses the causee of a causative construction with a transitive root verb in a postpositional phrase containing the instrumental postposition -*koṇṭə*, Tamil puts the causee in such constructions in the accusative case. That is, Tamil exhibits the double object constructions with derived causatives containing transitive root verbs expected from the l-s structure in (7.105). Other languages that merge the causative affix and root verb at l-s structure express the causee of l-s structures like (7.105) in the manner of goals, that is, as indirect objects; still others express the causee of such constructions however the displaced subject in a passive is expressed (see Comrie 1976 for examples of the various sorts of languages).[7] Since on the present analysis the causee in causatives built on transitive roots is an indirect syntactic argument, one would expect languages to treat these causees as they treat what are usually called indirect objects—technically, indirect syntactic arguments of verbs.

As predicted by the l-s structure in (7.105), the lower object, not the causee, becomes the subject of the passive of a Malayalam causative built on a transitive root. The lower object is the direct argument of the derived causative. Sentence (7.106) contains the passive of the verb in (7.100).

(7.106)
ammayaal aana ṇuḷḷik'k'appettu.
mother-INST elephant-NOM pinch-CAUSE-PASS-PAST
'The elephant was caused by mother to be pinched.'

Compare the passive in (7.106) with the ungrammatical (7.79b) from Chi-Mwi:ni and (7.86c) from Japanese. Only when merger of the causative affix and root verb takes place at l-s structure may the lower object of a derived causative passivize.

Recall that the Malayalam reflexive *swa-* 'self' requires an s structure subject for its antecedent. Because it is not a SUB at s structure, the causee of the Malayalam causative, unlike the causee of the Chi-Mwi:ni and Japanese causatives, may not serve as an antecedent for the Malayalam reflexive as illustrated in (7.99) in a causative containing an intransitive root and in (7.107) with a transitive root verb.

(7.107)
amma kuṭṭiyekkoṇṭə aanaye swaṇtam wiṭṭil weccə ṇuḷḷiccu.
mother child-INST elephant-ACC self's house at pinch-CAUSE-PAST
'Mother made the child pinch the elephant at mother's/*child's/ *elephant's house.'

This behavior of Malayalam causatives stands in direct contrast to the behavior of causatives in languages that keep the causative morpheme and root verb separate at l-s structure.

Turkish derived causatives, discussed in Aissen (1974), must also be analyzed as involving merger of the causative affix and root verb at l-s structure. Crucially, in the causative built on a Turkish transitive root verb it is the lower object and not the causee that exhibits behavior indicating it is the direct logical object of the derived causative verb. A causative of a Turkish transitive verb appears in (7.108a). Note the accusative case on the lower object. When the verb in (7.108a) is passivized, as in (7.108b), the lower object becomes the subject of the derived verb.

(7.108)
a. Mehmet Hasan-a bavulu aç-tir-di.
          -DAT suitcase-ACC open-CAUSE-PAST
   'Mehmet had Hasan open the suitcase.'

b. Bavul (Mehmet tarafından) Hasan-a aç-tir-il-di.
   suitcase (Mehmet by) Hasan-DAT open-CAUSE-PASS-PAST
   'The suitcase was caused (by Mehmet) to be opened by Hasan.'

Again, according to the present theory, the lower object may become the subject of the passive of a derived causative verb in a language only if merger of the causative affix and root verb takes place at l-s structure. The data in (7.108) indicate that the causative affix and root verbs merge at l-s structure in Turkish.

Aissen shows that the antecedent–anaphor relation between reflexive *kendi-* 'self' and its antecedent is clause bound, at least with a first person antecedent. Sentence (7.109) is ungrammatical with the indicated interpretation because the first person antecedent, *ben* 'I,' does not fall into the same s structure sentence as the reflexive *kendi-* 'self.'

(7.109)
*Ben Hasan-in kendim-i yika-masina sevindim.
          -GEN self-ACC wash-PART was-pleased
   'I was pleased that Hasan washed me.'

When merger of the causative affix and root verb takes place at l-s structure, the causative construction is monoclausal at s structure and the causer and lower object fall into the same s structure sentence. Thus a first person causer should be able to serve as antecedent for *kendi-* 'self' as lower object in a Turkish causative construction. As Aissen shows, this is precisely the case.

(7.110)
Hasan-a kendim-i yika-t-tim.
          -DAT self-ACC wash-CAUSE-PAST.1sg
   'I made Hasan wash me.'

Compare (7.110) with the ungrammatical Chi-Mwi:ni sentence (7.83c). When merger takes place at s structure, as in Chi-Mwi:ni, and the antecedent–anaphor relation is clause bound, the causer may not serve as antecedent for a lower object reflexive.

The causee is not an OBJ of the derived Malayalam or Turkish causative verb formed from a transitive root because these languages allow a verb to assign only one semantic role in the unmarked case. Percolation of the inherent semantic role assigning features of the transitive root verb to the derived causative verb prevents the derived verb from assigning the role of the predicate formed by the root verb. In a language that allows a verb to assign more than one semantic role in the unmarked case, one would expect that the derived causative could assign both the role of the root verb and the role of the predicate formed by this verb. In such a language, both the causee and the lower object could be direct logical objects of the derived causative verb, if causative merger occurred at l-s structure.

In section 7.1.1.2 I presented evidence that Kinyarwanda (Kimenyi 1980) allows a verb to assign two semantic roles in the unmarked case. Kinyarwanda also seems to merge its causative affix and root verbs at l-s structure. Example (7.111) is a Kinyarwanda causative built on a transitive verb stem.

(7.111)
Umugabo á-r-úubak-iish-a abákozi inzu.
man SP-PRES-build-CAUSE-ASP workers house
'The man is making the workers build the house.'

If my analysis is correct, both the causee *abakozi* 'workers' and the lower object *inzu* 'houses' should be direct logical objects of the derived causative in (7.111). Therefore, either should be able to correspond to the SUB of the passive of the derived verb. In fact, Kimenyi (1980) demonstrates that both the causee and lower object have direct object properties in (7.111) and that both will passivize.

(7.112)
a. Abákozi bá-r-úubak-iish-w-a inzu n'ûmugabo.
   workers SP-PRES-build-CAUSE-PASS-ASP house by-man
   'The workers are made to build the house by the man.'
b. Inzu í-r-úubak-iish-w-a abákozi n'ûmugabo.
   house SP-PRES-build-CAUSE-PASS-ASP workers by-man
   'The house is being made to be built by the workers by the man.'

Compare (7.112) with sentences (7.86b,c) from Japanese and (7.79) from Chi-Mwi:ni. Recall that since either the goal or the theme argument of Japanese *ataeru* 'give' may passivize (see (7.90)), Japanese, like Kinyarwanda, must be seen as allowing verbs to assign two semantic and syntactic roles—to take two direct logical and syntactic objects. Yet only the causee, not the lower object, may passivize when the passive affix is attached to a Japanese derived causative—compare (7.90) with (7.86). In contrast, either the causee or the lower object of a Kinyarwanda derived causative may passivize, as shown in (7.112). This difference between Japanese and Kinyarwanda is predicted under the assumption that the causative affix and root verb merge at l-s structure in Kinyarwanda but at s structure in Japanese.

7.2.4. Merger and Splitting

Merger is essentially nondirectional. In the chain of structures related by merger at any level of syntactic analysis stretching from the initial structure for that level to the final structure (see diagram (7.2)), two constituents in one structure may correspond to one constituent at the next or one constituent at the first structure may correspond to (split into) two constituents at the next. If a single constituent in one list of constituents and relations at s structure corresponds to two constituents in the next list at s structure, a single s structure word may correspond to two independent surface structure morphemes.

Although I have yet to work out the analysis in detail, it seems that French causative constructions (and Romance causatives in general) exploit this splitting option. It has often been remarked in the literature that the syntax of French causatives from a grammatical relational standpoint closely resembles the syntax of causatives in languages analyzed here as merging root verb and causative affix at l-s structure. Yet the surface structure of French causatives looks biclausal and leaves the causative and lower verbs as separate words. This behavior is just what one would expect if the causative and root verbs merged at l-s structure but split again at s structure, mapping two l-s constituents onto one s structure constituent and one s structure constituent onto two surface structure constituents.

Recall from section 4.3 that the expression of the causee in a French causative under *faire* depends on the transitivity of the lower verb. In general, the causee with an intransitive lower verb shows up as an unmarked postverbal NP, just like a canonical direct object. The causee with a transitive lower verb generally shows up in a prepositional phrase with *à*, the preposition used in French to mark indirect syntactic arguments of verbs.

(7.113)

a. Jean a fait partir Marie.
   John PAST make leave Mary
   'John made Mary leave.'

b. Jean a fait boire du vin à Marie.
   John PAST make drink of-the wine to Mary
   'John made Mary drink some wine.'

The French causatives in (7.113) superficially resemble the Malayalam and, particularly, the Turkish causatives, with the exception that the causative morpheme in French is not an affix but a higher, governing verb much like English *make*. The merger and splitting analysis makes it possible to account for the shared behavior of the French causatives both with the causative constructions that involve merger at l-s structure and with the causative constructions that involve distinct surface structure verbs.

The splitting analysis holds potential for analyzing various cases of discontinuous morphemes in a highly constrained manner. For example, English pseudopassives like those in (7.114) may be seen as involving the merger of verb and preposition at l-s structure with subsequent splitting at s structure.

(7.114)

a. This bed was slept in by the porcupine.
b. Porcupines are thought highly of by all our readers.

Since the preposition and verb merge at the l-s structures of (7.114), the logical object of the preposition becomes the logical object of the derived verb and may passivize in the mapping between l-s and s structure. If the preposition and verb split at s structure, adverbials may come between them in the surface structure tree, as in (7.114b).

7.3. Merger at Surface Structure

In light of a set of important data brought to my attention by Paula Pranka (see Pranka 1983), I have just begun to explore the consequences of merger at surface structure. Although some merger at surface structure is distinguishable from merger at s structure only in that it holds no consequences for grammatical relations, the particular nature of the relations at surface structure leads me to expect certain types of merger that find no counterparts at other levels. Merger of tense/aspect with the head verb of its sentential complement at s structure has the effect of making the subject of the sentence—by the Government Transitivity principle, an argument of tense/aspect—into a grammatical argument of the derived tensed verb (see section 7.4). On the other hand, since grammatical relations are represented at s structure, merger of tense/aspect with the lower verb at surface structure as in English has no effects on the grammatical relations in the sentence.

Given that adjacency is a relation at surface structure, one might find two morphemes merging simply because they are specified to be adjacent in a string. The merger in this case would express the adjacency relation between the merged constituents. Such merger might account for cases of suppletion that have proved troublesome for constrained theories of the interaction of morphology and syntax. Consider the cases of preposition and article suppletion in French, in which the prepositions *à* and *de* have special suppletive forms in combination with certain following articles: *à* plus a following masculine singular article *le* forms the morpheme *au,* for example.

Suppose when an s structure relation R(X, Y) is mapped onto an adjacency relation between the surface structure counterparts of X and Y, X' and Y', the relation is actually represented at surface structure as a relation between the last lexical item in the left-hand member of the relation and the first lexical item in the right-hand member.

For example, if the ROLE relation between French *à* and the NP *le garçon* is expressed as an adjacency relation, this relation would be represented as a relation between *à* and the first lexical member of *le garçon,* the article *le.* (Of course, what constitutes the first member of a constituent must be computed from the general principles and specific requirements of the language in question that determine linear order at surface structure for this language.) Merger of the preposition and the article would express an adjacency relation at surface structure. Since merger involves lexical affixation, one looks to the lexicon for the item consisting of *à* affixed to *le.* This derived word happens to have a special phonological form in French, *au* (the bound forms of the preposition and article do not project the phonological features of their independent forms). Thus *à le garçon* as a prepositional phrase shows up as *au garçon* in surface constituent structure.

Note that the theory predicts the French sort of suppletion only in cases where the adjacency between the suppleted elements is the expression of some s structure relation, not an accidental linear adjacency. Merger occurs between lists of constituents and relations mapped between levels of analysis. Fortuitous adjacency shows up only in the surface structure tree. So one would not expect to find a language exactly like French only postpositional, instead of prepositional, in which the postposition *à* of a PP would supplete with an article leading off an NP that just happened to fall to the right of the PP, as in (7.115). The present theory rules out cases like (7.115) in principle.

(7.115)

$_{PP}[. . . à]\ _{NP}[le . . .] \rightarrow . . . au . . .$

One should distinguish special affixal forms of items standing in the adjacency relation at surface structure from the more usual cases of sandhi. In sandhi, rules of phrasal phonology affect the phonological forms of the beginning and ends of words, depending on the immediately adjacent phonological elements. Phonological sandhi rules operate on phonological representations and are not sensitive to the identity of the morphemes they affect. The sort of situation for which merger at surface structure is required involves special forms of morphemes that depend on the particular morphemes involved, not simply on their phonological form. Thus the French case does not affect any word ending in . . . *à* followed by any word beginning in *le* . . . , but only the preposition *à* followed by the article *le*, which must head the object of *à* at s structure.

Sproat (1982) discusses a Welsh example very similar to the French case. Certain prepositions in Welsh cause a form of consonant mutation, lenition, on the first consonant of the first lexical element of their objects. For example, *i* 'to' and *Caerdydd* 'Cardiff' become *i Gaerdydd* 'to Cardiff,' with a lenited initial consonant on 'Cardiff.' Sproat argues convincingly that the lenited-initial form is expected under affixation; that is, the phonology of the example is predictable if the preposition is considered to affix to the first lexical item in its complement. Nevertheless, Sproat argues, the lenition is not predicted by a phrase level phonological rule (a sandhi rule) that might be triggered if the preposition somehow cliticized onto the following word. Rather, the predictions follow if the preposition affixes to the following word in the lexicon.

Again, this state of affairs is exactly what one expects from the merger analysis. Merger relates lists of constituents and relations that are independently generated with items from the lexicon. If merger re-

lates a list with an independent preposition P and some word X to a list
that contains the derived word P+X, then P must affix to X in the
lexicon.

Welsh also contains completely suppletive forms for combinations of
certain prepositions and their pronominal objects. In (7.116a) I list the
forms for the preposition *am* 'about' and pronominal objects. To show
the suppletion of the pronominal forms, I provide a paradigm for the
independent pronouns in (7.116b).

(7.116)

a.		Sg.	Pl.	b.		Sg.	Pl.
	1.	amdanaf	amdanom			mi	ni
	2.	amdanat	amdanoch			ti	chwi
	3.m.	amdano	amdanynt			ef	hwy
	f.	amdani				hi	

Pranka (1983) reports some suggestive data from Papago that high-
light the potential range of the merger at surface structure analysis.
Papago generally places the auxiliary element AUX in second position.
Where certain forms of the AUX would be expected to follow certain
sentence initial constituents, a suppletive word appears in sentence-
initial position instead. A plausible analysis of Papago might suppose
that the AUX, the surface counterpart of a sentential operator at
s structure (see chapter 3), stands in an adjacency relation with the
sentence at surface structure. It then always merges with the first
member of the sentence at surface structure according to the principles
of merger and my assumptions about the representation of adjacency
relations at surface structure. In the lexicon, AUX may affix to the
right of any element. Certain combinations of lexical items and AUX
have special suppletive forms in Papago.

The suggestion is that the AUX-second phenomenon in Papago is a
direct result of merger. The AUX is always affixed to (the right of) the
first element in the sentence to express an adjacency relation between
the AUX and the sentence. In certain cases, the resulting derived word
has a special phonological form. Perhaps many second-position effects
cross-linguistically may be explained by the merger of a syntactic sentential operator with its sentential complement, implemented to express an adjacency relation at surface structure.

7.4. Potential Extensions of Morphological Merger

In chapter 3 I suggested that tense/aspect is a propositional operator at l-s structure that exceptionally Governs into the sentential counterpart of its propositional argument at s structure. Since tense/aspect Governs the VP head of its s structure complement, by the Government Transitivity condition it must also head-Govern the subject of the VP. This analysis works in conjunction with the Surface Appearance principle to explain the dependence on tense/aspect of the expression of subjects in sentences.

On this analysis of tense/aspect, the subject of a sentence is a grammatical argument of tense/aspect. When, as in English, tense/aspect appears as morphology on the head verb of its sentential complement, it must merge with the head verb at s or surface structure. If merger occurs at s structure, the principles of merger dictate that the subject of the sentence, an argument of tense/aspect, should become an argument of the derived tensed verb. Chomsky (1981) has suggested that in languages, such as Italian, that allow free inversion of subject and verb, agreement may attach to the verb in syntax. On the other hand, languages such as French and English do not allow agreement to attach to the verb until the phonology. It seems likely that this analysis of what has been called the "pro-drop parameter" would translate into the present theory as a choice in the locus of the merger of tense/aspect with the root verb. Having agreement attach to verbs in the syntax corresponds to having tense/aspect merge with verbs at s structure. In the GB framework, such attachment implies that the verb will govern the subject, in a technical sense. In the present framework, merger of tense/aspect with root verbs at s structure will have the derived verb Govern the subject.

It is not yet clear to me how much of the GB analysis of pro-drop will carry over into the present theory on the assumption that Chomsky's analysis translates into a location of merger account. In particular, if tense/aspect merges with verbs at s structure, there is no reason to expect pro-drop itself, that is, the absence of a phonologically overt subject. This merger analysis accounts only for those properties of pro-drop languages that follow from having the subject governed by the tensed verb: free subject-verb inversion and violations of the *that*-trace generalization (see Chomsky 1981). There are other possible analyses of missing subjects in languages with overt subject agreement. For example, subject agreement could be treated as the surface structure counterpart of the s structure subject of the sentence that has merged with the verb at surface structure. On such an analysis, the verb would not Govern the subject in any sense.

Other possible extensions of morphological merger include analyses of object incorporation. It seems that object incorporation could be analyzed as the merger of (logical or grammatical) object and verb at some level of syntactic analysis. Preliminary work by M. Baker (1983) indicates that this line of research holds promise. Baker has examined incorporation in Greenlandic (Sadock 1980), Niuean (Seiter 1980), and various North American Indian languages. Of particular importance for the present theory are the arguments that Sadock provides indicating, in his terms, that incorporation must be syntactic rather than lexical. For example, although the head noun of a noun phrase incorporates into a verb in Eskimo, what seem to be other subconstituents of the noun phrase remain separate from the verb. This state of affairs precisely resembles derived causative constructions. In such constructions, although the lower verb incorporates with the causative morpheme, subconstituents of the proposition headed by the lower verb remain distinct from the derived causative verb. It is likely that, as with other problems in the interaction of morphology (and the lexicon) with syntax, morphological merger will provide a constrained theory in which to examine the peculiar aspects of noun incorporation.

Chapter 8
Theories of Grammatical Relations

I have presented and explored a theory of grammatical relations, a theory of the mapping between semantic interdependencies among sentential constituents and the expression of these interdependencies in surface structure. Having concentrated in previous chapters on demonstrating how the present theory makes a wide range of interesting and correct predictions about a variety of constructions in the world's languages, in this chapter I examine the present work in the context of previous investigations of grammatical relations.

The present theory falls into the class of theories containing projection principles (Chomsky 1981). According to such theories, the syntactic relations of a sentence are projected from the semantic relations it encodes. In section 8.1, I discuss some general properties shared by theories with projection principles in contrast to theories without. I also compare the present approach with two other projection-containing theories: the Government-Binding framework and Montague Grammar.

In section 8.2, I contrast the general approach to grammatical relations taken in this book with other approaches exemplified in the literature. In particular, I characterize approaches to grammatical relations according to the source that they propose for grammatical relations and according to the manner in which they account for generalizations that seem true of grammatical relations. The present theory locates the source of grammatical relations in logico-semantic interdependencies. Its approach to phenomena that implicate grammatical relations may be characterized as explanatory in that generalizations true of grammatical relations are shown to follow from fundamental principles of grammar and from inherent properties of grammatical relations. Most current theories of grammatical relations locate their source in semantic roles, not semantic interdependencies (relations), and are nonexplanatory in that they account for generalizations true of grammatical relations by reference to laws or rules that are independent of fundamental grammatical principles and of inherent properties of grammatical relations.

8.1. Theories with Projection Principles

Projection principles in syntactic theories forge direct and explicit links between relations of compositional semantics and grammatical and structural relations. The present theory contains two sorts of projection principles. The first explicitly relates the types of relations at each level of syntactic analysis to the types found at other levels. The second constrains the mapping between relations at different levels in the syntactic analysis of any sentence.

Recall from the discussion in 2.3.1 that there are two fundamental types of relations in the theory. One is a relation of asymmetric sisterhood—A and B stand in this relation if they are immediate constituents of the same element and one is singled out as the operator of the element. This relation has direct implications for constituency. The argument relations at l-s and s structure and the structural government and agreement relations at surface structure are of this first type. The second sort of relation also holds between A and B where one is singled out as the operator, but it holds no implications for constituency. The role assignment relations at s and surface structure and the adjacency and case marking relations at surface structure exemplify this second, constituent structure independent, sort of relation.

The theory of grammar thus projects the argument relation of l-s structure to the argument relation at s structure and the structural government and agreement relations at surface structure; it projects the role assignment relation of l-s structure to the role assignment relation at s structure and the adjacency and case marking relations at surface structure. However, these are type-to-type projections. As we saw in chapter 2, a particular relation r(a, b) at l-s structure need not correspond to R(A, B) at s structure, where R, A, and B are the s structure counterparts to r, a, and b respectively. Specific mapping principles constrain and determine the projection of particular tokens of relations from level to level.

Mapping principles essential to the projection of l-s relations to surface structure include principles (2.46) and M of chapter 2 mapping from l-s to s structure, and principles (2.83), (2.84), and (2.85) mapping from s to surface structure. These principles are not as strong as, say, a proposed isomorphy among all levels of syntactic analysis would be. Nevertheless, the workings of these mapping principles have been supported with data throughout this book.

Chomsky's Government-Binding theory (Chomsky 1981) includes a projection principle that served as the model for the projection principles in this book. Although there is little fundamentally incompatible between the present work and Chomsky 1981, there are significant differences. These differences fall into three categories. First, I have developed areas of syntactic theory that Chomsky (1981) does not discuss at great length. For example, the account of lexical entries and argument structures developed here fills in details left open by GB theory. Second, I chose to develop one line of research in certain areas where the GB line is consistent with the data and mainly consistent with the rest of the present theory. For example, although I sketch a treatment of trace binding in section 3.2.2 different from the GB account, the treatment is not forced by fundamental assumptions of the theory and I could adopt the GB treatment of traces without changing my analyses of the constructions discussed in chapters 4 through 7. Third and most important, some differences between the present theory and the GB framework implicate fundamental principles of the two theories. Adopting the GB position to reconcile differences of this last sort would completely alter the present theory. These differences include the choice of principle M and the principles of morphological merger over Chomsky's projection principle. I will discuss only differences of this third, fundamental sort.

For purposes of comparing the present theory with GB theory, I will sketch some basic features of the GB framework, but to comprehend the discussion in this section fully, the reader must consult Chomsky 1981. Consider the model of grammar in (8.1), suggested in Chomsky (1980b).

(8.1)

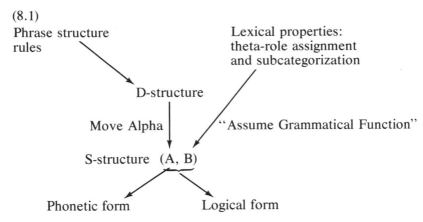

Phrase structure rules

Lexical properties: theta-role assignment and subcategorization

D-structure

Move Alpha

"Assume Grammatical Function"

S-structure (A, B)

Phonetic form   Logical form

In (8.1) the phrase structure rules of a grammar generate or constrain the construction of D-structures into which lexical items are inserted (as explained in Chomsky 1981 and Stowell 1981, the phrase structure rules of a language are derivative—determined from the settings of a limited number of parameters in X-bar theory and from other general principles and particular properties of the language). A general trace-leaving movement rule, Move Alpha, generates the structure labeled "A" from D-structure. Move Alpha may either move a constituent and (Chomsky-)adjoin it to a node or move a constituent and substitute it for a node (in structure preserving movement transformations). The lexical properties of theta-role (thematic role) assignment and subcategorization determine the structure labeled "B." Thematic or theta-roles are roughly equivalent to the semantic roles of the present theory; theta-role assignment is similar to semantic role assignment. A lexical item subcategorizes its arguments.

That an item assigns a theta-role or subcategorizes a certain argument establishes a structural relation at structure B between this item and the constituent to which it assigns a role or which it subcategorizes. For example, for X to assign a role to or subcategorize Y, both X and Y must be immediately dominated by the same node Z. This condition on the structural representation of theta-role assignment and subcategorization constitutes part of Chomsky's projection principle. Technically, the projection principle states that theta-role assignment and subcategorization are preserved at every syntactic level of analysis—in (8.1) the relevant levels are B and logical form. That is, the structural relations established by theta-role assignment and subcategorization are preserved in the course of a derivation. The pair consisting of structures A and B in (8.1) constitute S-structure. Rules of the logical form component derive a logical form from S-structure; rules of phonology map structure A onto a phonetic form.

Grammatical relations, or functions, are defined in GB theory in terms of structural relations at B. The rule "Assume Grammatical Function" in (8.1) allows a constituent to bear freely (assume) a structural relation (grammatical function) in structure B not dictated by theta-role assignment or subcategorization. To clarify further Assume Grammatical Function and to facilitate a comparison of (8.1) with the diagram of my framework in (1.4), (8.1) is redrawn as (8.2).

(8.2)

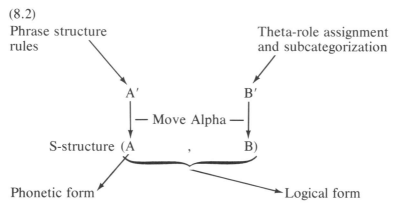

In (8.2), lexical properties determine structure B' instead of B. Assume Grammatical Function of (8.1) reduces to substitution Move Alpha between B' and B in (8.2); that is, a constituent assumes a grammatical function by moving to occupy a new structural position. Chomsky classifies languages along a continuum between the configurational and nonconfigurational. A language is configurational to the extent that the relation between structures A and B in (8.2) is identity. In nonconfigurational languages, there is some more complicated relation between structures A and B.

When Chomsky's 1980b model of grammar is diagrammed as in (8.2), it becomes clear that the present theory, associated with the model of grammar in (1.4), conforms to the general lines of GB theory. Structures A' and A correspond to surface structure, although in the present theory the Move Alpha relation holds at a level of analysis instead of mapping between levels. As B' is a projection of theta-role assignment and subcategorization, so l-s structure is a construction from the basic semantic relations, semantic-role-assigner–semantic-role-assignee and argument-taking-item–argument. Chomsky defines grammatical relations as structural relations at structure B; I encode grammatical relations in structural relations at s structure.

Despite these strong correspondences between the GB framework and the present theory, certain differences in fundamental assumptions clearly distinguish the two. First, Chomsky assumes that Move Alpha is crucially involved in raising to subject and in the promotion of objects to subject in passivization. That is, GB theory claims that there is a relation between a (moved) constituent and a structural position (the source of the moved constituent) in passive and raising constructions that shares some feature(s) with the relation between a constituent and a structural position in, for example, wh- questions and relative clauses. The assumed similarity between these two sorts of constructions is captured by having the relation between the constituent and the structural position in both cases established by Move Alpha. In the present theory, no direct connection is claimed to exist between passive and raising constructions, on the one hand, and constructions, like wh- questions, involving (adjunction) Move Alpha within the theory, on the other. The specification of head-Government in place of Government in principle M allows for the promotion of logical objects to subject in passivization, whereas raising implicates a transitivity condition on grammatical relations (see chapter 3).

Although in the GB framework passive and raising constructions are generated with the "same" Move Alpha rule used to generate wh- questions and relative clauses, Move Alpha in passivization and raising is a substitution rule whereas other examples of Move Alpha (e.g., Move Alpha in constituent questions) adjoin the moved constituent to a node. Furthermore, substitution Move Alpha leaves a trace that is identified as an anaphor with respect to the binding theory. In contrast, adjunction Move Alpha generally leaves a trace that is subject to the same clause of the binding theory as non-pronominal lexically filled NPs. In short, although the GB framework establishes a similarity between passive and raising constructions and constructions like wh- questions, it allows these constructions to differ in many important features. One feature the constructions must share by virtue of being generated through Move Alpha is that the connection between the moved constituent and its trace, which is assumed to be present in the constructions, must obey the subjacency condition on Move Alpha. The subjacency condition ensures a specific structural proximity between moved constituent and trace, keeping them close in a well-defined sense. As I have demonstrated (Marantz 1982e), however, the subjacency condition never plays a demonstrable role in constraining the relation between a moved constituent and a trace in passive and raising constructions because this relation is more highly constrained by the binding theory.

In terms of mechanical details, the GB treatment of raising and promotion in passivization differs markedly from the present treatment. Although I have found no empirical differences between the approaches to passivization, I have argued in favor of the present analysis of raising in section 3.1.

A second major difference between GB and the present theory involves GB "case filter" (Chomsky 1980a, 1981). Basically, the case filter demands that an NP with phonological content bear Case (abstract case) if it appears in surface structure. In general, an NP may be assigned Case if it is governed (in a structural sense that Chomsky makes clear) by a lexical category—either a V, a P, or an agreement element. Much of the work of the GB case filter is accomplished in the present theory by the Surface Appearance principle (2.86), which implies that a constituent (that is not an operator or the head of a phrase) will appear in surface structure only if it is Governed by a lexical item (or a structural position). Both the GB case filter and the Surface Appearance principle ensure that an NP with phonological content will bear a grammatical relation with respect to a lexical item in many situations. But the case filter and the Surface Appearance principle are clearly not equivalent, and they play distinct roles in their respective theories. For example, the GB case filter is instrumental in forcing the promotion of NP logical objects to subject in English passive constructions, whereas the Surface Appearance principle was exploited in the present theory to account for the distribution of PRO.

Another important discrepancy between the GB framework and the present theory lies in the connection the theories assume to exist between relational structure (structure B in (8.2) and s structure in (1.4)) and surface constituent structure (structure A in (8.2) and surface structure in (1.4)). Chomsky assumes that the relation between structures A and B in (8.2) is identity in configurational languages like English. To my knowledge, the GB framework says nothing explicit about the relation between structures A and B in nonconfigurational languages. In the present theory, because s and surface structures are fundamentally different sorts of representation, it makes no sense to claim that s structure is identical to surface structure in any situation. An s structure is a representation of the grammatical interrelations among constituents, while the surface constituent structure encodes linear order and constituent structure dominance relations directly relevant to phonological interpretation. The principles that govern the connection between s and surface structure are intended to apply to all languages whether configurational or nonconfigurational.

Although it is difficult to sort out fundamental empirical differences between the projection principles of GB theory and the present work, the merger constructions discussed in chapter 7 do seem to provide direct evidence in favor of the approach of this book. Recall that the connection between the structures B' and B in (8.2) is constrained by the projection principle, which insists that the structural relations established by thematic role assignment and subcategorization at B' are preserved at B. In contrast, I assume that the connection between l-s and s structures, which correspond roughly to B' and B respectively, is governed by principle M and by the principles of merger given in chapter 7. As a consequence, the present theory is able to predict the syntax of applied verb constructions (section 7.1) and derived causative constructions (section 7.2) calling upon the same general principles that govern the analysis of any sentence. For the GB framework, constructions that I would analyze as involving merger at l-s structure present a major problem. If the principles of the GB framework are interpreted in a straightforward manner, these constructions violate the projection principle. If the constructions are analyzed in such a manner as to preserve the projection principle, the GB framework offers no explanation of the syntax of these constructions comparable to that provided by the present theory.

As an example of the problems merger constructions present for the GB framework, consider the Malayalam causative construction discussed in section 7.2.3. Examining the semantic role assigning properties of the morphemes in the Malayalam sentence (8.3), I proposed the l-s structure shown in (8.4).

(8.3)
acchan kuṭṭiye kaṟayiccu.
father-NOM child-ACC cry-CAUSE-PAST
'Father made the child cry.'

(8.4)

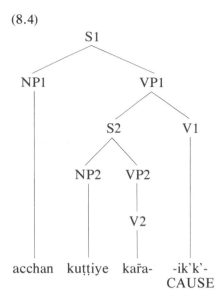

acchan   kuṭṭiye   kaṟa-   -ik'k'-
                                        CAUSE

Since B′ in (8.2) is a projection of thematic role assignment and sub-categorization, which correspond to semantic role assignment and argument taking, the GB structure B′ for (8.3) should look like (8.4) too. I argued in 7.2.3 that the correct s structure for (8.3) is (8.5), where X′ stands for the s structure counterpart of X.

(8.5)

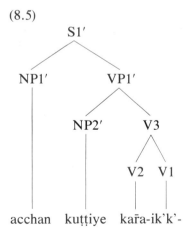

acchan   kuṭṭiye   kaṟa-ik'k'-

Using the same data presented in 7.2.3, one could argue that (8.5) is the proper GB structure B for (8.3) as well. However, the relation between (8.4) and (8.5) violates the projection principle. Technically, the structural relation between NP2 and VP2 in (8.4), which is established because VP2 assigns a theta-role to NP2, is not preserved in (8.5). Also, while NP2 is not subcategorized in (8.4) in the technical sense, it is subcategorized by V3 in (8.5).

To preserve the projection principle in merger constructions, one could claim that the l-s structures postulated in 7.2.3 for such constructions are not appropriate GB B' structures. Rather, the B' structure for a sentence like (8.3) should look like (8.5). If the correct structure B' for (8.3) is structurally isomorphic to (8.5), the analysis of (8.3) would not violate the projection principle. But if GB theory proposed (8.5) as the B' structure for (8.3), some additional account would need to be given for how V3 acquires the thematic role assigning and subcategorization properties reflected in (8.5). Also, postulating (8.5) as the B' structure for (8.3) would seriously endanger the explanatory force of the projection principle, which says that the lexical properties of theta-role assignment and subcategorization are structurally encoded in a specified manner at every syntactic level of analysis. If (8.5) were a syntactic structure for (8.3), the (semantic) lexical properties of the Malayalam causative affix -ik'k'-, that it takes a sentential argument and assigns a theta-role to this argument, would not be structurally represented at some syntactic level. If lexical properties of some items are not subject to the projection principle, how does one determine to which properties the principle applies?

Of course, another approach to merger constructions like (8.3) within the GB framework would be to modify the projection principle to accord with principle M and the principles of morphological merger found in chapter 7. These principles of the present theory share the basic insight of Chomsky's projection principle but capture this insight in a formally different manner.

Another theory that includes an explicit projection principle is the framework of Montague Grammar (MG). Although they apply to most Montague analyses, the majority of my remarks here are directed at the work of Dowty (1982a,b). Among linguists working within the Montague framework, Dowty has most directly addressed the issues and concerns of syntacticians outside the Montague school.

For MG, syntactic and compositional semantic structure are isomorphic. There are no levels of syntactic analysis mediating a mapping between grammatical structure and compositional semantics in the sense these terms have been used in the present work. MG incorporates a projection principle by insisting, in effect, that syntactic structure must be a direct reflection of semantic structure.

In discussing differences between MG and the present work, I translate the issues into the vocabulary of this book. That is, the comparison should not be seen as a fair weighing of the advantages and disadvantages of the two approaches; rather, I point out fundamentally different views on aspects of syntactic theory essential to my own work.

First note that where MG recognizes only one semantic/syntactic relation, the present work depends on two. For MG, the only relation corresponds to my argument-taker–argument relation; it is a relation that necessarily involves constituency. The present theory recognizes, in addition, a role assignment relation that does not hold implications for constituency. This second relation proved important for distinguishing direct and indirect arguments.

Second, as pointed out in section 2.1.3, the system of category types in the present theory, although related to the Montague system, places more stringent constraints on syntactic structure. Although for MG a category defined as a X/Y (takes an item of type Y and yields an item of type X) need not actually take a Y argument or head an X phrase in any sentence, a similarly defined category in the present theory (where X and Y are distinct) must in fact head an X phrase in syntax. The Nonmaximal Head principle (section 2.1.3), which demands that nonmaximal projections head phrases, thus ties the functional definitions of categories to the syntactic analysis of sentences much more tightly in the present theory than the functional definitions of MG are associated with Montague syntax.

Finally, although the projection principle of MG seems to claim a much stronger connection between compositional semantics and syntax than the projection principles of the present work, the exploitation of notational devices such as the lambda notation within MG in fact negates much of the force of its projection principle (see Marantz 1982b on this point). For example, within MG the inherent compositional semantics of a logically transitive verb might imply that it combines first with its logical object to create a sort of derived intransitive verb. The combination of verb and object combines with the subject to form a sentence. However, a lexical rule operating on the argument structure of the verb may change the relation between the verb's inherent compositional semantics and the way in which the verb actually combines with arguments in a sentence. By adding lambda notation to the argument structure of the verb, one may derive a verb that, in the construction of a sentence, actually combines first with that argument I have called the logical subject. The combination of verb and logical subject will combine with what I have called the logical object.

Dowty and others believe the power of adding lambda notation within lexical entries is necessary to account for alternations in the expression of a verb's semantic dependents like those described in chapters 4 through 7. But incorporating this power negates much of the force of the projection principle within MG. In fact, the compositional semantics in the sense of this book is not directly reflected in the syntax of MG. Rather, lexical rules may change the correspondence between what I have identified as compositional semantics and syntactic structure in ways that have not yet been completely explored. That is, MG employs lexical rules mapping from semantic to grammatical relations. These rules are currently unconstrained by any explicit projection principle. At the moment, the projection principles of the present work constrain the mapping between argument structures and syntax much more strictly than the seemingly stringent mapping principle of MG.

Lexical-Functional and Relational Grammars, which lack projection principles of the sort just discussed, in principle allow for any arbitrary association of (compositional) semantic relations and structural relations with grammatical relations. As far as the fundamental principles of these theories are concerned, the argument that combines first, semantically, with a logically transitive verb in a language might consistently be the syntactic subject while the argument that combines with the verb plus the first argument could consistently be the syntactic object. Also, a language could put all its subjects within a phrase structure VP while all its objects are sisters to its VPs. By tying semantic relations both to compositional semantics and to structural relations, projection principles rule out these possibilities.

Of course, if theories without projection principles did not link their grammatical relations to semantic notions or syntactic properties in universal grammar, it would not make sense to claim that such theories allow the argument that combines first semantically with a logically transitive verb to be the syntactic subject. For what would syntactic subject mean? All the major theories without projection principles found in the literature agree that certain grammatical relations should have certain properties. For example, subjects are canonically agents in canonical nominative-accusative languages, and subjects are controlled in structures of obligatory control. Canonical objects canonically passivize.

The explanatory problems of theories without projection principles would be clear even if they were not structured such that one could compare their treatment of subjects and objects with that supported by projection principle theories. These projectionless theories provide no principled account of the relation between compositional semantic relations and structural relations. Since they do not connect grammatical relations with these semantic and structural relations by fundamental principle and since they account for syntactic phenomena such as passivization, binding, and control in terms of grammatical relations, theories lacking projection principles also make no deep, principled connection between these syntactic phenomena and the semantic and structural relations.

8.2. Alternate Theories of Grammatical Relations

In comparing theories of grammatical relations, I will characterize them according to the source they attribute to grammatical relations and according to the approach they take toward accounting for syntactic phenomena that seem to implicate grammatical relations. Incorporating the projection principles I have described, the theory of this book locates the source of grammatical relations in logico-semantic relations. The theory is explanatory in that it attempts to explain generalizations true of grammatical relations by appealing to fundamental syntactic principles and to the inherent properties of grammatical relations. For example, the fact that grammatical subjects but not objects are controlled in control constructions like those described in section 3.2.1 follows in the present theory from the interaction of the Surface Appearance principle with inherent properties of subjects and objects. The Surface Appearance principle implies that a constituent bearing a grammatical relation with respect to a phrase will not appear in surface structure by virtue of bearing this relation. By the definition of these grammatical relations, subjects bear a grammatical relation with respect to a phrase, while objects bear a grammatical relation with respect to a lexical item (or structural position). In section 3.2.1, I showed how the Surface Appearance principle and these properties of subjects and objects allow PRO to occur as a subject but not as an object. Since PRO is what is controlled in control constructions, it follows that subjects but not objects may be controlled. I will classify as nonexplanatory those theories that, in order to account for generalizations true of grammatical relations, rely on rules or laws, independent of fundamental principles in the theories, that refer to specific grammatical relations. For example, a theory that accounts for the generalization that only subjects are controlled with a law stating that only subjects may be controlled would be classified as nonexplanatory.

8.2.1. Grammatical Relations from Structural Relations

Some theories define grammatical relations in terms of dominance relations in phrase structure trees. This approach to grammatical relations is usually associated with Chomsky's *Aspects of the Theory of Syntax* (Chomsky 1965, pp. 70–71). Since the appearance of *Aspects*, a great deal of literature, particularly in the Relational Grammar (RG) framework, has been devoted to demonstrating that there exist crosslinguistic generalizations referring to a set of grammatical relations that cannot be defined in terms of phrase structure configurations (see also Marantz 1982e). It has become clear that no universal definition of grammatical relations in terms of surface constituent structure would be adequate to capture these generalizations, where surface structure refers to the surface structure of the present theory or structure A of (8.2).

Although inadequate as construed in versions of Extended Standard Theory up to Chomsky 1980b, Chomsky's attempt to define grammatical relations structurally was generally explanatory. Fundamental principles of the theory were structurally based, and generalizations true of grammatical relations were shown to follow from these fundamental principles. For example, the fact that subjects but not objects are controlled in control constructions was shown by Chomsky (1979) to follow from the binding theory. The binding theory defines the structural domains in which anaphors must find their antecedents and in which nonanaphors must be free. Objects, by their definition as [NP, VP]'s, are governed with respect to the binding theory, while subjects, by their definition as [NP, S]'s, are not. Since, as Chomsky demonstrates, the binding theory implies that PRO must be ungoverned with respect to the binding theory, and since it is PRO that is controlled in control constructions, subjects but not objects are controlled.

Although neither GB nor the present theory defines grammatical relations in terms of surface phrase structure relations, both theories contain projection or mapping principles that strictly constrain the possible relations between grammatical and structural relations. Also, as explained in 8.1, both theories relate grammatical relations explicitly to structural relations. For example, structural government and the argument-taker–argument relations are both basic relations of asymmetric sisterhood.

8.2.2. Grammatical Relations from Semantic Roles

Semantic roles are implicitly or explicitly assumed to be the source of grammatical relations in most linguistic theories. Pedagogical grammars consistently define grammatical relations in terms of semantic roles. Although simple semantic definitions of grammatical relations have been generally recognized as inadequate for capturing generalizations in the mapping of semantic roles onto their expressions in sentences, more sophisticated attempts have been made to formalize the intuition that there is an inherent connection between certain semantic roles and certain grammatical relations.

For example, Starosta's (1978) Lexicase Grammar in effect views grammatical relations (he calls them "semantic relations") as grammaticalizations of semantic roles. Although it is not possible to determine the grammatical relation of a particular constituent on purely semantic grounds in Starosta's system, each grammatical relation class has a semantic core. Membership in a given class may be determined by grammatical as well as semantic criteria; if a constituent behaves syntactically like a core member of a class, it may be placed in this class regardless of its semantic features.

Some linguists take the position that many of the phenomena thought to implicate grammatical relations actually involve rules that refer directly to semantic roles. Ostler (1979) and Carter (1976) fall into this category, along with the Fillmore of "The Case for Case" (1968).

Two currently popular theoretical frameworks that claim to incorporate primitive grammatical relations are also associated with the view that semantic roles are the source of grammatical relations in some sense. Working within Bresnan's Lexical-Functional framework, Pinker (1981) has suggested that children learn language with the initial assumption that agents will be subjects and patients objects. Grammatical relations are flagged with semantic roles in the child's innate knowledge of language. Thus semantic roles serve as the developmental source of grammatical relations in the Lexical-Functional framework.

In assuming that constituents are assigned their initial grammatical relations on the basis of a universal initial assignment of grammatical relations to semantic roles, RG places semantic roles as the source of grammatical relations in the analysis of every sentence. RG's many-to-one mapping of semantic roles onto initial grammatical relations constitutes an extremely strong connection between semantic roles and grammatical relations, a connection that, as explained in Marantz 1982b, may be considered a definition of grammatical relations in semantic terms.

At least some versions of RG place this connection between semantic roles and grammatical relations at the core of syntax. The assumed universal initial assignment of grammatical relations to semantic roles (or relations) is perhaps the most fundamental principle of RG. This principle allows one to identify the initial grammatical relation that a sentential constituent will bear on the basis of its semantic role in the sentence. Without this principle, it would be extremely difficult for RG to derive predictions about particular constructions in particular languages because the theory would leave open too many possible analyses of any given construction.

In this book I have presented data that call into question the universal initial assignment of grammatical relations to semantic roles within Relational Grammar (the Universal Initial Assignment Hypothesis or UIAH). Recall the discussion of Sanskrit impersonal passivization in section 5.2.1. We saw in section 4.1.3 that the combination of the 1-Advancement Exclusiveness Law (1AEX) and the UIAH, taken with the RG analysis of impersonal passivization, predicts that intransitive verbs whose sole argument bears a theme or patient role (unaccusative verbs) may not undergo impersonal passivization. By the UIAH, the sole argument of such intransitive verbs is an initial object, which is promoted to subject. Since impersonal passivization of such verbs would involve the subsequent promotion of a dummy object to subject on the RG analysis, resulting in two advancements to subject in a single clause, the 1AEX rules out impersonal passivization with unaccusative verbs.

Ostler (1979) showed, however, that verbs in Sanskrit that would be identified in RG as unaccusative on semantic role grounds do undergo impersonal passivization (see section 5.2.1). Therefore, it seems that either the 1AEX or the UIAH is wrong as currently stated in RG. But, as Ostler also demonstrates, passive clauses in Sanskrit do not undergo impersonal passivization. Since RG relies on the 1AEX to prevent the impersonal passivization of passives, the Sanskrit data indicate that the 1AEX must be maintained in RG. Because Ostler's Sanskrit evidence not only demonstrates that the 1AEX and the UIAH cannot both be maintained but also provides support for the 1AEX, I am led to conclude that RG should drop the UIAH. That is, the sole semantic dependent of a Sanskrit verb that bears the theme or patient role should be allowed to bear the initial subject relation in violation of the UIAH, which would assign the initial object relation to such an argument.

The data in chapter 6 on ergativity also present a serious challenge to the UIAH. The initial grammatical relations of RG correspond roughly to the l-s relations of the present theory—at least the initial subject and object relations correspond to the logical subject and object (of a verb) relations. It was only on the assumption that agent and theme or patient arguments canonically bear different l-s relations in nominative-accusative languages from those they bear in ergative languages that the present theory was able to explain the differences between nominative-accusative and ergative languages described in chapter 6. It is unclear how RG could characterize the demonstrable differences between nominative-accusative and ergative languages without allowing the ergative languages to violate the UIAH. If the conclusions of chapter 6 are correct, the association of semantic roles and initial grammatical relations should be allowed to differ from language to language.

Without the UIAH, RG consists mainly of a series of universal laws concerning grammatical relations, none of which seem fundamental to the theory. The laws amount to generalizations over the behavior of various constructions in some number of languages. For example, RG accounts for the syntax of the derived causative constructions discussed in section 7.2 by stipulating what happens to the grammatical dependents of the causative affix and root verb under clause union— the union into a single sentence of the clause headed by the causative morpheme and the clause headed by the lower verb (see 7.2 for an explanation of the vocabulary used in discussing derived causative constructions). The RG laws of clause union predict the syntax of Comrie's paradigm case causative constructions by, in effect, stipulating the correspondences listed in (7.70).

As shown in 7.2.2, there is a type of derived causative that does not conform to Comrie's paradigm case—causative constructions in which the causative affix and root verb merge at s structure. Because the stated effects of clause union in RG, like most universals in the theory, are independent of fundamental principles, the existence of these derived causative constructions does not undermine the theory of RG. To account for this alternate type of derived causative construction, RG could simply add another option to the clause union laws. Languages like Turkish (section 7.2.3) would choose one option in these laws, while languages like Japanese (section 7.2.2) would choose the other. Or RG might claim that no clause union takes place in the second, Japanese sort of derived causative. Because RG includes no general principles determining the interaction of morphology and syntax, the fact that the causative verb appears as an affix on the lower verb of a causative construction holds no particular importance for the analysis of causative constructions in RG. That is, the affix status of the causative verb need not imply clause union in the theory.

In contrast to the RG analysis of derived causative constructions, the present theory predicts the syntax of these constructions from fundamental principles of the grammar. That a causative affix appears on the lower verb as an affix in a causative construction implies that it must merge with the lower verb at some level of syntactic analysis. General principles, like principle M, determine the consequences of merger at each level for the syntax of the causative constructions. Empirical discoveries could force changes in principles like principle M, but because it applies in the analysis of every sentence, any change in this principle would have far-reaching consequences throughout the grammar. The principles of the present theory have a tight interdependency and wide range of application not characteristic of the laws and rules of RG.

As for the explanatory force of tying grammatical relations to semantic roles, I am unaware of any serious attempts to provide an explanatory link between the semantic role source of grammatical relations and generalizations true of grammatical relations. Moreover, it is unlikely that any such link may be forged. If the agent role is somehow intimately associated with the subject relation, for example, this feature of subjects seems unlikely to enter into an explanation of why subjects but not objects are controlled in control constructions. Since semantic roles seem unconnected with syntactic properties of grammatical relations, theories that posit semantic role sources for grammatical relations are nonexplanatory.

8.2.3. Grammatical Relations from Clusters of Properties
Keenan (1976) defines "subject" in terms of a cluster of properties subjects share cross-linguistically. It is not clear to me whether Keenan is defining a theoretical term that might appear in principles or rules of grammar or a concept he believes speakers of languages acquire. His methodology seems geared to the latter task. As he writes (p. 312), "On this type of definition 'subject' does not represent a single dimension of linguistic reality. It is rather a cluster concept, or as we shall say, a

multifactor concept." Keenan assumes that people have pretheoretical intuitions about grammatical relations (p. 306): "We are not free to define a notion like 'subject' in any way that suits our purposes. There is a large body of lore concerning the notion, and any proposed definition must at least largely agree with the traditional, and to some extent, pretheoretical usage of the term." In defining "subject" in terms of a cluster of properties, Keenan's task is to capture the concept linguists have when they refer to subjects.

Keenan seems to be making a fundamental error, an error discussed in chapter 1. As Wittgenstein (1958) explains at length, just because we use some words to refer to objects, there need not be an object behind every word. That we use the word *subject* in a variety of situations does not imply that there is a definable concept 'subject,' even a cluster concept, that stands behind our use of the word in each of the situations. What Keenan (1976) does in his article is recount various ways in which linguists have used the term *subject*—an interesting exercise but of questionable importance to linguistic theory. There is a body of linguistic work that makes use of grammatical relational terms. Linguists are free to define grammatical relations in any way that contributes to an explanatory theory of grammar, ignoring intuitions about the appropriate use of grammatical relational terms and precedents for the use of the terms in the literature. They are not free to ignore any insights or generalizations in the literature that refer to grammatical relations.

Defining grammatical relations in terms of the cluster of properties that constituents bearing them seem to share is an inherently non-explanatory approach to grammatical relations. If, in fact, a set of constituents shares a cluster of properties, the explanatory task is to account for why these properties cluster together.

8.2.4. Grammatical Relations as Primitives

Proponents of Relational Grammar and Lexical-Functional Grammar have claimed that the grammatical relations in their theories are primitive. I made some general comments about this approach to grammatical relations in chapter 1. Here I wish to emphasize that, like the cluster-of-properties view of grammatical relations, the grammatical-relations-as-primitives position is inherently nonexplanatory. Nothing can follow from the nature of grammatical relations on such a position because grammatical relations lack a nature. RG and L-F theory resort to stipulated laws referring to particular grammatical relations to account for generalizations true of their grammatical relations.

For example, consider the 1-Advancement Exclusiveness Law of RG, which states that there may be no more than one advancement to subject ("1") within a given clause (see section 4.1.3). Because subjects and objects have no inherent properties in RG, there is no way to explain the existence of a 1AEX but no 2 (Object)-Advancement Exclusiveness Law by appealing to the inherent properties of these grammatical relations. Within RG, this asymmetry is taken as an arbitrary fact about universal grammar.

To take a similar example from the L-F framework, consider how this framework accounts for the generalization that only subjects are controlled in control constructions. Bresnan 1982a introduces a universal law of "functional control" that mentions only subjects—SUBs—as controllers. Because SUBs and OBJs have no inherent properties in the L-F system, the theory cannot explain why OBJ does not occur in the place of SUB in the law of functional control by referring to inherent properties of grammatical relations.

If a theory with so-called primitive grammatical relations contains universal principles that alone or in some combination uniquely pick out a particular grammatical relation, then this grammatical relation is in fact definable in the theory. For example, in RG one need only take a statement of the 1AEX, replace all occurrences of 1 (subject) in this statement with X, and place before the statement the phrase "1 is the grammatical relation X such that," and "1" (subject) will have been defined within the theory. Similarly, for Lexical-Functional Grammar SUB may be defined as the grammatical relation (function) that is functionally controlled. By claiming that their theories include primitive grammatical relations, practitioners of RG and L-F Grammar eschew explanation. It seems clear that they should be trying to explain why the grammatical relation that obeys the 1AEX or is controlled should display the other properties that subjects exhibit in these theories.

While exploring the nature of grammatical relations in this book, I have presented and developed a highly restrictive and explanatory syntactic theory. Most of the predictive power of the theory rests in a few very general principles and definitions, which interact to tightly constrain possible syntactic analyses. These principles do not refer to specific logico-semantic, grammatical, or structural relations, either basic or defined; in fact, the only distinguishing feature of relations that a principle mentions is the distinction between relations borne with respect to phrases and relations borne with respect to lexical items (see the Surface Appearance principle). In order to meet the goal of accounting for constructions that implicate grammatical relations, I have found it necessary to describe and constrain the possible interactions between morphology and syntax to an extent without precedence in the literature. I hope that the theory will provide a framework for further extensive cross-linguistic research.

Notes

Chapter 1

1. Binding theory should apply to s structure if it is correctly stated solely in terms of government and governing categories. Mohanan (1982a) has presented evidence from Malayalam and other languages that at least the determination of possible coreference between a pronoun and an NP is dependent on the linear order of these constituents in some languages. Because linear order is not a feature of s structure but only of the surface constituent structure tree, pieces of binding theory may need access to surface structure in (1.4).

Chapter 2

1. On Case Grammar, see Filmore (1968, 1977), Cook (1979), the papers in Abraham (1978), and the sources cited in these works.

2. In addition to the references mentioned in note 1, see Ostler (1979), Gruber (1976), and Carter (1976).

3. For the purposes of this book, it is only necessary to claim that a verb names a mapping from arguments onto predicates. If the verb maps each set of arguments onto a single predicate, it names a function. I will continue to use the term "function" for the mapping that a verb names even though it is not essential that verbs meet the uniqueness condition on functions.

4. Ken Hale has informed me that Navajo has a great number of idiomatic expressions that would be analyzed as subject idioms (with free object positions) on the basis of their English glosses. However, the identification of grammatical relations in Navajo is problematic. See Young and Morgan (1980, e.g., p. 313) for the Navajo data.

5. Referring to an earlier draft of this work, Hasegawa (1981) argues for subject/object compositional asymmetries in Japanese using arguments similar to these mustered from English. Lieber (1983) presents further evidence for the basic subject/object asymmetry in English based on constraints on English compounding.

6. Alternatively, these terms may be seen as naming features of semantic roles. For example, the logical subject of *run* in, *Elmer ran away from the rabid porcupine* might be [+agent], since *Elmer* is an active participant in the running, and [+theme], since *Elmer* undergoes a change of state (from a position near the rabid porcupine to a position farther away).

7. Recall that the logical object is a direct argument of a lexical item, a constituent that both receives its semantic role from and serves as argument to this lexical item. The logical subject is the direct argument of a predicate.

8. This hypothesis must be distinguished from the claim of GB theory (Chomsky 1981) that D and S-structure are structures of the same type. The constituents and relations of l-s and s structure are distinct, although the two structures for a given sentence could be isomorphic. In GB theory, the constituents and relations of D and S-structure are identical, but the D and S-structure for a given sentence could be distinct, e.g., related by a movement transformation.

9. I ignore here the distinction between a lexical item and its immediately dominating category node. I separate a lexical item from its category node only to follow the notational conventions in the literature—all category nodes could be eliminated from the representations of l-s and s structure without consequences for the theory. Each lexical item must in any case carry some indication of its category type. Note also that definition (2.47) will determine the s structure counterpart of an l-s category node by projection from the lexical item that it immediately dominates.

10. The combination of syntactic/semantic role assigner and indirect argument of a verb, e.g., *to Hortense* in *Elmer gave the porcupine to Hortense,* is not a constituent at l-s or s structure. Such a role assigner lacks an argument structure and thus does not form or head a phrase. Nevertheless, such role assigners may form constituents with their role assignees at surface structure, perhaps because they merge with their role assignees at surface structure (see section 7.3) or because general principles in the mapping from s to surface structure demand this constituency.

11. A grammatical subject might bear exceptional case marking determined by the tense or aspect marking in its sentence. As explained in chapter 3, tense/aspect marking may Govern SUBs at s structure. Since such marking is lexical, it may dictate special case marking on its syntactic role assignee, the SUB of the sentence.

12. It is important to distinguish this hypothetical situation from the very real phenomenon of noun incorporation, discussed briefly in section 7.4 (see, e.g., Sadock 1980).

Chapter 3

1. I assume that the [X, VP] position in English assigns a syntactic role unconditionally to a constituent of any s structure type except that of noun phrase. Modifiers with the internal structure of noun phrases will be modifiers, not

noun phrases, at s structure. Thus in *I consider Elmer the best man for the job*, the NP *the best man for the job* will receive a syntactic role from [X, VP] just as would the AP *fond of porcupines* in *I consider Elmer fond of porcupines*. Both phrases are of the s structure type modifier. The structural position [NP, VP] may also assign a syntactic role to s structure noun phrases in situations in which this position also assigns a semantic role. See section 5.1 for an analysis of dative movement constructions that depends on [NP, VP]'s assigning both semantic and syntactic roles.

2. My analysis of raising does not necessarily imply that the sequence *Elmer fond of porcupines* in *I consider Elmer fond of porcupines* is not a surface phrase structure constituent. *Elmer* does bear a grammatical relation with respect to the AP, and this relation must find some counterpart at surface structure. Although *Elmer* will not appear in the surface structure tree by virtue of bearing this surface relation, since it will appear by virtue of an OBJ relation it bears with respect to the raising verb, *Elmer* might appear as sister to the AP in a surface phrase to express the relation between it and the AP. Most of the arguments in the literature for or against raising to object (that are not simply confused) have actually been arguments for or against a surface constituent consisting of the raised object and the lower modifier.

3. See Steele (1981) for a discussion of the relation between the tense-aspect system and the expression of subjects in Luiseño.

4. The existence of a special mechanism whereby auxiliary verbs may exceptionally Govern the VPs of their sentential complements leads me to take special caution in evaluating the claim that raising from verb phrases is the marked case cross-linguistically. Where apparent cases of raising to subject from verb phrases are found, one must decide between a raising and an auxiliary analysis. Auxiliaries lack the semantic properties of raising items. As a result, auxiliaries will not generally take AP, NP, and PP modifiers in addition to VPs. Because of the possibility of an auxiliary analysis for apparent cases of raising to subject from verb phrases, I have used raising to object to illustrate the restriction on raising to AP, NP, and PP modifiers in the unmarked case.

5. Strong evidence has been presented that the raised object in raising to object constructions does not fall in the lower clause in the surface structures of Quechua (Cole and Hermon 1981) and Icelandic (Thráinsson 1980). Carden (1983) also argues for a raising to object analysis of constructions in a handful of languages.

6. The analysis does more closely resemble the accounts of raising in Bresnan (1982a) and Dowty (1982b), although the resemblance is superficial. Both Bresnan and Dowty link raising much more closely to control constructions than in the present theory, for example. As a result of such differences, these alternative analyses fail to make the same cross-linguistic predictions as the present account.

7. Suppose, as Chomsky does, that the coindexing that indicates the Move Alpha relation at surface structure is the same coindexing that operates in the theory of control, connecting PROs and their antecedents at s structure. A PRO

and its antecedent will be coindexed in precisely the same way as a binder and its trace. Suppose further that indices are borne by constituents at all levels of syntactic analysis and are only checked or interpreted by the theory of control or by the relation of Move Alpha. Given these assumptions, if a binder binds two traces, these traces will be coindexed at s structure as well as surface structure. If one c-commands the other, the lower trace will be identified by control theory as a PRO bound by the upper trace. But then a single empty category, the lower trace, would be identified as both a PRO and a trace, a contradiction. Since Niuean allows binders in projected positions, to make this explanation of the c-command restriction on parasitic gaps hold cross-linguistically, binders must not be recognized as potential antecedents by the theory of control.

Chapter 4

1. For present purposes I consider affixes those morphemes with word tree subcategorization features. Although systems of nonconcatenative morphology, such as that described in McCarthy 1981, raise some questions for the analysis of the interaction between morphology and syntax presented in this book, they do not pose any great problems. In a nonconcatenative system, in which the morphemes are prosodic templates (C-V skeleta) and phonemic melodies, what are the affixes and what the roots? One may simply provide subcategorization features to those morphemes that, for purposes of predicting the interaction of morphology and syntax, one wishes to identify as affixes, but independent motivation for such a move may be lacking.

2. I do not think it is an accident that the past perfect participle is used for the passive in English, though I am not aware of a theory that correctly predicts that this participle and not, say, the present progressive, will show up in passives.

3. The [−transitive] feature of passive participles might be provided to them by the markedness principle that [−log sub] verbs are [−transitive] in the unmarked case—see section 4.1.2. That is, the passive affix need not carry the feature [−transitive] to ensure that passive participles become [−transitive]. Nevertheless, the English passive affix -en must carry the feature [−transitive] because it attaches only to [+transitive] roots.

4. In the remainder of this work, I ignore the participle nature of the passive verb. In chapter 3 I suggested that auxiliaries should be analyzed as sentential operators that exceptionally Govern into their sentential complements at s structure, in effect causing raising to subject. Given this analysis of auxiliaries, one may treat the passive participle as a main verb heading a sentential complement to *be*.

5. Since the logical object of *by* is assigned its semantic role (indirectly) by a predicate and serves as an argument to a predicate, it is, in an important sense, a logical subject. If some rule or generalization in a language refers to logical subjects as a class, it is possible that it might apply to the logical object of *by*.

6. It is quite simple to collapse the account of the *by* phrase used with passive participles with that of the *by* phrase in nominalizations like *the city's destruction by Elmer,* but a number of interesting phenomena associated with derived nominals indicate that the connection between *the city's destruction by Elmer* and *The city was destroyed by Elmer* is not straightforward (see Kayne 1981, Rappaport 1980, 1983, Williams 1982, and the references cited in these sources).

If one did wish to collapse the account of *by* in passives with the account of *by* in nominals, one would suppose that certain nouns are associated with nominal-argument structures like those described in chapter 2, but that instead of nominals, nominal-argument structures like (i) produce functions from an argument to nominals.

(i)
'destruction' (*destroyed*)

The nominal-argument structure named by *destruction* takes in arguments bearing the destroyed role and yields an object, which may be called a nominal-producer, that assigns a destroyer role to a constituent and takes in a constituent bearing this role to yield a nominal. A derived nominal like *destruction* creates nominal-producers that assign the same semantic role as the predicates created by the P-A structure of the related verb *destroy.*

In addition to heading predicate modifiers, the preposition *by* may head a modifier of nominal-producers. Within NPs, *by* would assign to its logical object the semantic role assigned by the nominal-producer that is sister to the modifier *by* heads at l-s structure. Then *by* would apply the nominal-producer to its logical object to yield a nominal, identified as a degenerate nominal-producer. That is, *by* functions in nominals precisely as it functions in sentences.

This account of the function of *by* in nominals would allow one to generalize the use of *by* in passives to its use with nouns like *portrait* in (ii) which have no obvious verbal counterparts.

(ii)
The portrait of Elmer by the famous post-dadaist hangs in the public zoo.

Although *portrait* is not directly related (i.e., related by a productive morphological process) to a verb with a P-A structure, it names a nominal-argument structure, which takes in *Elmer* as an argument in (ii) and yields the nominal-producer *portrait of Elmer.* The nominal-producers that *portrait*'s nominal-argument structure yields take in an argument bearing the painter role, a role that *by* may assign in nominals.

The possessive marker, *'s,* is available to every noun phrase and serves a variety of functions. Like *of* (see section 2.2.3.2), *'s* may be provided to any noun to assign a syntactic role to the s structure counterpart of the noun's logical object, allowing this NP to serve as an indirect syntactic argument with respect to the noun at s structure.

(iii)
the city's destruction

In (iii), *destruction*'s logical object, *the city,* corresponds to an indirect syntactic argument of the noun at s structure, assigned its syntactic role by the possessive ending. In addition to serving as a syntactic role assigner with no l-s counterpart, as in (iii), the possessive *'s* may play the role of *by* in nominals, as in (iv).

(iv)
Elmer's destruction of the city

The possessive ending in (iv) serves the same function as *by* in (v).

(v)
the destruction of the city by Elmer

The resemblance between derived nominals and passive constructions in the present theory may be accounted for by the similarity between the nominalization and passive participle formation processes. Since nouns are by nature [−transitive], nominalization like passivization detransitivizes a verb. And since neither nominals nor nominal-producers are predicates, nominalization in effect makes an argument-taking verb [−log sub]. Unlike the logical subject semantic role of a predicate, which the predicate in certain situations (i.e., when the item that produces the predicate is [+log sub]) must assign, the semantic role assigned by a nominal-producer is never obligatorily assigned.

7. It has been suggested in the literature on the Extended Standard Theory that the [−log sub] and [−transitive] features of English passive participles need not be explicitly associated with passive morphology. In Marantz 1982e I showed why the [−log sub] feature of passive participles can not follow from the use of the copula in passive sentences and why their [−transitive] feature can not follow from their adjectival nature.

8. Not everyone considers the (b) sentences in (4.17)–(4.19) ungrammatical, but there is general agreement that (4.16b) is much better.

9. Williams (1979) makes a similar argument against a promotion analysis of passivization, and his article was the inspiration for this section. However, Williams's argument depends on allowing passivization to apply freely to intransitive verbs in English. As Williams points out, although he can account for the facts surrounding the sentential complements of *feel, reason,* etc., he cannot account for the ungrammaticality of sentences like *It was died.* Moreover, Williams fails to provide evidence against the obligatory sentential extraposition analysis of sentences like the (c) examples in (4.17)–(4.19).

10. A promotion analysis of passivization could account for the behavior of the sentential complements to passive participles if it postulated a special rule of impersonal passivization in English which applies only to verbs taking sentential complements. This impersonal passive rule would demote from subject status the logical subject of verbs taking sentential complements but would not promote to subject the sentential complements of these verbs. A dummy *it* would take over the subject function or position in such impersonal passives. Since, on an impersonal passive analysis, the sentential complements in (4.25a,b) and (4.26a,b) would be subjects at no stage in the derivation of these

sentences, such an analysis would make the proper distinction between these sentential complements and extraposed subjects.

Postulating a rule of impersonal passivization for verbs taking sentential complements, however, involves giving up the promotion analysis of passivization. In impersonal passivization with sentential complements, nothing promotes. Thus if one wished to save the promotion analysis for certain passives while maintaining an explanation for the use of the passive morpheme in the impersonal passives, one would have to claim that what makes passives passives is not the promotion of an object but the demotion of a subject. In any case, the impersonal passive analysis of English passives with sentential complements must invoke a number of ad hoc stipulations not required by the unified analysis of English passivization supported in this chapter.

11. Actually, general principles would not force the verbs in adversity passive sentences to be [−log sub] if morphological merger played a role in their analysis (see chapter 7 on merger). On a merger analysis of adversity passives involving a [+log sub] verb, the affix -rare would be a higher verb at l-s structure, taking a propositional complement. The predicted syntax of the resulting construction would parallel the syntax of the derived causative constructions described in section 7.2.2. But the expression of the subject of the root verb as a *ni* marked object regardless of the transitivity of the verb is not what one would expect on the merger analysis, as explained in connection with the discussion of causatives in section 7.2. Therefore, even if a morphological merger analysis is motivated for the adversity passives, the derived passive verb should be [−log sub] to account for the expression of the subject of the root verb.

12. The Chichewa verbal affixes glossed as pronouns are agreement morphemes. I follow Trithart (1977) in coindexing the agreement morphology with the NPs with which they agree. The initial agreement affix agrees with the subject; the agreement marker following the tense prefix generally agrees with a grammatical object of the verb, but may also agree with other constituents.

13. In chapters 5 and 8 I review Ostler's (1979) demonstration that Sanskrit data falsify the 1AEX within Relational Grammar. Although Ostler's data do suggest the need for fundamental changes in the principles of Relational Grammar, given one simple assumption about Sanskrit consistent with the present theory, they in fact support the explanation of the 1AEX provided in this section. That is, arguments like Ostler's work only against the 1AEX within Relational Grammar and not against any conceivable explanation of the data that the 1AEX predicts.

14. If the subjects in (4.43), the means and time arguments, are not logical subjects of the predicates in these sentences, they must be logical objects of the verbs. As we saw in section 2.2.3.2, only logical objects and logical subjects may in general correspond to syntactic subjects. Furthermore, the identification of the semantic roles for these arguments clearly depends on the verbs alone among the lexical items in the sentence. So one peculiar thing about the verbs *buy* and *find* in their uses in (4.43) is that they assign two semantic roles: *buy* assigns the bought and means roles; *find* assigns the found and time roles.

In addition to assigning two semantic roles, the verbs in (4.43) are unusual in two respects. First, they are highly marked in being both [−log sub] and [+transitive], in violation of markedness principle (4.32). Second, the verbs must specify in some manner which of their logical objects will correspond to their syntactic object at s structure. The logical objects bearing the means and time roles, not those bearing the bought and found roles, show up as subjects in (4.43).

15. It is not the *door* ('by') phrase in (4.48b,d) that renders the sentences ungrammatical. As Perlmutter shows, impersonal passives of unaccusative verbs are ungrammatical without *door* phrases.

16. Some sentences containing the passive participles of unaccusative verbs might look grammatical because such passive participles are often homophonous with passive participles of related transitive verbs. The grammatical readings of such sentences would implicate the passive participles of the transitive verbs, not of the homophonous unaccusatives. English has transitive *wilt* in, *The sun wilted the flowers,* and unaccusative *wilt* in, *The flowers wilted.* The passive participle, *wilted,* in, *The flowers were wilted,* is formed from the transitive root. The passive sentence must contain the logically transitive verb because it implies an agent—someone or something wilted the flowers. The unaccusative verb has no agentive implications.

17. If passivization were viewed as a process changing a [+log sub] verb into a [−log sub] verb, and if passive morphology were viewed as a flag or marker of this process, the impossibility of passivizing unaccusative verbs would follow immediately without the NVAP. One would not find passive morphology on inherently [−log sub] verbs because it is impossible for such verbs to undergo the process of changing from [+log sub] to [−log sub]. The only processes associated with passivization in the present framework are the mechanisms of affixation and feature percolation. Thus I am committed to explaining the ungrammaticality of passives of unaccusative verbs with a condition on word formation. If the proposed constraint against vacuous affixation should prove untenable, the process view of passivization would gain support.

18. Postal (1977) reports examples of what he calls antipassivization in a variety of languages, but most of the constructions Postal discusses would be analyzed in the current theory as examples of indefinite object deletion—see section 5.2.2. Whereas antipassivization is a productive affixation process, indefinite object deletion constructions involve an alternation in the argument structure of verbs not productively mediated by affixation.

19. Gerdts (1981) provides a convincing demonstration that Halkomelem Salish includes an antipassivization process.

20. The choice of a verb meaning 'wash' to illustrate lexical reflexivization is perhaps misleading. It is possible that the intransitive forms of verbs like 'wash' and 'dress' in a language will have reflexive implications regardless of whether the language has an identifiable reflexive verb form; Benstein (1983) suggests that modern Hebrew is such a language. Consider English *Elmer washed/ dressed before dinner.* The relation between transitive and "reflexive" (intrans-

itive) *wash* in a language like English should be treated in the same manner as the anticausative alternation discussed in section 5.2.1. The analysis provided in this section extends only to languages for which verbs beyond the narrow semantic class including 'wash' and 'dress' may appear in the reflexive verb form with reflexive meaning.

21. Like the passive affix in a language that exhibits impersonal passives (see section 4.1.2), the reflexive affix could carry just the feature [−log sub]. The implication in (4.32) would provide the [−log sub] reflexive verb with the feature [−transitive]. I do not know of any evidence to indicate whether or not the reflexive affix should carry the [−transitive] feature.

22. In chapter 7, I consider evidence that binding theory applies at the initial s structure, i.e., the list of constituents and relations mapped directly onto l-s structure. Morphological merger allows multiple lists of constituents and relations at each syntactic level.

23. When its subject is plural, the Albanian reflexive verb may have a reciprocal interpretation. This reciprocal reading is possible for the reflexive verbs of many languages.

24. In addition to the fact that the reflexive verb form in the Romance languages often has a passive reading, the syntax of reflexive constructions shares many features with the syntax of passive constructions containing passive verb forms not homophonous with the reflexive (see Burzio 1981).

Chapter 5

1. This prediction holds only for nominative-accusative languages, in the sense of chapter 6. See section 6.2 for a discussion of dative shift in ergative languages.

2. Dutch (Zaenen, personal communication) and Korean (Shibatani 1977) present potential counterexamples to the predictions of the theory concerning double object constructions. I have been unable to find a group of Dutch speakers who agree on the crucial data, however, and the situation in Korean is complicated by a number of interesting factors.

3. Double object constructions in Swahili proper exhibit the same behavior as that described for Chi-Mwi:ni double object sentences (see Ashton 1944).

4. Jane Simpson informs me that double object constructions in the closest neighboring languages to Yindjibarndi behave as do their Yindjibarndi counterparts.

5. Burzio (1981) argues explicitly that English anticausatives are unaccusative in the sense of section 2.1.2.

6. This difference between the the argument structures of (5.25) and (5.26) is nowhere represented explicitly. Note in particular that the [−log sub] features in (5.26) do not indicate that the predicates produced by the argument structures do not assign semantic roles. Passive verbs are [−log sub], but the predicates they produce do assign semantic roles.

The fact that anticausative verbs create predicates that do not assign semantic roles is not explicitly encoded in the lexical entries for these verbs because this information is not exploited by the grammar. Some P-A structures produce role-assigning predicates and some do not, but this is not information that can be accessed by the syntax or lexicon. For example, an affix could not subcategorize for a root that produces role-assigning predicates. If one distinguished verbs that produce role assigners from verbs that do not with an explicit feature, one would have no explanation for why this feature plays no role in grammar.

7. Actually the situation in Japanese is rather complicated (see Jacobson 1982). Some anticausatives with morphologically related transitives are morphologically simple; some such anticausatives are morphologically derived.

8. Other analyses of the indefinite object deletion alternation are conceivable. Nevertheless, if it is to account for the connection between the *eat*'s in (5.23a) and (5.23b), the grammar must prevent the *eat* in (b) from assigning the patient role that *eat* assigns in (a); or allow *eat* not to assign the patient role in (b); or bind *eat*'s patient argument in (b) to some nonovert indefinite NP. Regardless of which of these analyses is correct, no percolation of features from an affix attached to the *eat* in (5.23a) could create a derived verb with the properties necessary to serve as the *eat* in (5.23b).

9. Although the antipassive affixes discussed in section 4.2 may have the effect of allowing logically transitive verbs to appear without overt logical objects, in all cases of true antipassivization the logical object of a verb may appear overtly with the verb's antipassive form as a syntactic indirect argument. The antipassive affix does not generally indicate the absence of the logical object from the sentence.

10. Benstein (1983) applies the analyses of section 5.2 to Modern Hebrew, whose nonconcatenative morphology contrasts with the systems of affixation employed by the languages I have discussed.

Chapter 6

1. On ergativity see Dixon (1979b), Comrie (1973), and the papers and references in Plank (1979). For a discussion of Dyirbal's ergativity, see Dixon (1979a), Heath (1979), Mel'čuk (1979), Schmerling (1979), and the references cited in these works.

2. As Dixon (1977, pp. 388–392) explains, the Yidin coordination constructions differ in many respects from the Dyirbal topic chain constructions, but these differences are not relevant to the point I am making here.

3. Levin (1983) derives further predictions from my analysis of ergative languages and tests them in languages not discussed in this book. Her work strongly supports the proposed distinction between nominative-accusative and ergative languages.

4. For this analysis to work, I must assume that comitative case assigns the theme role in (6.9b). As far as I can tell, there is no independent reason to

believe that the comitative case should be able to assign the theme role in Arctic, but we have already seen that the nominative-accusative analysis of Arctic dative shift constructions fails to predict the case marking on the theme argument.

5. Relational Grammar provides no natural explanation for the ungrammaticality of (6.25) on the nominative-accusative analysis of Arctic. Dative shift in Relational Grammar is analyzed as indirect to direct object (3 to 2) advancement. Antipassivization (see Postal 1977) is the demotion of a subject to object, which puts the current object "en chômage," then the subsequent advancement of the demoted subject back to subject. Since data from the Bantu languages precludes the postulation of a 2-Advancement Exclusiveness Law that would block a rule putting a derived object "en chômage" (see Perlmutter and Postal 1978a), no current laws of Relational Grammar prevent dative shift and antipassivization in the same clause. Therefore, the laws of Relational Grammar do not block (6.25) if Arctic is considered nominative-accusative.

6. My various sources on Greenlandic employ different orthographies. I reproduce each example sentence in the orthography of its source.

7. The present theory provides a straightforward analysis for alternations like those illustrated in (6.41). Basically, they should be treated as I treated the English benefactive alternations in section 5.1.2. The lexical entries of the transitive verbs in the alternations should embed the P-A structures of their intransitive counterparts. In addition, the transitive verbs contain the argument structures of heads of predicate modifiers similar to English directional prepositions. The transitive verbs assign roles to the arguments of these predicate modifier producers. For example, the P-A structure of transitive *tikippaa* 'he has come to it' in (6.41a) should look like (ia); the P-A structure of its intransitive counterpart *tikippuq* 'he has come' in (6.41b) should look like (ib).

(i)
tikipp-   a. ('come' ($\emptyset$) 'to' (*direction*))
         b. 'come' ($\emptyset$)

The relation between the transitive and intransitive versions of *tikipp-* 'come' in (i) should be parallel to the relation between dative shifted and non-dative-shifted *bake* (see section 5.1.2).

Chapter 7

1. I need not specify anything about the category type of the applied affix. Its argument structure determines that it will be the head of a modifier when it is an independent l-s constituent; that is, it names a function from an argument to a modifier of predicates. The Merger principle (7.8), which determines the argument structure of derived words under merger, dictates that the derived words that the applied affix will head must be verbs: they must name functions from arguments to predicates. By (7.8) the argument structure of a derived applied verb will be the argument structure of the applied affix applied to the argument structure of the root verb. Such a derived argument structure is a predicate

argument structure—a function from arguments to predicates. Since it is associated with a predicate argument structure, the derived applied verb must in fact be a verb.

2. Except in certain cases when the NP that depends on the applied affix—the applied object—bears an instrumental role.

3. The applied verb constructions in Fula, described by Sylla (1979), behave essentially as do the Chi-Mwi:ni applied verb constructions just analyzed. An exception is the the Fula instrumental applied verb construction, to be discussed in section 7.1.2.

4. Note again that *make* and the causative affixes under discussion might actually take predicates or modifiers rather than propositions as arguments. This alternative does not substantially affect the present analysis of causatives. On the analysis assumed here, by Governing into their sentential complements at s structure, causative affixes, morphology, and verbs Govern the VP heads of these sentences. Therefore, by the Government Transitivity principle, the causative items must head-Govern the subjects of the VPs. On the alternate analysis in which predicates or modifiers are the l-s arguments of the causative morpheme, the causative will Govern the lower VP directly at s structure and thus must head-Govern the subjects of the VP.

5. The passivization data in (7.90) provide additional support for the proposed biclausal s structure of Japanese causatives. The surface structures of (7.90a) and (7.86a), a causative containing a transitive lower verb, are apparently identical: each contains a verb, a subject, an *o* marked argument, and a *ni* marked argument. Yet only the *o* marked argument of (7.90a), not that of (7.86a), may passivize. The biclausal analysis of (7.86a) yields a straightforward explanation of the facts.

6. Note that *ni* is a marker for subjects in other constructions and thus is a natural case marking for the causee subject in a derived causative, if the causee cannot receive the canonical OBJ marking for its OBJ status. Also, the *ni* marking on the causee of causatives built on transitive root verbs brings the surface case marking pattern for such causatives in line with that for underived two-argument verbs like 'give' in the Japanese (see, e.g., sentence (7.90a)).

7. Malayalam passives use the instrumental case as *by* is used in English passives, but this instrumental case is distinct from the instrumental postposition that marks the causee in a causative construction with a transitive root verb.

References

Abasheikh, M. I. (1979). *The Grammar of Chimwi:ni Causatives*. Doctoral dissertation, University of Illinois, Urbana, 1978. Distributed by University Microfilms.

Abraham, W., ed. (1978). *Valence, Semantic Case and Grammatical Relations*. John Benjamins B. V., Amsterdam.

Aissen, J. (1974). "Verb Raising." *Linguistic Inquiry*, 5, 325–366.

Anderson, S. R. (1982). "Where's Morphology?" *Linguistic Inquiry*, 13, 571–612.

Andrews, A. (1981). "The Representation of Case in Modern Icelandic." In Bresnan 1982b, pp. 427–503.

Aronoff, A. (1976). *Word Formation in Generative Grammar*. Linguistic Inquiry Monograph Series No. 1, MIT Press, Cambridge, Massachusetts.

Ashton, E. O. (1944). *Swahili Grammar*. London.

Baker, C. L. (1979). "Syntactic Theory and the Projection Problem." *Linguistic Inquiry*, 10, 533–581.

Baker, M. (1983). "Verbs that Noun-Incorporate." Unpublished paper, MIT and Harvard University, Cambridge, Massachusetts.

Benstein, J. (1983). *The Verbal System of Modern Hebrew: Transitivity and Other Syntactic Issues*. Senior thesis, Harvard University, Cambridge, Massachusetts.

Boatner, M. T., and Gates, J. E. (1975). *A Dictionary of American Idioms*. Barron's Educational Series, Woodbury, New York.

Borer, H. (1980). "Empty Subjects in Modern Hebrew and Constraints on Thematic Relations." In Jensen 1980, pp. 25–37.

Bresnan, J. (1980). "Polyadicity." In T. Hoekstra et al., eds., *Lexical Grammar*, Foris Publications, Dordrecht.

Bresnan, J. (1981). "The Passive in Lexical Theory." In Bresnan 1982b, pp. 3–86. Also, MIT Center for Cognitive Science Occasional Paper No. 7, Cambridge, Massachusetts.

Bresnan, J. (1982a). "Control and Complementation." *Linguistic Inquiry,* 13, 343–434. Also in Bresnan 1982b.

Bresnan, J. ed., (1982b). *The Mental Representation of Grammatical Relations.* MIT Press, Cambridge, Massachusetts.

Burzio, L. (1981). *Intransitive Verbs and Italian Auxiliaries.* Doctoral dissertation, MIT, Cambridge, Massachusetts.

Carden, G. (1983). "Raising Rules and the Projection Principle." With L. Gordon and P. Munro. Paper presented to the Harvard Linguistic Circle, Cambridge, Massachusetts.

Carter, R. (1976). "Some Linking Regularities." Unpublished paper, MIT, Cambridge, Massachusetts.

Chomsky, N. (1965). *Aspects of the Theory of Syntax.* MIT Press, Cambridge, Massachusetts.

Chomsky, N. (1979). "On Markedness and Core Grammar." Paper presented at the 1979 Generative Linguists of the Old World Colloquium, Scuola Normale Superiore, Pisa, Italy.

Chomsky, N. (1980a). "On Binding." *Linguistic Inquiry,* 11, 1–46.

Chomsky, N. (1980b). "On the Representation of Form and Function." Paper presented at CNRS Conference, Royaumont, France, June 1980. To appear in *Linguistic Review.*

Chomsky, N. (1981). *Lectures on Government and Binding.* Foris Publications, Dordrecht.

Chomsky, N. (1982). *Some Concepts and Consequences of the Theory of Government and Binding.* Linguistic Inquiry Monograph No. 6, MIT Press, Cambridge, Massachusetts.

Chung, S. (1976). "An Object-Creating Rule in Bahasa Indonesia." *Linguistic Inquiry,* 7, 1–37.

Cole, P., and Hermon, G. (1981). "Subjecthood and Islandhood: Evidence from Quechua." *Linguistic Inquiry,* 12, 1–30.

Cole, P., and Sadock, J. M., eds. (1977). *Syntax and Semantics, Vol. 8: Grammatical Relations.* Academic Press, New York.

Comrie, B. (1973). "The Ergative: Variations on a Theme." *Lingua,* 32, 219–253.

Comrie, B. (1976). "The Syntax of Causative Constructions: Cross-Language Similarities and Divergences." In Shibatani 1976a, pp. 261–312.

Comrie, B. (1977). "In Defense of Spontaneous Demotion: The Impersonal Passive." In Cole and Sadock 1977, pp. 47–58.

Cook, W. A. (1979). *Case Grammar: Development of the Matrix Model (1970–1978)*. Georgetown University Press, Washington, D.C.

DeLancey, S. (1981). "An Interpretation of Split Ergativity and Related Patterns." *Language*, 57, 626–657.

Dixon, R. M. W. (1972). *The Dyirbal Language of North Queensland*. Cambridge University Press, Cambridge, England.

Dixon, R. M. W. (1977). *The Grammar of Yidin*. Cambridge University Press, Cambridge, England.

Dixon, R. M. W. (1979a). "Corrections and Comments Concerning Heath's 'Is Dyirbal Ergative?'" *Linguistics*, 17, 1003–1015.

Dixon, R. M. W. (1979b). "Ergativity." *Language*, 55, 59–138.

Donaldson, T. (1980). *Ngiyambaa*. Cambridge University Press, Cambridge, England.

Dowty, D. (1981). "Quantification and the Lexicon: A Reply to Fodor and Fodor." In T. Hoekstra et al., eds., *The Scope of Lexical Rules*, Foris Publications, Dordrecht.

Dowty, D. (1982a). "Grammatical Relations and Montague Grammar." In Jacobson and Pullum 1982.

Dowty, D. (1982b). "More on the Categorial Analysis of Grammatical Relations." In A. Zaenen, ed., *Subjects and Other Subjects*, Indiana University Linguistics Club, Bloomington, pp. 115–153.

Dowty, D. R., Wall, R. E., and Peters, S. (1981). *Introduction to Montague Semantics*. D. Reidel, Dordrecht.

Engdahl, E. (1981). "Parasitic Gaps." Paper presented at Sloan Workshop on Processing of Unbounded Dependencies, January 1981, University of Massachusetts, Amherst.

Farmer, A. (1980). *On the Interaction of Morphology and Syntax*. Doctoral dissertation, MIT, Cambridge, Massachusetts.

Fillmore, C. J. (1968). "The Case for Case." In E. Bach and R. Harms, eds., *Universals in Linguistic Theory*, Holt, Rinehart and Winston, New York.

Fillmore, C. J. (1977). "The Case for Case Reopened." In Cole and Sadock 1977, pp. 59–81.

Fodor, J. A., and Fodor, J. D. (1980). "Functional Structure, Quantifiers, and Meaning Postulates." *Linguistic Inquiry*, 11, 759–770.

Fodor, J. A., Fodor, J. D., and Garrett, M. F. (1975). "The Psychological Unreality of Semantic Representations." *Linguistic Inquiry*, 6, 515–531.

Fodor, J., Garrett, M., Walker, E., and Parker, C. (1980). "Against Definitions." *Cognition,* 8, 263–367.

Gary, J. O. (1977). "Implications for Universal Grammar of Object-Creating Rules in Luyia and Mashi." *Studies in African Linguistics,* Supplement 7, pp. 85–95.

Gerdts, D. (1981). *Object and Absolutive in Halkomelem Salish.* Doctoral dissertation, University of California at San Diego.

Grimshaw, J. (1981). "On the Lexical Representation of Romance Reflexive Clitics." In Bresnan 1982b, pp. 87–148. Also MIT Center for Cognitive Science Occasional Paper No. 5, Cambridge, Massachusetts.

Gruber, J. (1976). *Lexical Structures in Syntax and Semantics.* Linguistic Series No. 25, North-Holland, Amsterdam.

Hale, K. (1980). "On the Position of Warlpiri in a Typology of the Base." Distributed in 1981 by the Indiana University Linguistics Club, Bloomington.

Harris, A. (1982). "Georgian and the Unaccusative Hypothesis." *Language,* 58, 290–306.

Hasegawa, N. (1981). *A Lexical Interpretive Theory with Emphasis on the Role of Subject.* Doctoral dissertation, University of Washington, Seattle.

Heath, J. (1979). "Is Dyirbal Ergative?" *Linguistics,* 17, 401–463.

Hodges, K. S. (1977). "Causatives, Transitivity and Objecthood in Kimeru." *Studies in African Linguistics,* Supplement 7, pp. 113–125.

Horvath, J. (1981). *Aspects of Hungarian Syntax and the Theory of Grammar.* Doctoral dissertation, UCLA, Los Angeles, California.

Huang, C-T. J. (1982). *Logical Relations in Chinese and the Theory of Grammar.* Doctoral dissertation, MIT, Cambridge, Massachusetts.

Hubbard, P. L. (1979). "Albanian Neapolitan Morphology." In P. L. Hubbard and P. M. Tiersma, eds., *Linguistic Notes from La Jolla,* No. 6, University of California, San Diego, pp. 55–86.

Jackendoff, R. (1972). *Semantic Interpretation in Generative Grammar.* MIT Press, Cambridge, Massachusetts.

Jackendoff, R. (1976). "Toward an Explanatory Semantic Representation." *Linguistic Inquiry,* 7, 89–150.

Jackendoff, R. (1977). *X-bar Syntax: A Study of Phrase Structure.* Linguistic Inquiry Monograph Series No. 2, MIT Press, Cambridge, Massachusetts.

Jacobson, P., and Pullum, G., eds., (1982). *On the Nature of Syntactic Representation.* D. Reidel, Dordrecht.

Jacobson, W. (1982). *Transitivity in the Japanese Verbal System.* Doctoral dissertation, University of Chicago, Illinois. Distributed by the Indiana University Linguistics Club, Bloomington.

Jaeggli, O. (1980). "Remarks on *To* Contraction." *Linguistic Inquiry,* 11, 239–245.

Jensen, J. T., ed. (1980). *Cahiers Linguistiques d'Ottawa,* Vol. 9, April 1980. (Proceedings of Tenth Annual Meeting of the North Eastern Linguistic Society), University of Ottawa, Ottawa, Canada.

Johnson, M. R. (1980). "Ergativity in Inuktitut (Eskimo), in Montague Grammar and in Relational Grammar." Distributed by the Indiana University Linguistics Club, Bloomington.

Kayne, R. (1981). "Unambiguous Paths." In R. May and J. Koster, eds., *Levels of Syntactic Representation,* Foris Publications, Dordrecht.

Keenan, E. L. (1976). "Toward a Universal Definition of 'Subject.'" In C. Li, ed., *Subject and Topic,* Academic Press, New York.

Kimenyi, A. (1980). *A Relational Grammar of Kinyarwanda.* University of California Press, Berkeley.

Kiparsky, P. (1981). "Case, Control, and Ellipsis in Pāṇini's Grammar." Unpublished paper, MIT, Cambridge, Massachusetts.

Kiparsky, P., and Staal, J. F. (1969). "Syntactic and Semantic Relations in Pāṇini." *Foundations of Language,* 5, 83–117.

Kisseberth, C. W., and Abasheikh, M. I. (1977). "The Object Relationship in Chi-Mwi:ni, a Bantu Language." In Cole and Sadock 1977, pp. 179–218.

Klokeid, T. (1976). *Topics in Lardil Grammar.* Doctoral dissertation, MIT, Cambridge, Massachusetts.

Kuno, S. (1973). *The Structure of the Japanese Language.* MIT Press, Cambridge, Massachusetts.

Kuno, S. (1976). "Subject Raising." In Shibatani 1976c, pp. 25–49.

Kuno, S. (1980). "A Note on Ostler's Nontransformational Analysis of Japanese Case-Marking." In Otsu and Farmer 1980, pp. 93–113.

Levin, B. (1983). *On the Nature of Ergativity.* Doctoral dissertation, Department of Electrical Engineering and Computer Science, MIT, Cambridge, Massachusetts.

Levin, L. (1981). "Lexical Representations of Quirky Case in Icelandic." Unpublished paper, MIT, Cambridge, Massachusetts.

Levin, L., Rappaport, M., and Zaenen, A., eds. (1983). *Papers in Lexical-Functional Grammar.* Indiana University Linguistics Club, Bloomington.

Levin, L., and Simpson, J. (1981). "Quirky Case and Lexical Representations." Paper presented at the annual meeting of the Chicago Linguistics Society, April 30, 1981, Chicago, Illinois.

Lieber, R. (1980). *On the Organization of the Lexicon*. Doctoral dissertation, MIT, Cambridge, Massachusetts, distributed by the Indiana University Linguistics Club, Bloomington.

Lieber, R. (1983). "Argument Linking and Compounds in English." *Linguistic Inquiry*, 14, 251–285.

McClosky, J. (1982). "Raising, Subcategorization and Selection in Modern Irish." Paper presented to the Harvard Linguistic Circle, December, 1982, Cambridge, Massachusetts.

Manzini, M.-R. (1983). "On Control and Control Theory." *Linguistic Inquiry*, 14, 421–446.

Marantz, A. (1978). "Embedded Sentences Are Not Noun Phrases." In M. J. Stein, ed., *Proceedings of the Eighth Annual Meeting of the North Eastern Linguistic Society*, University of Massachusetts, Amherst, pp. 112–122.

Marantz, A. (1980). "English S is the Maximal Projection of V." In Jensen 1980, pp. 303–314.

Marantz, A. (1981a). "Grammatical Relations, Lexical Rules, and Japanese Syntax." In A. Farmer and C. Kitagawa, eds., *Coyote Papers* Vol. 2, Department of Linguistics, University of Arizona, Tucson, pp. 123–144.

Marantz, A. (1981b). *On the Nature of Grammatical Relations*. Doctoral dissertation, MIT, Cambridge, Massachusetts.

Marantz, A. (1982a). "On the Acquisition of Grammatical Relations." *Linguistische Berichte*, 80–82, 32–69.

Marantz, A. (1982b). "Grammatical Relations and Explanation in Linguistics." In A. Zaenen, ed., *Subjects and other Subjects*, Indiana University Linguistics Club, Bloomington, pp. 1–24.

Marantz, A. (1982c). "The Interaction of Morphology and Syntax." Paper presented at the University of Texas at Austin, October, 1982.

Marantz, A. (1982d). "Re Reduplication." *Linguistic Inquiry*, 13, 435–482.

Marantz, A. (1982e). "Whither Move NP?" In A. Marantz and T. Stowell, eds., *MIT Working Papers in Linguistics* Vol. 4, MIT, Cambridge, Massachusetts, pp. 123–162.

Marantz, A. (1983). "Raising and Category Types in Japanese Syntax." In Y. Otsu et al., eds., *Studies in Generative Grammar and Language Acquisition*, Editorial Committee, Monbusho Grant for Scientific Research, Tokyo, pp. 29–47.

Martin, S. E. (1975). *A Reference Grammar of Japanese*. Yale University Press, New Haven, Connecticut.

Mel'čuk, I. A. (1979). "The Predicate Construction in Dyirbal." In P. T. Roberge, ed., *Studies in Dependency Syntax*, Karoma Publishers, Ann Arbor, Michigan.

Miyagawa, S. (1980). *Complex Verbs and the Lexicon. Coyote Papers* Vol. 1, Department of Linguistics, University of Arizona, Tucson.

Mohanan, K. P. (1982a). "Grammatical Relations and Anaphora in Malayalam." In A. Marantz and T. Stowell, eds., *MIT Working Papers in Linguistics* Vol. 4, MIT, Cambridge, Massachusetts, pp. 163–190.

Mohanan, K. P. (1982b). "Grammatical Relations and Clause Structure in Malayalam." In Bresnan 1982b, pp. 504–589.

Mohanan, K. P. (1983). "Move NP or Lexical Rules? Evidence from Malayalam Causativisation." In Levin et al. 1983, pp. 47–111.

Nash, D. (1980). *Topics in Warlpiri Grammar.* Doctoral dissertation, MIT, Cambridge, Massachusetts.

Neidle, C. (1982). "Case Agreement in Russian." In Bresnan 1982b, pp. 391–426.

Nichols, J. (1982). "Head-marking and dependent-marking morphology." Paper given at the Annual Meeting of the Linguistic Society of America, December 1982, San Diego, California.

Ostler, N. D. M. (1979). *Case-Linking: A Theory of Case and Verb Diathesis Applied to Classical Sanskrit.* Doctoral dissertation, MIT, Cambridge, Massachusetts. Distributed by Indiana University Linguistics Club, Bloomington.

Ostler, N. D. M. (1980). "A Non-Transformational Analysis of Japanese Case-Marking and Inflexion." In Otsu and Farmer 1980, pp. 63–91.

Otsu, Y., and Farmer, A., eds. (1980). *MIT Working Papers in Linguistics Vol. 2: Theoretical Issues in Japanese Linguistics.* Department of Linguistics, MIT, Cambridge, Massachusetts.

Perlmutter, D. M. (1978a). "Empirical Evidence Distinguishing Some Current Approaches to Syntax." Paper presented at the annual meeting of the Linguistic Society of America, December 1978, Boston, Massachusetts.

Perlmutter, D. M. (1978b). "Impersonal Passives and the Unaccusative Hypothesis." In J. Jaeger et al., eds., *Berkeley Linguistics Society* Vol. 4, pp. 157–189.

Perlmutter, D. M. (1980a). "Relational Grammar." In E. A. Moravcsik and J. R. Wirth, eds., *Syntax and Semantics Vol. 13: Current Approaches to Syntax.* Academic Press, New York.

Perlmutter, D. M. (1980b). "Syntactic Representation, Syntactic Levels, and the Notion of Subject." In Jacobson and Pullum 1982.

Perlmutter, D. M., ed. (1983). *Studies in Relational Grammar 1.* University of Chicago Press, Chicago.

Perlmutter, D. M., and Postal, P. M. (1978a). "The 1-Advancement Exclusiveness Law." To appear in D. M. Perlmutter, ed., *Studies in Relational Grammar 2,* University of Chicago Press, Chicago.

Perlmutter, D. M., and Postal, P. M. (1978b). "Some Proposed Laws of Basic Clause Structure." In Perlmutter (1983).

Perlmutter, D. M., and Postal, P. M. (1980). "Impersonal Passive and Some Relational Laws." Unpublished paper, University of California at San Diego.

Pesetsky, D. (1982). *Paths and Categories*. Doctoral dissertation, MIT, Cambridge, Massachusetts.

Pinker, S. (1981). "A Theory of the Acquisition of Lexical Interpretative Grammars." In Bresnan 1982b, pp. 655–726. Also MIT Center for Cognitive Science Occasional Paper No. 6, Cambridge, Massachusetts.

Plank, F., ed. (1979). *Ergativity: Towards a Theory of Grammatical Relations*. Academic Press, New York.

Poser, W. (1983). "The 'Double-O Constraint' in Japanese." Paper presented at the Second Annual Meeting of the West Coast Conference on Formal Linguistics, University of Southern California, February, 1983, Los Angeles, California.

Postal, P. (1977). "Antipassive in French." *Linguisticae Investigationes*, I, 333–374.

Pranka, P. (1983). *Syntax and Word Formation*. Doctoral dissertation, MIT, Cambridge, Massachusetts.

Rappaport, M. (1980). "On the Derivation of Derived Nominals." Unpublished paper, MIT, Cambridge, Massachusetts.

Rappaport, M. (1983). "On the Nature of Derived Nominals." In Levin et al. 1983, pp. 113–142.

Reed, I., Miyaoka, O., et al. (1977). *Yup'ik Eskimo Grammar*. Alaska Native Language Center and Yup'ik Language Workshop, University of Alaska, Fairbanks.

Saksena, A. (1980). "The Affected Agent." *Language*, 56, 812–826.

Sadock, J. M. (1980). "Noun Incorporation in Greenlandic." *Language*, 56, 300–319.

Schein, B. (1981). "Small Clauses and Predication." Paper presented at the Twelfth Annual Meeting of the North Eastern Linguistic Society, MIT, Cambridge, Massachusetts.

Schein, B. (1982). "Non-Finite Complements in Russian." In A. Marantz and T. Stowell, eds., *MIT Working Papers in Linguistics* Vol. 4, pp. 217–243, MIT, Cambridge, Massachusetts.

Schein, B. (in press). "Small Clauses and Predication." To appear in *Linguistic Inquiry*.

Schmerling, S. F. (1979). "A Categorial Analysis of Dyirbal Ergativity." In C. S. Smith and S. F. Schmerling, eds., *Texas Linguistic Forum* Vol. 13. Department of Linguistics, University of Texas at Austin, pp. 96–112.

Seiter, W. (1980). *Studies in Niuean Syntax*. Garland Publishing Co., New York.

Seiter, W. (1983). "Subject-Direct Object Raising in Niuean." In Perlmutter 1983, pp. 317–359.

Shibatani, M., ed. (1976a). *Syntax and Semantics Vol. 6: The Grammar of Causative Constructions*, Academic Press, New York.

Shibatani, M. (1976b). "The Grammar of Causative Constructions: A Conspectus." In Shibatani 1976a, pp. 1–40.

Shibatani, M., ed. (1976c). *Syntax and Semantics Vol. 5: Japanese Generative Grammar*. Academic Press, New York.

Shibatani, M. (1977). "Grammatical Relations and Surface Cases." *Language*, 53, 789–809.

Shukla, S. (1981). *Bhojpuri Grammar*. Georgetown University Press, Washington, D.C.

Silverstein, M. (1976). "Hierarchy of Features and Ergativity." In R. M. W. Dixon, ed., *Grammatical Categories in Australian Languages*, Australian Institute of Aboriginal Studies, Canberra, pp. 112–172.

Smith, E. E., and Medin, D. L. (1981). *Categories and Concepts*. Harvard University Press, Cambridge, Massachusetts.

Sproat, R. (1982). "Redundancy Rules and Welsh Mutation." Unpublished MIT ms.

Starosta, S. (1978). "The One Per Sent Solution." In Abraham (1978), pp. 459–576.

Steele, S. (1981). "The Luiseño Absolutive, and the Other Syntactic Operators." Unpublished University of Arizona ms.

Steele, S., Akmajian, A., et al. (1981). *An Encyclopedia of AUX: A Study in Cross-Linguistic Equivalence*. Linguistic Inquiry Monograph Series No. 5, MIT Press, Cambridge, Massachusetts.

Stowell, T. (1980). "Subjects Across Categories." *Linguistic Review*.

Stowell, T. (1981). *Origins of Phrase Structure*. Doctoral dissertation, MIT, Cambridge, Massachusetts.

Swadesh, M. (1944). "South Greenlandic (Eskimo)." In H. Hoijer, ed., *Linguistic Structures of Native America*, New York: Viking Fund Publications in Anthropology, pp. 30–54.

Sylla, Y. (1979). *Grammatical Relations and Fula Syntax*. UCLA doctoral dissertation, distributed by University Microfilms.

Thomas-Flinders, T. (1982). "On the Notions 'Head of a Word' and 'Lexically Related': Evidence from Maricopa Verbal Morphology." In D. P. Flickinger et al., eds., *Proceedings of the First West Coast Conference on Formal Linguistics*, Stanford, California, pp. 168–178.

Thráinsson, H. (1980). *On Complementation in Icelandic*. Harvard University doctoral dissertation, 1979. Published by Garland Press, New York, 1980.

Trithart, M. L. (1977). *Relational Grammar and Chichewa Subjectivization*. Distributed by Indiana University Linguistics Club, Bloomington.

Valfells, S. (1970). "Middle Voice in Icelandic." In H. Benedicktsson, ed., *The Nordic Languages and Modern Linguistics*, Vísindfélag Íslendinga, Reykjavík, pp. 551–571.

Williams, E. (1979). "Passive." Unpublished paper, University of Massachusetts, Amherst.

Williams, E. (1980). "Predication." *Linguistic Inquiry*, 11, 203–238.

Williams, E. (1981). "Argument Structure and Morphology." *Linguistic Review*, 1, 81–114.

Williams, E. (1982). "The NP Cycle." *Linguistic Inquiry*, 13, 277–295.

Williams, E. (1983). "Against Small Clauses." *Linguistic Inquiry*, 14, 287–308.

Wittgenstein, L. (1958). *Philosophical Investigations*. Third edition. Macmillan, New York.

Woodbury, A. (1977a). "Greenlandic Eskimo, Ergativity, and Relational Grammar." In Cole and Sadock 1977, pp. 307–336.

Woodbury, A. (1977b). "The Greenlandic Verbal Suffix *-ut-:* Interactions of Linguistic Form and Grammatical Function." In K. Whistler et al., eds., *Berkeley Linguistics Society* Vol. 3, Berkeley, California, pp. 251–269.

Wordick, F. J. F. (1979). *The Yindjibarndi Language*. Australian Institute of Aboriginal Studies.

Young, R. W., and Morgan, W. (1980). *The Navajo Language*. University of New Mexico Press, Albuquerque.

Index